elites
and
masses

An Introduction
to Political Sociology

elites
and
masses

An Introduction
to Political Sociology

Martin N. Marger

Northern Kentucky University

Wadsworth Publishing Company
Belmont, California
A Division of Wadsworth, Inc.

ISBN 0-534-25410-1

(Previously ISBN 0-442-25410-5)

Copyright © 1981 by Litton Educational Publishing, Inc.

Library of Congress Catalog Card Number: 80-51094

10 9 8 7 6 5 4 3 2

ACKNOWLEDGMENTS

Acknowledgment is made to the following publishers and individuals for permission to reprint material:

Ben Bagdikian. *The Information Machines*. Copyright © 1971 by the Rand Corporation. Published by Harper & Row, Publishers, Inc. (p. 328).

Kenneth M. Dolbeare. *Political Change in the United States: A Framework for Analysis*. Copyright © 1974, McGraw-Hill, Inc. Used with the permission of McGraw-Hill Book Company. (pp. 24, 151, 234).

G. William Domhoff. *The Powers That Be: Processes of Ruling-Class Domination in America*. Copyright © 1978 by G. William Domhoff. Published by Random House, Inc. (p. 229).

Murray J. Edelman. *The Symbolic Uses of Politics*. Published by University of Illinois Press, 1964. (pp. 265, 293).

Ted Robert Gurr. *Why Men Rebel*. Copyright © 1970 by Princeton University Press (Princeton Paperback, 1971): Figs. 1, 2; pp. 47, 51. Reprinted by permission of Princeton University Press. (pp. 358, 360).

Robert J. Havighurst and Bernice L. Neugarten. *Society and Education*. Fourth Edition. Copyright © 1975 by Allyn and Bacon, Inc., Boston. Reprinted with permission. (p. 197).

Joan Huber and William H. Form. *Income and Ideology: An Analysis of the American Political Formula*. Copyright © 1973 by Joan Huber & William H. Form. Reprinted by permission of the Free Press a Division of Macmillan Publishing Co., Inc. (pp. 37, 307, 310, 318, 319).

Floyd Hunter. *Top Leadership, U.S.A.* Copyright © 1959 The University of North Carolina Press. (pp. 216, 217).

Suzanne Keller. *Beyond the Ruling Class: Strategic Elites in Modern Society*. Copyright © 1963 by Random House, Inc. (pp. 82, 223).

V. O. Key, Jr. *Public Opinion and American Democracy*. Published by Alfred A. Knopf, Inc. By permission of Charles Y. Wadsworth and Samuel P. Newbury, Trustees of the Luella Gettys Key Trust. (pp. 324, 328, 333).

Gerhard E. Lenski. *Power and Privilege: A Theory of Social Stratification*. Copyright © 1966 by McGraw-Hill, Inc. Used with the permission of McGraw-Hill Book Company. (pp. 21, 23, 122).

Seymour M. Lipset and Reinhard Bendix. *Social Mobility in Industrial Society*. Published by University of California Press, 1959. (pp. 205, 206).

Robert Michels, translated by Eden and Cedar Paul. *Political Parties*. Copyright © 1962 by the Crowell-Collier Publishing Company. Reprinted with permission of Macmillan Publishing Co., Inc. (pp. 70, 71, 72, 110, 338).

Lester W. Milbrath. *Political Participation*. Published by Rand McNally, Inc., 1965. By permission of the author. (p. 269).

Ralph Miliband. *The State in Capitalist Society*. Published by Basic Books, Inc., 1969. (pp. 102, 107, 155, 217, 231, 331).

C. Wright Mills. *The Power Elite*. Published by Oxford University Press, Inc., 1956. (pp. 26–27, 54, 124, 212, 213, 232, 234).

vi Acknowledgments

Frank Parkin. *Class Inequality & Political Order: Social Stratification in Capitalist and Communist Societies.* © 1971 in London, England by Frank Parkin. Published by Praeger Publishers, Inc., 1971. Reprinted by permission of Holt, Rinehart and Winston. (pp. 27, 99, 317).

John Porter. *The Vertical Mosaic: An Analysis of Social Class and Power in Canada.* © University of Toronto Press, 1965. (pp. 146, 201, 227).

Kenneth Prewitt and Alan Stone. *The Ruling Elites: Elite Theory, Power, and American Democracy.* Figure "Class Bias in Recruitment of the Elite" (p. 137). Copyright © 1973 by Kenneth Prewitt and Alan Stone. Reprinted by permission of Harper & Row, Publishers, Inc. (p. 195).

David Riesman, et al. *The Lonely Crowd.* Published by Yale University Press, 1950. (pp. 224–225).

Arnold M. Rose. *The Power Structure.* Published by Oxford University Press, Inc., 1967. (pp. 44, 221–222).

Sidney Verba and Norman Nie. *Participation in America.* Table 2-1 (p. 31). Copyright © 1972 by Sidney Verba and Norman H. Nie. Reprinted by permission of Harper & Row, Publishers, Inc. (p. 270).

preface

Unlike most subareas of sociology, political sociology lacks a sizable collection of texts that comprehensively introduce the field to students. *Elites and Masses* was written to help fill that need.

One of the fundamental purposes of sociology is to provide a different mode of looking at and explaining society, one that often exposes the conventional views and explanations as incomplete, flawed, or perhaps entirely inaccurate. The goal of this book is to encourage readers to rethink some of their long-held ideas about power and politics. Although intended primarily for a college and university audience, general readers will also find it informative and thought provoking.

The subject matter of political sociology is broad, straddling both sociology and political science. Any text in the field, therefore, must necessarily be selective in its coverage. In my view, the core of political sociology is the structure of power in societies. Although I have chosen to focus mainly on power in American society, particularly in Parts Three and Four, most of the ideas discussed are applicable to other advanced capitalist societies as well. I have also presented an examination of the three major theoretical perspectives in political sociology to show several ways in which the analysis of power in societies can be approached.

While my theoretical preferences are clearly set forth, I have created a reasonable balance by citing various schools of thought on the topics discussed in each chapter. Perhaps in no subarea of sociology is the cleavage between proponents of different theoretical perspectives more apparent than political sociology. This cleavage is unfortunate, for it makes studying the field more demanding and sometimes confusing. Political sociologists, however, are not immune to the same social forces that inspire conflicting and often volatile political views among the general populace.

I have tried to remain objective, but my analysis is obviously not free of bias. A vast literature has accumulated over the past several decades concerning the practice (and practicality) of objectivity in the social sciences, and it seems neither appropriate nor constructive to enter the ongoing debate here. In studying political sociology, it is especially difficult to remain "above the arena" as dispassionate and unaffected observers. In a world of constantly generated mass communication, where political and economic institutions reach into virtually every area of social life, it is unlikely that any of us can remain detached for long as we investigate politics and power in society.

In order to enhance the value of *Elites and Masses* as a learning and teaching tool, I have prepared an Instructor's Manual for the text, with questions, exercises, and suggested readings for each chapter. The Manual is available to instructors from the Publisher.

I would like to thank the following reviewers who read various sections of the manuscript and provided helpful criticisms and suggestions: Ford W. Cleere, University of Northern Colorado; Henry Etzkowitz, State University of New York, Purchase; J. W. Freiberg, Boston University; Thomas Guterbock, University of Virginia; John Kramer, State University of New York, Brockport; Jan Smith, Ohio Wesleyan University; and Ira M. Wasserman, Eastern Michigan University. In addition, I would like to thank Paul R. Abramson, Michigan State University, and Christopher Boehm, Northern Kentucky University, for reviewing specific chapters. A special word of thanks is due James B. McKee, Michigan State University, who not only read several sections of the manuscript, but furnished much valuable advice and encouragement throughout the project. I would like to acknowledge Mary Ellen Ryan for research assistance and finally my wife, Joette, who served as a sounding board for many ideas.

contents

elites
and
masses

An Introduction
to Political Sociology

part one

politics
and power
in society

chapter 1

introduction

*Good sociology should begin with the application
of radical skepticism and criticism to one's own
society, to one's place in it, and, by extension, to
all social behavior. Sociology should, in short, be*
alienating.

Pierre L. van den Berghe

All of us occupy certain positions on the social hierarchy and thus enjoy more or less of our society's rewards: wealth, prestige, justice, education, health, and so on. This unequal distribution of rewards is an outcome which is not the result only, or even mainly, of our individual efforts and capacities. Instead it is determined in largest part by the process of societal politics—most simply the interplay of power, for this is what politics is basically about. To understand our place in the social scheme, we must therefore understand the society's institutions of power—what they are, how they work, and who makes their vital decisions.

Most commonly we assume that to comprehend politics and power in society, we need but look at the personalities and events of government and political parties, abundantly described on the front pages of daily newspapers and the nightly televised news. We often refer to this as the "political world," and it is here that we assume power is wielded. But politics, and thus power, is part of every realm of social life. Thus, to limit our view of power and the powerful to the most obvious political milieu, government, is to acquire a partial and perhaps inaccurate picture.

Political sociology, unlike the common thought, makes few presumptions about power. Indeed, the questions "Who has power?" and "How is power exercised?" might be said to be the starting points of this discipline. As we will see, power takes many forms, some not easily seen and measured. As a result, answers to questions of who has it and how it is wielded are never as straightforward as they may seem. Furthermore, power is never exercised in a vacuum. Power actions always produce social consequences—some benefit and others lose. One of the major objectives of political sociology, then, is to determine not only who has power and how it is exercised but also in whose interests power is applied. In Part Three we will investigate these issues, particularly as they are manifest in contemporary America.

Political sociology is also concerned with how power in societies is contested, sustained, and given legitimacy. Is the power of ruling groups a product of the popular will or is it created by the powerful themselves through their successful manipulation of public opinion? In either case, the power of ruling groups is never unrestrained and permanent. In all societies the powerful are periodically challenged, not only through the acceptable methods of political competition but sometimes by efforts outside the official system. The techniques by which ruling groups maintain power and the manner in which they are challenged are the focus of Part Four.

Before we can analyze the nature, distribution, and methods of power in societies using the approach of political sociology, however, we must familiarize ourselves with how political sociologists uniquely view power and politics. A key difference between the sociological and the more customary analyses of politics is that the former uses more rigorous terms and concepts. Some of these principal ideas are discussed in the following chapter; most of them will be dealt with in the remainder of the book.

The sociological approach to politics and power also differs from the layman's approach in that sociologists try to relate what they observe to a body of theory. Some theories are quite specific, while others are more encompassing and less formalized. The latter are theoretical perspectives, sometimes called models or paradigms, which basically comprise a set of general assumptions concerning the "who, how, and why" of politics and power. All of us create theoretical models in our minds about why political or other institutions take a particular shape or why people behave as they do. Rarely are we conscious of doing so, however. When trying to explain corruption, war, riots, or other political and social maladies, for example, or when accounting, on the other hand, for displays of cooperation or altruism, reference is often made to "human nature." That is, certain behavior patterns are assumed to be basic human social characteristics. Such assumptions are similar to the theoretical models or perspectives constructed by sociologists; they are merely less complex and sophisticated.

The basic themes of each of the major theoretical perspectives in political sociology —the pluralist, the elite, and the class —are dealt with in Part Two; reference to them will be made in our succeeding discussions of power in America and other advanced capitalist societies. Since each of these models or perspectives makes different assumptions about the shape of power structures, in whose interests power groups act, and what motivates political behavior, it should not surprise us to find several conflicting accounts of power in America or, for that matter, any society. We might think of it as a choice of several different routes leading to the same destination. What is seen and encountered on each will vary. Thus, travelers may disagree on which is the fastest, safest, or most scenic route. In a similar way, sociologists will differ on which is the most valid or productive theoretical perspective.

This book's analysis of power in America and societies which are similar in political and economic structure has been guided by certain assumptions of the class and elite perspectives. These will become clearer as our analysis proceeds. The conclusions we reach using these assumptions will therefore not always coincide with those of the pluralist model, which has been more popular as a guiding framework of political analysis in the United States. Both class and elite perspectives are more critical of the workings and outputs of dominant political and economic institutions and, predictably, do not sit well with common notions of how and in whose favor the American system works. Pluralism, expressing as it does ideas more compatible with the tenets of liberal democracy, has been the preferred model of politics and power in the United States, and most of us have been trained—either explicitly or subtly—to think in those terms.

Of course, even though they may seem like radically opposing views, different theoretical perspectives are not necessarily "either-ors." In some ways their explanations may overlap, and in others they may each simply focus more sharply on certain aspects of power and politics. For example, if we assume that the basic function of government is the maintenance of order and stability in society, we will reach noticeably different conclusions about the uses and origins of political power than if we assume that government is only a mechanism for protecting the interests of a privileged class. Those who view government as an institution assuring social order—as most pluralists do—emphasize the unifying, consensus-building functions of the political system. Those who see government as an instrument of a privileged few—elite and class theorists take this view—stress those aspects of the system which generate conflict and inequality in the distribution of the society's wealth. One sees the overriding influence of order, the other of conflict. Neither, however, would deny that at different times and in different ways government is both a societal unifier and a defender of special group interests.

Political Economy

Political sociology is not a new field of study. Its roots reach well back to the nineteenth century. Yet, political sociology is today a field which is not clearly defined. This is partially due to the fact that much of its content is marginal to both sociology and political science. Although sociologists and political scientists often find themselves pursuing answers to similar questions, speaking the same analytic language, using similar theoretical models, and employing common techniques of inquiry, there are nonetheless certain differences in their approaches to and explanations of politics in society.

Perhaps chief among these differences is their scope of inquiry. Political scientists are concerned mainly with power as it is exercised by formal bodies and leaders of authority—that is, the state. Political sociologists, on the other hand, are more inclined to probe the underlying or hidden structures of power in society rather than those attached to the state alone. Also, the sociological approach considers the state not in isolation but as an institution which affects and in turn is affected by other societal institutions. In modern societies, economic institutions in particular interrelate closely with the state. Thus, much of the analysis of the political is unavoidably an analysis of the economic as well.

In addition, economic decision makers in modern societies, like state leaders, have vast powers in their own right that enable them to influence the distribution of various life chances — perhaps even life itself — for all members of the society. Given their far-reaching power, we would be seriously remiss if our analysis of societal politics failed to include economic leaders and organizations.

The thrust of this book's approach, then, is **political economy**, a view of politics and power that recognizes the essential interweaving of state and economic institutions and the coequal place of both political and economic leaders in the power structure.

Change and Conflict

A second key difference between sociologists and political scientists in their approaches to power and politics lies in the treatment of change and conflict. Political sociologists have traditionally been more conscious of power structures in societies as changing phenomena and have thus made greater use of historical factors in their analyses. Political scientists, on the other hand, have usually focused on the workings of political systems as they exist at particular times, in a snapshotlike fashion. While the political scientist is likely to ask questions about how the parts of the political system function, the political sociologist is more likely to ask how the system has come to be constructed as it is and how the society's various groups stand to gain or lose from that arrangement.

Because of their stress on the changing nature of power and politics, political sociologists generally come to see the polity and other institutions of power as arenas of conflict, not necessarily structures of cooperation and consensus. With its emphasis on conflict, dissent, and movements that challenge the prevailing institutions, political sociology is apt to be seen quite naturally as a "radical" discipline. In any case, students of political sociology must be prepared to examine critically the dominant political arrangements of their society and the official rationales which justify them.

In this book many of the orthodox ideas about who has power, and how and on behalf of whom it is exercised in the United States and similar societies, will be challenged. The intent is not to persuade but to expose the reader to an unconventional view of politics and to stimulate new ways of thinking about political events, personalities, and structures. The major institutions of our society —government, the corporation, the educational system, the mass media, the various religious bodies —all encourage a basically favorable view of the prevailing sociopolitical system. Thus, until one is exposed to a *critical* analysis of politics in society, an analysis which does not begin with the assumption that the dominant system necessarily functions in a beneficial manner for all or even most people, one cannot make intelligent decisions about political happenings or the process of power in general.

chapter 2

power in societies

*Power has to do with whatever decisions men
make about the arrangements under which they
live, and about the events which make up the
history of their times. Events that are beyond
human decision do happen; social arrangements
do change without benefit of explicit decision.
But insofar as such decisions are made, the
problem of who is involved in making them is the
basic problem of power. Insofar as they could
be made but are not, the problem becomes who
fails to make them?*

C. Wright Mills

Consider for a moment our power as social actors. Most of us have a great deal of freedom in making decisions that affect us within the realm of personal activity. We have the power, for example, to choose to wear a particular outfit one day and change it the next, eat what and when we want or forego a meal entirely, opt for a television show in place of a book, or select one make of car over another. More importantly we have the power to make certain decisions regarding our family and work situations. We may choose to marry or remain unattached, have ten children or none, and live in a central city or a rural area. Within certain obvious limits, we may work where we desire, change jobs, or drop out of the mainstream work force. These are all instances of power over individual actions within very circumscribed private boundaries.

Once we move beyond this rather narrow range of personal actions, however, our power diminishes. Most of the major decisions which affect us on a long-range basis will be made by others who are not subject to our direct influence. What will be the quality of the air we breathe or the water we drink? What will our incomes be, and how much will we have to pay for the needs of subsistence and the wants of luxury? What will be the content of our formal education, and to what ends will we be able to apply it? Will peace be preserved or will nuclear weapons be unleashed, creating global devastation? It is clear that most of us simply lack the capacity to affect such decisions significantly. However, a small number of people in the society *do* have the power to decide these and other vital issues that basically shape our lives.

There are, then, great differences in power among a society's populace, a fact well expressed in C. Wright Mills' assertion (1959:181) that "men are free to make history but some are much freer than others." It is the differentials in societal power between the few and the many that is the general focus of political sociology. Specifically, political sociology is most concerned with relationships and structures of power as they appear within the larger, more encompassing institutions of society, where decisions have wide-ranging impact. As we shall see, these institutions are primarily the state and the economy.

In the chapters that follow we will look carefully at the power systems of societies, particularly the United States. In doing so we will pose questions about politics and power which do not ordinarily enter our minds. Basically, sociologists try to discover and explain the unseen social forces which govern our behavior in various ways. As a subarea of sociology, political sociology is concerned with finding and analyzing those *political* forces which weigh most heavily upon us but of which we may have little comprehension. Most of us are so familiar with political and economic institutions that we give little thought to why they operate as they do, why they consistently seem to benefit some groups more than

others, and why they remain essentially unchanging over many generations. Beyond those small groups such as the family and the peer group
within which we conduct our personal day-to-day activities, not only does
our power dwindle but our understanding of who makes decisions, how,
and on what basis is greatly reduced. Public surveys frequently reveal
how relatively little the average citizen understands about the personnel
and functions of government agencies or how decisions are reached on
particular issues. Even more incomprehensible to almost all of us is the
power of economic institutions despite the fact that what occurs in the
executive offices of giant industrial and financial corporations can have
as much impact on our lives as the actions of government officials.

Before we can analyze the structure of power in America and other
societies, however, we must first make clear with what we are actually
dealing. Unfortunately many of the ideas of political sociology are not
used consistently and unambiguously by different analysts. Our purpose
in this chapter is therefore to clarify the meaning of some key terms and
concepts, especially *power*. Laymen sometimes accuse social scientists of
"telling us what we already know in highfalutin terms." In all too many
cases, such accusations are well founded. But precision in the use of
terms is one of the major factors separating social science from more
casual explanations of social occurrences or from journalistic reportage.
If our analyses of social phenomena are to be systematic and generaliz-
able, we must necessarily adopt a less informal and more exact terminology.

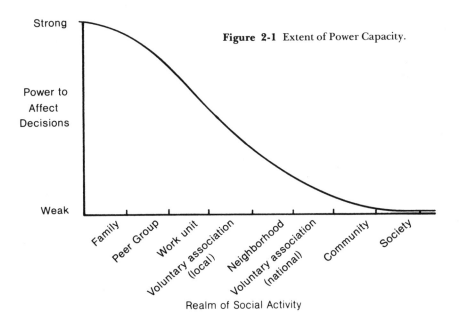

Figure 2-1 Extent of Power Capacity.

SOCIETAL POWER

It would seem, at first glance, that "power" should be a term easily understood by everyone and having a minimum of ambiguity. However, nothing could be further from the truth. Power, it seems, is one of those terms we all understand and can explain—until asked to do so.

Adding to the confusion surrounding this concept is the fact that it has acquired a nasty connotation; that is, it is frequently used in a derogatory manner. We often hear phrases such as "power mad," "power hungry," or "only out for power," each implying a clearly negative—perhaps even sinister—meaning. In the realm of world politics the term power is often used in describing the actions of tyrants, dictators, or totalitarian forms of government. Even sociologists sometimes view power as a basically adverse notion. Marvin Olsen (1970:5) writes that "Those sociologists who see power as only a negative process often speak of it as 'control over others' and explore its occurrence because of an underlying ideological belief that power is undesirable in social life."

Power, however, is not exercised only in adverse social contexts. Rather it is fundamental, indeed inherent, in human interaction of any kind at any social level. Whether we are looking at whole societies of several million persons or families of two or three members, power relationships will be evident. Charles E. Merriam (1934:16), an early leader in political science, notes that "Power is first of all a phenomenon of group cohesion and aggregation, a child of group necessity or utility, a function of the social relations of men." And Michael Crozier (1973:212) admits that one might even say that "without power, neither integration nor society is possible." We are all political actors and thus, unavoidably, users and targets of power. With this fact in mind we can broaden our understanding of power, realizing that whether applied in positive or negative ways, intentionally or unintentionally, consciously or unconsciously, within small or large groups, it is a constant foundation of social interaction. As political sociologist Amitai Etzioni (1968:321) has put it, "The notion that evil is imposed by power while goodness flies on its own wings assumes an optimistic view of human nature and societal institutions that has little evidence to support it. The application of power is a principal way of getting things done." It should not be assumed, of course, that power, though always present, is necessarily functional and beneficial for the society as a whole. Power may at different times and under different circumstances serve the interests of both social cohesion and conflict.

Although power is evident at all social levels, we have explained that the focus of political sociology is primarily upon power as it is exercised and pursued at the macrosocial level—that is, within large-scale or societywide institutions. This is *societal* rather than *interpersonal* power. The latter is apparent in the relationships, for example, between husbands and wives, parents and children, employers and employees, and teachers and students. In none of these cases do the consequences of the actions by any party extend much beyond the immediate group. However, when the effects of an organization's or individual's decisions are felt, either directly or indirectly, by vast segments of the society, we may refer to societal power.

The actions of the state are the clearest examples of such widespread power. Virtually no one is immune to the effects of decisions made by government leaders. Societal power, however, lies not only within the realm of the state. Large-scale economic organizations in particular also display similar influence. For example, the decision by one or a few steel companies to raise the price of steel will ultimately rebound not only to the purchasers of steel but to the society as a whole, given the importance of this item to other sectors of the economy. Jobs in most industries, market prices of almost all goods, and the fate of countless public and private projects will be fundamentally affected. The policies and decisions of private organizations, such as steel companies, can therefore be as public as the policies and decisions of government agencies. *Societal* power, then, refers to power which is exercised by individuals and organizations, public and private, whose scope of activity is broad enough to affect many, if not all, elements of the society.

Power, of course, whether societal or interpersonal, is not an object to be possessed or a substance in some clearly visible form. It is a *relationship* that is understood by those parties involved. A power action thus necessarily implies not only the use or application of power but also compliance. Discovering who has power and how it is exercised is essentially the uncovering of power relationships. Power therefore should not be thought of as a permanent or inherent attribute of a particular person or group. To say that person X or group Y has power is meaningless until we specify "over whom" and "under what conditions."

Also we should not think of power as exercised randomly by individuals or groups. Rather there is a *structure* of power in societies in which relatively enduring relations are apparent between leaders and led. When sociologists speak of social structures or social orders, they are denoting stable and regular relations, those that are understood by the interacting parties and that produce expected and predictable actions. A social structure is comprised of various social positions occupied by persons playing appropriate roles. A mutual awareness of the patterns of behavior called for in these roles is what generates ordered interrelations among social actors. Such ordered, predictable relations essentially distinguish a functioning, viable society from an unorganized, chaotic mass. Whenever humans find themselves grouped together for a common purpose, a social order is established, perhaps without recognizable intention, so that they may interact easily.

A society's *power* structure, then, denotes the relatively stable interrelations among powerful groups and individuals and the manner in which they exercise their power in relation to the general populace. We might similarly think of power structures within particular groups and organizations. Union officials, for example, have certain powers, such as the right to bargain with management, that rank-and-file members do not. Likewise, stockholders in a corporation have very limited powers in comparison with corporate managers. Political sociology, however, has been traditionally concerned with power structures of the larger society or community.

FORCE, AUTHORITY, AND INFLUENCE

Political sociologists have constructed numerous typologies describing the various forms of power, all of which have been debated intensely. To simplify matters, we will break down societal power into three basic categories: force, authority, and influence. Each is closely interrelated.

Probably the most often quoted sociological definition of power is that given by Max Weber, one of the preeminent figures in sociological and political theory. Weber defined power as the ability of persons or groups "to realize their own will in a communal action even against the resistance of others who are participating in the action" (Gerth and Mills, 1946:180). Power in this sense is based on the capacity to make people comply either (1) by force or (2) through authority.

Force

Force (or coercion) may be seen simply as power whose basis is the threat or application of punishment. Applying or threatening physical measures or withholding valued items constitutes such power. Force may be used either legitimately or illegitimately. The actions of criminals illustrate the former while the actions of police in apprehending criminals illustrate the latter.

Although force is ultimately at the base of a wide variety of power actions, it is only in unusual situations that societal power actually takes this form. If a society's institutional system is accepted as legitimate by most of the populace, force is rarely necessary as a means of assuring compliance. Authority and influence are the principal forms.

Authority

Most simply, authority is socially approved power. It is a right held by persons in certain positions to command others. Sociologist Robert Mac-Iver (1965:63) specifically defines it as "the established *right*, within any social order, to determine policies, to pronounce judgments on relevant issues, and to settle controversies, or, more broadly, to act as leader or guide to other men." Authority may be distinguished in at least two ways: it is legitimate and impersonal.

Legitimacy. First, authority is socially acceptable; it is, in other words, *legitimate* or institutional power. Sociologist Gerhard Lenski (1966:54) has described the difference between force and institutional power basically as the difference between the rule of might and the rule of right. Because people of a society recognize certain power as acceptable, they approve of its use and accede to its demands routinely. What is understood is that certain persons are empowered to act on behalf of the society. Their actions and decisions are recognized as appropriate, and compliance is thus voluntary.

In the United States, where the institutional structure is quite stable, the vast majority of power is exercised in this manner. For most of us it is only in rare instances that we abide by a law or a social norm because we are directly coerced into doing so. Our compliance is primarily based on our understanding of the expectation to obey and our commitment to the society's normative code. Such understandings are internalized early in life, and through the socialization process we come to accept as normal and largely unquestioned certain limitations on personal freedom.

What is perhaps most important is that the regulators of legitimate power are mostly unconscious and automatic. With internalization of the society's normative code, a code enforced and rationalized by the state more than any other institution, compliance with authority becomes almost reflexive. Automobile drivers, for example, routinely observe certain rules of the road, but not because an agent of the state is sitting beside them compelling them to do so. All of us stop at red lights even when no traffic is approaching on the intersecting road or when no law enforcement officials are present. Such instances demonstrate how thoroughly most of us have internalized those norms or expected patterns of behavior which take the form of law. As MacIver (1965:58) explains, "Men obey because they are social beings —or, if you prefer it, because they are socialized beings, trained and indoctrinated in the ways of their society. All the motivations that are evoked and active in their social circle conspire to make them, on the whole, law-abiding."

Understanding legitimacy enables us to understand why actions of the powerful are generally accepted by most people even when they stand to suffer from their consequences. Committing the society to war, for example, or imposing severe economic restraints can make life uncomfortable. Yet, the powerful are rarely challenged in any serious manner on such decisions.

Impersonality. A second characteristic of authority is that it is, for the most part, *impersonal*. Individuals command others or direct the allocation of social resources not on the bases of personal traits or achievements but simply because they occupy a particular position. Governor, teacher, employer, and parent all represent positions or roles to which are attached certain powers, obligations, and privileges. The incumbents of such institutional positions may change frequently, but so long as the definition of positional rights and duties remains the same, whoever occupies them will assume the same capacity to exercise power. Thus it is that one can be a peanut farmer one day and president of the United States the next, or vice versa.

Usually we think of the state as that societal institution which exercises authority —that is, where officials' decisions are acknowledged as binding on all members of the society. Authority, however, is evident in relationships within economic and other societal institutions as well. We recognize the right of teachers to discipline students, of employers to hire and fire employees, and of parents to control their children. As with governmental authority, these cases represent rights attached to particular positions.

Ownership of property may also involve the exercise of authority. If, for example, a home is forcibly entered and the occupants harm the intruder, they will probably be acquitted of any wrongdoing because their authority in this case as "homeowners" or "residents" is recognized. Individuals or groups are also entitled to transfer their property to others as they see fit. Businesses may sell goods at a price they choose and may place them on the market or withhold them in such a way as to maximize their profits. In capitalist societies the authority attached to property is most critical.

The State as Ultimate Authority

Although authority is exercised within various societal institutions, the state more than any other retains *ultimate* authority simply because it has a monopoly on the legitimate use of violence. Only the state may, through its agents, coerce, physically harm, or even kill as a means of assuring its will. As Bertrand Russell (1969:37) has observed, "The ultimate power of the Law is the coercive power of the State." In modern societies it is the state which is responsible for enforcing the social code and meting out justice. Vigilantes, those who attempt to take the law into their own hands, do not act with authority and are therefore apt to be penalized for their actions. For instance, storeowners who apprehend burglars on their premises are required by law to turn the felons over to the police —that is, the representatives of the state. Storeowners themselves cannot deal out punishment as they may see fit. Even the previously mentioned homeowners protecting their property against intruders will have to answer to the state, though their actions may eventually be ruled justifiable. In short, only the state is granted the right to use force to sustain its policies.

Of course, when a government is recognized as legitimate by the people of a society, it rarely must resort to the use of forceful measures to assure compliance with its policies. As already explained, people most often obey reflexively. In his research, psychologist Stanley Milgram (1975) has demonstrated how frighteningly resolute obedience to authority may be, even when it conflicts with moral standards. Milgram showed in a series of experiments that a majority of his subjects were willing to inflict what they believed to be great pain on other persons so long as they understood their actions to be a correct response to an order of authority.

At the same time, however, we should not think that obligations to authority are so thoroughly internalized as to make us automatons who respond on cue and who voluntarily accept the will of the state without thought. Authority is, in the final analysis, always founded upon coercion (Bierstedt, 1954:79). There is, in other words, an element of force as well as consent in such power relationships. Political scientist Carl Friedrich (1963:166) notes that coercion and consent are not mutually exclusive but are in most power situations both operative "in varying degrees and combinations." Occasionally when authority breaks down we get a glimpse of how shaky its foundations may actually be. In 1969, for example, the entire police force of the city of Montreal walked off the job in a labor dispute with city officials. Though the strike lasted only one day, vandals and looters caused approximately a million dollars' worth of property damage. One observer of this event explains that a wide variety of people abandoned their inhibitions: "Essentially, it was not the rise in professional crime — 12 times the normal — that counted. It was the way political grievances, and private and group frustrations, shot to the surface when no one was around to enforce the law" (Clark, 1975:441). Similar outbreaks seem to occur during large-scale disasters, such as floods and blackouts, when law enforcement agencies are unable to police the community adequately.

The Sources of Authority

What is it that confers upon some groups and individuals the right to command others or to make significant decisions that affect the lives of all or a substantial part of the society's population? And why do members of a society in most cases abide by the commands and decisions of leaders? Why, in short, do they consent to be ruled? In what has become a classic theoretical description, Max Weber suggested three different bases of authority or legitimate rule.

Tradition. First, authority may be the product of tradition. Certain families or groups have ruled in the past, and their claims to authority are sustained over many generations merely on the basis of custom. In such cases, leaders are not selected on the basis of their qualifications but rather acquire their positions as the result of inheritance. This form of legitimate rule, according to Weber, is most apparent in simple societies with relatively uncomplicated divisions of labor and preindustrial economic systems. Hereditary monarchies and tribal chieftainships are examples of traditionally based authority.

Just as leaders emerge by customary practices, people in such societies accept rules as a matter of tradition because "it has always been this way." Such systems of rule are typically found where sacred values predominate — that is, where people do not recognize their ability or propriety in changing well-established practices.

Although traditional authority has been predominant throughout most of human social development, systems with traditional bases of authority in the pure sense are increasingly difficult to find in the contemporary world. Elements still remain strong in certain societies, however (Coleman, 1960; LaPalombara, 1965).

Legal-rational. More typical of modern societies is what Weber called legal-rational authority. Here leaders are given authority and their decisions obeyed because they have been selected for their positions in accordance with formalized, standard procedures. People are elected or assigned for a fixed period of time to specific posts whose legal boundaries (that is, what they can rightfully do in those posts) are clearly spelled out. Thus, power is invested in the position itself rather than in the individual who temporarily occupies it.

In sociopolitical systems with a legal-rational basis, then, people submit not to particular persons but to a system of rules administered by those in leadership positions. The president of the United States, for example, is inordinately powerful but only within the boundaries of his office. He may have the power to allocate enormous societal resources and to command a vast admin.strative machine, but for all this he cannot issue a simple parking ticket! His power, in other words, cannot be applied outside his authorized area. Nor can he utilize illegitimate means to sustain his presidential powers.

The case of Richard Nixon and his coterie demonstrates what may happen when persons of authority choose to disregard the limitations which are placed upon their actions within a legal-rational system. In many of their activities, these men went beyond the formally defined powers of their offices. The powers of the president and his staff did not include the use of government agencies to harass political adversaries and pursue personal vendettas, nor did they include burglarizing and other illegalities to stifle opposition. Subsequently some of their misdeeds were discovered, and they were divested of authority.[1] Also in this case Nixon's aides violated a basic principle of a legal-rational order which requires loyalty to the system rather than to particular personalities who for a period of time make up its constituent parts.

A legal-rational basis of authority typifies all organizations in modern industrial societies, not simply agencies of government. Corporate officials hold power through appointment or election by rational procedures, as do labor union leaders, educational leaders, and officers of the entire range of voluntary associations from churches to fraternal groups and social clubs. What is most important in all of these cases is that power is clearly limited by well-defined guidelines.

Weber explained that the transition from traditional to legal-rational systems is a natural result of the increasing complexity of societies and the corresponding emergence of bureaucratic organizations. Bureaucracy, according to Weber, is part of the tendency in modern societies toward ra-

---

1. The literature describing and commenting on Nixon and what has come to be known in general as "Watergate" is vast. One of the more comprehensive treatments of the incidents and personalities of this period is by Lukas (1976). For an insightful analysis of the crisis of legitimacy which Watergate created, see Vidich (1975).

tionalization of all social life. A bureaucracy represents ideally a form of social organization in which nothing is left to chance, where the actions of its various parts are subject to clearly specified rules and regulations. Theoretically positions are filled on an impersonal basis—need and qualification—and the transitory nature of one's appointment or selection is understood. This is the essence of legal-rational authority. Although bureaucratic organization is most often associated with the state, in modern societies all major institutions except the family are so organized.

Charisma. Weber explained that authoritative power may occasionally be founded upon the sheer strength of personal appeal. In such cases, leaders will assume their positions as a result of their ability to capture the allegiance of large numbers of people. Weber called this charismatic authority.

Charisma implies a certain electrifying quality, a capacity on the part of an individual to attract and hold the attention and loyalty of others. Those who follow charismatic figures believe them to be extraordinary, perhaps even superhuman. Loyalty and compliance are given not to a rational "system" or even to custom but to a particular personality. History is replete with charismatic figures who have ascended to leadership of various societal institutions: religious personalities such as Christ, Muhammad, and Gandhi; military figures such as Caesar and Napoleon; and political leaders such as Lenin, Hitler, Zapata, Mao, and Castro.

Sociopolitical movements designed to change the society's distribution of power are led by charismatic personalities, at least for a necessary period of time. For example, if we look at the black civil rights movement in the United States during the 1960s, we immediately associate certain key figures—Martin Luther King, Malcolm X, Stokely Carmichael—with the movement itself. Such personalities are able to articulate the movement's objectives and may serve as forces of cohesion for what may be an otherwise unorganized mass. In focusing attention on the movement, they become, in a sense, its very embodiment. Revolutionary movements are especially personified in their early stages by charismatic figures. Almost all observers of the Cuban Revolution, for example, claim that in its early years Fidel Castro *was* the revolution. One writer describes his role as the country's "new hero":

> In the eyes of his countrymen, not only had he waged a prolonged and successful guerrilla struggle, but he had also done so against seemingly impossible odds. Thus, having proven himself, Fidel took

on the classic attributes of a charismatic leader—by performing as a prophet in miraculously deposing Batista as he had originally promised, by proving his valor all along as a heroic warrior, and by ultimately delivering the Cuban people from tyranny (Gonzalez, 1974:88–89; see also Fagen, 1965).

Charismatic authority is fundamentally different from either traditional or legal-rational authority in that it is a product of social crisis or rapidly changing social conditions. It is thus an inherently unstable form of authority which eventually must give way to, or at least incorporate some elements of, either a traditional or legal-rational system. The latter types are relatively permanent and sustain themselves by meeting the general needs of the society or by successfully creating societal acceptability through control of information and ideology. When a society experiences radical changes that create serious social strain, however, extraordinary personalities may appear who promise quick and certain solutions to the crisis.

But as suddenly as charismatic personalities may arise, so they may disappear or lose their appeal. The emergence of charismatic leaders and their assumption of authority are in the end dependent upon people's perception of them as extraordinary persons, whether or not they in fact possess such characteristics. Weber explains that "it is recognition on the part of those subject to authority which is decisive for the validity of charisma" (1947:359; see also Davies, 1954). Also, if sociopolitical movements are too firmly associated with their leaders, the removal of such persons from the scene may result in dissipation of the movement itself. To avoid this, charismatic leaders must stabilize their authority by reinforcing it with or transforming it into one of the other types.

Furthermore, every governing system must eventually face the tasks of meeting everyday problems of administration. This requires a more permanent and formalized ruling structure, which in modern societies takes the form of bureaucracy. Weber referred to this process as "the routinization of charisma" (Gerth and Mills, 1946:297). A revolution or any other type of sociopolitical movement thus becomes institutionalized at that point when its key figures can permanently exit while the movement's structure remains intact. The movement no longer must incorporate the personality of its leaders into its policies and decisions. Those societies which have undergone social revolution in the twentieth century—Mexico, the Soviet Union, China, and Cuba—all illustrate this phenomenon.

Weber's three bases of authority should be understood as "ideal types," useful as analytic tools but not meant to describe precisely any single sociopolitical system. No particular case will fit perfectly one or the other category; rather it is more likely that any institutionalized ruling system will encompass elements of all three. Nonetheless we can certainly recognize various examples of authority which more closely fit one descriptive type or the other. Though John F. Kennedy surely exhibited charisma more than any American president since Franklin D. Roosevelt, his power was, of course, based essentially upon legal-rational grounds. His charisma, however, was valuable as a means of attracting public support for his political actions. Here, then, we have a case in which one type of authority clearly is dominant, though another is present to some degree. Similarly, the retention of symbolic monarchies in England and several other European states represents the blending of legal-rational authority with traditional authority, the latter only slightly meaningful in substance.

Pseudocharisma. Before leaving Weber's typology, we should note the modern usage of the concept of charisma. Today public personalities in various areas of social life—politics, entertainment, sports, and so on—are frequently described as "charismatic," but their charisma is largely contrived by advertising and public relations efforts. Bensman and Rosenberg (1976:431–433) have referred to this as "pseudocharisma."

Attempts at building charismatic images are most evident in large-scale political campaigns, especially those which rely heavily on television. A good illustration is the 1968 presidential campaign of Richard Nixon, described by Joe McGinniss in his book *The Selling of the President 1968* (1969). McGinniss relates how advertising men, recognizing Nixon's lack of a forceful and credible image vis-à-vis the American public, successfully created a positive, "winning" image largely with the techniques of television campaigning.

The process of image creation in politics is essentially no different from the way in which "stardom" in the entertainment world is virtually created by vast public relations blitzes. Just as the performer is packaged and presented to a carefully prepared public through a meticulously planned campaign, so too the potential winning candidate is presented to his constituency. Appearances are staged, press conferences rehearsed, and "spontaneous" displays of public enthusiasm may be contrived well in advance. Little is left to chance. Selling a president or a senator becomes no different from selling soap or automobiles (see, for example, Bloom, 1973; MacDougall, 1977). Once in office, the politician must maintain the image, and so the efforts of image creation continue.[2]

Of course, the use of public relations techniques to create favorable images in personalities, objects, or beliefs is a commonly accepted practice of almost every institutional area of modern societies whether it be politics, entertainment, business, or even religion. In a sense, institutional leaders become "celebrities" (Boorstin, 1962).

It may be argued that leaders with charisma are demanded by the public, and if they do not possess such characteristics, advertising and public relations techniques serve to create them. In a complex, often incomprehensible society, people cling to social myths which give them assurance and confidence in the rightness and logic of the prevailing sociopolitical system. Among the more common of these myths is the notion that societal leaders are superior persons in knowledge and insight who can therefore be relied on to make critical, far-reaching decisions (Edelman, 1971:83).

Influence

The confusion in defining terms of political sociology is quite evident in differentiating *influence* from *power*. Some simply do not consider the difference meaningful and use the two terms interchangeably (French and Raven, 1959; Goldhamer and Shils, 1939; Polsby, 1963; Simon, 1953), while others feel the need to keep them conceptually separate (Bierstedt, 1950; Coser, 1976; Etzioni, 1968; Hunter, 1953). We will consider influence a type of power distinct from force and authority though often overlapping with the latter.

Basically we may think of influence as noncoercive or *persuasive* power. Bachrach and Baratz (1963:637) explain that "one person has *influence* over another within a given scope to the extent that the first, without resorting to either a tacit or an overt threat of severe deprivations, causes the second to change his course of action." Lenski (1966:57) defines it as "the ability to manipulate the social situation of others, or their perception of it, by the exercise of one's resources and rights, thereby increasing the pressures on others to act in accordance with one's own wishes." Influence as a form of power is indirect and subtle, where "command" is not a com-

---

2. Loewenstein (1966) argues that modern forms of communication actually tend to diminish rather than increase the spell of charisma. Through constant exposure, particularly on television, rulers become personalized in a way that could not have occurred in earlier times. As he explains, "the leader who shows himself daily . . . is less magical and magnetic than the leader who is not seen at all, or only rarely on occasions especially favorable to him" (p. 85).

ponent of the relationship between the interacting parties (Friedrich, 1963:199). Persuasion rather than coercion or formal sanctions is the chief means of eliciting compliance.

Most of the reported news of the day is comprised of descriptions of the actions of politicians, those who are part of the formal governmental apparatus. Authority, specifically political authority, is, in other words, that type of power which most often engages our attention. Only the most naive, however, would understand power in societies as the monopoly of those who occupy positions of authority. Most people recognize the underlying effects of influence, a form of power which is, unfortunately, not as easily seen and thus not as easily scrutinized as authority. As Friedrich (1963:203) points out, the workings of influence are elusive "because most influence changes the conduct of people without any outward appearance of change."

While authority is clearly limited to a position in a particular social organization, influence is not at all so circumscribed. One may be influential not only in his or her own specialized realm but in others as well. Corporation officials, for example, exercise authority within the corporate organization but have no legitimate power to make decisions within government agencies. If those same corporation officials, however, are able to convince a group of legislators to take certain actions favorable to the corporation's interests, actions they otherwise would not have taken, they have exerted influence.

Also the power and prestige gained by occupying a formal position of authority in one area may strengthen one's influence in other unrelated areas. Consider again the corporate officials. If they happen to be attached to a firm which relies heavily on defense contracts, their services will be considerably more valuable if their past experience includes a position in the Pentagon. Presumably their influence among military leaders, acquired through associations and knowledge while with the Defense Department, will carry over in their current position.

Influence and authority may, of course, be coincidental and mutually reinforcing. In seeking to bolster their authoritative power, officials will often use the inherent influence of their formal positions to gather support for policy decisions. For example, it is a common tactic of the president to attempt to sway congressmen on particular legislation by inviting them to the White House, individually or in small groups, or through personal telephone calls. The resultant prestige or psychological rewards obtained are often effective inducements to a change of mind.

Of course, attempts to use personal influence are apt to be more successful by some than others. We frequently hear reference to "weak" or "strong" presidents, congressmen, or other public and private officials.

Essentially what is referred to in these cases are the relative abilities of officeholders to carry out their policies effectively through the use of influence. In this sense, it is possible that persons may occupy positions of substantial authority but wield little influence, thus diminishing their effective power. By the same token, officials may sometimes hold positions of limited authority but exercise considerable influence. Henry Kissinger, for example, while still a presidential advisor, was, by all indications, actually conducting many of the affairs of foreign policy ordinarily carried out by the secretary of state.

In addition to personal forms of influence, economic influence is especially important in modern societies. We have noted that the state is unique among societal institutions in that it has powers that extend to the society as a whole. Only the state may establish rules and make decisions that are binding on all persons, and only it can enforce its will to the maximum extent. As a result, those who are not part of this formal decision-making structure attempt to influence those who are. Although expertise, prestige, skills, access to information, and various other things may be potential bases of influence, in modern capitalist societies economic resources are the primary means by which state influence is sought. Therefore those who control substantial parts of the society's productive and distributive systems can by that fact alone be extremely influential in almost all areas of public policy. In short, to the extent that individuals and organizations own or control in great quantity those things in the society which are valued and scarce, they can influence those with formal authority to act in their interests.

In order to understand power in societies, then, it is necessary to look beyond the formal actions of officials within the political arena and to consider the informal, persuasive tactics of influence. Unfortunately, though influence and authority "are quite distinct on the analytical level, they are often hopelessly intertwined on the empirical" (Lenski, 1966:57).

POWER AS RESOURCE CONTROL

To this point we have described power as taking forms which are *behavioral* in nature. That is, power presumably lies with those who actually wield it. This behavioral conception of power is valuable in that it lends itself to empirical techniques; we can observe or detect who is or is not applying power in any particular situation. But power is not always so easily discerned. Put simply, power lies not only in the actions and decisions of people but also in their possession or control of the society's valued items. This is power as **resource control**.

By conceptualizing it as control of resources, we need not assume that power necessarily involves actual participation in the decisions of political and other important societal institutions, or even in the attempts to influence those who make the decisions. Power is also the *potential* or capacity to act on or influence others. Thus, some groups or individuals may exert power effortlessly or even unintentionally through the sheer weight of their resource base. As Anderson (1974:20–21) has stated, "Power inheres in the social relations which regulate or control the flow of material and human resources in a society. Thus, power may be measured by the degree to which a person or group controls the application and distribution of a society's (or the world's) resources." Dolbeare (1974:4) similarly defines power as "a capability in people, each of whom possesses certain resources (money, talent, reputation, institutional position, etc.) that may affect the thoughts and action of others in various ways."

All power, of course, in whatever form, is founded on power resources that can take many forms, including wealth, property, prestige, formal office, arms, control of communications, control over values, knowledge and expertise, and votes (Clark, 1968; Dahl, 1961; Rossi, 1960). These various power resources, however, are not of equal weight; obviously some are more significant than others.

In capitalist societies, wealth, particularly institutional wealth, is an especially crucial resource. Those who own or control industrial corporations and banks and other financial institutions are able to regulate the society's flow of income, jobs, and other forms of economic livelihood. Indeed, so critical are economic resources that they overshadow most others in significance. In societies such as the United States, elites who control great institutional wealth are thus enormously influential, not only in their own private realms but also in the arena of public politics.

In a sense, just as governmental decisions are binding on all members of the society, so too the decisions of giant corporations in the United States and other modern capitalist societies are compulsory, given everyone's dependence on these organizations for needed goods and services. It is true, of course, that corporations and other economic institutions, unlike the state, cannot enforce their will through the threat of coercion. One can, for example, ignore the local power company's rate increase by burning candles for light or firewood for heat. That is, the power company cannot literally force one to accede to its demands, as the state can do. Yet, the difference in power between the state and key economic institutions may be meaningful only in the abstract. If corporate executives are able fundamentally to affect the distribution of the society's material wealth, their power may be equal to and in many ways even exceed that of government officials, though they occupy no formal political offices or may choose not to exert influence purposefully on those who do. Furthermore, the mere possession or control of such massive resources by these groups forces political decision makers to take them into account on public policy matters whether or not corporations choose to involve themselves.

Nondecision Making

By viewing power as control of resources, we may consider the more subtle forms it may take. One such hidden, almost imperceptible form of power is referred to by Bachrach and Baratz (1962) as "nondecision making." Let us look more closely at this notion.

It is obvious that when the president of the United States orders the movement of troops or when corporate officials announce plans to lay off or hire personnel, power in a most direct form has been exercised. But if we concentrate only on such clearly observable and intentional actions or decisions, we may overlook the important effect of what is called the "mobilization of bias" —that is, the extent to which the society's dominant groups have shaped the values, rules, and attitudes of the prevailing political system (Schattschneider, 1960). Thus, certain issues may be automatically channeled into the political arena, while others are prevented from ever arising. Bachrach and Baratz (1963:641) explain:

> When the dominant values, the accepted rules of the game, the existing power relations among groups, and the instruments of force, singly or in combination, effectively prevent certain grievances from developing into full-fledged issues which call for decisions, it can be said that a nondecision-making situation exists.

In other words, power is exercised when dominant groups in the society or community are able to reinforce cultural values and institutional practices which are inherently favorable to their interests.

Influence on particular issues need not be thought of in this way as a conspiracy operating behind the scenes. Those exerting such power may not even be aware of it themselves "simply because their position of dominance has never seriously been challenged" (Bachrach and Baratz, 1962:952). Thus, when political leaders are naturally disinclined to raise questions or create issues unfavorable to the interests of the society's dominant groups, the latter have exercised power, perhaps unintentionally and perhaps even unconsciously. In such cases the latent power of groups controlling key resources is well understood and their reactions to decisions are anticipated by political leaders.

Resource Control and Other Power Forms

Understanding societal power as control of resources does not mean that those who command great societal resources can always realize their interests. Having a strong power base does not automatically assure influence (demonstrated, for example, by President Carter's decision in 1977 not to finance the building of the B-1 bomber despite warnings from corporation and labor union officials that thousands of jobs would be lost), and the mobilization of bias enforced by dominant groups may sometimes be neutralized (the pressing of black civil rights in the South during the 1960s, for instance). However, cases such as these should not be mistaken as common.

In sum, power is not simply an action in which social parties engage. It is also the capacity to determine societal values and to control and allocate vital human and material resources. Command of such resources constitutes the very foundation of a society's power structure, and those who are able to make basic decisions in this regard are by definition powerful. Understanding power in this way enables us to visualize the pursuit of politics as extending well beyond the formal sphere of government decision makers and also makes us cognizant of significant covert forms of power. Weber defined politics as "striving to share power or striving to influence the distribution of power, either among states or among groups within a state" (Gerth and Mills, 1946:78). If power is conceived of as the control of human and material resources, politics is simply the striving of groups and individuals to influence the distribution of those resources in their favor. Politics, is, then, not limited to politicians.[3]

None of the three main forms of institutional power we have described—authority, influence, and resource control—is necessarily mutually exclusive. On the contrary, they are apt to overlap strongly in most cases. Moreover, they are mutually supportive; possession of one generally leads to others. By controlling scarce societal resources, persons are inherently influential and thus at least potentially powerful. In addition, control of resources inheres primarily in various institutional positions of authority. "No one . . . can be truly powerful," writes Mills, "unless he has access to the command of major institutions, for it is over these institu-

---

3. Whether power should be defined as participation in decision making or as resource capacity is a key issue of debate among political sociologists. Although the two conceptions may not be wholly incompatible, they are distinguishable nonetheless. This becomes an important methodological point since one's initial understanding of what power *is* will naturally affect one's ultimate findings of who *has* power.

tional means of power that the truly powerful are, in the first instance, powerful" (Mills, 1956:9).

With an understanding of these three forms of societal power, we may combine them into a working definition: Power is the capacity to make decisions which affect the society as a whole, or to influence those who do, through authoritative position in important institutions or through control of vital resources. Our concern, then, is with institutional rather than inter-personal power, and our focus will be upon those institutions—chiefly the state and the economy—within which control and direction of the human and material resources of the society lie.

ELITES AND MASSES: THE STRATIFICATION OF POWER

However we conceptualize power, we will find those who have much of it and those who have, by comparison, little. Moreover, this unequal dis-tribution of power is relatively persistent over long periods of time. The same groups from one generation to the next seem to occupy the society's important positions and either own or control the bulk of the society's wealth. Power is, in other words, *stratified*.

When sociologists refer to stratification, they mean a stable and endur-ing structure of inequality among a society's groups. Modern societies are stratified along several dimensions: wealth, prestige, and power.[4] We are most concerned with the power dimension, but in a basic sense power underlies all forms of stratification. Wealth and prestige are essentially mirrors of a society's power arrangement. British sociologist Frank Parkin (1971:46) has described this relationship:

> To speak of the distribution of power could be understood as another way of describing the flow of rewards; the very fact that the dominant class can successfully claim a disproportionate share of rewards *vis-à-vis* the subordinate class, is in a sense a *measure* of the former's power over the latter. In other words, power need not be thought of as something which exists over and above the system of material and social rewards; rather, it can be thought of as a concept or metaphor which is used to depict the flow of resources which constitutes this system.

---

4. Weber's (Gerth and Mills, 1946:180–195) is the classic statement of the multidimen-sionality of stratification in modern societies. Another more current explanation of multidimensional stratification systems is Lenski's (1966).

Thus, the powerful usually are also the wealthy and the prestigious. Wealth, power, and prestige generally move in a circular flow. Like the proverbial chicken and egg dilemma, it is often difficult to determine whether one or the other is the initial component in the cycle; but once either is established, the others tend to follow. In modern industrial societies, however, wealth and prestige seem largely determined by the distribution of power (Lenski, 1966:75).

The Correlates of Power

Of special importance in political sociology is the way in which the stratification of societal power relates to other social variables, such as class, ethnicity, sex, and age. Looking at the correlations between societal power and other social variables enables us to know how open or closed is the society's power structure. Do people of different social origins commonly enter powerful decision-making and influential groups, or do top leaders remain tightly knit in self-sustaining units?

In all societies correlations between certain social characteristics and power positions are quite evident. As we shall see, no matter how open the power structure may seem, the social backgrounds of leaders tend to be relatively consistent for long periods of time. Those who hold leadership positions are generally replaced by persons of similar social origins, and these repetitive patterns of replacement come to be commonly expected. In the United States, for example, it is not accidental that the top power holders in almost all institutional areas have traditionally been and continue to be upper or upper middle class, white, Protestant, of northwest European origin, male, and generally middle-aged. The manner in which political and economic institutions operate, as well as social expectations and widely held beliefs regarding leaders (for example, "women are physically and mentally ill equipped to make crucial societal decisions"), tend to perpetuate the replacement of those at the top with others who possess dominant class and status backgrounds.

Elites and Masses

The stratification systems of modern societies such as the United States are highly complex, with a great range of class, status, and power groupings. But in deciding those issues which affect all or great parts of the society, it is only the few at the top who are able to make their influence felt. Only on issues that affect limited and specific parts of the society do most people have any input.

To simplify matters, then, we may divide the society into two main power strata: elites and masses. **Elites** are those who occupy the society's top positions of power and wealth. They are the people who exercise authority, influence, and control of resources within the society's important organizations. They formulate policies, guide the activities, and decide the significant issues of government, the corporation, education, and other major societal institutions. They own the bulk of the society's wealth. And, perhaps most importantly, they are able to impose on the society as a whole their explanation and justification for the dominant political and economic systems.

Masses or nonelites are those who comprise the vast majority of the society's populace, whose power, wealth, and prestige are limited. Obviously there are great differences in power, wealth, and prestige among nonelites. However, in deciding the fundamental issues of the political and economic systems—in political scientist Harold Lasswell's (1936) oft-quoted phrase, "who gets what, when, how?"—these differences decline in significance. The important distinction is basically between the few at the very top and the remaining populace.

It is an axiom of political sociology that in any society a relatively small number of people—an elite—always rules, regardless of what kind of social system is evident or what form of political or economic ideology is proclaimed. Given the prevalence of elite rule and privilege in societies, the principal questions which have absorbed the attention of political sociologists concern the makeup and change of elites and the relationship between elites and masses. The key analytic problems are thus not only "*Who* are the significant decision makers and influentials in society?" but also "*Whose interests* do elites serve and how do the masses try to hold elite power in check?" These points will form the crux of our analysis of power in America in Part Three. They are also integral to the major theoretical models of political sociology, to which we will turn in Part Two.

SUMMARY

Power, the fundamental concept of political sociology, is inherent in all human interaction. Political sociologists, however, are most interested in **societal** power—that is, power which is pursued and exercised by groups and individuals whose actions and decisions have societywide impact. Three major types of societal power are authority, influence, and resource control.

Authority is the right given to particular persons and organizations to exercise power on societal issues. It is legitimate, socially approved power and is impersonal in application. Weber suggested three bases of authority in societies: traditional, legal-rational, and charismatic. **Traditional** authority is founded on custom, whereas **legal-rational** authority is based on clearly prescribed rules. In a legal-rational system, leaders assume power and people obey on the basis of objective procedures. **Charismatic** authority rests on the ability of an individual to attract the allegiance of great numbers of people through his or her personal attributes. It is an intrinsically unstable form of authority and necessarily gives rise to either a legal-rational or traditional system. **Pseudocharisma** is a modern phenomenon whereby charisma is "manufactured" through media techniques.

Influence is a subtle, indirect form of societal power whose chief effect is persuasion rather than coercion. Authority often overlaps with influence, but the two are not necessarily collateral.

Power is also measured by the degree to which persons or organizations control the society's vital resources, wealth in particular. Power as **resource control** is a potential form of power and is exerted in indirect, sometimes hidden fashion. In modern capitalist societies economic decision makers exercise great public power in the same way as government leaders on the basis of their control or ownership of the society's productive resources.

Authority, influence, and resource control generally overlap. Regardless of the form it takes, societal power is always distributed unequally. The unequal distribution of power is structured, resulting in little change over long periods of time. Power is thus **stratified**. Those at the top of the hierarchy of power, exercising maximum authority, influence, and control of resources, are **elites**. Those beneath them, the vast majority of the society's populace, are **masses** or nonelites. Power is the foundation of other forms of social stratification including wealth and prestige.

Most of the overriding questions and issues of political sociology revolve around the sociological makeup, interrelations, and actions of the society's elites and the extent to which they are controlled by masses.

REFERENCES

Anderson, Charles. 1974. *Toward a New Sociology.* (Revised ed.) Homewood, Ill.: Dorsey.

Bachrach, Peter, and **Morton Baratz.** 1962. "Two Faces of Power." *American Political Science Review* 56(December):947–952.

———————————. 1963. "Decisions and Nondecisions: An Analytical Framework."

American Political Science Review 57(September):632–642.

Bensman, Joseph, and **Bernard Rosenberg.** 1976. *Mass, Class, and Bureaucracy: An Introduction to Sociology.* New York: Praeger.

Bierstedt, Robert. 1950. "An Analysis of Social Power." *American Sociological Review* 15(December):730–738.

_____. 1954. "The Problem of Authority." In Morroe Berger, Theodore Abel, and Charles H. Page (eds.), *Freedom and Control in Modern Society.* New York: Van Nostrand.

Bloom, Melvyn. 1973. *Public Relations and Presidential Campaigns.* New York: Crowell.

Boorstin, Daniel J. 1962. *The Image.* New York: Atheneum.

Clark, Gerald. 1975. "What Happens When the Police Strike." In William J. Chambliss (ed.), *Criminal Law in Action.* Santa Barbara: Hamilton.

Clark, Terry N. 1968. *Community Structure and Decision-Making.* Scranton: Chandler.

Coleman, James S. 1960. "The Politics of Sub-Saharan Africa." In Gabriel Almond and James S. Coleman (eds.), *The Politics of the Developing Areas.* Princeton, N.J.: Princeton U. Press.

Coser, Lewis. 1976. "The Notion of Power: Theoretical Developments." In Lewis Coser and Bernard Rosenberg (eds.), *Sociological Theory.* (4th ed.) New York: Macmillan.

Crozier, Michael. 1973. "The Problem of Power." *Social Research* 40(Summer): 211–228.

Dahl, Robert. 1961. *Who Governs?* New Haven: Yale U. Press.

Davies, James C. 1954. "Charisma in the 1952 Campaign." *American Political Science Review* 48(December):1083–1102.

Dolbeare, Kenneth M. 1974. *Political Change in the United States.* New York: McGraw-Hill.

Edelman, Murray. 1971. *Politics as Symbolic Action.* Chicago: Markham.

Etzioni, Amitai. 1968. *The Active Society.* New York: Free Press.

Fagen, Richard. 1965. "Charismatic Authority and the Leadership of Fidel Castro." *Western Political Quarterly* 18 (June):275–284.

French, John R. P., and **Bertram Raven.** 1959. "The Bases of Social Power." In Dorwin Cartwright (ed.), *Studies in Social Power.* Ann Arbor: Institute for Social Research, University of Michigan.

Friedrich, Carl J. 1963. *Man and His Government.* New York: McGraw-Hill.

Gerth, Hans, and **C. Wright Mills.** 1946. *From Max Weber.* New York: Oxford U. Press.

Goldhamer, Herbert, and **Edward Shils.** 1939. "Types of Power and Status." *American Journal of Sociology* 45(September):171–182.

Gonzalez, Edward. 1974. *Cuba Under Castro: The Limits of Charisma.* Boston: Houghton-Mifflin.

Hunter, Floyd. 1953. *Community Power Structure.* Chapel Hill: U. of North Carolina Press.

LaPalombara, Joseph. 1965. "Italy: Fragmentation, Isolation, Alienation." In

Lucian W. Pye and Sidney Verba (eds.), *Political Culture and Political Development*. Princeton, N.J.: Princeton U. Press.

Lasswell, Harold. 1936. *Politics: Who Gets What, When, How?* New York: McGraw-Hill.

Lenski, Gerhard. 1966. *Power and Privilege*. New York: McGraw-Hill.

Loewenstein, Karl. 1966. *Max Weber's Political Ideas in the Perspective of Our Time*. Amherst: U. of Massachusetts Press.

Lukas, J. Anthony. 1976. *Nightmare: The Underside of the Nixon Years*. New York: Viking.

MacDougall, Malcolm D. 1977. "How Madison Avenue Didn't Put a Ford in Your Future." *New York* 10(February 21):46–54.

MacIver, Robert. 1965. *The Web of Government*. New York: Free Press.

McGinniss, Joe. 1969. *The Selling of the President 1968*. New York: Trident.

Merriam, Charles E. 1934. *Political Power*. New York: McGraw-Hill.

Milgram, Stanley. 1975. *Obedience to Authority*. New York: Harper & Row.

Mills, C. Wright. 1956. *The Power Elite*. New York: Oxford U. Press.

———. 1959. *The Sociological Imagination*. New York: Oxford U. Press.

Olsen, Marvin. 1970. "Power as a Social Process." In Marvin Olsen (ed.), *Power in Societies*. New York: Macmillan.

Parkin, Frank. 1971. *Class Inequality and Political Order*. New York: Praeger.

Polsby, Nelson. 1963. *Community Power and Political Theory*. New Haven: Yale U. Press.

Rossi, Peter. 1960. "Theory, Research, and Practice in Community Organization." In Charles R. Adrian (ed.), *Social Science and Community Action*. East Lansing: Michigan State U. Press.

Russell, Bertrand. 1969. *Power: A New Social Analysis*. New York: Norton.

Schattschneider, E. E. 1960. *The Semi-Sovereign People*. New York: Holt, Rinehart and Winston.

Simon, Herbert A. 1953. "Notes on the Observation and Measurement of Power." *Journal of Politics* 15(November):500–516.

Vidich, Arthur J. 1975. "Political Legitimacy in Bureaucratic Society: An Analysis of Watergate." *Social Research* 42(Winter):778–811.

Weber, Max. 1947. *The Theory of Social and Economic Organization*. Trans. A. M. Henderson and Talcott Parsons. Glencoe: Free Press.

part two

major theoretical perspectives in political sociology

chapter 3

pluralism

In no country in the world does the law hold so absolute a language as in America; and in no country is the right of applying it vested in so many hands. The administrative power in the United States presents nothing either centralized or hierarchical in its constitution; this accounts for its passing unperceived.

Alexis deTocqueville

The first theoretical model of politics in society with which we will deal is one most familiar to Americans. It is essentially a description of how modern democratic sociopolitical systems are supposed to work. As we shall see, the other two major theoretical models coincide on the notion that societal power is held by a small, self-serving group —a ruling elite or ruling class. Americans, however, are reluctant to think of politics as the covert actions of elites or the conflict between social classes. Pluralism breaks sharply from these ideas. Societal power is seen as decentralized rather than as resting in the hands of a relatively centralized and cohesive few. In short, the pluralist view is that no one group in the society can exert its will on all significant issues.

In a more specific way, pluralism can be contrasted with elite and class models on two major points: (1) the scope of power in a society and (2) the relations between leaders and masses. On the first point, pluralists see the power pie divided into many pieces; elitists and class theorists see it as uncut. On the second point, pluralists see average citizens as having meaningful input into decision making, thus exerting effective power over leaders; elitists and class theorists see the average citizen as having little real control over leaders and thus having little or no say in the shaping of societal decisions.

It is clear, then, why pluralism is more palatable to the American political mind: It is based on the democratic image of the American sociopolitical system into which we are socialized from our earliest school experience. "Government of, by, and for the people," "equality before the law," and "separation of powers" are phrases which describe the civics book picture of power in America, and pluralism certainly fits this image more snugly than class or elite models. The distrust of an all-powerful government is also a fundamental part of the American political tradition, and again pluralism complements this belief quite well. Most simply, pluralist systems are usually seen as *democratic* systems, and there is a tendency to equate the two. A correctly functioning pluralist system is one in which no single group among many diverse groups is able to impose its will on the society as a whole. This is contrasted to a totalitarian system in which a single group rules with no accountability to the citizenry.

Of the three major theoretical models in political sociology, pluralism is the least systematically integrated since it encompasses several theories with a common basis. That common basis is the understanding that power is widely shared; it is fragmented and diffuse, deriving from many sources. Sociologists Joan Huber and William Form's definition of pluralism seems simplified and general enough to include most variations. They describe a political system as pluralistic "when a variety of groups or factions can influence policy in such a way that no single or no small number of groups can control it or, conversely, when all legitimate interest groups have an appreciable share of influence" (Huber and Form, 1973:132).

The idea of pluralism has been used in a number of ways to describe not only sociopolitical systems but whole societies, communities, and organizations of all kinds. *Social* pluralism refers to a society in which a number of diverse ethnic, racial, or religious groups live under the same general cultural system while retaining and respecting each other's unique life-styles, values, and cultural identities (Gordon, 1964). *Political* pluralism is founded on the same essential idea: There is a variety of power bases corresponding to many different interest groups, each of which is able to have its say in the political arena through a process of negotiation and compromise within a mutually respected common political framework. In fact there is a strong relationship between social and political pluralism. Those who favor pluralism see it as a perspective uniquely suited to the politics of a modern heterogeneous society. In a sense, a decentralized, complex, and varied society leads to a decentralized, complex, and varied political system.

Pluralism, then, is a perspective of power suitable mainly to industrial societies of the modern world where there are many varied social groups — political, occupational, ethnic, religious, fraternal, and so on. But its applicability is even further narrowed to societies with democratic sociopolitical systems, in particular the Anglo-American societies. Modern pluralism has been largely created and favored by American political scientists of the post-World War II era, and its proponents have focused almost exclusively upon the United States. This paradigm therefore is not as broadly applicable to many societies as is either of the other perspectives at which we will look.

THE THEORETICAL ROOTS OF AMERICAN PLURALISM

In tracing its historical roots, pluralist theory may be seen as a response to the industrialization and urbanization of Western society in the nineteenth century. The traditional way of life centering on the institutions of family, religion, and community was now shattered by these twin processes. Where these institutions had in the past served as sources of material and spiritual needs, their roles were now diminished as social life became structured within centralized, specialized, impersonal forms. Bureaucracy increasingly characterized not only the state but work, education, and the church as well. The alienating effects of these processes were of great concern to early sociologists, including Marx, Durkheim, and Weber.

Sociology at this time was a budding field of study, and one of its chief questions was the manner in which a society of individuals, no longer restrained by the authority of traditional institutions, could be bound together and function without serious disruption. French sociologists Alexis deTocqueville (1805–1859) and Emile Durkheim (1858–1917) were especially concerned that a society of unorganized, atomized individuals would be defenseless against a centralized political power. Such an unchecked power, they feared, would create the potential for despotism in which individual liberties would be destroyed. Their answer to this problem was the development of a plurality of centers of power. Government itself would be divided into separate units and, most importantly, individual citizens would be able to find guidance, security, and expression of their vital interests within a variety of voluntary associations. These voluntary associations would serve as a kind of buffer between the state and the individual.

In addition to the rise of industrialization and bureaucracy, the early nineteenth century was characterized by the spread of democratic ideas throughout Europe, spurred in largest part by the American and French revolutions. DeTocqueville had closely studied these events and saw the ascendance of democracy as an irreversible trend of modern industrial societies. America, he felt, represented that society in which the structural conditions needed for a democratic system —the disappearance of distinction of class or rank and a uniformity of living conditions —had been most successfully developed to that time. Himself a French aristocrat, deTocqueville visited the United States in the early 1830s with the purpose of observing and reporting on life there; at that time America was still a new and relatively exotic nation to Europeans. From his sojourn came a most insightful description and commentary on American society, *Democracy in America*, a volume many of whose findings remain amazingly pertinent even today. The patterns of democracy he found in the United States —equality in application of the law and equality of economic opportunity —were seen by deTocqueville as forerunners of what eventually would occur in European societies, and this belief galvanized his interest in studying American institutions.

Voluntary Associations

A consequence of the diffusion of democratic ideas and the ascent of industrialization is the demise of a social aristocracy, a group which had traditionally served as an intermediary between the ruling monarch and the masses. In preindustrial societies an aristocracy stood as a stabilizing and generally benign force, acting as a filter of sorts through which the monarch's power was moderated as it passed down to the lower social levels. DeTocqueville felt that without such an intermediate level of power, a society might easily be swept up by, on the one hand, an all-powerful tyrant or, on the other, a "tyranny of the majority."

In modern democratic societies such as the United States, however, deTocqueville sees no aristocracy. What, then, substitutes for this important middle level of power? His answer is a network of well-organized voluntary associations, representing economic, political, and religious interests. "Public security, trade and industry, and morals and religion all provide the aims for association in the United States" (deTocqueville, 1966:174–175). DeTocqueville was especially impressed with the American tendency to form innumerable autonomous and private organizations whose purposes were to further an almost endless variety of goals and activities.

In deTocqueville's view, this middle layer of organizations between rulers and masses serves a dual purpose. First, it prevents elites from exerting unmitigated power, and second, it provides the citizenry a means of input into the power process. In other words, it is through these organizations that citizens are able to influence societal leaders and hold them accountable. DeTocqueville explains:

> In aristocratic nations secondary bodies form natural associations which hold abuses of power in check. In countries where such associations do not exist, if private people did not artificially and temporarily create something like them, I see no other dike to hold back tyranny of whatever sort, and a great nation might with impunity be oppressed by some tiny faction or by a single man (deTocqueville, 1966:177).

The existence of pluralism within government itself is also seen by deTocqueville as highly significant in the maintenance of political democracy. He was convinced that the American system of separation of powers, as well as the proliferation of many state and local units of government, were additional safeguards against the growth of an all-powerful state. Thus, many competing power centers, deTocqueville observed, typify the politics of American society both inside and outside its governmental institutions.

Tyranny of the Majority

One of deTocqueville's main points is that centralized authority can easily become tyrannical since it tends to destroy independence of thought and action. Hence the importance of *many* power centers. But in an ironic way, equality too can limit individual liberty, and of such a "tyranny of the majority" deTocqueville was equally fearful. Tyranny, in other words, can flow from the bottom of the social order as well as the top.

The ability of the majority to stifle nonconforming or unpopular beliefs and actions may not be as direct and intimidating as the tyranny of a dictatorship, but it can be quite effective nonetheless. DeTocqueville had already observed the power of the majority to dampen freedom of expression. "In America the majority has enclosed thought within a formidable fence. A writer is free inside that area, but woe to the man who goes beyond it" (deTocqueville, 1966:235).

Such is the subtle terror and intimidation which may be created by democracy. DeTocqueville's fear is well expressed in this poignant passage from *Democracy in America*:

> When a man or a party suffers an injustice in the United States, to whom can he turn? To public opinion? That is what forms the majority. To the legislative body? It represents the majority and obeys it blindly. To the executive power? It is appointed by the majority and serves as its passive instrument. To the police? They are nothing but the majority under arms. A jury? The jury is the majority vested with the right to pronounce judgment; even the judges in certain states are elected by the majority. So, however iniquitous or unreasonable the measure which hurts you, you must submit (deTocqueville, 1966:233).

In the end, however, deTocqueville was optimistic that the negative capabilities of a democratic system —both an all-powerful state and a tyranny of the majority —could be averted by the maintenance of pluralistic social and political structures. Strong private and autonomous voluntary associations were a primary component of these structures.

MODERN PLURALISM:
THE INTERPLAY OF INTEREST GROUPS

DeTocqueville's portrait of the American democratic system has become the theoretical groundwork of modern pluralism. Following a similar line of thought, political scientists in the 1950s developed an updated theory which took as its central theme the interplay of many varied interest or pressure groups. Perhaps the major exponent of this version of the pluralist idea was David Truman, who, in *The Governmental Process* (1951), presented a picture of the American political system as basically revolving around the workings of such groups. Like deTocqueville, Truman saw organizational membership as the chief means by which individuals could influence and ultimately control political decision makers. Interest group theory gained much favor among political scientists, and many of its basic points remain vital to an understanding of the pluralist perspective of power.

Again it is important to bear in mind that Truman and other interest group theorists are concerned primarily with the American system. Despite the intention of creating a paradigm applicable to any modern democratic society, almost all discussions and examples are drawn from the United States. Thus one must be careful to consider the limited relevance of this approach to any but those societies with very special structural conditions: a heterogeneous population, a widespread network of diverse private associations, and a relatively fragmented government consisting of many units at different levels. To all intents and purposes, then, interest group theory is directed exclusively at American society.

Interest Group Activity

A basic assumption of interest group theory is that political behavior takes place within and between groups rather than as interaction between individuals. Realistically it can be no other way in a modern complex society. Particularly when one is dealing with governmental institutions in trying to strengthen or protect one's interests, only through group action may favorable results be realized.

It is the workings of such interest or pressure groups that constitute the nucleus of the political process. Truman defines an interest group as a group of persons who share a similar attitude (interest) that makes certain claims upon other groups in the society. "If and when it makes its claims through or upon any of the institutions of government, it becomes a political interest group" (Truman, 1951:37). Most interest groups, since they at one time or another seek out the institutions of government in pursuing their objectives, do become political groups. Thus they usually offer financial support to political candidates who are sympathetic to their causes and use lobbying and other techniques in attempting to influence lawmakers and political parties.

It is important to emphasize the voluntary nature of interest group membership. Persons may choose any number of associational ties depending on their needs and desires. Not all the organizations to which one belongs, of course, will necessarily be interest groups in the sense that they are politically motivated. Once groups seek to influence societal issues in their favor, however, they are political groups.

To illustrate interest group activity, consider two cases, one local and one national in scope.

In a residential area of a community, a rash of traffic accidents has occurred at a busy intersection. It is obvious that a stoplight is needed. Persons who live in the area might petition the city council to install one by writing letters or perhaps personally visiting the council. These would be costly and time-consuming methods, however. Furthermore the council would not likely act on the request of single individuals. A neighborhood organization such as a block club or homeowners improvement association, however, would have as its very purpose attending to such issues. Individuals would not be acting alone and would have the benefit of the group's financial and other organizational resources. Moreover the council would be more responsive to the organization's request since it represents a relatively large number of persons whose votes may be critical at the next election. The organization, then, can achieve what persons acting as individuals cannot.

At the same time, of course, other groups may apply counterpressures on the council *not* to install the light. Local businessmen, for example, might claim that it would slow traffic and cause inconvenience to commuters, discouraging them from passing through the area and thereby hurting their trade. Their argument might be presented to the city council by local business and trade associations. The advantages of group action by the businessmen are the same as for those who want the light installed: It is costly to act alone and, most importantly, the council will be more receptive to the argument of an organized group than of scattered individuals.

In this case the council presumably will act as an umpire, weighing both sides of the issue and ruling in favor of one.

At the societal level, environmentalists may seek to raise air pollution standards by, among other methods, compelling industries nationwide to install newer and more efficient filtering systems. Only by action of the federal government, however, might such a measure be enforced. Thus, efforts will be made to influence lawmakers, but the most effective of these will be activities tied to a national group such as the Sierra Club or the Committee for Environmental Defense. Such organizations can mobilize large numbers of people and resources behind an issue such as this in a manner that single individuals or even local groups cannot. Through lobbying efforts and promises of electoral support—or nonsupport—these associations will attempt to persuade federal lawmakers to pass stricter air pollution standards.

Meanwhile, industrialists will be fighting to *lower* clean air standards in order to minimize profit losses. They too will engage in organized activities in their attempts to sway lawmakers. The National Association of Manufacturers or the Chamber of Commerce, groups which represent the collective interests of business, will pressure government with a campaign that individual firms might find too costly, inefficient, and unproductive. Many corporations, of course, are large enough to be interest groups in their own right.

As at the local level, it is presumed that the government (in this case the federal) will act as a referee, considering both sides and ultimately reaching a decision which will be in the interests of the society as a whole.

In dealing with the federal government, it is obviously far more difficult for individuals to appeal their complaints or pursue their special interests alone. Thus voluntary associations naturally form around various interests. Labor unions, professional societies, trade associations, farmers' groups, veterans' organizations, ethnic and religious groups, and consumer groups are examples of a seemingly endless variety of such voluntary associations acting as interest groups.

In the pluralist view, then, politics becomes essentially a struggle of competing groups within an arena supervised by the state. Pluralists explain that as a society becomes increasingly complex, there is a natural increase in the number and variety of interest groups. As Truman states, "Diversity of interests is a concomitant of specialized activity, and diversity of groups is a means of adjustment" (Truman, 1951:502). Although associations operating as political interest groups may represent a multiplicity of social activities, the most significant appear to be economic groups, specifically those representing business, labor, agriculture, and the professions. Following World War II, economic associations in the United States such as labor unions, trade associations, professional associations, and farm bureaus made increasing claims on or through the state by well-organized and financed lobbying of legislatures and other agencies of federal, state, and even local governments. Thus most of the examples of interest group activity offered by pluralists involve such economically based organizations.

In sum, the interest group version of pluralism sees associations acting as pressure groups upon government, supporting issues and political actions of importance to their members. They serve as a means by which individuals with common interests may exert influence on decision makers by collective action. If citizens cannot realistically apply political pressure individually, they can do it through their organizations. Sociologist Arnold Rose describes the function of the voluntary association for political participation by the average citizen:

Through the voluntary association the ordinary citizen can acquire as much power in the community or the nation as his free time, ability, and inclinations permit him to, without actually going into government service, provided he accepts the competition for power of other like minded citizens. . . . Political power or influence, in the United States is not concentrated in the government, but is distributed over as many citizens, working through their associations, as want to take the responsibility for power (Rose, 1967:247).

In this view, voluntary associations are vital to the functioning of the political system in enabling average citizens to exert at least some control over leaders. Through their organizations' activities, people's desires are made known to political leaders and are responded to in some degree.

The Stability of the Interest Group System

Given the apparent laissez-faire nature of such a sociopolitical system, one might logically ask why it does not disintegrate into a chaotic muddle. How can the general well-being of the society be assured when each organization is pursuing its own selfish ends? Furthermore, what prohibits an overly powerful group or groups from dominating the system? Pluralists point out several safety valves which prevent the system from breaking down.

The balance of group power. First there is presumably a natural balance of power among the various interest groups which is preserved through the "veto power" of each. Since they realize that no single group can win on every issue, they must bargain and compromise with each other. There is, in other words, a give-and-take among them. Regarding air and water pollution, for example, the steel industry may win on one occasion while environmental groups will win on another. As one observer has put it, "Today's losers may be tomorrow's winners" (Latham, 1952:391). Understanding this, none dares to ride roughshod over the others even when it has the capacity to do so.

Each group pursuing its own particular goals ironically assures that the welfare of the society as a whole will be promoted. It is much like the "invisible hand," a term used by classical economist Adam Smith (1723– 1790) in describing the workings of a capitalist economic system. Smith explained that, in an uncanny way, the interests of everyone were assured by all individuals pursuing their own material interests. In the same manner, equilibrium among self-serving political groups assures the public interest. Political scientist Earl Latham (1952:390) describes this effect: "What may be called public policy is actually the equilibrium reached in the group struggle at any given moment, and it represents a balance which the contending factions of groups constantly strive to weight in their favor."

As the interest group system works, the state acts as a kind of bargaining agent through which the political give-and-take between groups takes place. Political leaders take on the role of mediators, turning the proper dials and pushing the right buttons, keeping the system in a more or less shaky balance. Political scientist V. O. Key (1964:20) explains:

> One class or group becomes discontented with existing conditions, and the processes of politics go into operation to create a new equilibrium. The politician finds himself in the middle — and belabored from all sides — as he seeks to contrive a formula to maintain peace among conflicting interests.

Moreover the state, in its role as overseer of the political process among competing groups, has no interests of its own. As Key (1964:150) claims, "A major preoccupation of government is the policing of conflicts of interest." The state, then, is primarily an umpire.

Separation of governmental powers. A second factor which contributes to the smooth functioning of a pluralist system is the division of powers within government itself. Just as there is a plurality of nongovernmental groups in the political arena, there is also a plurality of competing governmental agencies, divisions, and branches. As various social and economic groups vie for power, governmental groups do the same. And as the give-and-take among private interest groups limits their individual power, likewise the separation of powers within the state serves to preclude the dominance of any single branch or agency (Latham, 1952).

The competition for power is exemplified even at the acme of American politics. Political scientist Richard Neustadt pictures the American presidency as a position of utmost formal power, but power which its occupant cannot exert without bargaining with and influencing other political officials and agencies. Neustadt (1976:78) asserts that despite his authoritative powers, the president "does not obtain results by giving orders" and despite the status of his office "does not get action without argument."

Competition among political parties also helps to mitigate state power and prevents any one group from dominating government. The political "ins" understand that they will eventually have to relinquish power to the political "outs" and thus do not act intolerantly toward them. As Raymond Aron (1950:11) states, "Government becomes a business of compromise."

In the pluralist view, then, the power of those in high places is deceptive. In reality they are only arbitrators among competing groups for whose support they too must bargain (Presthus, 1964:15–16).

Finally the separation of powers provides private interest groups with more than one agency within government to which they can appeal their cases. Thus groups or individuals who fail to get a successful hearing of their demands from one official body can turn to others (Mitchell, 1962:64–65; Truman, 1951:264). There are, in other words, various points of access to government decision makers.

Crosscutting group membership. A third important feature of a pluralist system which assures its stability is the overlapping nature of group membership among individuals. Individuals will belong to many organizations rather than to any one exclusively. Furthermore, their simultaneous memberships will often be crosscutting, the purposes and goals of one group conflicting with the purposes and goals of another. Thus, it is argued, since persons do not find themselves consistently on one side of all social and political issues, compromise rather than polarization will typify the system. Different groups pull people in opposite directions, but this, pluralists claim, makes for political stability since they are not totally committed to one group and thus do not form unyielding factions. Instead, temporary alliances are formed around particular issues, forcing moderation and bargaining rather than a "fight to the death."

Mr. X, for example, might be an auto worker, white, Catholic, a Democrat, a veteran, a member of the auto workers' union, and a member of the American Legion. These multiple group memberships will create cross-pressures and will force him to shift his political allegiance on different issues. As part of the white majority, he may resist the racial integration of his neighborhood; but the local Catholic diocese may call upon its parishioners to accept such a move. Or his labor union may favor reestablishing trade relations with Cuba while the American Legion will call for the opposite. On these issues Mr. X will be forced to weigh the constraints of conflicting group pressures.

If the society were made up of individuals who found themselves within *coinciding* rather than crosscutting political groups, there would be little basis for compromise and the degree of antagonism between political factions would be great. Politics would therefore be extremely polarized, with frequent violent confrontations and persistent disagreements. Instead of a precarious though consistent equilibrium, characterized by incremental and gradual changes, the political system would operate as a series of enormous and radical shifts in power, depending on who was able to dominate at any one time.

Consensus of values. Another critical feature of a pluralist system is a widely held acceptance of the basic political framework within which the competition among various interest groups takes place. We might think of this as the "rules of the game," about which there is no disagreement.

When the majority of a society seems to demand conformity to a general set of norms or values, sociologists speak of a "consensus." Certain political norms and values in the United States compel an almost automatic compliance, and it is these widely accepted characteristics of the system that pluralists stress. Democratic procedures, for example, simply are not questioned by any organized interest group; they are accepted by all as givens. No individuals or groups can be denied entry into the political process so long as they adhere to democratic procedures. All interests are entitled to be heard, and if they can muster enough support they may prevail on any particular issue.

It is assumed that there is a mutual awareness of the democratic tradition and that fundamental principles of egalitarianism are to be upheld, thereby protecting the rights and interests of even those who are not part of well-organized interest groups. If undemocratic techniques are proposed by certain groups or factions of them, they will be overridden by other interest groups or the majority within the group itself. The consensus of basic political norms and values may be seen as another check against extreme and rapid sociopolitical change.

Potential groups. Pluralists maintain that shared attitudes constitute group interests. Thus, people who feel the same way about a particular issue can organize and enter the political arena. In fact, even nonorganized groups can be brought into the public policy-making picture. Truman calls these "potential groups," a concept which can be broadly defined to include almost everyone in the society. People may have strong feelings about certain issues but for various reasons will not express them through political activism. But such persons are always *potential* actors, and therefore decision makers can never entirely discount them. Not all taxpayers, for example, are formally organized in pressure groups. But a tax-related issue might arouse enough public concern to rally together vast numbers of people who are usually among the unconcerned and nonparticipating. Political leaders must therefore take these broad and largely unexpressed interests into account. Vice President Spiro Agnew's demagogic appeals in the late 1960s and early 1970s to the "silent majority" would seem to be a reference to these potential groups.

The unorganized, then, are not completely closed off from political input, at least on major issues. Truman (1951:511–512) explains that

". . . the possibility that severe disturbances will be created if these submerged, potential interests should organize necessitates some recognition of the existence of these interests and gives them at least a minimum of influence."

ELITE-PLURALISM

Rare is the theorist who adheres intractably to a single, narrow theory; by the same token, rare is the theory which does not evolve into some new form which seems more compatible with current "reality." Such is the case with pluralism. Although the general outline of interest group theory has not been rejected, in recent years pluralists have recognized that small leadership groups —that is, elites —do and must make the society's major decisions regardless of democratic institutions. This, as we shall see, is a fundamental tenet of the elite model of societal power.

But modern pluralists have synthesized the reality of elite rule with the view of a *pluralistic* elite structure, a characteristic which presumably assures a form of democracy. Their position is that despite elite dominance, the American sociopolitical system and others like it are still basically democratic systems, but democratic systems in which citizen input is more indirect and less effective than earlier interest group theorists seemed to suggest.

It is recognized that mass participation in any area of societal decision making is simply not possible in large, complex societies. There is no denial that leadership is and must be exercised by elites. But although elites dominate the political process, the new pluralists reject the idea of a single, unified, and cohesive elite controlling all key sociopolitical issues. Instead they see many *competing* elites, representing diverse spheres of social life. Through competition among elites the democratic process is preserved. In a sense, the plurality of competing *groups* which had previously been stressed is now narrowed to the competition among a plurality of *elites*. Thus we have a theory which has been variously referred to as "strategic elites" (Keller, 1963), "democratic elitism" (Bachrach, 1966), "plural elitism" (Dye and Zeigler, 1978), and "polyarchy" (Dahl, 1967). Let us consider the last more closely.

Dahl's Polyarchy

The term "polyarchy" has been used by political scientist Robert Dahl (1967; 1972) to describe political systems which fall short of the democratic ideal (no state with "perfect" democratic characteristics exists) but which approach this ideal more than others. The American system falls into this category.

Dahl concedes the critical role played by elites in societal decision making in the United States but does not see them as a single integrated unit. Rather he sees numerous elites who do not agree on all issues. Moreover there is disagreement even within any particular elite. This competition between and within elites is the key means by which the power of leaders is held in check. Elites oppose each other (Democrats versus Republicans, labor leaders versus business leaders, and so on), and differing views are held by different members of any one particular elite (liberal Democrats versus conservative Democrats, labor leaders who support heavy military spending versus labor leaders who support cuts in military spending, and so on).

What is most important in Dahl's theory is the division of political power into many different seats. In Dahl's words, "The fundamental axiom in the theory and practice of American pluralism is, I believe, this: Instead of a single center of sovereign power there must be multiple centers of power, none of which is or can be wholly sovereign" (Dahl, 1967:24).

Bargaining, negotiation, compromise —these are still the basic characteristics of the American pluralist system, according to Dahl, but it is now bargaining, negotiation, and compromise *among elites* which preserves democracy. With multiple centers of power, one can be pitted against another, thus reducing coercion to a minimum. Negotiation among various power elites makes for peaceful solution of issues and a cognizance of the need for mutual rather than partisan solutions to problems.

As with the interest group version of pluralism, an assumption of balance is made: No elite has access to so many power resources that it can achieve all its major goals at all times. Likewise, even *within* elites there is never unanimous agreement on major goals or issues. To win out on an issue generally requires a coalition of different sets of leaders who have diverse goals.

Citizens in this system of elite rule are not entirely left out of the political process, however. An intermediate level of power consisting of voluntary associations and state and local governments contributes to citizen participation. Moreover, although they may not actually take part in decision making, citizens are able to hold elites (at least those in the governmental realm) accountable through periodic elections involving competing parties (Dahl and Lindblom, 1953:277–278).

In short, Dahl's theory of polyarchy is an effort to fuse the reality of elite rule with the central principles of democratic thought. If democracy in the ideal sense is a chimera in modern societies, then the next best thing is a system wherein leaders are held accountable to the citizenry. This is accomplished by the competition among diverse elites, by periodic elections, and by providing channels of influence upon elites for those elements of the masses who choose to be politically active.

Elite-Pluralism and Democracy

Although elite-pluralists do not see the citizenry as a whole as powerless, there is no presumption of large-scale mass political participation. It is assumed that in any case only a minority will have significant influence on elites, whether it is consumers appealing to corporations, rank-and-file members making demands on union leaders, or citizens petitioning government officials. As to the last, Dahl (1956:132) asserts that elections and political competition simply "increase the size, number, and variety of minorities whose preferences must be taken into account by leaders in making policy choices." Organizational constraints and mass apathy are assumed to deter the activism of large numbers of people.

What is more, mass participation is seen not as a desirable goal to be striven for but as a potential threat to the continued stability of the sociopolitical system. "If the uninformed masses participate in large numbers, democratic self-restraint will break down and peaceful competition among elites, the central element in the elitist [elite-pluralist] theory, will become impossible" (Walker, 1966:287).

Despite its anti-democratic overtones, proponents of elite-pluralism defend this arrangement as a version of democracy modified to fit the conditions of modern society. Thus French sociologist Raymond Aron (1968:28) claims that "The fundamental difference between a society of the Soviet type and one of the Western type is that the former has a unified elite and the latter a divided elite." What distinguishes democratic societies from nondemocratic societies, in this view, is not the number of people who participate in political decisions and the shaping of public policy but the number and diversity of *elite groups* making decisions and formulating policy. So long as there is, in Aron's terms, a "dissociation of powers" (Aron, 1950:11), the basic framework of democratic rule is in place.

A CRITIQUE OF PLURALISM

The pluralist model of politics in society has been applied chiefly to the United States, and as a result most of the debate concerning its validity has centered on its interpretation of the American power structure. In the past two decades its detractors have disputed its basic conclusions about who has power and how it is exercised, at both local and societal levels. Many claim this model to be a rationale for the status quo and a defense of the current American political system. Given its emphasis on equilibrium, stability, and gradual change, it is hard to deny that pluralism is in fact a conservative perspective.

Pluralism's somewhat parochial focus is, of course, a key criticism in itself; it is simply inapplicable to most of the contemporary world. But narrowly focused as it is, does pluralism even present an accurate portrait of power in American society? Some of the specific questions concerning the validity of this perspective will be dealt with in the following chapters. At this point we might briefly consider some of its general features which have been challenged.

Voluntary Associations

In every variation of the pluralist theme from deTocqueville to elite-pluralism, voluntary associations play a major role. They are seen as safeguards against the development of overly powerful groups and individuals, and they provide a mechanism by which individuals may influence decision makers. Do such intermediate-level organizations actually play such a role in modern political life?

If they are a fundamental requisite to a well-functioning pluralist system, we must assume that such organizations will be, on the one hand, small enough so that each individual member can have some meaningful say in the group's decisions and, on the other, large enough to exert some clout with larger, primarily governmental, institutions. Organizations meeting both of these requirements seem improbable. Those which are small will generally lack the resources to make themselves heard, and those which may effectively influence decision makers are ordinarily so large that individual members' voices are lost.

This, as we shall see, raises a basic point of the elite model. As one critic of pluralism has pointed out:

> The demand of traditional pluralist theory for individual participation in the policy-forming process through primary groups has been made sentimental by modern organizational conditions. When we accept these conditions, it becomes meaningless to exhort individuals to share in making the decisions of their organizations (Kariel, 1961:182).

Thus, instead of linking the individual to societal decision makers, large interest groups only place one more set of remote leaders and one more bureaucratic structure between them (Mills, 1956:307). Some might argue that the rank-and-file of such organizations recognize their lack of competence in making decisions and thus voluntarily relegate power to their leaders. But it might also be argued that the members do not participate because they simply recognize the futility of their efforts at controlling organization leaders who shape policy. French sociologist Jacques Ellul, for example, attributes the seeming indifference of political party or labor union members to a realization on their part that participation is useless and fictitious: "I have yet to see in any group a true debate starting at point zero and taking all opinions into account" (Ellul, 1972:175). What emerges is not organizational democracy but what Ellul calls "bureaucratic authoritarianism." The organizations which pluralists claim protect the individual against a monolithic government have themselves become oligarchically governed bureaucracies by which individuals are swallowed.

The Class Bias of Interest Group Activity

Even if we disregard the inherent oligarchic tendencies of large associations, is participation in such groups actually as widespread as most pluralists assume? If it is not, the group basis of pluralism is thrown into serious doubt.

The description of the United States as a "nation of joiners" has been common ever since deTocqueville first commented on the tendency for Americans to form associations for almost any conceivable purpose (Lerner, 1957:630; Zimmer and Hawley, 1959:198). But sociological studies show that this characterization is highly exaggerated. Not only is there a comparatively narrow range of participation in voluntary organizations of all kinds, but the joiners are consistently the better educated, the wealthier, and those of higher social status (Curtis, 1971; Hyman and Wright, 1971; Verba and Nie, 1972:41–43, 180–181; Wright and Hyman, 1958). As we proceed down the class and status hierarchies, organizational membership declines. Who, then, represents or speaks for those at or near the bottom? Can potential groups be relied on to fill their needs? Or are the unorganized simply disregarded?

Political scientist Michael Parenti studied the response of local governmental officials to three issues actively fought by the residents of a ghetto area of Newark in the mid-1960s. Based on his findings with regard to these issues, he concluded that "The belief that lower-strata groups exercise a constant, albeit indirect, power remains an article of faith rather than a demonstrated proposition" (Parenti, 1970:519). Since lower-class groups were unsuccessful in influencing decision makers when *active*, Parenti felt that there was even less reason to think they might wield influence when *in*active.

As we shall see in chapter 11, participation of almost any kind in the political process is limited to higher class and status groups. But the interest group system in particular is overwhelmingly dominated by business and upper-class groups. Thus it is not surprising that the wealthier and better organized few will generally have their way on issues affecting their interests. As political scientist E. E. Schattschneider (1975:34−35) has put it, "The flaw in the pluralist heaven is that the heavenly chorus sings with a strong upper-class accent. Probably about 90 percent of the people cannot get into the pressure system."

Moreover, as economist Mancur Olson (1971) has posited, individuals in any case have little incentive to join large interest groups since their investment in time and effort usually exceeds any tangible payoff. Most political groups (those with which pluralists are concerned) dispense what Olson calls "collective" or "public" goods which everyone receives whether or not they are activists. If a consumers' group, for example, successfully lobbies for a truth-in-advertising law, *all* members of the community benefit, not simply those who are members of the group. Smaller groups, Olson points out, are generally more successful in obtaining support because they can offer noncollective goods. Those large groups that *are* effective lobbies attract members by offering what Olson calls "selective incentives," not by offering collective benefits. If steelworkers' jobs depend on union membership or if doctors are afforded prestige by membership in the American Medical Association, these are the primary motivations to join. The incentive in these cases is individual interest, not the collective political interests of "steelworkers" or "doctors," even though through lobbying efforts those collective interests may be served.

Inequality of Power Resources

Perhaps the most fundamental ingredient of a successful pluralist system is a balance of power among various institutions and organizations, particularly as they pressure government to act on their behalf. Such a belief naively assumes, however, that diverse institutional spheres and organizations and their leaders are comparable in terms of real or potential power. They are not. Can we equate big business with organized religion? The National Association of Manufacturers with the National Council of Churches? General Motors with the Methodist Church? Obviously these institutions and organizations perform different functions and display vastly unequal capacities to pressure government and to affect societal policies in general.

The equilibrium view of power grossly discounts the pervasiveness of economic institutions, especially the corporation, in the social and political life of capitalist societies—those in which the pluralist model is most applicable. As Prewitt and Stone (1973:127) contend, all elites, whether those of business or any other societal area, must operate in the milieu of the business world: "There is little that is done by any of the elites for which business support and approval is not required." As we shall see, giant corporations do in fact dominate the sociopolitical system quite consistently.

Finally, what does a power balance mean if huge segments of the society are unrepresented by organizations or their elites? Mills (1956: 246) has written that:

> "Balance of power" implies equality of power, and equality of power seems wholly fair and even honorable, but in fact what is one man's honorable balance is often another's unfair imbalance. Ascendant groups of course tend readily to proclaim a just balance of power and a true harmony of interest, for they prefer their domination to be uninterrupted and peaceful.

In other words, a balance of power may exist which, as it is composed, automatically favors some and disregards the interests of others. Only in recent years, for example, have blacks, consumers, and women begun to be recognized and to petition government and other powerful societal institutions successfully *as groups*.

The Role of the State

Pluralists assume that the state is chiefly a neutral mediator in the political give-and-take of various interest groups and their leaders. It is as if the state enforces a set of rules which are given and unchangeable. Obviously, however, it constantly revises and reinterprets those rules, providing different means of political access to various groups. The changed stance of the government toward organized labor in the 1930s or toward blacks during the past two decades are noteworthy examples.

Also public problems and issues which are debated in the pluralist arena do not emerge "naturally" but are monitored by ruling elites who control the political agenda. Thus problems, issues, and groups may be kept off the political agenda if they appear to threaten the dominance of established power groups. And in the same way, other problems, issues, and groups may be given undue attention. As Parenti (1970:521) notes, "One of the most important aspects of power is the ability not only to prevail in a struggle but to predetermine the agenda of struggle, that is, to determine whether certain questions ever reach the competition stage." For example, poverty became a "problem" in American society after it was recognized as such by the federal government in the 1960s. But to think that poverty was not problematic before the government called attention to it is absurd. The fact of poverty amidst the affluence of post-World War II America had been known and publicly attested to for years by many social critics who were either ignored or scoffed at. Only when the established powers recognized the issue of poverty did it become part of the political debate.

In the same way, it is not simply accidental that socialist alternatives in American politics have never been given serious consideration in attacking social problems. During the 1970s, for instance, when the United States first encountered an energy crisis, nationalization of oil companies was not considered as a possible governmental action to alleviate the problem. The crisis was perceived solely in terms of the continued production and distribution of oil by private companies. These boundaries of the problem and its possible solutions, however, were by no means arrived at neutrally, with all voices being given equal weight. Rather, they were defined by the state and dominant economic groups, not necessarily in collusion but by a common understanding of what is "problematic" and what are "feasible" solutions.

Consensus of Political Values

Pluralists assume that any group may enter the arena so long as it abides by the "rules of the game." Presumably there is widespread agreement —a consensus —on the political rules. But just as we were forced to question a balance of power *among whom*, likewise we must ask, a *consensus* among whom? If the rules are set by those already in power, dissident groups, offering truly alternative approaches to the society's major issues, will find it difficult to garner the resources needed to compete with established interest groups. Indeed, they may never be heard. Minority parties, for example, have never been able to challenge seriously the predominance of the two major parties throughout most of American history. Various groups and leaders tend to be coopted by the established power elements, none of which questions any of the basic assumptions of the status quo. Politicians with truly innovative ideas are deradicalized by establishment forces, not necessarily because they consciously "sell out" (though many do) but because they find that to be given a hearing on *any* issue requires that they accede to establishment rules. Reputedly, newly elected U.S. congressmen are admonished that to "get along" they must "go along."

If a group or party is perceived as a threat to the established system, outright suppression may be employed. Many, particularly those of the left, have been routinely harassed and intimidated by agents of the government. For example, in 1976 it was revealed that the FBI had infiltrated and sabotaged perfectly legal political activities of the Socialist Workers Party for at least fifteen years (Schneir and Schneir, 1976). This and numerous other revelations of the systematic harassment or outright elimination of dissident groups from the public arena during the past three decades by various governmental groups ranging from the CIA, FBI, and Internal Revenue Service to state and even local police have led to serious questions about the meaning of consensus.

Truman, in *The Governmental Process* (1951), concedes that a pluralist system will not work as it is supposed to if strong class divisions develop or if certain groups are restricted in a castelike fashion. In such cases, access to government will be limited, and the political rules may not be seen by these out-groups as sacrosanct. But Truman and other pluralists pay only minimal attention to these "potential" problems. Writing in the 1950s and early 1960s, they apparently either did not recognize or chose to discount the significance of the relative absence of political participation in the United States by lower classes and racial minorities. Thus pluralists were unprepared for the noninstitutionalized political behavior often employed by blacks and other minorities in the late 1960s and early 1970s.

Finally, although pluralists have claimed that consensus characterizes the American sociopolitical system, this term has never been applied in a consistent manner (Horowitz, 1962). There is a consensus of some kind but, as one political scientist has stated, "Rarely . . . have writers on consensus attempted to state what the fundamentals must include, how extensive the agreement must be, and *who* must agree" (McCloskey, 1964:362). One is not certain if by consensus pluralists mean agreement among the entire citizenry or only the politically active element, or what specifically comprises agreement. Is it on all political norms and values, a majority of them, or only a few fundamental ones? As we shall see in chapter 12, most Americans show little consistency in their interpretations (or even understanding) of democratic political values.

Pluralism and Democracy

Proponents of pluralism believe that a pluralist system is the best that modern complex societies can hope for since it comes closest to assuring at least a semblance of democracy. Democracy, of course, has been acclaimed by almost every regime in the modern world, from the freest to the most repressive. The essence of Western democracy, however, is the influence and participation of the *individual* in the political process. But the power of the individual to shape policies or determine the scope of issues of modern societies has deteriorated with the spread of bureaucracy and its attendant oligarchies. Modern pluralism has compensated for this undeniable tendency by offering a democratized version of elitism. The diminished place of the individual in an increasingly elite-dominated system is acknowledged, but democracy, it is believed, is still intact so long as power elites are held in check through dispersion and competition.

This revised model of democracy is defended as more realistic in terms of the conditions of modern societies. Yet no matter how one explains it, this is a system in which elites — even if they are plural, competitive, and dispersed — make the vital decisions of the society; there is a minimum of input by nonelites. Many, therefore, see it not as a modernized form of democracy but as a perversion of it (Bachrach, 1966). As one critic has explained, in the contemporary version of democracy "popular rule means only the popular choice at periodic elections of governors who make policy decisions. The extent of popular participation which is *essential* to political democracy is no more than that" (Davis, 1964:44 – 45).

We have already noted the basic mistrust by elite-pluralists of mass participation in politics. This has prompted other accusations of the "antidemocratic" nature of this perspective. Studies have revealed quite consistently that a commitment to the basics of American democratic ideology is much stronger among the politically active minority than among the citizenry as a whole (Dahl, 1961; Lane, 1962; Lipset, 1963; McCloskey, 1964). Pluralists recognize this fact but do not view it with concern. What is most important in their estimation is the consensus on democratic values among *elites*, not masses. The minimal participation of the masses is also not cause for alarm among pluralists. In fact, to some extent it is better that the masses remain politically inactive and ignorant lest they become the easy prey of demagogues or mass political movements — that is, victims of either of the tyrannies of which de Tocqueville warned. But critics point out that this assumes a sense of social responsibility on the part of elites and irresponsibility on the part of masses, neither of which is necessarily the case (Walker, 1966:288).

The Governmental Focus of Pluralism

Those who have adopted the pluralist perspective — whether the interest group or elitist version — have confined their analyses mainly to the actions of government officials and the links between them and the masses, in particular, the electoral process. It is believed that key societal decisions are made within the institution of government, and it is here that the arena of power exists (Connolly, 1969:9). But as was pointed out in chapter 2, nongovernmental institutions such as the corporation, the school, and the media are also sources of critical power decisions which basically affect our lives.

Let us assume for the moment that the pluralist model is essentially accurate, that it does in fact describe the political process in the United States and other like societies. Perhaps there is a give-and-take between various interest groups or their leaders; perhaps there is a balance among them; perhaps there is a consensus of political values and that government is an effective and impartial umpire. Even if all of this were true, it would still describe politics only in the *public* sector of societal life. It certainly would not describe the process of politics in the *private* sector.

Pluralists argue that through elections, political competition, and the activities of voluntary associations, the society is protected against the excessive power of government. But private corporations, for whom most of us work (or will in the future) and from whom all of us must buy the necessities of life, are not subject to such citizen regulation. Nor are universities, labor unions, the press, or television networks, despite their great public power. How are corporate elites, education elites, communications elites, or elites in any other nongovernmental area controlled? In what ways are they held accountable for their decisions? How is their power restrained? What are the formal and informal mechanisms which the citizenry can use to influence them? Pluralism does not explain —or even pose —these questions.

In a well-known statement which elite-pluralists would not deny, Joseph Schumpeter (1950:284–285) bluntly asserted that "Democracy means only that the people have the opportunity of accepting or refusing the men who are to rule them." But as for private institutional leaders, most people do not have even this opportunity. Citizen control of these elites is minimal at best and nonexistent at worst. Therefore, looking at the actions of governmental leaders and organizations alone will give us only a partial picture of societal power and one that overstates the accountability of elites to masses.[1]

The pluralist view of power and the assumptions on which it rests do not correspond with the broader definition of power we have

1.   Because it is so narrowly confined to the governmental sphere, sociologists have been less prone than political scientists to adopt the pluralist perspective.

employed. Political power is not confined to the governmental realm but is exercised by other institutions in modern capitalist societies, in particular the corporation. Pluralism views governmental and economic institutions as separate rather than overlapping power sources. But the two in capitalist societies are hardly distinguishable. As we examine power in American society in Part Three, we shall see that their goals, actions, and personnel are very much the same.

SUMMARY

If the meaning of pluralism can be condensed into two phrases, they might be "the interplay of diverse political groups" and "diffusion of power." The first phrase describes the *process* by which a pluralist system operates, the second its end *product*. In this view, group interaction is the nucleus of political society; and it is the competition between political groups or their leaders which assures a wide distribution of power.

Specifically, the basic premises of pluralism are: (1) Political power is dispersed among a great number and variety of competing interest groups and their leaders, who make claims upon and through the state. (2) The chief methods by which group conflicts are resolved and issues decided are bargaining and compromise. Deep-seated schisms are minimized by a consensus of political rules. (3) The various interest groups and their leaders are in a delicate equilibrium, each checking the demands of the others. Thus radical or rapid societal change is deterred. (4) All persons in the society are represented by some group(s) or potential group(s) so that their basic interests are protected. The degree of power exercised by particular groups or individuals is dependent on the amount of political activism they choose to undertake.

The classical pluralist structure is thus a tri-level arrangement in which a congeries of voluntary associations stand between the masses and the state, "influencing and checking the latter so as, in some limited way, to represent the former" (Hamilton, 1975:241).

A modern version of pluralism is elite-pluralism, in which the need for political elites to make societal decisions at some distance from the masses is recognized. These are competing elites, however, presumably assuring that no single interest will constantly be served by the state.

The validity of the pluralist model as a description of politics and power in the United States and other similar societies is questionable on several grounds. First, most people are not represented by organized interest groups, and those who are find themselves in bureaucratic organizations with little control over leaders who speak for the group.

Second, the interest group system in general is monopolized by dominant economic groups representing upper-class interests. In addition, the state does not arbitrarily set the agenda of political debate but is subject to the dictates of these dominant groups. Finally, pluralism overemphasizes the role of government as the major focus of power, disregarding significant private power institutions such as the corporation.

REFERENCES

Aron, Raymond. 1950. "Social Structure and the Ruling Class." *British Journal of Sociology* 1 (March/June): 1–17; 126–144.

――――――. 1968. *Progress and Disillusion: The Dialectics of Modern Society*. New York: Praeger.

Bachrach, Peter. 1966. *The Theory of Democratic Elitism*. Boston: Little, Brown.

Connolly, William E. 1969. *The Bias of Pluralism*. New York: Atherton.

Curtis, J. 1971. "Voluntary Association Joining: A Cross-National Comparative Note." *American Sociological Review* 36 (October): 872–880.

Dahl, Robert A. 1956. *A Preface to Democratic Theory*. Chicago: U. of Chicago Press.

――――――. 1961. *Who Governs?* New Haven: Yale U. Press.

――――――. 1967. *Pluralist Democracy in the United States: Conflict and Consensus*. Chicago: Rand McNally.

――――――. 1972. *Democracy in the United States: Promise and Performance*, 2nd ed. Chicago: Rand McNally.

――――――, and **Charles E. Lindblom.** 1953. *Politics, Economics, and Welfare*. New York: Harper and Bros.

Davis, Lane. 1964. "The Cost of Realism: Contemporary Restatements of Democracy." *Western Political Quarterly* 17 (March):37–46.

deTocqueville, Alexis. 1966. *Democracy in America*. J. P. Mayer and Max Lerner (eds.). New York: Harper and Row.

Dye, Thomas R., and **L. Harmon Zeigler.** 1978. *The Irony of Democracy*. 4th ed. North Scituate, Mass.: Duxbury.

Ellul, Jacques. 1972. *The Political Illusion*. New York: Vintage.

Gordon, Milton. 1964. *Assimilation in American Life*. New York: Oxford U. Press.

Hamilton, Richard. 1975. *Restraining Myths: Critical Studies of U.S. Social Structure and Politics*. New York: Sage.

Horowitz, Irving Louis. 1962. "Consensus, Conflict and Cooperation: A Sociological Inventory." *Social Forces* 41 (December): 177–188.

Huber, Joan, and **William H. Form.** 1973. *Income and Ideology*. New York: Free Press.

Hyman, Herbert H., and **Charles R. Wright.** 1971. "Trends in Voluntary Association Memberships of American Adults: Replication Based on Secondary Analysis of Sample Surveys." *American Sociological Review* 36(April):191–206.

Kariel, Henry. 1961. *The Decline of American Pluralism.* Stanford: Stanford U. Press.

Keller, Suzanne. 1963. *Beyond the Ruling Class.* New York: Random House.

Key, V. O., Jr. 1964. *Politics, Parties, and Pressure Groups.* 5th ed. New York: Crowell.

Lane, Robert E. 1962. *Political Ideology.* New York: Free Press.

Latham, Earl. 1952. "The Group Basis of Politics: Notes for a Theory." *American Political Science Review* 46 (June): 376–397.

Lerner, Max. 1957. *America as a Civilization.* New York: Simon and Schuster.

Lipset, Seymour M. 1963. *Political Man.* New York: Anchor.

McCloskey, Herbert. 1964. "Consensus and Ideology in American Politics." *American Political Science Review* 58 (June): 361–382.

Mills, C. Wright. 1956. *The Power Elite.* New York: Oxford U. Press.

Mitchell, William C. 1962. *The American Polity: A Social and Cultural Interpretation.* New York: Free Press.

Neustadt, Richard. 1976. *Presidential Power: The Politics of Leadership with Reflections on Johnson and Nixon.* New York: Wiley.

Olson, Mancur. 1971. *The Logic of Collective Action.* Cambridge: Harvard U. Press.

Parenti, Michael. 1970. "Power and Pluralism: The View from the Bottom." *Journal of Politics* 32 (August): 501–530.

Presthus, Robert. 1964. *Men at the Top.* New York: Oxford U. Press.

Prewitt, Kenneth, and **Alan Stone.** 1973. *The Ruling Elites.* New York: Harper and Row.

Rose, Arnold. 1967. *The Power Structure.* New York: Oxford U. Press.

Schattschneider, E. E. 1975. *The Semisovereign People.* Hinsdale, Ill.: Dryden (orig. published 1960).

Schneir, Walter, and **Miriam Schneir.** 1976. "Square Target of the FBI." *Nation* 223 (September 25): 272–277.

Schumpeter, Joseph A. 1950. *Capitalism, Socialism, and Democracy.* 3rd ed. New York: Harper and Bros.

Truman, David B. 1951. *The Governmental Process.* New York: Random House.

Verba, Sidney, and **Norman H. Nie.** 1972. *Participation in America.* New York: Harper and Row.

Walker, Jack L. 1966. "A Critique of the Elitist Theory of Democracy." *American Political Science Review* 60 (June): 285–295.

Wright, Charles R., and **Herbert H. Hyman.** 1958. "Voluntary Association Memberships of American Adults: Evidence from National Sample Surveys." *American Sociological Review* 23 (June): 284–294.

Zimmer, Basil G., and **Amos H. Hawley.** 1959. "The Significance of Membership in Associations." *American Journal of Sociology* 65 (September): 196–201.

chapter 4

the elite model

*In all societies — from societies that are very mea-
gerly developed and have barely attained the
dawnings of civilization, down to the most advanced and powerful societies — two classes of
people appear — a class that rules and a class that
is ruled.*

Gaetano Mosca

The second major theoretical model of politics in society stands in distinct contrast to the pluralist model we have just reviewed. Elite theorists see not an informed populace holding leaders accountable through elections and pressure groups but a deceived and apathetic public unable to secure information about elite decisions and having virtually no input into those decisions. The fundamental notion of the elite model, then, is the unrestrained power of the ruling few over the masses.

This perspective obviously runs counter to the common American view of how leaders relate to citizens and how the power of the former is kept in check by the latter. But the dominant relationship of elites to masses is prevalent in *all* societies, explain elitists, even those nominally democratic. Most simply, regardless of the nature of the society, a small group—an elite—always holds the bulk of power. Who ultimately decides fundamental issues of right and wrong in the society? Who writes and interprets the society's laws? Who commands the society's vital resources? Elite theorists answer that such decisions are never the responsibility of the people as a whole. Rather, they are determined by an elite. The composition of the elite and the basis of its power may vary at different times and in different societies, but the essential fact of elite rule remains unchanged.

Once elites hold power, they exert whatever means are necessary to retain it. They may use legitimate power resources attached to the positions they hold in the state, the major economic organizations, the media, and so on. And since they control the production of ideology, elites can create legitimacy for their rule where it may not already exist. On these points there is general agreement among elite theorists.

But on other details of elite rule there is a wide range of thought. In fact, much controversy has centered on the philosophical and practical justification for elite rule. Do elites use their power for the society's welfare or for personal gain? Are they necessary or might their functions be assumed by other forms of leadership? The actual nature of elite rule has also been widely debated, especially as regards the United States. Are elites closed and cohesive units or are they open and diverse? Is there only one ruling elite or are there several? If there is more than one, what is the relative importance of each? Finally, the characteristics of elites themselves have been subject to much investigation. From what social classes, ethnic groups, and other social categories do elites come? How do patterns of elite circulation change, enabling those of different social origins to enter into positions of power and privilege? Much research has been carried out regarding these patterns in American society, and we will discuss many of the findings in Part Three.

THEORETICAL ROOTS OF THE ELITE MODEL

The development of elites in society has been approached theoretically in two distinct yet often overlapping ways. First, some have maintained that there is a fundamental psychological difference which sets elites apart from masses. The argument here is that leaders emerge through "natural" processes. Elites develop in societies not because they control great material resources or because they occupy powerful positions of authority (these, of course, follow) but because of personal resources such as intelligence, cunning, or skill. Elite theorists who have been apologists for totalitarian systems such as Nazi Germany or Fascist Italy, for example, have justified power elites in terms of innate superiority.

A second approach has emphasized the development of elites as an unavoidable product of modern social organization. The essence of this thesis is that organizational complexity necessitates a leadership group. That is, leaders give cohesion and direction to a disparate, specialized social structure, whether it be a government, a corporation, an educational institution, a baseball team—in short, *any* social group of sufficient size with a specialized division of labor. Elites in modern societies, then, are functionally necessary and cannot be dispensed with. Their power lies in their positions of authority in key political and economic organizations and the material and human resources they thereby control. Modern elite theory has rested its case primarily on this explanation of elite rule.

The crux of either approach, however, is that in any society there are those who rule (those who occupy positions of authority and influence) and those who do not (the masses). The composition of the elite may change. It may be relatively permanent and closed or it may provide access to those from below, and even counterelites may replace currently dominant elites. But in any case, rule by the few is perpetual.

Pareto and Mosca

The idea of elites extends at least as far back in Western thought as Plato. But Vilfredo Pareto and Gaetano Mosca, Italian scholars writing in the early twentieth century, are most frequently credited with firmly establishing this concept in modern social science. Their basic conclusions are quite similar, though their reasoning is somewhat different.

Pareto. Pareto's definition of elites is clear: the highest achievers in any area of human activity, whether it be politics, the arts, business, and so on. The distinction between such top achievers and the rest of society—that is, the masses—is, according to Pareto, subject to empirical verification and requires no esoteric scientific formula to discern. Top achievers are obvious in the society.

This is a very broad, inclusive definition, and Pareto further breaks down the elite into two components: the governing elite (those who play some part in government) and the nongoverning elite (Figure 4-1). It is the former which is of chief concern to Pareto, and his contribution to elite theory turns on that group.

Pareto argues that elites govern the masses through "force and fraud"—that is, by means of coercion and through guile or cunning. Elites are able to utilize physical as well as moral and intellectual persuasion. Generally, however, they exhibit a preference for one or the other. This corresponds to the two groups of political leaders, whom Pareto calls "lions" and "foxes." Those who fall into each group are endowed with certain psychological proclivities, which Pareto labels "residues." Here we see a fundamental psychological orientation in Pareto's thesis.

Pareto also discusses what he calls the "circulation of elites," the movement of those who excel among the subordinate masses into the ranks of the elite. Such constant regeneration of elites is necessary for them to remain vibrant and effective ruling groups. Pareto (1970:118) states that:

> The governing class is restored not only in numbers, but—and that is the more important thing—in quality, by families rising from the lower classes and bringing with them the vigour and the proportions of residues necessary for keeping themselves in power.

Pareto, then, sees changes in elites but not in the basic dichotomy of power: elites at the top, masses at the bottom. This class division is simply inherent in the nature of society.

Mosca. Mosca presents essentially the same theme as Pareto—the inevitability of a ruling class—though with a different twist. Pareto seemed to rely almost exclusively upon psychological—and what he defined as basically irrational—variables in explaining elites. Mosca's explanation, however, is more sociological in that he stresses structural and organizational factors as well as personal characteristics. For Mosca, the power of the ruling class results from its being an organized minority confronting an unorganized majority. Given the ruling class's organization and the ease of communication among its relatively few members, it becomes difficult for the governed majority to counterorganize and resist the will of the ruling minority:

The power of any minority is irresistible as against each single individual in the majority, who stands alone before the totality of the organized minority. At the same time, the minority is organized for the very reason that it is a minority. A hundred men acting uniformly in concert, with a common understanding, will triumph over a thousand men who are not in accord and can therefore be dealt with one by one. Meanwhile it will be easier for the former to act in concert and have a mutual understanding simply because they are a hundred and not a thousand (Mosca, 1939:53).

Mosca also introduces a subelite in his depiction of societal power, a group made up of intellectuals, technocrats, civil servants, managers, and other organizational specialists who are today referred to as the "technostructure" (Galbraith, 1967) or the "new class" (Parker, 1972). "Below the highest stratum in the ruling class there is always, even in autocratic systems, another that is much more numerous and comprises all the capacities for leadership in the country" (Mosca, 1939:404). Mosca considers these people extremely critical to the functioning of the political mechanism, for they are in more direct contact with the masses than elites themselves. Mosca compares this subelite group to lower-ranking officers in the military: "The higher stratum in the ruling class corresponds to the general and staff, the second stratum to the officers who personally lead the soldiers under fire" (1939:405). It is these people who staff the bureaucracies and who actually run the state. The elite at the top, as well as this subelite group, constitute what Mosca refers to as the political class (Figure 4-1).

Although structural factors are more prominent in Mosca's view of elites, like Pareto, he too points to the importance of certain "superior" personal characteristics—intellectual, material, moral—of the ruling minority, lacked by the majority of the society's people. In Mosca's descriptive terms, they "have some attribute, real or apparent, which is highly esteemed and very influential in the society in which they live" (1939:53).

Mosca also recognizes the significance of control of valued resources, which he calls "social forces." These may be skills of various kinds, material items, moral suasion, and so on. Whatever their form, certain social forces seem to predominate in a society at any particular moment in its history. We might think of social forces as "interests" which are represented by various groups and leaders, some obviously of more weight than others. In contemporary America, for example, we might say that business and the general values of property and profit that are integral parts of the business system are the predominant social forces of our

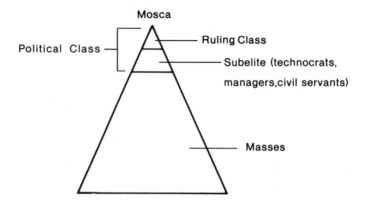

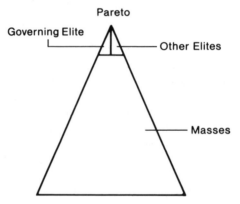

Figure 4-1 Two Versions of the Elite Model.

time. Whatever they are in any society, it is the elite who have easier access to them and thus can reinforce and sustain their power through them.

The elite, in sum, have *organization, personal attributes,* and *social forces,* which in combination assure their continued place at the top of the political hierarchy. There is one additional advantage which elites are able to employ in sustaining their power: a ruling class ideology, which Mosca calls a "political formula." On the surface, at least, this element of Mosca's theory resembles, as we shall see, the Marxian notion of ruling class ideology. Ruling classes justify their domination over the majority by a myth—in Mosca's terms, a "formula"—which more or less reflects the character and function of the ruling class currently in charge. This myth or formula will essentially express the "spirit of the time" of the society (Meisel, 1962:16– 17). Mosca explains:

> No political class, however constituted, will say outright that it rules because . . . its members are the ones most fit to rule. Instead, that class will always try to justify its power on the ground of an abstraction which we shall call the political formula. To say that all officials derive their authority from the official sovereign, who, in turn, derives it from God, is to make use of a political formula; another version is expressed in the phrase that all power resides in the people (Meisel, 1962:55).

The political formula, however, is not an ideology imposed on the majority solely to assure the continued rule of the minority. There is an additional positive social function which is derived from this formula, the answer to a "real need in man's social nature." This, explains Mosca, is the need "of governing and knowing that one is governed not on the basis of mere material or intellectual force, but on the basis of a moral principle" (Mosca, 1939:71).

Unlike Pareto, Mosca recognizes that changing elites may bring about changes in the social structure, particularly political institutions. Also new social trends, technologies, and ideologies may produce new types of elites. But whatever the type, there is no difference from one political system to another in the eventuality of a ruling class. Even in representative democracies, representatives "have themselves elected" or "have their friends elect them" (Mosca, 1939:154). Those who have superior intellectual and material means will always find themselves able to impose their candidacies upon the majority. The candidates who are ultimately successful are those who "are championed by groups, by committees, by *organized minorities*" (Mosca, 1939:154).

Mosca is not altogether pessimistic in his view of the elite-mass relationship, however. He does not carry his ruling class analysis to the point of endorsing or advocating antidemocratic or authoritarian political systems. On the contrary, he believes these to be, other than anarchy, the least desirable ruling types.

But we should not go too far in attributing to Mosca a belief in any "ideal" qualities of democratic governments. In the end, they too are not immune to the same developments which produce and sustain a ruling class. Mosca calls for a balanced and moderate system, one that maximizes equilibrium among the various organized social forces, an idea which, as we have seen, is not basically unlike the modern notion of political pluralism. In Mosca's view, this is the best that can be realistically hoped for.

Michels' Iron Law of Oligarchy

Of the three preeminent elite theorists, German sociologist Robert Michels is for modern political sociology the most important figure. In his now classic work *Political Parties*, written in 1911, Michels strikes squarely at the seemingly unavoidable emergence of elite rule created by the structure of modern social organizations. His theory is viable even today and might well be consulted by those who wish to understand more fully why large organizations work as they do. Unlike Pareto's and even Mosca's, Michels' analysis is founded most basically on the key sociological variables of social organization and division of labor rather than on psychological factors or innate human tendencies.

Moreover, Michels' work is more closely patterned in the style of modern social science; his thesis is based on empirical data, not simply selected historical examples. In comparison with Mosca and Pareto, "it was Michels who marshaled his evidence most carefully and whose writings come closest to contemporary standards of scientific investigation" (Hughes, 1958:257–258).

Although Michels focused his study on political parties—specifically the German Social Democratic party—his analysis is generally applicable to all kinds of organizations, public and private alike: government bureaucracies, corporations, labor unions, universities, professional associations, fraternal groups, religious bodies, and so on. In short, it is a theory that fits the organizational form of politics in modern societies. Michels did not arbitrarily choose the German Social Democratic party for analysis. Rather, he purposely set out to show that if the tendency to oligarchy—that is, rule by a few—was evident in a party such as this which openly declared and presumably practiced democratic principles, it is unavoidable in *any* large, complex organization.

Like Pareto and Mosca, Michels assumes that a craving for power and recognition is an inherent human psychological trait. But as an explanation of the oligarchical nature of large social groups, this innate tendency is clearly secondary to the general needs of organization. It simply augments and perhaps impels social processes which are already in place. Michels explains:

> The apathy of the masses and their need for guidance has as its counterpart in the leaders a natural greed for power. Thus the development of the democratic oligarchy is accelerated by the general characteristics of human nature. What was initiated by the need for organization, administration and strategy is completed by psychological determinism (Michels, 1962:205).

Oligarchy, then, even in democratic organizations, inevitably arises out of the complexity and size of the organization. It is simply not possible for large numbers of persons to make decisions in an efficient manner as a unit. The only realistic alternative is to invest officers with power to make decisions on behalf of the collectivity as a whole. With such delegation of powers, a stable—and eventually self-serving—leadership group is established. Thus Michels advances his often quoted dictum: "Who says organization, says oligarchy" (1962:365).

When collectivities reach a certain dimension, a division of labor emerges, even among the leadership group. Positions are created that are held by persons with special expertise, persons who thereby become indispensable to the functioning of the organization:

> Just as the patient obeys the doctor, because the doctor knows better than the patient, having made a special study of the human body in health and disease, so must the political patient submit to the guidance of his party leaders, who possess a political competence impossible of attainment by the rank and file (Michels, 1962:114).

Because of their specialized expertise, elites are further enabled to perpetuate themselves in high positions. Political leaders can point to the masses' lack of knowledge in any particular area, asserting that they must therefore be given the power to make important decisions. Furthermore leadership groups can control the training and recruitment process of *future* leaders, thereby creating a self-reproducing class. Thus the gulf between leaders and masses becomes increasingly wider.

Once in power, elites devote more and more of their energies to maintaining their positions rather than working toward the ostensible goals of the organizations they lead. In a sense the organization now becomes an end in itself, and its perpetuation becomes the paramount goal. Sociologists have referred to this organizational phenomenon as "goal displacement" (Merton:1957).

Lack of mass response. One would assume that all of these developments would ordinarily be met with strong resistance by the masses. On the contrary, however, the masses seem content to turn over the affairs of the state (or any other organization) to the leadership group. Michels explains that this is due to apathy, insufficient time, lack of expertise, and in some cases a predisposition to be led. In short, the masses are not only incapable of ruling themselves but are indifferent about relinquishing decision-making power to elites. As Michels puts it, "Though it grumbles occasionally, the majority is really delighted to find persons who will take the trouble to look after its affairs" (1962:88). This indifference and incapability, of course, considerably strengthen the positions of the leadership and make more unlikely the development of countermovements among the masses.

Such movements stand little likelihood of success even if they do materialize since the elite has all the power cards stacked in its favor: information which the masses do not have, control of the flow of that information, credibility and prestige which automatically accrue to incumbent office-holders, and, perhaps most important, cohesive organization. This last point, it will be recalled, was also fundamental in Mosca's explanation of elite power. Through all of these power resources the dominant leadership is able to monitor carefully the selection of new elites.

Cooptation.   In addition, there is a coopting process which tends to lessen the challenge of new leaders who may emerge from the masses. In a sense, political opponents are bought off by being brought into the folds of power. Thus challenge from below is met not with total resistance but with the skillful use of organizational resources. Challengers are usually not immune to the allure of power, privilege, and prestige which can be offered by the established leadership. In describing the relations of labor union leaders to the rank-and-file, for example, Michels states that the influence exercised by leaders and the financial security of their position "become more and more fascinating to the masses, stimulating the ambition of all the more talented elements to enter the privileged bureaucracy of the labor movement" (1962:170). The cooptation process is quite evident in the United States where, as in most societies, the political "outs," calling for change, often accuse the political "ins" of enjoying sumptuous life-styles at tax-payers' expense but seem to take on similar life-styles when they become the "ins." The same kind of transformation, of course, occurs among neophyte officials of *any* organization, public or private.

The conservative nature of elites.   The demands of retaining power make all leadership groups conservative no matter how radical their causes may initially be:

> As soon as the new leaders have attained their ends, as soon as they have succeeded (in the name of the injured rights of the anonymous masses) in overthrowing the odious tyranny of their predecessors and in attaining to power in their turn, we see them undergo a transformation which renders them in every respect similar to the dethroned tyrants. . . . The revolutionaries of today become the reactionaries of tomorrow (Michels, 1962:187).

Part of this conversion, Michels explains, is psychological, the result of individuals responding to the acquisition of power and its various perquisites. But the greater part of such change is the result of the tactical needs of the organization itself. So long as leaders are necessary—and this is simply basic to any large collective body—over a period of time they will become more professionalized and will turn into a stable, well-entrenched group. Their expertise, professionalism, and power lead to increasing separation from the organization's general membership, and they begin to pursue policies which stabilize or enhance their own power, not the collective interests of the organization.

Michels, then, points out not only the inevitability of oligarchy but also the abuse of power which accompanies leadership in organizations. The interests of the elite become predominant over those of the masses they supposedly are serving. This occurs whether or not their original intentions are honorable.

Weber and Bureaucracy

The great German sociologist Max Weber (1864–1920) is not generally grouped with the elitists, but his theory of bureaucracy certainly dovetails with Michels' iron law of oligarchy in its implications for political society. Michels and Weber were contemporaries, and no doubt their ideas were mutually influential.

In essence Weber and Michels offer very similar explanations of political rule in modern societies. Weber, like Michels, sees the fact of modern social organization as the most significant force which compels the formation of ruling groups. But Weber's explanation stresses the nature of bureaucracy and how this uniquely modern organizational form creates elite power.

With the modernization of society and the movement toward legal-rational authority, there arises an increasing professionalization of leadership. Rulers come to be more and more dependent on skilled bodies of specialists and experts—bureaucracies—to advise and ultimately carry out critical decisions. Greater and greater power comes to be concentrated in bureaucracies which maintain control over vast human, material, and intellectual resources. Political bureaucracies, both public and private, thus become additional societal power groups, in some ways exercising dominance even over elected officials in democratic societies or self-appointed leaders in authoritarian systems. In turn, control over bureaucracies constitutes an immense power resource.

The nature of bureaucracy. Weber saw the historical development of societies as a movement toward rational forms of organization—that is, groups organized not on the basis of the authority of personalities and traditions but on the basis of specific functions to perform or objectives to meet (that is, legal-rational authority). In modern industrial societies this type of social organization primarily takes the form of bureaucracy. Bureaucracy as a form of social organization enables vast numbers of persons playing specialized roles to blend into cohesive, well-functioning units. It is, in a sense, a "social machine," whose purpose is to instill efficiency, speed, and precision into organized human effort. "The decisive reason for the advance of bureaucratic organization," Weber notes, "has always been its purely technical superiority over any other form of organization" (Gerth and Mills, 1946:214). Indeed it seems unlikely that the complex political, economic, and educational institutions of modern societies could be arranged in any other way.

Of course, just as bureaucracy spells a great technical advance for humanity, it also produces alienation by increasingly removing individuals from direct control of their social environment and by turning them into depersonalized objects. Weber was concerned about the alienating effects of bureaucracy but was pessimistic in his prognosis for controlling their development. Marx saw man in capitalist society alienated as a result of his inability to control his economic destiny; but in the end Marx was optimistic in his belief that socialist revolution might alleviate that condition. Weber, however, has no vision of a bureaucracy-less society. Variations in the economic and political systems of modern societies make little difference; none can avoid the imperatives of bureaucratic organization.

Sources of bureaucratic power. Political bureaucracies in modern societies take on great power in their own right. As Weber admits, "Under normal conditions, the power position of a fully developed bureaucracy is always overtowering" (Gerth and Mills, 1946:232). By what means is a bureaucracy able to wield such power? There are two main devices: (1) its monopoly of expertise and (2) its capacity to implement policies made by powerful leaders.

First, modern organizations such as governments cannot operate without the technical knowledge of specialized experts. At the level of the federal government, for example, matters pertaining to transportation, agriculture, foreign affairs, housing, fiscal policy, and so on will be dealt with by those who are trained in these specific fields. A distinct bureaucratic hierarchy will be formed around each particular policy area.

With their possession of expertise, bureaucrats may attempt to control the flow of information to both policymakers and the public in order to protect and maximize their power. When they are successful, policymakers are virtually at their mercy. Weber (1947:338) notes that:

The question is always who controls the existing bureaucratic machinery. And such control is possible only in a very limited degree to persons who are not technical specialists. Generally speaking, the trained permanent official is more likely to get his way in the long run than his nominal superior, the Cabinet minister, who is not a specialist.

Another means by which the bureaucracy exercises great power is its discretion in carrying out decisions made by political leaders. Laws may be made, but they can be enforced only by a bureaucracy which can choose to vigorously carry them out or, at the other extreme, ignore them. Although political leaders—government or private—may be quite powerful in making top-level decisions, the vast majority of day-to-day business is handled by the lower levels of the bureaucracy.

One would assume that people in positions of great political power would be able to bypass the discretionary power of bureaucracies. But this is never the case. In fact, bureaucracies may frustrate and inhibit even the power of political rulers at the very top. As imposing a position of power as the U.S. presidency, for example, is not immune to the neutralizing effects that bureaucracies may inflict on policies and actions. Noting the frustrations of dealing with the federal bureaucracy, political scientist Richard Neustadt (1976:77) relates the comment of President Truman in 1952, contemplating the possibility of General Eisenhower succeeding him in office: "He'll sit here and he'll say 'Do this! Do that!' *And nothing will happen*. Poor Ike—it won't be a bit like the Army."

With their monopolies of expertise and policy administration, bureaucracies become the most stable elements of a political system, outlasting many changes in top leadership. Given the built-in intransigence of a stabilized bureaucracy, Weber felt that societal change must often be impelled by strong charismatic leaders, those who are free of the constraints of bureaucratic office. Such dynamic personalities become catalysts of change and represent extremely important revitalizing forces in society. But as was noted in chapter 2, charisma is always a temporary phenomenon and ultimately becomes "routinized." In modern societies charismatic authority is eventually transformed into legal-rational authority, thus coming full circle to a restoration of bureaucracy. Indeed, Weber fittingly remarked that the idea of eliminating bureaucracies "becomes more and more utopian" (Gerth and Mills, 1946: 229).

The prevalence of bureaucracy in modern society has two major effects on the structure and relations of power. First, with the centralization of power in encompassing bureaucracies, those who control and direct these social machines command enormous power resources on a scale without precedent. Despite their capacity to frustrate the process of policy enforcement, bureaucracies do not rule in their own right. In the end they still must carry out policies made by ruling elites (Bottomore, 1966:86). In capitalist America these are the heads of giant corporations, top officials of government agencies, Pentagon officials, and leaders of labor unions. Elite power, then, is expanded with the ever increasing concentration of economic and political power into fewer and fewer vast organizations.

Second, bureaucracies make citizen control of political and economic decision makers more difficult. A bureaucratic elite, comprising those at the top of vast organizations, is remote and unanswerable to the citizenry, whatever the status of democratic politics in the society. In the political realm, bureaucratic elites are for the most part civil servants, not elected officials obligated to a particular constituency. Thus, with the concentration of power in bureaucratic organizations, the citizen is further removed from control of and input into political decision making.

An Assessment of Classical Elite Theory

Michels, like Mosca, is quite clear in his belief that, despite its inherent inconsistencies, democracy is "the least of evils" (Michels, 1962:370). Yet it is not difficult to see how his theory, as well as Pareto's and Mosca's, was viewed by many as the intellectual foundation of the totalitarian systems of Fascist Italy and Nazi Germany in the 1920s and 1930s. If the elite theorists are basically correct, the whole idea of representative democracy is thrown into question. Thus, as might be expected, elite theory has not been enthusiastically embraced by political sociologists in the United States.

But despite its lack of appeal to many for ideological reasons, there is simply no denying the applicability of many aspects of elite theory to the politics of modern societies, including those with democratic systems. We need only take notice of the current politics of public and private governments to appreciate its persuasiveness, particularly Michels' contribution. Regardless of their sphere of activity, leaders in democratic societies are constantly accused of losing touch with those they are obligated to serve, solidifying their power, and pursuing their personal ends. Such accusations are routinely leveled at politicians, union leaders, corporation executives, school officials—in short, leaders of the entire range of institutional political life.

Leaders, in turn, respond with justifications for their power. Important decisions require the expert judgment of professional politicians, managers, or administrators. The membership of an organization or the citizenry as a whole is simply not equipped to deal with the complex and esoteric problems which must be managed by a properly trained elite. Moreover the citizenry cannot render meaningful input into important decisions since they lack adequate information, held exclusively by the elite.

Examples which illustrate the iron law of oligarchy are everywhere around us. In the realm of national government the critical societal issues of foreign affairs, the economy, and the environment, as well as less compelling issues, are left to governing and administrative oligarchies. And within those organizations which are designed to represent closer-to-home interests—local governments, labor unions, professional associations, and so on—oligarchy remains the order of the day. School boards, for example, are staffed by professionals whose policy decisions may not express the desires of the community. Labor leaders evolve into professional groups who increasingly detach themselves from the rank-and-file. Even professional societies such as legal and medical associations, whose memberships are smaller and more aware of leaders' activities, are typified by oligarchic traits. Consider the American Medical Association, for instance. Its leadership is made up of physicians, but not *practicing* physicians. Rather, they are professional administrators who are concerned chiefly with maintaining the organization. They may have little understanding of how doctors in the field actually feel about key issues concerning the medical profession and cannot consult them on a regular basis. Thus they may in reality represent neither the views nor the interests of the majority of physicians.

Perhaps most unsettling to those who would deny the validity of elite theory is the overwhelming evidence of mass apathy toward government leaders and the leaders of more localized groups. Michels' observation that elite rule is facilitated in large part by the general unconcern of the masses is evidenced over and over again. How many union members attend their local meetings? How many students participate in student government? How many persons keep apprised of current political issues? How many even vote in elections —at any level of government? The answer in each case is a minority. Examples of mass apathy abound at all organizational levels and seem to verify Michels' contention that most persons prefer to have leaders make decisions for them.

The applicability of Weber's theory of bureaucracy as an accessory of the elite perspective is equally apparent in modern societies. The ever-increasing size and complexity of governments, corporations, schools, labor unions, and voluntary associations makes the need in all of these cases for increasing organizational integration and coordination imperative. This means, in a word, bureaucracy. Bureaucracy, in turn, creates, by its very nature, elites—those who occupy the positions of centralized control and specialized expertise.

In short, whether one looks with favor or displeasure on the development of these leadership groups, it is difficult to dispute their inevitability in technologically advanced and socially complex societies. As political scientist Robert Presthus (1964:80) has written:

> The more highly differentiated structure of modern society results in elites, which tend to become separated from the members of their various groups both by their interest in maintaining themselves in power and by the demands of technology and strategy which require secrecy, dispatch, flexibility, and skills generally not characteristic of mass behavior.

CONTEMPORARY ELITE THEORY

We have now looked at the classical elite theories of Pareto, Mosca, and Michels and have also considered Weber's theory of bureaucracy as an adjunct of this approach. Whatever the variation, each presents a picture of politics in society which emphasizes the power of a few to make the major decisions for the society as a whole. And elitists see the inevitability of elite rule regardless of changing social and economic institutions. Pareto and Mosca take a conservative view of the elite-mass relationship. The masses are seen as unable to rule themselves, and therefore the place of elites in society is both necessary and desirable. As for Michels, he too is distrustful about the place of the masses in the ruling scheme of any modern society given the advent of complex organizational life.

Modern applications of the elite model, however, have been founded for the most part on different assumptions of the elite-mass relationship. Whereas the classical (or conservative) elitists see masses as apathetic, incompetent, and unwilling or unable to govern themselves, contemporary elitists see them as manipulated and exploited by elites who rule in their own interests, not those of the larger society. This modern view of elites and masses, particularly as it has been applied to the United States, is generally referred to as **radical elitism**.

Radical elitism is not a description of "what must be," as the classical theorists posit, but rather an empirical description of "what is." Elite rule is seen not as necessarily inevitable but as a state of affairs which currently exists in the United States and other industrial societies. Great power is concentrated in a few hands, but this is not an unavoidable development. Moreover, according to radical elitists, power elites rule in their own personal or class interests, and their actions therefore have a negative effect on the society; elite rule is not, as Pareto and Mosca contend, necessary and desirable.

Radical elitists stress elite control of key power resources: corporate wealth, governmental authority, and the society's communication system. By controlling the latter, elites are able to regulate the flow of ideas and information and can therefore engineer public opinion in their favor. Radical elitists are thus not distrustful of the masses, as are the classical or conservative elitists, but view them as kept in a state of ignorance by the direct and indirect machinations of ruling elites. This also accounts for the general nonparticipation of the masses in politics. Conservative elitists maintain that masses lack the ability to make rational decisions and are eager to have elites act for them; as a result they relinquish societal power willingly. Radical elitists, however, assert that masses are not given the information needed to understand the roots of social problems and are thus unwittingly guided into accepting elite rule.

Finally, radical elitists see power holders in the United States and similar societies as a cohesive group made up of socially alike persons drawn disproportionately from the upper class. New members of the elite may at times be recruited from lower social ranks, but they are coopted into accepting the basic legitimacy of the established power structure. Thus elites tend to perpetuate themselves through selective recruitment and socialization to elite values. In this regard, at least, the radical elitists' view does not differ from that of the classical elitists.

Perhaps the most significant of the radical elite theorists is the late C. Wright Mills, who, in his important work *The Power Elite* (1956), portrayed the power structure of mid-twentieth-century America as a relatively cohesive elite of big businessmen, a few top government officials, and high-ranking military chiefs. Societal power, according to Mills, rests in control of key societal institutions, and in contemporary America it is the corporation, the executive branch of the federal government, and the Pentagon which comprise such institutions. Those in the top positions of these institutions are therefore the power elite. We shall look closely at Mills' analysis of the American power structure, as well as those of other contemporary elite theorists, in chapter 9.

The radical elite view represents a clear refutation of the more popular pluralist perspective of power in America and will guide much of our discussion in Part Three. Here we might briefly compare some of the major themes of radical elitism and pluralism.

1. Pluralists see a power system in America in which masses influence leaders through elections and pressure group tactics. Elitists, however, see minimal accountability of elites by masses. The power of elites is solidified through their authority in key institutions such as government and the corporation, their control of expertise and information, and their ability to shape political ideology.
2. Pluralists view voluntary associations as important links between leaders and masses. But elitists consider such groups of minimal significance on big issues which are decided by power elites above the level of interest group politics. Moreover such groups in themselves constitute bureaucratically organized, elite-run associations which do not represent the interests of their memberships.
3. Pluralists see a power system accepted by the society in general. Elitists see the legitimacy of the system created by elites themselves through the propagation of an ideology that favors their interests. Thus masses find it difficult to contest the virtually unbridled power of elites not only because they lack control of the institutions of power but because they are effectively deluded by the dominant ideology justifying elite rule.
4. Pluralists see a balanced power system of competing interests and elites, none of which is able to dominate. Elitists see a highly unbalanced power system with big businessmen predominating on most important issues. Competition takes place only at the middle range of power, not at the very top where key societal issues are decided. Disagreements which occur at the top do not concern basic aspects of the system of political and economic relations.

A CRITIQUE OF THE ELITE MODEL

In the context of modern societal conditions, elite theory is highly persuasive. Not only does it account for the extreme (and growing) distance between citizens and leaders but, as Prewitt and Stone (1973:22) have written, it also "provides an explanation for why political and social structures change so gradually, if at all." Why is it that leaders come and go but political and economic systems seem to stay the same? Why are zealous reformers, if and when they attain power, almost always mollified, taking on more conservative attitudes? Elite theory provides substantial leads in accounting for these paradoxes.

Elite theory also helps to explain why powerful elites, controlling the formation of political values and the flow of information, have usually been able to effectively placate discontented masses by granting moderate reforms or symbolic changes, neither of which threatens their power. As we shall see, only a few sweeping social revolutions have occurred in all of modern times. Elite theory points to the irony of such mass movements even when they are successful. When the masses are not conciliated by token or symbolic handouts of elites and finally compel fundamental sociopolitical change, a new elite inevitably emerges and the process begins anew.

But despite the impressive evidence which supports its basic suppositions, the elite perspective, in both its classical European forms and its modern American applications, has been subject to important points of criticism. Let us look at some of the more cogent counterarguments.

Elite Inevitability

First, the classical elitists see elite rule as an inevitable feature of social life. This is a point which critics of elite theory have found most difficult to counter. Since all societies beyond the most technologically primitive are stratified, a hierarchy of power is implied. And this, of course, means an elite at the top of that hierarchy. If elites are defined strictly in terms of power, there is no gainsaying their inevitability, at least in modern societies.

But the existence of *powerful persons* in a society need not be equated with *elites*. Elite theorists define elites not simply as powerful groups but also as cohesive, self-sustaining, and self-serving groups. The latter characteristics, however, cannot be presupposed as a certainty under all societal conditions. Although it is surely an unusual social arrangement in the modern world, the Israeli kibbutz is an example of a community which seems to have resisted the development of a stable power elite with undue privileges (Spiro, 1970).

Thus we cannot make assumptions about future, or even all present, sociopolitical forms. Indeed, as we have seen, the inevitability of elite rule is a point on which radical elitists part company with the classical elite theorists. Radical elitists recognize the power of elites in contemporary America and other modern industrial societies but do not see this as a necessity.

As for Michels' iron law of oligarchy, some have pointed out that the persistence of democratic tendencies, despite the seemingly inevitable regeneration of oligarchy, may just as easily prove an "iron law of democracy" (Gouldner, 1955). In this view Michels' analysis dwells solely on the ways in which organizational needs inhibit democracy, ignoring the other side of the coin —those ways in which organizations tend to discourage authority.

Although Michels' iron law may be evidenced more commonly than not, exceptions sometimes appear. One such case is described in a sociological study of the International Typographers Union (Lipset and Trow, 1956). Contrary to what might have been expected, the researchers found that the rank-and-file membership were able to prevent the formation of a permanent leadership group by maintaining an effective two-party system within the union. An organized opposition to the incumbent leadership was always in place, and the membership was presented with distinct alternatives. Under these conditions the development of a firm oligarchy was avoided.

Finally, as we have seen, pluralists pose the question of whether *any* group or groups need necessarily dominate the power structure of a society or community at all times. They argue that coalitions may just as easily typify a long-term power arrangement when issues change from moment to moment.

Elite Cohesiveness

One analyst of the classical elite theorists writes that Pareto and Mosca credit elites with "the three C's: group consciousness, coherence, and conspiracy" (Meisel, 1962:4). That is, an elite is not simply a functioning group, acting out its leadership role. In addition, its members are cut from the same sociological mold and are aware of themselves *as a group*, sharing similar interests and social perspectives. Even modern exponents of the elite model such as Mills assume that power elite members are typified by similar social origins, education, and interests. Such group consciousness, it is believed, reinforces elite power.

In modern societies, however, where many elites emerge in different institutional areas —the economy, the polity, education, and so on —it may be difficult to sustain such a unified and homogeneous leadership group. Suzanne Keller (1963:70) maintains that the increasing complexity of modern societies precludes the development of socially cohesive elites:

> Specialization . . . affects the strategic elites no less than the general population and makes of that common centripetal core group a divided and separate series of specialists. The consequences of this are the greater autonomy and independence of these elites, their smaller degree of cohesion, and the decreasing likelihood that any single elite can long exert absolute, arbitrary power.

Before we can assume elite cohesiveness, then, careful analysis of the origins and activities of a society's formal decision makers as well as other influential persons must be made.

Elite-Mass Relations

Both classical and radical elite theorists postulate a minimal influence of elites by masses. It is assumed that, given the highly unequal distribution of power resources, elites can, for the most part, rule as they wish. In doing so they pursue their own interests rather than those of the society or the membership of a particular organization. Power becomes an end in itself.

Viewing elite power as unbridled, however, negates the accountability functions of electoral politics and public opinion in democratic societies. The degree to which either of these means actually controls leaders will, of course, vary from institution to institution and from organization to organization. Such controls are bound to be more effective within government, for example, than within the corporation. But whatever the real potency of these constraining forces (and this has been debated since the advent of democratic political systems), their effects cannot be totally discounted.

Viewing elites as self-serving also denies the possibility that they may at times act on altruistic motives. In some cases leaders may be genuinely desirous of serving the people and thus remain very much aware of and obligated to public interests. Moreover different social origins, as well as numerous personality factors, will produce diverse motives of elite behavior (Putnam, 1976).

Elitists view bureaucracies commanded by elites as having become ends in themselves, serving mainly their own internal interests. But this tends to ignore, as Alford (1975:151) explains, "The concrete social and economic interests actually served by bureaucratic organizations." In short, elites and bureaucracies, no matter how self-reproducing and self-serving they may be, do serve the interests of certain groups and classes in the society. Concentrating solely on the structure and regeneration of elites and bureaucracies thus neglects what may be a more important question: "Who, in addition to themselves, benefits from their actions?" Radical elitists have been more concerned with this point, and it is, as we shall see, critical in the class model of societal power as well.

The Place of the Masses

As we have seen, conservative and radical elitists each interpret the nonparticipation of the masses in politics quite differently. The conservative elite theorists portray the masses as incompetent and unwilling to assume their own governance, while radical elitists see them as manipulated and rendered powerless by elites and bureaucracies.

Whatever the reasons, empirical studies have shown consistently that political apathy does indeed characterize large segments of all classes in modern societies. But these studies have also shown that it occurs less frequently as social class rises. That is, those who work in higher-status occupations, are wealthier, and are more educated tend to participate in governmental and organizational politics more than those who rank lower on these class indicators. Thus to talk of one amorphous, inert mass is to draw an oversimplified picture of the political behavior of nonelites.

The Two-Class Power Structure

Although both classical and radical elite theorists recognize a group immediately below the elite but not submerged in the general mass (that is, a subelite), they basically posit a dichotomous structure of power: rulers and ruled. However, the stratification systems of industrial societies are highly complex and not typified by such a simple division. There are apt to be several fairly distinct levels of power even among those making the most critical decisions of the society. In short, the simple two-class model of societal power may be too simple.

Even within particular organizations, the idea of a power order consisting of a ruling oligarchy versus the rank-and-file membership is perhaps too sweeping a generalization. There are different degrees of oligarchy among different groups. Corporations will not resemble universities, which in turn will differ from government agencies. Some may be quite clearly dichotomous—a leadership group and a powerless membership—but others may exhibit more complex hierarchies of power.

SUMMARY

The fundamental premise of the elite model of societal power is the prevalence of rule by the few. Classical elite theorists Pareto and Mosca explain the development of elite rule as inevitable; a ruling class combines skills, cunning, organization, and legitimation of social values to sustain its power. New groups and individuals do enter the elite, but the elite-mass dichotomy is not changed. The masses are viewed as incompetent, not capable of self-rule. Elites therefore are necessary and beneficial to society.

Michels explains elite rule as a product of the nature of social organization in industrial society. Large, complex organizations demand specialized experts who become functionally indispensable. Organization

thus breeds elite rule in all areas of societal life, including most importantly the polity and the economy. Leaders inevitably lose contact with
the masses and pursue their own interests. Weber's explanation of bureaucracy serves as an adjunct to Michels' theory. Weber points out that
as greater and greater power comes to be concentrated in bureaucracies,
such bodies not only provide great power to those who control them but
also become powerful in their own right.

Radical elite theorists who have applied the elite model to American
society recognize elite power as inherent in control of institutional resources, particularly the wealth and authority of the giant corporation
and the federal government. As with classical elite theory, power elites
are seen as unaccountable to the masses. But radical elitists do not see
elites as either inevitable or necessarily functional. The power elite in the
United States is viewed as retaining its power through manipulation of
the masses. The latter are thus not seen as incapable of participating in
important societal decisions but rather as deceived and misinformed by
the ruling elite.

Despite its compelling thesis, elite theory leaves certain questions
unanswered. Must elites inevitably emerge, as Pareto, Mosca, and Michels maintain? Are elites cohesive and necessarily self-serving? Are the
masses always unable to assert control over elites? Is a "rulers versus
ruled" dichotomy too simple a description of the structure of power in
modern societies? In spite of these questions, elite theory remains a
forceful description of political structure and behavior in modern
societies. The reality of elites has been recognized by almost all political
analysts and observers, regardless of ideological or theoretical leanings.
Indeed many of the basic tenets of elitism are now taken for granted. So
convincing is the fact of elite rule that some American sociologists and
political scientists who have favored pluralism, a basically converse
theoretical perspective, have, as we have seen, been forced to fuse the
fundamental premises of democratic politics with elitism.

If the evidence supporting many aspects of elite theory is substantial, then the important points of sociopolitical inquiry do not revolve
around whether elites or masses rule; rather, the more meaningful questions concern the nature and composition of the elite structure. Who are
elites in terms of sociological characteristics? How are new elites selected?
What is the process by which elites relinquish and acquire power? How
unified or diverse are elites? What is the relationship between elites and
masses at particular times in a society's history? How is elite rule
legitimized? From where do counterelites emerge and how do mass
movements arise? And, most important, whose interests do elites serve?
Political sociologists who have adopted the elite perspective concentrate
their efforts on answering such questions.

REFERENCES

Alford, Robert R. 1975. "Paradigms of Relations Between State and Society." In Leon N. Lindberg, Robert Alford, Colin Crouch, and Claus Offe (eds.), *Stress and Contradiction in Modern Capitalism*. Lexington, Mass.: Lexington.

Bottomore, T. B. 1966. *Elites and Society*. Baltimore: Penguin.

Galbraith, John K. 1967. *The New Industrial State*. Boston: Houghton-Mifflin.

Gerth, Hans, and **C. Wright Mills.** 1946. *From Max Weber*. New York: Oxford U. Press.

Gouldner, Alvin S. 1955. "Metaphysical Pathos and the Theory of Bureaucracy." *American Political Science Review* 49 (June):496-507.

Hughes, H. Stuart. 1958. *Consciousness and Society*. New York: Vintage.

Keller, Suzanne. 1963. *Beyond the Ruling Class*. New York: Random House.

Lipset, Seymour M., and **Martin Trow.** 1956. *Union Democracy*. New York: Free Press.

Meisel, James H. 1962. *The Myth of the Ruling Class: Gaetano Mosca and the Elite*. Ann Arbor: U. of Michigan Press.

Merton, Robert K. 1957. *Social Structure and Social Theory*. Glencoe: Free Press.

Michels, Robert. 1962. *Political Parties*. Trans. Eden and Cedar Paul. New York: Free Press.

Mills, C. Wright. 1956. *The Power Elite*. New York: Oxford U. Press.

Mosca, Gaetano. 1939. *The Ruling Class*. (Ed.) Arthur Livingston. New York: McGraw-Hill.

Neustadt, Richard E. 1976. *Presidential Power: The Politics of Leadership with Reflections on Johnson and Nixon*. New York: Wiley.

Pareto, Vilfredo. 1970. "Elites and Force." In Marvin Olsen (ed.), *Power in Societies*. New York: Macmillan.

Parker, Richard. 1972. *The Myth of the Middle Class*. New York: Harper and Row.

Presthus, Robert. 1964. *Men at the Top*. New York: Oxford U. Press.

Prewitt, Kenneth, and **Alan Stone.** 1973. *The Ruling Elites*. New York: Harper and Row.

Putnam, Robert D. 1976. *The Comparative Study of Political Elites*. Englewood Cliffs: Prentice-Hall.

Spiro, Melford. 1970. *Kibbutz*. New York: Schocken.

Weber, Max. 1947. *The Theory of Social and Economic Organization*. Trans. A. M. Henderson and Talcott Parsons. New York: Oxford U. Press.

chapter 5

the class model

Political power, properly so called, is merely the organised power of one class for oppressing another.

Karl Marx and Friedrich Engels

We have now examined two contrasting models of power in societies: pluralism and elitism. The pluralist model views societal power as inherent in the competition between various interest groups, each vying for the society's economic, political, and social resources. This competition, it is presumed, assures the dispersion of power and guarantees citizen input into the power process. The elitists, on the other hand, see societal power as concentrated in elite groups who control the resources of key social organizations and are not accountable to the masses. The class model, which we now consider, is similar to the elite model in viewing societal power as concentrated in the hands of a few. However, the origins of societal power in this view lie not in the control of social organizations but in the institutions of property and the class relations which derive from them.

THEORETICAL ROOTS OF THE CLASS MODEL

The class model relies primarily on the social and political theories of Karl Marx. In fact, so fundamental is Marx to this perspective that some simply refer to it as the "Marxist model."

Marx

To call Karl Marx the "father of political sociology," as some have, would not be overstating his significance. Though he lived and wrote more than a hundred years ago, his theories remain vibrant and form the basis not only of much of contemporary political sociology but all the social sciences. So sweeping was the range of his thought that few areas of social life remain untouched by his analysis. As a result, in the context of modern-day academic disciplines, Marx would be hard to categorize. Sociology, political science, and economics each can claim a Marxian tradition. Indeed it has often been remarked that all of social science since Marx's time has, in one form or another, involved a response to his ideas. In the case of political sociology this is surely true. Before one can investigate the various competing ideas of political behavior and structure, one must come to grips with Marx.

It would not be possible in just a few pages to attempt a detailed examination of Marx's contribution to the study of political society. Many scholars have devoted their entire careers to such a task, and literally thousands of volumes have been compiled dealing with interpretations, critiques, defenses, and refutations of his works. In fact one of the difficulties in any study of Marx is the extremely wide range of interpretations which have been offered by various analysts. One factor that has contributed to the proliferation of theoretical Marxisms is the rather unsystematic manner in which Marx's writings were presented. Friedrich Engels was a close working associate of Marx and organized much of his work, in the process supplementing it with ideas of his own. Also Marx's extremely broad scope of social analysis has undoubtedly helped to open the door to conflicting interpretations.

There is perhaps no avoiding the debate among proponents of the Marxian perspective; one must simply be prepared to endure a spate of "correct" versions. Ralph Miliband (1977:5) has tersely summarized the dilemma: "There are many worse slogans than 'Everyone his own Marx.' For in the end, there is no 'authoritative' interpretation—only personal judgement and evaluation." And Raymond Aron (1968:145) likewise reminds us that "if only there were not so many millions of Marxists, there would be no question at all about what Marx's leading ideas are or what is central to his thought." We might take comfort in knowing that the dilemma is not new in our era. The many different interpretations and applications of his work, even in his own time, prompted Marx to declare that he was "not a Marxist" (Lewis, 1972:9).

Marx's Political Theory

As well as explaining political power in societies, Marxian thought encompasses a sweeping theory of sociohistorical change, a full explanation of the capitalist economic system, and a utopian vision. Each of these units of thought are, of course, essentially interrelated and cannot be considered independently. Furthermore, within the context of the Marxian perspective one cannot isolate any single aspect of society, such as the state, since Marx sees societies as *total*, wherein the specific elements can be understood only in relation to the whole. It is important to understand, then, that Marx's theory is a theory of society, not of politics or the state. In fact, the state does not occupy a primary place in Marx's vast writings. Thus a "Marxist politics" must be constructed or reconstructed from much varied and fragmented material (Miliband, 1977:2).

Given the scope of Marx's theory, we will highlight only those elements which seem especially important in explaining the structure and dynamics of societal power.

The Economic Foundation

Fundamental to Marxian political theory is the pivotal role of a society's economic institutional structure. Most simply, power flows from economic relations, as does virtually every aspect of social life. Prior to Marx, most political theorists had simply assumed that in its most significant forms, power lay in the state and its various organizations. Thus to discuss politics and power meant discussing the state or government. Marx broke with this time-honored tradition, and it is here that we can begin to see the revolutionary impact of his theory. It was not the state that exercised ultimate societal power, nor was that institution its source. Instead Marx believed that power was to be found in the society's economic institutions; consequently those who were in dominant economic positions would by that fact also dominate political institutions. To the first question of sociopolitical analysis —who rules? —Marx's answer is clear: those who control economic resources.

The predominance of a society's economic institutions is so overwhelming, in Marx's estimation, that they are the determinants of the entire system of society. More than anything, Marx saw the dynamics of society originating in economic activity—securing food, shelter, and all other necessities of life: " . . . life involves before everything else eating and drinking, a habitation, clothing, and many other things. The first historical act is thus the production of the means to satisfy these needs, the production of material life itself" (Tucker, 1972:120).

It is out of this economic reality, the process by which people fulfill their material needs, that a society's culture arises: its various structures of law, religion, education, politics, and the belief systems attached to these structures. In short, the manner in which people organize to produce their needs and the relations which develop out of these activities essentially determine all other aspects of social life.

This system of production by which people provide for their material existence may be called a society's economic foundation or, as Marx put it, the "mode of production." As the economic foundation changes, so too people's ideas change, but it is fundamental that the former impels the latter. In a famous passage, Marx (1968:182) explains this process:

> The mode of production of material life conditions the social, political and intellectual life process in general. It is not the consciousness of men that determines their being, but, on the contrary, their social being that determines their consciousness.

The idea of economic reality, how people solve the problem of survival, is, then, the basic starting point for understanding the nature of power in societies. Political institutions and the ideologies which underlie them are products not of human philosophies but of the cold, hard reality of economic production. Therefore changes in a society's political system also develop out of changes in its productive system.

The Structure of Societies

Marx pictured societies as structured in two vertical dimensions. The economic base, or mode of production, comprises, as we have seen, the sum of economic activity; most simply, it is the society's productive system. Built upon this foundation is a superstructure consisting of all other social institutions: the state, the family, religion, education—in short, the remainder of organized social life. Let us look more closely at these two components.

The mode of production. The mode of production is more precisely composed of two parts: the *forces of production* and the *relations of production*. The forces consist of the technological and physical elements of production, what Marx called the "means of production," as well as the social arrangement by which production is organized. In industrial societies the means constitute such things as factories, machines, scientific know-how, and so on.

The relations of production refer to the relations between those who own the means of production and those who do not. Essentially the relations of production are *property* relations. In feudal societies a few own the land and the tools which are needed to make it productive; in industrial societies a few own the factories, machines, and other productive resources, while most own merely their own labor. Marx was not concerned with petty forms of private property but with *productive* property, that which can be used to create wealth. Basically, then, the relations of production denote the society's class structure. Class is a pivotal idea in the Marxian scheme, and we will return to it in a moment.

Societies at different stages of economic development will adopt different modes of production, corresponding to their particular circumstances. Hunting societies will differ from agrarian societies, which in turn will differ from industrial societies. Each form defines a way in which people have organized their productive activities in order to clothe, feed, and house themselves.

The noneconomic superstructure. Whatever form the economic base takes requires a whole superstructure of noneconomic activity and thought. This superstructure of noneconomic institutions necessarily reflects the foundation on which it is raised. The economic activity of an agrarian society, for example, is centered on the land. What the society produces for survival derives primarily from the soil, and most people will engage in occupations that relate to agriculture: farming, maintaining agricultural tools, and so on. To complement this mode of production, a set of noneconomic institutions will develop that helps sustain an agrarian economic system. The family will be large in order to provide as many hands as possible to work the land; religious rites will coincide with planting and harvesting times; the legal system will be concerned primarily with the ownership rights and inheritance of land; and the political system will be designed to protect the economic and social interests of those who own the land and the tools with which it is worked.

All of these institutions are shaped to fit the needs of an agrarian society; they would not accommodate an industrial mode of production. As a society's economic base changes, therefore, the form and content of its noneconomic institutions—the family, religion, education, the state—must also change. Marx thus explains societal change as the result of changes in the mode of production:

> In acquiring new productive forces men change their mode of production, and in changing their mode of production, their manner of gaining a living, they change all their social relations. The windmill gives you society with the feudal lord; the steammill, society with the industrial capitalist (Marx, 1920:119).

The economic base of a society should not be thought of as automatically giving rise to or "causing" the development of particular social and political institutions. What the economic structure does is to predispose a certain type of superstructure (Meyer, 1970:31). We might draw the analogy of finding a comfortable pair of shoes. Wearing shoes which are too tight or too loose will suffice, but eventually our feet will get sore and we will want to find the size that correctly fits. So too people in societies arrange institutions which best fit the needs of a particular mode of economic production. On this point Joseph Schumpeter (1950:11) explains that "Marx did not hold that religions, metaphysics, schools of art, ethical ideas and political volitions were either reducible to economic *motives* or of no importance. He only tried to unveil the economic *conditions* which shape them and which account for their rise and fall."

The primacy of the economic mode cannot be overemphasized. For Marx the central fact of all human history is the necessity for societies, in every epoch, to provide the necessary goods and materials for sustenance. How do people in society organize in order to provide these things? That is the fundamental question with which any societal analysis must begin. Thus to understand politics and power, as well as all other social phenomena, correctly, one must look not to the dominant philosophy of a historical period but to the dominant economic form. It is this "historical materialism" which is the cornerstone of Marxian thought.

Social Class and Political Power

The notion of class is central to Marxian political theory for it is in the relations between classes that we see the manifestations of political power. A class, for Marx, comprises those who stand in a common position with regard to the productive process. Although many subclasses are recognized, Marx sees the eventual emergence of two encompassing classes: those who own and control the means of production and those who do not. In capitalist societies these two classes are the bourgeoisie or capitalist owners, and the proletariat or industrial working class, who own no productive property and can offer only their human labor in exchange for material needs.

It is important to understand that class in the Marxian sense goes well beyond merely describing one's place in the productive system; it represents the essential mold of social existence for all persons. Where one stands in relation to the means of production—ownership or non-ownership—not only affects one's economic status in society but determines one's actions, thoughts, beliefs—in short, one's entire social being.

It is only natural, then, that Marx should see political behavior as basically an expression of social class. Marx believed that classes ultimately become political groups in the sense that individuals come to recognize their common socioeconomic interests and are prepared to engage in struggle to protect and enhance them. It is this power struggle between opposing classes that produces social change.

Political parties or organizations represent *class* interests. Political power is centered therefore not in the state but in the nature of class relations. The dominant class is, in effect, the dominant political group; it is a *ruling* class. That is, those who control the means of production are able to command the government as well. In capitalist societies the state basically reflects the interests of the bourgeoisie. Marx's view of the state is neatly summarized in the *Communist Manifesto*: "The executive of the modern State is but a committee for managing the common affairs of the whole bourgeoisie . . . " (Tucker, 1972:337).

In its most simple form, political life in the Marxian view is an outgrowth of class relations. Therefore, to understand the structure of political institutions in a society, the behavior of political actors, and the actions of political elites, it is first necessary to investigate the society's class structure. Instead of asking "Who rules?" or "Who are the governors of a society?" the Marxian political analyst asks, "Who owns and controls the means of production?" Answering this question—that is, determining those who are dominant in the economic realm—is tantamount to determining who dominates in all other societal realms, including, most importantly, the state.

The Hegemony of the Ruling Class

Why is the power of the capitalist class so irresistible? What enables it, as a ruling class, to thwart any resistance on the part of the subordinate classes? Marxian theory relies on two explanations: economic and ideological.

First, in capitalist societies, workers must submit to the rules established by the capitalist class because in the end they have no other choice. Without access to the means of production, workers must sell their labor to the capitalists and must accept what the capitalists will pay. Under these conditions there is little likelihood that workers can save enough eventually to possess productive property and become capitalists themselves. Thus Marx felt that any basic changes in the class structure could be realized only by a revolutionary movement which would divest the bourgeoisie of its control of the means of production.

The control of ideas and values by the bourgeoisie is perhaps as important as control of the means of production in assuring compliance with the social order of capitalist society. Some have referred to this as the "ideological hegemony" of the ruling class. Marx asserted that "The ideas of the ruling class are in every epoch the ruling ideas: i.e., the class which is the ruling *material* force of society, is at the same time its ruling *intellectual* force" (Tucker, 1972:136). In this view, the rules and values of the sociopolitical system are created, disseminated, and enforced by the dominant class and are ultimately accepted by the society as a whole.

Lacking class consciousness —that is, being unaware of their own class interests —the proletariat regards the ideas of the ruling class as "natural." The prevailing sociopolitical system is thus seen as working in the interests of *all* social classes, not simply the capitalists. Marxists refer to this as "false consciousness." The institutions of education, religion, and the state aid in socializing persons to the dominant values. And by controlling the means of communication (the press, and in modern societies radio and television), the capitalist class is able to stifle opposing ideas effectively. If he were able to witness American television, Marx might point out, for example, how simple it is for oil companies with almost limitless funds to communicate to the American people their explanation of the energy crisis, whereas counterexplanations, expressing the interests of less powerful groups, cannot be transmitted so easily.

Obedience to a social system created by the ruling (capitalist) class, then, is founded not so much on coercion as on (1) the virtual dependence of the working class on the capitalist class for subsistence and (2) the false consciousness of the workers, enforced by the effective control of the communication of new ideas and values by the capitalist class.

Class Conflict and Societal Change

Class conflict, Marx explains, is a certainty in societies so long as private ownership of property is sanctioned, thereby enabling one class to control the productive process, the distribution of wealth, and the communication of ideas. But it is class conflict which generates social change, eventually giving rise to a new mode of production and thereby creating a new ruling class. The transition of societies to new modes of production is the result of the eventual incompatibility between the relations of production (that is, class relations) and the forces of production. How do the forces and relations come into conflict so as to produce this modal change?

The development of capitalism. To demonstrate this process, let us look at the transition from feudal society to capitalist industrial society. Marx explained that feudal society in Europe was characterized by legal and religious institutions which served and rationalized an agrarian economy, not the industrial one that was beginning to emerge in the eighteenth and early nineteenth centuries. This emergent industrialism demanded a system which would facilitate the easy movement of labor from one location to another, the development of natural resources, and trade and commerce within an open market. Property law and custom (that is, the relations of production) in feudal society provided none of these. On the contrary, workers were tied to the land by the system of serfdom, natural resources were immobilized by legal restrictions such as primogeniture, and trade and commerce were hindered by various legal restraints. In short, the entire system of institutions relating to property favored and expressed the interests of the dominant land-owning class.

To change all of this, it was necessary to displace the landed aristocracy as the ruling class. The needs of the developing industrial system required the ascendance of a capitalist class. Ruling economic classes, Marx observed, are progressive bodies when they initially come to power, fostering the development of the new economic system. But eventually they become conservative in their attempts to stabilize and fend off threats to their dominance. Thus the landed aristocracy had been a positive force when societies moved from a state of primitive agriculture to a feudal system; but the coming of industrialism represented a challenge to their supremacy, giving rise to conflict with the new capitalist class.

In the contest between the old ruling class and the emergent capitalists, the latter eventually prevailed. But the victory of the bourgeoisie should not be interpreted as the result of direct confrontation between factory owners and landowners. Such actions were not absent but, most importantly, irreversible historical and economic forces were on the side of the capitalist class, making their ascendance inevitable.

The breakdown of capitalism.   In the same way, of course, the capitalist system will give way to a more advanced form of social and economic organization as the relations of capitalist society are no longer capable of supporting new productive forces. The increasing complexity of industrial production, for example, calls for centralized planning and a high degree of coordination among producers; but the prevailing relations of production—private ownership and competition—encourage the very opposite: individualistic pursuit of profit. Periodic breakdowns in the form of overproduction and unemployment thus become common. With each economic downturn, smaller, less productive capitalists find it more difficult to compete. They drop into the ranks of the proletariat, thereby leaving fewer and fewer producers with increasingly greater power.

Clearly, then, a system whereby the means of production are collectively rather than privately owned is necessitated. And just as capitalism replaced feudalism, the demise of capitalism and its replacement by a socialist productive system was felt by Marx to be an unavoidable future development. The momentum behind the passing of capitalism and the emergence of socialism is the conflict between capitalists and workers. Once the workers become conscious of their true class interests, they are transformed into a political group, prepared to engage in revolutionary confrontation with the bourgeoisie. And just as the irresistible historical and economic forces had previously favored the capitalist class in its conflict with the landowning class, they now favor the working class.

As to the nature of the revolutionary struggle, Marxian theory is not specific. Advancing industrialization and increasing worker exploitation, Marx felt, would eventually propel such a movement. But the organizational details of the revolution were left to practitioners such as Lenin to clarify and implement, well after Marx himself had died in 1883 and Engels in 1895.

The nature of postcapitalist society is also left largely to speculation and it is here that Marx becomes more a visionary than a social scientist.

The broad outlines of postcapitalism, however, were well-formulated thoughts. Following the revolution, two stages were envisioned, ultimately climaxing in a classless society. The first phase, socialism, was seen as a transitional period in which the workers would now control the means of production. By this fact alone power relations would be radically changed, bringing worker exploitation to an end. The state would necessarily still be present but it would now be a proletarian state, which Marx called the "dictatorship of the proletariat." The details of this worker's government were not made clear by either Marx or Engels, but, as noted, Lenin fashioned its actual working order, at least in the Soviet Union.

The length of the socialist stage is indeterminate and we may look at current "communist" societies such as China and the Soviet Union as contemporary versions of this intermediary societal form between capitalism and communism. Needless to say, they may resemble only slightly—if at all—the Marxian vision.

It is only with the total abolition of social classes that the final stage of postcapitalism might emerge. The classless society is manifestly utopian, characterized by the complete socialization of the productive system, the cessation of all economic exploitation, and the appearance of individuals no longer impelled by acquisitive and individualistic values. It is at this point that the well-known dictum "from each according to his abilities; to each according to his needs" is fulfilled. With these conditions in place, the state withers away since there are no longer class interests to protect and no need to impose social controls.

One should keep in mind that capitalism, to Marx, was a very beneficial system when compared with previous ones. It had created the technology and material abundance which now made it possible for people to enter into a social condition in which poverty, both material and psychological, would no longer exist. But to make that condition a reality required the organization of society into a socialist productive system. Capitalism had had its place; indeed it had been a necessary step in societal development. But its utility by the middle of the nineteenth century, Marx felt, was ended.

Marxian Political Theory in Summary

In a few pages we have distilled from the many volumes of Marx and Engels—and the far more numerous volumes of their interpreters—some semblance of the Marxian political idea. To further simplify it, the theory may be boiled down to a few key premises. It is these assumptions which form the starting point for political analysis using the Marxian approach.

1. Reality consists not of ideas but of the constant production of basic life needs — food, clothing, shelter. Reality is essentially the world of human effort, in one simple term, "work." Through work, people realize themselves, and it is around this productive process that history unfolds.
2. Societies in different stages of social and technological development create different productive systems. Economic institutions (that is, the productive system) are the most significant dynamic forces in society; they shape the general nature of beliefs and practices in all other areas of social life, including the political. Thus societal power is most basically a product of economic forces.
3. In all societies a class division evolves. Those who own or control the society's productive resources are inevitably in conflict with those who do not. Class struggle is a struggle between these two primary and opposing classes, and it is here that the dynamic forces of society lie. Class struggle is the generator of societal change.
4. Since classes are political groups — that is, groups seeking to enhance their societal power — political conflict is class conflict. Therefore political behavior and structures are products of class dynamics. To understand politics in a society, one must look first at the class structure.
5. Economic dominance in a society is effectively translated into power in all other societal realms, most importantly the state. Those who own or control the society's productive resources are able to dominate noneconomic sectors, including government. Therefore the dominant *economic* class is a ruling *political* class.

An Assessment of Marxian Theory

Critics have repeatedly pointed out the apparent inappropriateness of specific Marxian propositions to contemporary societies. Though the details of Marx's model of power and politics are certainly refutable in light of recent history, his theoretical contribution is, in a more general sense, of lasting and fundamental significance. Marx proferred a comprehensive theory of society which identified the unequal distribution of power as the key force of change. And given the economic resources on which power rests, society was shown to be subject to inevitable conflict. This theory is valuable not in its specific points but rather as a broad outline which forces us to look beyond the obvious in examining the processes and structures of power.

Just as certain elements of the classical elite theories of Pareto, Mosca, and Michels are distasteful to American ideology but valid nonetheless, so too several general aspects of Marxian analysis seem persuasive even though they do not conform to common American political thought.

Class. First, Marx emphasized the overriding importance of class as a determinant of political behavior and as the key ingredient in the formula of political power. Americans are prone to minimize the social significance of class, but this aspect of Marxian analysis seems well founded, particularly in the realm of politics. A considerable body of modern research shows that people's political actions and attitudes are commonly determined by class factors. Explaining political behavior and structures using class as a key independent variable is a method ordinarily employed by political sociologists and political scientists of all theoretical leanings.

Ideology. Second, the Marxian perspective demonstrates the way in which our social and political worlds are ideologically created. We are attuned to a certain way of thinking about and seeing political society. Rarely are any of us able to consider seriously alternative belief systems or alternative ways of organizing sociopolitical systems. Yet the prevailing modes of thought are not "natural" in the sense that they produce themselves without input from the social environment. Most simply, we *learn* to perceive our world in a particular way. And our learning is confined to that which we are offered by the society's socializing agents—the family, the state, the school, the media—all disseminators of the dominant ideology. Social and political behavior and attitudes we consider "normal" or "just" are in fact defined for us through this ideology. As Michael Harrington (1976:192) has explained, the Marxian perspective "asserts that the common sense of any given society is a rationalization for that society, that vocabularies normally conceal as well as communicate, particularly when they speak of anything that has to do with power."

Our concepts regarding the rights and wrongs of politics and power, then, do not simply come upon us. Rather the ideas and values of the dominant class generally become those of the society as a whole. As such they create a legitimacy for the structure of power and contribute to its perpetuation. As Parkin (1971:83) notes:

> Dominant values are in a sense a representation of the perceptions and interests of the relatively privileged; yet by virtue of the institutional backing they receive such values often form the basis of moral judgements of underprivileged groups. In a way, dominant values tend to set the standards for what is considered to be objectively "right."

This being the case, it should not surprise us that those who are seemingly oppressed by a sociopolitical system often become its staunchest defenders.

The power of economic institutions. Finally, the power of economic institutions in influencing the state and other societal institutions is recognized by almost all social analysts. As we shall see, disagreement concerns only the extent of that influence.

CONTEMPORARY CLASS ANALYSIS

All political sociologists today recognize the validity of at least some aspects of Marx's analysis. But obviously some are more strongly committed to this approach than others. What must be made clear is that among those who do lean more favorably toward this approach, Marx is not interpreted in an absolute or mechanical fashion. Instead Marxian ideas are accepted primarily as a *method* for explaining society rather than a definitive explanation itself. C. Wright Mills has referred to this group of scholars as "plain Marxists" who "are generally agreed that Marx's work bears the trademarks of the 19th century society, but that his general model and his ways of thinking are central to their own intellectual history and remain relevant to their attempts to grasp present-day social worlds" (Mills, 1962:98). Only among the dogmatic or "vulgar" Marxists, then, should we expect to find attempts to apply Marxian ideas in a literal sense to societies of the present age.

Although parts of it are pertinent to the whole course of human social development, Marx's analysis is concerned primarily with the structure and dynamics of capitalist industrial societies. It is in such societies that Marx foresaw the occurrence of the workers' revolution. Obviously this has failed to materialize. It is thus paradoxical that socialist revolutions of modern times have occurred in those societies in which the economic and social conditions required for the kind of movement Marx forecast were least present. Russia in 1917, as well as China and Cuba in more recent eras, were societies in which capitalist development was not great.

Whether the socialist systems of these societies represent Marxism in anything but ideology, then, is unlikely. Clearly they are aberrations of the Marxian legacy and must be seen as unique social orders. On few of these societies' essential problems does Marxian theory shed any light (Harrington, 1973). They have set their own goals, created their own forms of social, political, and economic organization, and developed their own methods of administration. Their policies could be the same had Marx never lived.

The meaning of Marx for contemporary socialist societies remains a point of intense debate among intellectuals and political leaders. What is more important for our purposes, however, is to explain the changed conditions of modern capitalist societies—particularly the United States—and how class theorists have revised and applied the Marxian idea in light of those changes.

The Changing Class Structure

To begin with, class struggle in advanced capitalist societies has not become more acute, as Marx had predicted. Instead the working classes of these societies have seemed to settle for an accommodation with the capitalist system. The fundamental objective of workers has become a more sizable share of the capitalist product, not a change in the productive system itself. Labor unions, for example, appear to be less political organizations than groups designed to operate on behalf of workers within the accepted rules of union-management relations. Particularly in the United States, unions are forces of stabilization, not of radical change. Marx had seen workers' organizations as potential political groups, designed to instill consciousness and alter the prevailing power structure, rather than simply as bargaining agents that would represent labor's interests vis-à-vis the capitalist class.

One reason serious class conflict has been averted in advanced capitalist societies is that the polarization of classes has not progressed as Marx felt it would; rather the very opposite has occurred: an increasingly complex and diverse class structure. The Marxian formula called for a growing contraposition of the two major classes, capitalists and workers. The former would become smaller and more concentrated while the latter would swell in size, gradually absorbing more and more of the marginal capitalists, mainly small entrepreneurs.

Instead with advancing technology the industrial proletariat has declined in size. Automation and centralization of production continue to eliminate traditional manual laboring (that is, working-class) occupations. Accompanying the decline in blue-collar occupations has been a growth of the white-collar laboring force, sometimes referred to as the "new middle class." This is not the middle class of small entrepreneurs, as in the past, but of salaried workers in clerical, sales, professional, and other nonmanual occupations. Today this class represents the largest element of the work force of industrial societies. But the place of white-collar workers is not well defined or overly important in the traditional Marxian model.

In addition to the increasing complexity of the working classes, their collective material state has not deteriorated but has improved markedly in the past 100 years. The standard of living and the objective conditions of work have been altered positively from the degrading conditions typical of Marx's time. These improvements are the result of various social forces and institutions, chief among which are the intervention of the state in dealing with the vacillations of a capitalist economy and the developing power of labor unions, the latter also aided considerably by state intervention.

In short, class conflict in the United States and other advanced capitalist societies has not intensified. The ascendance of a strong labor movement which has blended into the established capitalist system, an increasingly complex class structure, and a significant rise in material standards have been important factors in accounting for this development.

Contemporary class theorists acknowledge the transformation of the class system of advanced capitalist societies into a more diverse and complex arrangement (Harrington, 1979; O'Connor, 1973). Yet, in their view, the structure of power remains basically divided into two parts: those who own and/or control the means of production on the one hand, and those who can offer only their labor on the other. Miliband (1969:16), for example, asserts that despite the appearance of a variety of classes,

> The economic and political life of capitalist societies is *primarily* determined by the relationship, born of the capitalist mode of production, between these two classes—the class which on the one hand owns and controls, and the working class on the other. Here are still the social forces whose confrontation most powerfully shapes the social climate and the political system of advanced capitalism.

The diversity of the class structure is, then, of diminished significance if there still exists a class that owns or controls the bulk of the society's productive resources. As we shall see in chapter 6, there is a great deal of evidence to support this view. The distribution of wealth and property in the United States and other modern capitalist societies is highly concentrated among the affluent few, and the notion of a massive prosperous middle class is grossly exaggerated.

The Ruling Class

As noted, in the Marxian sense a ruling class is that class which, by virtue of its ownership and control of the society's productive resources, can exert the greatest influence on government policies and actions. Does such a class exist in capitalist societies today?

Much of the difficulty in trying to identify a ruling class in present-day capitalist societies arises from the fact that since Marx's time a great change has occurred in the property relations of these societies. Today the corporation is the dominant organizational form of economic production, a radically different type of enterprise from the family-owned and -operated company of the past. In the modern corporation, ownership resides with stockholders, and the actual day-to-day operation of the firm is left to a group of managers. Thus, it is argued, the Marxian notion of a capitalist class in the sense of owners of productive means is no longer valid (Berle and Means, 1932).

But the fact that corporate managers are not necessarily among the chief owners should not lead to the belief that they are simply a select group of hired employees. On the basis of their *control* of corporate resources, they are immensely powerful. Furthermore, as we shall see, in American society high-ranking corporation executives are commonly among the largest shareholders in the firms they manage. They are, then, key owners as well as managers of corporate capital. In any case, corporate wealth is highly concentrated among a tiny percentage of the populace. Together, then, the corporate owners and managers comprise the new capitalist class.

If the economic power of the modern capitalist class is as great as or greater than that of the capitalist class of an earlier time, the question remains as to whether that power is transferable to the political realm. Is the corporate capitalist class able to dominate government? Is it, in other words, a ruling class?

This is an issue which has been debated among class theorists. Simple Marxist views of the state conjure up images of big businessmen behind the scenes pulling the strings of government officials, much like puppeteers. The political (or state) elite may give the appearance of independence, but in fact it is the capitalists who direct the state. Contemporary class theorists, however, have pointed out the oversimplicity of this view. There is no question that the state serves the interests of the capitalist class, but there are different explanations among current class theorists as to how it accomplishes this. Basically two views have been evident, one stressing the strong ties of the capitalist class to the political elite, the other stressing the structural constraints imposed on the political elite by the very nature of the capitalist system.

The instrumentalist view. The first view is that the capitalists do not necessarily govern in the sense of occupying political offices, but that they *rule* by controlling political officials and institutions. This is very close to the traditional Marxian view of the linkages between the capitalist class and the state. The state is seen as functioning "in terms of the instrumental exercise of power by people in strategic positions, either directly through the manipulation of state policies or indirectly through the exercise of pressure on the state" (Gold, Lo, and Wright, 1975a:34). The critical question is, then "Who are the people in strategic positions?" Class theorists using this perspective have investigated the relations between top corporate and political decision makers, usually finding them to be of similar social backgrounds with a strong understanding of common purpose.[1] The service of government to capitalist class interests is thus natural and self-enforcing.

In addition to the direct political influence of the corporate elite through their exchange of strategic positions with government leaders, campaign financing, lobbying, and participation in public policy planning groups, there are indirect influences through the imposing of capitalist values on public education and the mass media. What is accomplished is acceptance by the society's various classes of the belief that societal interest and business interest are one and the same.

At minimum, then, corporate leaders act in concert with political and other institutional leaders to protect capitalist interests and to assure preservation of the prevailing class system. As we shall see in Part Three, there is much evidence to support this view.

The structuralist view. Another group of contemporary class theorists contends that the interpersonal linkages between political and economic elites are of little importance in assuring the maintenance of capitalist class interests by the state. They argue that the structure of political and economic institutions in capitalist society makes it imperative that the state serve those interests regardless of whether or not big businessmen directly or indirectly take part in state affairs. Attempts to influence government policymakers through campaign contributions, lobbying, and so on are merely "icing on the cake." Plainly the state cannot carry through anticapitalist policies because of mechanisms built into the modern capitalist political economy (Block, 1977:14: Poulantzas, 1973).

1. The studies of Domhoff (1967; 1971), Baltzell (1958; 1964), and Mills (1956) are the chief expositors of the functional and social linkages between state and economic elites in the United States. Porter's (1965) and Clement's (1975) studies have demonstrated similar elite linkages in Canada. These works will be discussed in greater detail in chapter 9.

These theorists reject the importance of social and strategic ties among corporate and government leaders. Since the viability of the state is dependent on a healthy economy, they argue, state leaders *must* promote the interests of big business (that is, the corporations) regardless of who they are or what their views may be. If the economy declines, tax revenues dry up, imperiling government programs and weakening public support for elected officials and other government leaders. The general interests of the capitalist class are thus naturally served. Indeed state leaders may be more aware of the general need for maintaining a stable social order (that is, a capitalist system) than profit-oriented capitalists. The state, in this view, is able to transcend the narrow, parochial interests of individual capitalists and protect the long-range, general interests of the entire capitalist class. As Reich and Edwards (1978:40) explain, "Since capitalists compete with each other for profits, state policies that are in the common interest of the whole capitalist class may actually conflict with particular interests of specific capitalists." There is, then, some autonomy for the state in dealing with individual capitalists on behalf of *all* capitalists.

Whether it is due to personal direction and influence or to the structural nature of the political economy, contemporary class theorists agree that within the context of a capitalist system, the state sooner or later must weigh the interests of the capitalist class more heavily than others. Moreover, the nature of the political economy in modern capitalist societies makes the distinction between government leaders and leaders of the corporation—the chief institution of the capitalist class—less meaningful. Given the active role of government in the making of economic policy, the various forms of public financial support given to private corporations, and the constant crossover of personnel from one sphere to the other, it is commonplace that key economic and political decisions are made by officials of government and corporation in concert.

The State

The class perspective of politics in society stresses the notion of political economy—that is, the meshing of state and economic institutions in both structure and functions. In trying to determine the shape of power, class theorists look first at the manner in which the society is economically organized. How are its material needs met—in Marx's terms, what is its mode of production? Which groups control and direct the economic system and which groups benefit from the prevailing institutional arrangement? In contrast to the pluralist perspective, which sees the state as the dominant power institution in society, class theorists see the state as an institution basically shaped by the system of economic production and thus subject to the direction of the dominant economic class. Economic institutions, then, even more than political ones, are of major importance.

In this view the state in capitalist society is not an independent intermediary which functions to maintain order between opposing interest groups, acting here on behalf of one, there on behalf of another. Nor does it actively pursue the common good of the society. Rather it is an institution which represents more than any other the society's dominant economic interests.

Contemporary class theorists recognize the important role of the state in modern capitalist societies in maintaining and reproducing the capitalist system and its attendant class relations. As the dominant institution of authority, the state protects the system of property relations and also helps to regenerate the system through the fostering of capitalist ideology. Thus laws pertaining to private property are enforced by the state and dissent is repressed, sometimes through violent means but more commonly through the propagation of dominant (that is, capitalist) values in schools, the media, and other societal institutions.

A second important function of the state in advanced capitalist societies is capital accumulation. Marxist theories have traditionally explained the role of the state as a guarantor of the conditions necessary for capitalist production. This means assuring social peace and generally providing an atmosphere conducive to investment and the expansion of economic activity. In modern capitalist systems, however, the role of the state in economic activities has increased considerably. With the advent of monopoly capitalism (see chapter 6), in which giant corporate enterprises are no longer competitive in the manner of traditional capitalist enterprises, there emerges a growing interdependence of the state and the corporation in assuring economic growth. Now the state does not simply guarantee the conditions which assure a healthy capitalist system; it also intervenes directly in that process by means of tax policies, spending, and even production of its own. (These functions will be further discussed in chapter 7.)

Thus the state assists in accumulating capital which is necessary to the private, particularly the corporate, sector. For example, the state directly subsidizes various industries; it builds roads and transportation systems vital to industrial development and commerce; it trains people in schools and colleges who enter the private work force; it finances research and development which aids various industries; it spends billions on countless items, especially military hardware. In short, state activities in the economy are critical to the development of capital and the profits which accrue to the capitalist class. As Miliband (1969:78) has noted, capitalist enterprise "*depends* to an ever greater extent on the bounties and direct support of the state, and can only preserve its 'private' character on the basis of such public help. State intervention in economic life in fact largely *means* intervention for the purpose of helping capitalist enterprise."

Some have theorized that the abilities of the state in advanced capitalist societies in solving the contradictions created by monopoly capitalism are becoming more difficult and are creating contradictions within the state itself. Economist James O'Connor (1973) has explained, for example, what he calls the "fiscal crisis of the state." One main function of the capitalist state, according to O'Connor, is accumulation—that is, financing economic growth, primarily in the monopoly (corporate) sector of the economy. But the state cannot simply impose the costs of capital accumulation on subordinate classes since this would create dissension and possible revolt. Thus in accumulating capital for the monopoly sector, the state must also try to assure social harmony—this O'Connor calls the "legitimation function"—by providing public benefits such as welfare, unemployment payments, and so on. These two functions, accumulation and legitimation, are often contradictory since accumulation for the monopoly sector leads to surplus capacity and surplus labor power, thereby threatening social and economic stability by creating unemployment and other disruptive forces which the state must alleviate through its own programs. The state's budget is thus increasingly strained. In short, demands on the state by capitalists and by increasingly dispossessed—especially nonunion—workers outrun its ability to raise revenues to finance them. This, then, is the state's fiscal crisis.

O'Connor's model demonstrates the changed place of the state in advanced capitalist societies. The state remains devoted to capitalist interests, but in doing so it now takes on independent features. It becomes not simply a state serving capitalist class interests because of direct capitalist influence or even because of the constraints imposed by the economic system, but because of internal characteristics of its own.[2] In a sense, the traditional Marxian distinction between the society's economic base and the state as an element of the superstructure is no longer meaningful; the state itself has become part of the productive base.

2.   This is a view of the capitalist state also explained in the works of German political sociologist Claus Offe (1974; 1975). Offe's translated works are quite cumbersome, however, and a good general summation of his theory is found in Gold, Lo, and Wright (1975b).

Key issues of both accumulation and legitimation are now decided within the political system, and class conflict becomes increasingly politicized as various groups seek state support. In other words, class struggle now takes place not within the sphere of economic production but within the sphere of state administration. As the state fails to solve the crisis produced by increasing public expenditures to assure private capital accumulation and profits, its legitimacy is also more difficult to sustain. Failure to pacify subordinate classes through social services (which are more difficult to finance) necessitates increased repression, which in turn creates more intense class conflict (Quinney, 1977:78–90).

A CRITIQUE OF THE CLASS MODEL

Despite its many cogent arguments regarding the nature of power and politics in modern capitalist societies such as the United States, the class model, like pluralism and elitism, has been criticized along several lines. Let us look at some key points.

The Emphasis on Class

Critics have pointed out that with its primary emphasis on class as a determinant of power and politics, there is a tendency for the class or Marxian model to discount or minimize other social variables. As Alford (1975:151–152) notes, the class paradigm plays down the extent of social and cultural diversity within classes, "although this class heterogeneity may have decisive implications for the potential for class consciousness, solidarity, and conflict." Pluralists argue, for example, that not all corporation executives, any more than all working-class people, will see eye-to-eye on each issue that affects them. Religion, sex, age, and other social factors in addition to class motivate people in the political arena. The abortion controversy, for example, seems to be a politico-religious issue encompassing a variety of class members on each side.

Also ethnicity and nationalism are two extremely powerful social forces of the twentieth century, each of which has created social movements and conflicts within and between societies to a far greater extent than class differences. Indeed so strong are they that many neo-Marxists have felt compelled to refocus the Marxian revolutionary idea upon them. Revolutionary struggle is thus seen as a confrontation of emerging societies (and minority peoples within industrial societies) against capitalist societies (Baran and Sweezy, 1966:9). In this view blacks in the United States and South Africa, Catholics in Northern Ireland, and peasants in various Third World nations exemplify the new revolutionary forces. Such revolutions are not those of a captive working class but rather a captive society or part of a society, struggling against the control of capitalist governments.

The Power of Economic Institutions

Just as pluralists have seemed to overemphasize the state as the center of societal power, class theorists have been accused of overstating the power of economic institutions and their leaders.

In his writings Marx devoted considerably less attention to the structure and workings of the political system of capitalist society than to its economic institutions. Indeed it must be remembered that his theory is not of the "state" but of "society." This neglect of the political machinery reflects his view that the shape and actions of the state are basically dependent on economic structures and relations. Although both Marx and Engels qualified their presumed reliance solely upon economic factors in explaining social and political dynamics, as Mills has put it, for Marx "economic causes are 'the basic,' the ultimate, the general, the innovative causes of historical change" (Mills, 1962:93). Undue reliance on economic factors as explanators of all social and political behavior, however, seems too narrow an approach for analysis of contemporary societies of whatever economic or political mold.

Political forces in the form of the state and its ancillary bureaucratic agencies must be recognized as equally important—and often dominant—factors in shaping social life and the motivations behind social change. In short, the state has become an overwhelming institution in modern societies with substantial independent power capacities. This is true of *all* modern societies, whether nominally capitalist or socialist. It is obvious in the extreme, for example, that in noncapitalist societies such as the Soviet Union, where productive property is no longer privately owned and controlled, the state has not diminished in power and presence. On the contrary, it has become more pervasive and forceful in determining the nature of the society. As we have seen, contemporary class theorists have been forced to account for the increasing autonomous powers of the state in advanced capitalist societies as well, particularly the United States.

The Inevitability of Elites

Perhaps the most convincing criticism of the class or Marxian model is its neglect of the elite imperative in modern societies. Most simply, the complexity and scale of modern industrial societies unavoidably give rise to impersonal bureaucracies led by elites. Marxists, however, have generally maintained that ideally a socialist society can emerge in which leaders will not display the oligarchic tendencies of elites in capitalist society. Indeed the utopian Marxist vision is of an eventual classless society wherein government and other institutions of authority are no longer necessary.

Among the major elite theorists, Michels seems to offer the most cogent refutation of the possibilities of an eliteless society. Replacing old leaders with new ones, even those who at first truly represent the masses, only has the effect of creating a new oligarchy that eventually separates itself from the subordinate classes. Michels explains this tendency:

> In proportion as the profession of politician becomes a more complicated one, and in proportion as the rules of social legislation become more numerous, it is necessary for one who would understand politics to possess wider experience and more extensive knowledge. Thus the gulf between the leaders and the rest of the party becomes ever wider, until the moment arrives in which the leaders lose all true sense of solidarity with the class from which they have sprung, and there ensues a new class-division between ex-proletarian captains and proletarian common soldiers (1962: 108–109).

Historical example seems to bear out Michels on this point. Nowhere has the realization of his prophecy been more obvious than in the contemporary socialist societies, in which the Communist parties have evolved into elite organizations, creating what some have called a "new class" (Djilas, 1957). One observer has described the transformation of the Soviet Communist Party, for example, "from an ideologically committed, revolutionary elite to an 'establishment' of vested interests, from a crusading minority bent on radical social change to a privileged elite interested in the maintenance of the status quo and improving the efficiency of the existing system" (Hollander, 1973:53). As Michels had earlier predicted, "The socialists might conquer, but not socialism, which would perish in the moment of its adherents' triumph" (1962:355).

In what is strikingly similar to Michels' observation regarding the inevitable emergence of oligarchy, Weber (1947:338) describes bureaucracy: "When those subject to bureaucratic control seek to escape the influence of the existing bureaucratic apparatus, this is normally possible only by creating an organization of their own which is equally subject to the process of bureaucratization." Thus with the need to coordinate political and economic activities in society, an authority system is created, thereby assuring the subordination of the many to the dictates of the few (Giddens, 1975:125).[3]

Michels and Weber respond to Marx by noting the critical nature not of the means of *production* but of the means of *administration*. No matter who controls the means of production, the administration of social wealth will be necessary, and therein lies unavoidable bureaucracy and elite rule. In the end, socialist societies will resemble capitalist societies so long as industrialism characterizes each. As Weber explains:

> The primary source of the superiority of bureaucratic administration lies in the role of technical knowledge which, through the development of modern technology and business methods in the production of goods, has become completely indispensable. In this respect, it makes no difference whether the economic system is organized on a capitalistic or a socialistic basis (1947:337–338).

Weber claims that socialism would, in fact, require an even higher degree of bureaucratization than capitalism. Again the status of current socialist societies seems to bear out Weber's prediction with great clarity.

SOME COMPARATIVE NOTES

We have now looked at three major models of power and politics in society as well as some variations of each. All seem to offer both compelling points as well as apparent shortcomings in explaining political behavior and structure. Let us briefly compare some of their key points, particularly as they relate to American society.

As is seen in Table 5-1, the class model of power and politics differs most sharply from the pluralist model. Pluralists view power not as the exclusive possession of one class but as a shifting product of competition among diverse groups, mediated by and filtered through the state. Class theorists do not deny that competition exists among various political groups in the society, but they point out that such competition is limited by the dominant class to "safe" issues which do not threaten the continuity of its power. This is accomplished not simply by direct methods but indirectly through propagation of the dominant (that is, ruling class) ideology. Disagreements are thus only on superficial or symbolic issues, not on the fundamentals of the capitalist political economy.

Looking at American political history, it seems obvious that move-

---

3. Ralf Dahrendorf (1959) has remodeled the Marxian idea by explaining authority relations rather than property relations as most significant in modern societies.

TABLE 5-1 Societal Power as Seen by the Three Models

Model	Chief source of power	Key power group (s)	Role of masses	Function of state
Class	Control of society's productive resources (wealth)	Ruling class (owners and controllers of the corporate system)	Manipulated and exploited by the ruling class	Protect capitalist class interests; reproduce class system
Elitist	Control of key institutions, primarily the corporation and the executive branch of the federal government	Relatively cohesive power elite, made up of top corporate and government leaders	Manipulated and exploited by the power elite	Protect interests of dominant elites and their institutions
Pluralist	Various political resources, including wealth, authority, and votes	Elective political officials; interest groups and their leaders	Indirectly control elites through competitive elections and interest group pressures	Referee the arena of interest groups; create political consensus

ments to alter the prevailing sociopolitical system in a basic way are very uncommon. When they do emerge, they are generally feeble efforts. Pluralists have interpreted this as a broadly based agreement on political norms and values. But class theorists interpret it as evidence of the success of the dominant class in imposing its set of presumptions on the society as a whole. As Parenti (1978:16) has noted:

> To assume that the absence of opposition to the existing social order is evidence of a freely arrived at consensus is to rule out the possibility of a manipulated consensus. It is to assume there has been no indoctrination, no socialization to conservative values, no control of information, no limitation of the agenda, no predetermination of interest choice, that power has not been operative in the shaping of interest definition.

Competitive politics, then, may be limited only to those groups who display establishment credentials, even if nonestablishment groups may sometimes represent the interests of a broad range of the society's classes.

Another critical difference between class and pluralist perspectives is the tendency of the latter to take the currently functioning sociopolitical system as "given." That is, the innate features of the system which automatically favor some interests over others are not a decisive point for pluralists. As Milton Mankoff (1970:419–420) has described it, pluralism is an ahistorical perspective in which "All current participants in competition over scarce resources (political, economic, military) appear to be stripped of any built-in advantages afforded by their strategic location in an ongoing society with a particular economic and cultural history." For example, why giant corporations and labor unions should be the chief participants in and beneficiaries of the power game run by government while small business and unorganized labor play only a minor role is a question never raised. Analysis is confined to the politics of various groups within the given power structure. But how and why that structure took its present shape or how other power structures might work in its place are not considered. These issues, however, are basic to the class model.

In several ways the contemporary class model of politics and power in America is quite similar to and overlaps with the elite perspective, particularly the radical elite version represented by Mills (1956). First, on the fundamental notion of elite rule there is no disagreement between the two; both share the assumption that political control is exercised by a ruling class or power elite that either directly or indirectly pulls the strings which manipulate the society or is prevented by the structure of the political economy from serving any but dominant group interests. Moreover elitists and class theorists agree that elites use their power to further their own interests or the interests of their class.

Second, both models also recognize a basically two-part power structure: rulers and ruled. There is, of course, some difference between the two in their understanding of the basis of elite power. Elitists regard power as a product of control of organizational resources, while class theorists see it as derivative of control of the productive system. Both agree, however, on the negative societal impact of ruling elites or ruling classes.

Third, elite and class models, in contrast to pluralism, minimize the place of the masses in the system of power. Pluralists see masses as participants, at least to some degree, in the political process. Through elections and interest group activities, political officials are held accountable and cannot favor the interests of only one or a few groups on all issues. The system remains relatively balanced and tranquil through compromise among the competing groups and their leaders. But elite and class theorists see the masses as manipulated by a cohesive ruling group which keeps them oblivious to the true functions of the state: to serve the interests of the society's dominant class. Compromise and consensus, so basic to the pluralist explanation, are only shams employed by powerful groups who control the resolution of truly significant issues in their favor.

As we shall see, political sociologists who have adopted a critical approach in their analyses of power in America have used elements of both radical elite and class models. The overlapping of the two, distinct from pluralism, will become apparent in chapter 9.

SUMMARY

The class model of politics in society is founded essentially on the theories of Karl Marx. Marx saw societal power as a product of class relations. In all societies two main classes are evident: those who own the means of production and those who do not. Political dynamics revolve around the relations between these two classes. Those who own or control the means are the dominant class and enlist the state to serve their interests. They, therefore, constitute a *ruling* class. The ruling class perpetuates its dominance through control not only of productive property but also of the formation and communication of ideology.

In advanced capitalist societies such as the United States, class conflict has not intensified as Marx had predicted and the class structure itself has become more complex and diverse. Also the ruling class in such societies is more difficult to distinguish since the traditional capitalist owners have been replaced by a managerial elite that runs the giant corporations, the chief institutions of the capitalist system. Nonetheless as controllers of the society's wealth, the corporate elite remains the core of the capitalist class. Contemporary Marxist theorists see this new capitalist class as also a ruling class on the basis of either (1) its control of state policymakers or (2) the structural nature of the capitalist political economy, which makes imperative the state's service of capitalist class interests.

According to class theorists, the state in advanced capitalist societies functions to protect prevailing class relations and to reproduce the sociopolitical system through the fostering of capitalist ideology. The state also guarantees the conditions necessary for capitalist production and intervenes in the economic process, assisting in the accumulation of capital necessary to the corporate sector of the economy.

The Marxian or class perspective is valuable in forcing us to understand the structural nature of power and politics and the place of ideology in perpetuating political systems. Also the importance of class dynamics in explaining political behavior is now a well-accepted part of social science analysis.

The class model has been criticized, however, as overly focused on class and economic factors in explaining power and politics while neglecting other social variables. Also it fails to consider the elite impera-tive in modern societies: The few dominate the many regardless of the nature of property relations.

Looking at pluralist, elite, and class models in comparison, the latter two overlap on several points and stand clearly apart from pluralism. Elite and class theorists basically see politics as dominated by powerful ruling groups who manipulate the general populace in securing support for their actions and policies. Pluralists, on the other hand, see the pow-erful in competition with each other and ultimately accountable to the masses.

REFERENCES

Alford, Robert R. 1975. "Paradigms of Relations Between State and Society." In Leon N. Lindberg, Robert Alford, Colin Crouch, and Claus Offe (Eds.), *Stress and Contradiction in Modern Capitalism*. Lexington, Mass.: Lexington.

Aron, Raymond. 1968. *Main Currents in Sociological Thought*. Vol. I. New York: Anchor.

Baltzell, E. Digby. 1958. *Philadelphia Gentlemen*. New York: Free Press.
_____. 1964. *The Protestant Establishment*. New York: Random House.

Baran, Paul, and **Paul Sweezy.** 1966. *Monopoly Capital*. New York: Monthly Review.

Berle, A. A., Jr., and **Gardiner C. Means.** 1932. *The Modern Corporation and Pri-vate Property*. New York: Macmillan.

Block, Fred. 1977. "The Ruling Class Does Not Rule: Notes on the Marxist Theory of the State." *Socialist Review* 7 (May-June):6–28.

Clement, Wallace. 1975. *The Canadian Corporate Elite*. Toronto: McClelland and Stewart.

Dahrendorf, Ralf. 1959. *Class and Class Conflict in Industrial Society*. Stanford: Stanford U. Press.

Djilas, Milovan. 1957. *The New Class*. New York: Praeger.

Domhoff, G. William. 1967. *Who Rules America?* Englewood Cliffs: Prentice-Hall.
_____. 1971. *The Higher Circles*. New York: Vintage.

Giddens, Anthony. 1975. *The Class Structure of the Advanced Societies*. New York: Harper and Row.

Gold, David A., Clarence Y. H. Lo, and **Erik Olin Wright.** a:1975. "Recent De-velopments in Marxist Theories of the Capitalist State." *Monthly Review* 27 (October):29–43.
_____. b:1975. "Recent Developments in Marxist Theories of the State: Part 2." *Monthly Review* 27 (November):36–51.

Harrington, Michael. 1973. *Socialism*. New York: Bantam.
_____. 1976. *The Twilight of Capitalism*. New York: Simon and Schus-ter.

_____. 1979. "The New Class and the Left." *Society* 16(January/February):24–30.

Hollander, Paul. 1973. *Soviet and American Society*. New York: Oxford U. Press.

Lewis, John. 1972. *The Marxism of Marx*. London: Lawrence and Wishart.

Mankoff, Milton. 1970. "Power in Advanced Capitalist Society: A Review Essay on Recent Elitist and Marxist Criticism of Pluralist Theory." *Social Problems* 17 (Winter):418–430.

Marx, Karl. 1920. *The Poverty of Philosophy*. Trans. H. Quelch. Chicago: H. Kerr.

Marx, Karl, and Friedrich Engels. 1968. *Selected Works in One Volume*. New York: International.

Meyer, Alfred G. 1970. *Marxism: The Unity of Theory and Practice*. Rev. ed. Cambridge: Harvard U. Press.

Michels, Robert. 1962. *Political Parties*. Trans. Eden and Cedar Paul. New York: Free Press.

Miliband, Ralph. 1969. *The State in Capitalist Society*. New York: Basic.

_____. 1977. *Marxism and Politics*. New York: Oxford U. Press.

Mills, C. Wright. 1956. *The Power Elite*. New York: Oxford U. Press.

_____. 1962. *The Marxists*. New York: Dell.

O'Connor, James. 1973. *The Fiscal Crisis of the State*. New York: St. Martin's.

Offe, Claus. 1974. "Structural Problems of the Capitalist State." In Klaus von-Beyme (ed.), *German Political Studies*. Vol. I. London: Sage.

_____. 1975. "The Theory of the Capitalist State and the Problem of Policy Formation." In Leon Lindberg, Robert Alford, Colin Crouch, and Claus Offe (eds.), *Stress and Contradiction in Modern Capitalism*. Lexington, Mass.: Lexington.

Parenti, Michael. 1978. *Power and the Powerless*. New York: St. Martin's.

Parkin, Frank. 1971. *Class Inequality and Political Order*. New York: Praeger.

Porter, John. 1965. *The Vertical Mosaic*. Toronto: U. of Toronto Press.

Poulantzas, Nicos. 1973. *Political Power and Social Classes*. London: NLB and Sheed and Ward.

Quinney, Richard. 1977. *Class, State, and Crime*. New York: McKay.

Reich, Michael, and Richard Edwards. 1978. "Political Parties and Class Conflict in the United States." *Socialist Review* 8 (May-June):37-57.

Schumpeter, Joseph. 1950. *Capitalism, Socialism, and Democracy*. 3rd ed. New York: Harper and Bros.

Tucker, Robert C. (ed.). 1972. *The Marx-Engels Reader*. New York: Norton.

Weber, Max. 1947. *The Theory of Social and Economic Organization*. Trans. A. M. Henderson and Talcott Parsons. New York: Oxford U. Press.

part three

power in
advanced
capitalist societies

chapter 6

corporate power

*The clichés of private enterprise survive but
serve primarily to disguise the essentially public
character of the great corporation, including its
private exercise of what is, in fact, a public
power. . . . To recognize that the great corporation is essentially a public entity is to accept that
its acts have a profoundly public effect.*
John Kenneth Galbraith

Societal power has been defined as taking three major forms: authority, influence, and control of resources, the three most often occurring in combination. But, as explained, none of these forms of power can be potent outside an institutional setting. To reiterate Mills, to be truly powerful requires command of major institutions. Or as sociologist Floyd Hunter has put it, "power of the individual must be structured into associational, clique, or institutional patterns to be effective" (1953: 6).

Thus to look at the structure of power in the United States and other industrial societies requires that we first identify those institutions wherein decisions made by leaders affect the society as a whole, where influence exerted on decision makers is of greatest consequence, and where the most substantial material and human resources lie. After locating the institutional sources of power, the next step is to identify power elites, those who are in the command positions of these institutions.

In the first three chapters of this part, these issues are explored at the national level of American society. Although the United States is only one society, the patterns of power here resemble those in other Western industrial societies closely enough that some broad generalizations may be made regarding all of them. We begin with a description of the structure and relations of the most important institutions (chapters 6 and 7) and then look more closely at the personnel who actually wield power in these settings (chapters 8 and 9). In chapter 10 we will look at the structure of power at the level of the community. Finally, the place of the masses in the structure of power must be considered. How do they relate to leaders and what means of control—if any—do they have over power elites? In chapter 11 we will consider these issues.

THEORETICAL ASSUMPTIONS

The analysis of power in the United States and other advanced capitalist societies in recent decades has boiled down to a debate between pluralists, elitists, and class theorists, whose basic arguments we have now examined. Our analysis of the American power structure is built around several theoretical assumptions drawn mainly from the class and elite perspectives.

Political Economy

First, political power in a society can be understood only as a synthesis of the actions of governmental and economic institutions. In advanced capitalist societies such as the United States, power is always an interplay of government and business. Thus to explore power in America is to look at business institutions as well as government, and the interrelations between the two. It is within these two institutional spheres that authority and influence are most crucial for the society as a whole and where societal resources are most highly concentrated. The consequences of the actions of business and government leaders affect all people; the far-reaching issues —jobs, prices, war or peace, public services, the environment —are settled by them. The importance of elites in other areas of social life such as education, communications, medicine, and so on is not disputed; but particularly in capitalist societies their activities are essentially shaped by business and government (see Form and Miller, 1960).

The system of power in advanced capitalist societies is best described, then, as **political economy**. In such a system understanding the relationship between economic and governmental institutions is a first step in discovering the nature and distribution of power.

Ruling Elites

Second, power within these two spheres is highly centralized and concentrated among a relatively few organizations and, within these organizations, a relatively few individuals. Important decisions affecting the society are made by an elite who are effectively separated from the relatively powerless masses. Only a handful of individuals actually wield great power within business and government. In the United States it is obvious that fewer and fewer economic organizations control larger and larger elements of the economy as a whole. Leaders of such organizations are largely unaccountable and hardly even identifiable to those outside the highest circles of power. As for government, important decisions with societywide impact are increasingly made within the executive branch of the federal government rather than the more broadly based Congress. With the exception of the President, none of these positions of executive power are elective; all are appointive and thus less sensitive to the constraints of public opinion.

The power of a few governmental agencies is, then, similar to the power of a few large corporations. And this increasing concentration of power within the economic and governmental realms has been accompanied by an increasing interaction between the two, so much so that it is often difficult to separate them analytically. Their interests coincide, and they overlap in policy and personnel. They are essentially mutually supportive. This interplay between government and economy in the United States is evident in many specific areas, which will be discussed in the following chapters.

Wealth and Power

The unequal distribution of wealth in society is most critical in determining the structure of power for "wealth conditions the exercise of power and, through power, determines much of the inequality of social life" (Turner and Starnes, 1976:45). To say that wealth and power are always related is erroneous, but the association between the two is strong. Sociologist Gerhard Lenski has neatly summarized the relationship:

> If privilege is defined as possession or control of a portion of the surplus produced by a society, then it follows that *privilege is largely a function of power, and to a very limited degree, a function of altruism.* This means that to explain most of the distribution of privilege in a society, we have but to determine the distribution of power (1966: 45).

In modern capitalist societies, the most important form of privilege is corporate wealth since, as we shall see, it is in the corporation that the bulk of the society's productive resources lie. The corporation thus becomes, with the state, one of the two key institutions of power. It is on the power of the corporation that we will focus in this chapter.

AMERICA AS A CAPITALIST SOCIETY

Before examining the power of the corporation in American society, we first need to understand the capitalist framework within which it operates. Three basic characteristics shape the system of production and its complementary social institutions in capitalist society: the private ownership of property, the competitive pursuit of profit, and inequality in the distribution of social wealth. On all three counts the American socioeconomic system is fundamentally capitalist.

Private Ownership

The American economic system has often been described as "mixed," denoting the participation of both public and private institutions. However, it is mixed only in the sense that government and private enterprise each participate in various ways in shaping economic policy and stimulating a sound economic climate. Although in a few instances the state supplies services (for example, postal delivery, roads, and in some cases electricity), the vast bulk of the American economy is privately owned and controlled. In this regard the United States is unique even within the capitalist world since in almost all other modern capitalist societies at least some of the more basic industries are publicly owned. In Great Britain, for example, power companies, railroads and airlines, coal mining, and steel production are state enterprises. In socialist societies, of course, state ownership is the norm in all industries.

Profits

That profits are the motivational underpinnings of capitalism needs little discussion. Persons in capitalist societies are expected to maximize their wealth by competing with each other for the society's product. But the society's wealth and the means by which it is produced are primarily private. This means that profits generated are *private* profits. Pursuing self-interest is certainly common in all societies, but what is so distinctive about this feature of capitalism is that such activity is considered socially beneficial and morally correct. Given the predominance of this value in American society, public needs are met only to the extent that they minimally affect private gain. Moreover public programs such as health, education, housing, and so on are generally dependent on private firms and individuals for materials and services, in which case public investment results in private profits.

Inequality

As a system founded upon individualistic competition, capitalism automatically generates inequality in the distribution of the society's product. Quite simply, some get more than others. What is of greatest consequence, however, is the unequal distribution of capitalist or productive property, that which can be used to create further income and wealth. Most people in capitalist societies own various amounts of property such as their clothes, their cars, their household appliances, and for many, their homes. But these personal forms count for little. Rather it is such items as factories, machines, real estate and, most importantly, financial capital which are the critical forms; these constitute the means of production. By possessing or controlling these, one is able to convert them into increasing amounts of income and wealth.

The inequality in personal income generated by capitalism is extremely great in American society (Table 6-1), but inequality in wealth or productive property is even more acute. As seen in Table 6-2, there is a huge gap between the few who own and/or control large amounts of wealth and the many who own little or none. Furthermore studies have shown these patterns of maldistribution in income and wealth to be very

TABLE 6-1 Income of U.S. Families as Percent of Total (by income fifths)

	1950	1955	1960	1965	1970	1976
Lowest fifth	4.5	4.8	4.8	5.2	5.4	5.4
Second fifth	12.0	12.3	12.2	12.2	12.2	11.8
Middle fifth	17.4	17.8	17.8	17.8	17.6	17.6
Fourth fifth	23.4	23.7	24.0	23.9	23.8	24.1
Highest fifth	42.7	41.3	41.3	40.9	40.9	41.1
Highest 5 percent	17.3	16.4	15.9	15.5	15.6	15.6

Source: *Statistical Abstract of the United States*, 1978, p. 443.

consistent throughout American history (Kolko, 1962; Parker, 1972; Turner and Starnes, 1976).

In capitalist society, wealth is the most essential power resource since it is most easily transformed into authority and influence. In contemporary America and other capitalist societies, the possessors of greatest wealth are the giant industrial and financial corporations and the few superaffluent families and individuals, the latter of less significance. As Dye and Zeigler write, "Individuals may control millions but institutions control billions" (1978:101). Of course, even those with great personal fortunes find that their wealth is primarily in the form of corporate wealth such as stocks and bonds. As Mills has written:

> The pyramid of wealth cannot be understood merely in terms of the very rich; for the great inheriting families ... are now supplemented by the corporate institutions of modern society: every one of the very rich families has been and is closely connected — always legally and frequently managerially as well—with one of the multi-million dollar corporations (1956:9–10).

To all intents and purposes, then, the corporation is the source of economic wealth in American society. In this position the corporation becomes dominant in the shaping of public policy, both inside and outside of government.

CORPORATE CAPITALISM

The overriding characteristic of the American economy today is the dominance of the corporation as the chief form of enterprise. This has developed with the evolution of the United States as an industrial power during the past 100 years.

Prior to the Civil War, the American economy had been predomi-

TABLE 6-2 Personal Wealth Held by Top 1 Percent of All Persons

Form of Wealth	1958	1962	1969	1972
Real estate	15.1	15.3	14.4	15.1
Corporate stock	75.4	62.0	50.8	56.5
Bonds	41.4	40.6	53.4	60.0
Cash	15.2	15.3	14.3	13.5
Debt instruments (notes, mortgages, security credit)	37.3	42.3	40.9	52.7
Life insurance	14.1	11.4	10.8	7.0
Trusts	92.1	NA	92.3	89.9
Miscellaneous	7.9	13.9	10.9	9.8
Total assets	25.5	26.2	24.4	24.1

Source: *Statistical Abstract of the United States*, 1978, p. 464.

nantly an agrarian one, with two-thirds of the labor force engaged in agriculture, mainly in family owned and operated farms. Manufacturing was typified by the small plant, also primarily individually owned and operated. There was, then, little concentration of economic power. During the 50 or so years following the Civil War, the entire economic structure was radically changed. From an agrarian system of many individual entrepreneurs with little consolidation among them, the productive system became an industrial one in which large corporate enterprises began to dominate most aspects of economic activity. By 1929, only one-fifth of the labor force was engaged in agriculture. And by this time the convergence of economic power among fewer and fewer industrial firms was evident, the 200 largest controlling almost one-half of the assets of all nonfinancial corporations (Means, 1964:8–9).

Concentration of Corporate Wealth

Regardless of the measure used —profits, assets, number of employees, value of sales — it is clear that the process of corporate concentration has continued unabated to the present time. A good starting point for understanding the extent of concentrated economic power is a look at the New York Stock Exchange, which lists the common stock of approximately 1,500 companies. These are the companies that dominate the American —and world —economy, and they represent a cross section of its diverse sectors including industrial, financial, utility, transportation, and retail trade firms. In 1971 these companies represented less than 0.1 percent of the approximately 1.7 million American corporations. Yet these few firms controlled 40 percent of total corporate assets and had sales or revenues of about 60 percent of total corporate revenues. What is perhaps most striking is that almost 90 percent of net income of all corporations was received by these 1,500 firms (Blumberg, 1975:16).[1]

As we approach the top of the corporate hierarchy, the picture of concentration becomes even sharper. In 1976, among the 500 largest American corporations, the *typical* firm held $2 billion in assets and had sales of about $1.4 billion. The smallest of these 500 had sales of $618 million (*Forbes*, 1977:156). The industrial sector of the American economy is generally recognized as the most important, and here the 100 largest firms in 1972 had 41 percent of the sales of all industrial corporations, 47 percent of all assets, and over 51 percent of total net income (Blumberg, 1975:30 – 31). The top 5 industrial firms — Exxon, General Motors, Texaco, Ford, and Gulf — alone controlled 10 percent of all industrial assets (Dye, 1976:20).

To the purely financial aspects of corporate power must be added the control of jobs. In 1972, the 100 largest industrial corporations employed 8.5 million persons and the 200 largest, 12.3 million (Blumberg, 1975:31 – 33). The American Telephone and Telegraph Company, the largest single corporation in the United States, alone employed almost 1 million persons in 1976. In that year, the 500 largest private employers together paid the salaries of about 20 percent of the society's entire work force (*Forbes*, 1977:285). What is perhaps more critical than the direct employment of persons by giant corporations is the indirect impact such companies have on jobs in all other sectors of the economy.

The enormity of the power of a few giant corporations is well described by economist Robert Heilbroner (1966:10), who asserts simply that if the 150 top corporations in America disappeared, the society would come to a virtual standstill.

Interlocking Directorates

Looking only at figures showing assets, employees, or profits actually understates the concentration of economic power in the United States. An additional characteristic of the corporate system which magnifies the power of a few firms is the interlocking directorate. An interlock occurs when a director of one corporation sits on the board of one or more other corporations at the same time. Through such close coordination, competition among firms is diminished and policies can be made which serve the mutual advantage of the interlocked companies. Thus a small

---

1. The degree of concentration of corporate wealth is even more remarkable if we consider that there are about 12 million businesses — corporate or noncorporate — in the United States.

number of key corporate officials are enabled to wield great influence over increasingly large elements of the total economic system.

How common is this practice? Several studies have verified the widespread nature of interlocking directorates among firms of various types. Sociologist W. Lloyd Warner and his associates studied 5,776 directors of one or more of the 500 largest corporations and found that they held over 20,000 directorships. The study concluded that "less than 4000 managers of large corporations hold the directorships that interconnect the elite classes of officers and managers of the major corporations that employ most of the workers and do most of the business in American life" (Warner et al., 1967:157). Similar findings were reached by economist Peter Dooley, who reported interlocking among almost all of the 250 largest industrial, merchandising, financial, utility, and transportation firms (1969:320; see also Allen, 1974).

Monopoly Capitalism

Perhaps the key principle of a capitalist economic system is competition among producers in an open and free market. Where competition among producers exists, it is the market which tells them what goods consumers want, how many should be produced, and who will get them in what amounts. Hence the basic economic problems of the society —production, distribution, and consumption—are answered by the market. Without the pressure of authority or the influence of tradition, the social good is assured, curiously, by people pursuing their self-interests. Ideally competition in the market results in the production of those goods society actually needs and wants, in the quantities it desires, and at the prices people are prepared to pay. This is the way Adam Smith and other classical economists of the eighteenth and nineteenth centuries described capitalism, and much of even modern economic thought still retains this theoretical picture.

Such an ideal competitive market system, of course, has never existed, even in Smith's time. But prior to the emergence of the modern corporation, competition among a great number of small businesses and manufacturers was the norm. Monopoly, where only one firm controls the production or distribution of an item, was held to a minimum, and producers and sellers were generally too small and numerous for any one to capture an inordinate share of the market. Also the doctrine of laissez-faire deterred government from significant intervention in the market process, limiting its role basically to enforcing property rights.

The present-day form of capitalism, however, bears little resemblance to the market economy of earlier times. The concentration of power in a few giant corporate enterprises in almost every area of economic activity has created a capitalist system in which basic decisions of production and distribution for the most part are no longer made in the marketplace. With basically monopolistic powers, corporations themselves are able to set prices, determine quantities of goods to be produced and marketed, and generally make those decisions which theoretically, and to a large extent realistically, were previously made by the supply-and-demand dictates of the market. This modern form of capitalism has been called **monopoly capitalism** or **corporate capitalism**.

Oligopoly. Monopoly in the classical sense, in which a single company completely dominates the production and distribution of a commodity, exists in only a few cases. Public utilities such as telephone service and electric power are prime examples. What is more common, however, is the dominance of the production and distribution of certain goods by a *few* giant producers, a condition referred to as **oligopoly**. In a sense, an oligopoly is a monopoly shared by a few. Thus prices are controlled and consumer demand is managed not by a single dominant firm but by a small number of firms which together dominate the market. Perhaps the most obvious example in American society is the automobile industry. Here almost 100 percent of all domestically produced vehicles are manufactured and sold by three companies: General Motors, Ford, and Chrysler. So complete is their control of the industry that it is virtually impossible for other producers to challenge them seriously. Competition among these three firms in terms of price is suspended; one firm declares a price increase and the others reflexively follow. Any competition among them is limited to product differentiation and more effective advertising. Thus automobile companies may rival each other in the design of their cars or in the catchiness of their television commercials, but they do not compete on the basis of price.[2]

The degree of oligopoly in different industries varies, but it is a clear tendency in all. In the pharmaceutical industry, for example, the bulk of the market is shared among 20 to 30 firms. Thus it is not as concentrated as the automobile, steel, or electronic data computer industries, in each of which three or four firms control virtually the entire market. In neither case, however, is there competition in the classic

2. The system of price leadership in one extremely oligopolistic industry, steel, is described by one economist in the following way: "Typically, U. S. Steel sets the pace and the other companies follow in lockstep—both in their sales to private customers and in their secret bids on government contracts. Often, steel producers shipping from different locations will quote delivered prices identical to the thousandths of a cent per pound" (Adams, 1977:107).

sense. Whether it is airplanes, tractors, beer, or cornflakes, the pattern is the same: an increasing concentration of fewer and fewer firms controlling more and more of the market.[3] As economists Walter Adams and Horace Gray have written, "If monopoly is used to denote not merely a single firm but a small group of firms who possess substantial economic power, America's is accurately a monopoly capitalist system" (1955:vii).

The development of conglomerates, corporations which own or control a series of economically diverse companies, has further intensified the concentration of corporate power (see Mintz and Cohen, 1971:34–75). Mergers and takeovers by powerful firms have created a situation in which major corporations act as holding companies for what are basically unrelated industries. ITT is a well-known, but by no means atypical, example. Although ostensibly a firm specializing in communications systems, ITT's subsidiaries include Wonder Bread, Avis Rent-a-Car, Sheraton Hotels, and the Hartford Insurance Group (Sampson, 1973).

The Multinational Corporation

The most powerful American corporations are, almost without exception, multinational companies whose operations span the globe in an octopuslike fashion. The ubiquitous Coca-Cola signs, as glaringly evident in Peruvian villages as in Atlanta or Chicago, or the golden arches of McDonald's in Tokyo or Paris, are symbolic of the world presence of American corporate enterprise. In addition to growth and concentration, internationalization is a chief characteristic of the corporation in the post-World War II era. While these firms remain American-based, increasingly their business operations are conducted on an international scale. The top 300 United States-based corporations earn 40 percent of their entire net profits outside of the United States (Barnet and Müller, 1974:16).

The world character of the giant corporations has made them, in a sense, sovereign units themselves whose economic and political power exceeds that of many governments. Indeed, so vast are the resources of world corporations that in some ways they have become political rivals to the nation-state as we know it. The gross income of many of the largest firms exceeds the gross national product of most countries of the world (Table 6-3). Corporations independently engage in trade negotiations

---

3. The latter two industries are good examples of the steady decline in producers. The largest four cereal makers accounted for 68 percent of the market in 1940, 84 percent in 1950, and 91 percent in 1970 (Kohlmeier, 1976). As for beer, in 1947 the top five companies accounted for only 19 percent of the industry's sales; by 1974 their share was 64 percent (Elzinga, 1977:227).

TABLE 6-3 Gross National Products of Countries and Net Sales of Companies Interspersed, by Rank, 1970

Rank	Country or company	GNP or sales (billions)
1.	United States	$974.0
2.	Soviet Union	485.7
3.	Japan	196.7
4.	West Germany	184.8
5.	France	146.3
6.	People's Republic of China	121.0
7.	United Kingdom	116.3
8.	Italy	91.7
9.	Canada	78.0
10.	India	52.5
11.	Poland	46.0
12.	Brazil	40.4
13.	East Germany	39.6
14.	Mexico	33.2
15.	Australia	32.9
16.	Spain	32.5
17.	Czechoslovakia	32.5
18.	Sweden	31.5
19.	Netherlands	31.3
20.	Belgium	25.0
21.	Romania	24.4
22.	Argentina	23.9
23.	Switzerland	20.6
24.	GENERAL MOTORS	18.8
25.	Yugoslavia	18.5
26.	Pakistan	17.9
27.	South Africa	17.8
28.	AMERICAN TELEPHONE AND TELEGRAPH	17.0
29.	STANDARD OIL (NEW JERSEY)	16.6
30.	Denmark	15.8
31.	FORD MOTOR	15.0
32.	Indonesia	14.0
33.	Austria	13.7
34.	Bulgaria	11.7
35.	Norway	11.2
36.	ROYAL DUTCH/SHELL	10.8
37.	Venezuela	10.3
38.	Finland	10.2
39.	Iran	10.1
40.	Philippines	9.8
41.	SEARS, ROEBUCK	9.3
42.	Greece	9.2
43.	South Korea	8.9
44.	GENERAL ELECTRIC	8.7
45.	Turkey	8.6
46.	Chile	8.4
47.	IBM	7.5
48.	MOBIL OIL	7.3
49.	Colombia	7.0
50.	CHRYSLER	6.9
51.	UNILEVER	6.9
52.	Thailand	6.8

TABLE 6-3 (continued)

Rank	Country or company	GNP or sales (billions)
53.	ITT	6.4
54.	TEXACO	6.3
55.	Egypt	6.3
56.	WESTERN ELECTRIC	5.9
57.	A & P	5.7
58.	Peru	5.6
59.	Israel	5.6
60.	Taiwan	5.5
61.	GULF OIL	5.4
62.	SAFEWAY STORES	4.9
63.	U.S. STEEL	4.8
64.	VOLKSWAGEN	4.3
65.	WESTINGHOUSE ELECTRIC	4.3
66.	STANDARD OIL (California)	4.1
67.	PHILIPS'	4.1
68.	J.C. PENNEY	4.1
69.	BRITISH PETROLEUM	4.1
70.	NIPPON STEEL	4.0
71.	Malaysia	3.9
72.	Ireland	3.8
73.	LING-TEMPCO-VOUGHT	3.8
74.	KROGER	3.7
75.	STANDARD OIL (Indiana)	3.7
76.	BOEING	3.6
77.	DuPONT	3.6
78.	SHELL OIL	3.5
79.	IMPERIAL CHEMICAL	3.5
80.	BRITISH STEEL	3.5
81.	North Korea	3.5
82.	GENERAL TELEPHONE & ELECTRIC	3.4
83.	HITACHI	3.3
84.	Morocco	3.3
85.	RCA	3.3
86.	SIEMENS	3.2
87.	GOODYEAR TIRE & RUBBER	3.2
88.	SWIFT	3.1
89.	FARBWERKE HOECHST	3.0
90.	UNION CARBIDE	3.0
91.	DAIMLER-BENZ	3.0
92.	PROCTER & GAMBLE	3.0
93.	AUGUST THYSSEN-HUTTE	2.9
94.	BETHLEHEM STEEL	2.9
95.	BASF	2.9
96.	MONTECATINI EDISON	2.8
97.	MARCOR	2.8
98.	EASTMAN KODAK	2.8
99.	KRAFTCO	2.7
100.	GREYHOUND	2.7

Source: U.S. Senate, *Role of Giant Corporations*, Hearings Before the Subcommittee on Monopoly of the Select Committee on Small Business, 92d Cong., 1st sess., Part 2, Corporate Secrecy: Overviews (1971), p. 1198.

with governments, bypassing the traditional channels of the state, and even participate in diplomacy, financially supporting or helping to undermine parties and governments in various countries. The efforts of ITT to unseat the government of Salvador Allende in Chile in 1972 is an obvious example. Revelations of financial contributions to political parties in Italy and other countries by United States corporations have indicated the routine nature of such operations for many years.

The Banking Sector

Banks constitute a key element in the modern capitalist economy, for they have the power to control the flow of money and the supply of credit. In many ways they represent the heart of the economic system. Not only do individuals rely on banks for loans and other forms of credit, but corporations are also dependent on them to supply financial capital when they are unable to generate such funds themselves.

The same patterns of corporate power which are evident in the industrial sector, where a few hundred firms manufacture and supply the bulk of the society's material goods, also typify the financial sector. Here too, growth, concentration, and internationalization are the principal features.

A few figures illustrate the extent of concentration among American banks. Of the more than 14,000 commercial banks, about 50 have more assets than all the rest combined (Salamon, 1975:xxii). The top 10 alone hold over 15 percent of assets and 17 percent of deposits (U.S. Bureau of the Census, 1977:526). As in the manufacturing sector, an increasing amount of these banks' business is conducted abroad. In 1977, 8 of the 9 largest American banks relied on foreign sources for more than 40 percent of their total deposits (Aronson and Stein, 1977:50).

Perhaps the most significant aspect of banking power, however, lies in these institutions' influence in other sectors of the corporate economy through their control of stocks and other corporate assets. In their study of New York-based Citibank, the nation's second largest, Leinsdorf and Etra (1973:xxiv–xxv) describe the immense resources of this one bank:

> Only AT&T, Prudential Life and Metropolitan Life have more assets.
> In addition to the $26 billion of assets owned by FNCB [Citibank],
> the bank's trust department manages another $14 billion in assets
> for pension funds, personal trusts, investment advisory accounts,
> and estates and has exclusive investment discretion over almost half
> of these assets.

We will further discuss the ownership by banks of huge corporate assets later in this chapter.

The Dual Economy

Although American ideology continues to extol the virtues of a free enterprise, competitive economic system, it is quite evident that for the most part the system is presently neither free, in the sense that anyone can enter as producer or seller, nor competitive, at least price-wise. However, at the same time that the productive resources of the society are concentrated mainly in a few hundred corporations, there is a relatively competitive sector of the economy which operates alongside the corporate sector. This is the world of small business, in which a large number of producers and sellers still operate in a more traditional market setting. But the status of small businesses is continually perilous, and they do not represent a significant counterelement to the dominant corporations. The latter set the tone of the entire economy, and small or even medium-sized businesses respond to the direction of the supercorporations, just as consumers do. There is, then, a dual economy, with one part overwhelmingly dominant (Galbraith, 1973).

THE CORPORATION AND SOCIETY

The concentration of wealth in the United States and other modern capitalist societies is an inescapable fact. To put it most simply, the productive resources of these societies are controlled by a relatively few giant corporations and their leaders. But what does this agglomeration of economic resources mean for the average citizen? In what ways does the power of the corporation affect the society as a whole? In short, what does this fact tell us of the structure of power?

Control of Investment

Perhaps the most critical decision-making power which corporate leaders possess is the power to decide where, when, and in what amounts corporations will invest their resources. The number and types of jobs available, the location of plants and equipment, and the kinds and numbers of goods and services that will be available are all determined by these decisions. In effect, they define the economic status of the society. The power to make investment decisions is, in Andrew Hacker's words, "the power to decide what kind of a nation America will be" (1964:139).

The crucial nature of corporate investment is reflected in the efforts of state and local governments to lure industries to their communities. Financial incentives such as tax breaks and the use of public lands are used to attract industry and the resultant jobs and revenues. Pennsylvania, for example, put together a package of state incentives worth $80 to $100 million in 1976 to induce Volkswagen to build its American production facility in that state. Propositions of this kind are used so extensively that in a sense the traditional lobbying process is reversed, with government becoming, in effect, a lobbyist itself.

Patterns in the way people and facilities are distributed in the society are also very much affected by corporate investment decisions. The decision to locate a plant in a particular area, for example, will not only create jobs, but will have a lasting impact on the entire sociological face of the area: population, housing patterns, schools, and so on. Indeed the repercussions of corporate investment decisions can spell virtual life or death for cities and regions.

The prerogative of corporations to invest their resources in projects outside their firms is also critical. The development of the Renaissance Center in Detroit, a $500 million building complex, provides an excellent example of the effects of outside corporate investment. This project has become the nucleus of the envisioned redevelopment of the entire downtown area of Detroit, but it did not germinate until Henry Ford II committed substantial corporate funds (and induced other corporate leaders to do the same) to its development. An earlier similar case occurred in Pittsburgh in the 1950s and early 1960s, when the investments of the Mellon family and other corporate magnates contributed to a renewed downtown area. Such examples are evident in cities and towns of various sizes. It would be no exaggeration to say that the demographic shape of the society is dependent more than anything else on corporate investment decisions.

Control of Jobs

Corporate decision makers control jobs — what kind and how many — not simply in their own industries but on a larger scale for the society as a whole. The number of jobs provided by General Motors or AT&T is substantial, but the indirect effects of such firms on the general employment picture are more significant. A decision to lay off several thousand workers at an auto plant, for example, will affect not only the auto workers themselves but also numerous other businesses and industries which supply the plant and its work force. Similarly, the decision of large firms to automate creates a long-range effect not only on workers but on the very nature of work itself. Or the choice of corporations to relocate abroad, where wages are considerably lower and thus profits higher, have incalculable effects on the entire work force. In short, corporations have immense direct and indirect power to create jobs and, if they deem it necessary, to destroy them as well.

The countervailing power of labor unions in this regard becomes essentially a power to bargain for wages and benefits for jobs already assured. The ability to create new jobs or even to protect old ones, however, is in the hands of the corporate elite. Given the resources at its disposal, a large firm may choose simply to move on to a new location rather than compromise with the demands of organized labor. A less entrenched labor movement and lower wage levels explain much of the general movement of American industry in the past decade from the Northeast and Midwest to states of the Southern tier as well as to foreign locations.[4]

The Corporation and Education

The kinds of jobs required by the corporation will, in turn, affect the nature of education in the society, particularly higher education. To a large extent, educational institutions basically respond to the needs of the society's dominant economic institutions. The growth of the industrial economy requires the availability of a highly trained, technically proficient labor force, and universities and colleges, subsidized by public funds, take on this function. As one observer notes, "Far from merely 'serving corporate capitalism' by providing occasional research and consulting services, the universities have become a basic point of production" (O'Connor, 1972:315).

The relationship between the needs of a corporate industrial system and the content and direction of higher education is most evident in the fields of science, engineering, and management, where research and applied technologies are jointly developed by corporation and university. But even in nonscientific areas, the ties are often noticeable. Consider the remark of an official of the Modern Language Association, an organization of college and university teachers of English, on the need for feedback from the business community to fulfill classroom duties adequately: "We would like to go to 10 major corporations and learn just what kind of writing they do, what kind of writing they need, within their organizations. It would be useful for us to know" (*Cincinnati Enquirer*, 1978).

Corporations also influence the nature of higher education by dominating university and college boards of trustees, who set general policies and make long-range decisions regarding the uses of the institutions' personnel and facilities. In the 1970s, the University of California

---

4. The effects on the American labor force of multinational corporations shifting their production facilities abroad to accommodate profit needs is well described by Barnet and Müller (1974, ch. 11).

Board of Regents, for example, consisted of 24 members, 20 of whom were representative of the highest echelons of the corporate world. The remaining four were ex-officio politicians. Among them they held directorships in 60 corporations. Many of these firms were among the nation's as well as California's largest (Smith, 1974:29–31, see also Hartnett, 1969).

Finally, through financial contributions to universities and colleges, corporations can have much to say about the content of academic programs and the nature of research and scholarship.

Control Over Material Goods

What goods will be available for purchase, and at what price are questions answered not by an objective consumer market but by the needs of corporate enterprise. The foods we eat, the clothes we wear, the cars we drive, and the television programs we watch are determined by corporate decision makers.

Corporate capitalism relies not simply on meeting the material needs of the society but, more importantly, on *creating* needs. Marx noted the requirement of a capitalist system to expand continually, to develop new markets, to create demand for goods. Constant growth is required to maximize profits, and meeting only the existing demand for consumer products obviously cannot generate such growth. This is one aspect of Marxian economic theory which seems to have been borne out in modern capitalist systems (see Weisskopf, 1978). Thus corporations must continually stimulate demand by creating markets through planned obsolescence, expansion into foreign countries, and, perhaps most importantly, advertising and other sales strategies. As economist John Kenneth Galbraith states, "The purpose of demand management is to insure that people buy what is produced—that plans as to the amounts to be sold at the controlled prices are fulfilled in practice" (1967:203). In managing consumer demand, advertising becomes a key mechanism. Businesses annually spend billions of dollars in various media advertising—that is, creating needs and thereby creating demand for their products. Soap and detergent firms, for example, spend 20 percent of all sales revenues on advertising, and drug firms spend four times more on advertising than on research (Green, 1972:13). Procter and Gamble, the nation's leading advertiser, alone spends almost half a billion dollars annually on various forms of advertising (Zim, 1978:54).[5]

5. On the historical development of advertising as a demand control mechanism, see Ewen (1976).

Control Over Technological Change

When and at what rate technological changes are introduced in the society are determined by the corporation more than any other institution, for only it possesses the economic resources to maintain substantial research and development programs. Here too there is extreme concentration among the largest few. A 1967 Senate hearing revealed that 384 corporations, each employing 5,000 or more workers, accounted for 85 percent of all industrial research and development expenditures. The largest four corporations alone accounted for about 22 percent (U.S. Senate, 1967:5).

Also *which* technologies will be developed are determinations made basically within the giant corporation (see Schmookler, 1959). Here as in other aspects of corporate enterprise, choices are made primarily on the basis of profit needs rather than societal needs. The search for more efficient and accessible forms of energy serves as an illustration. Whether the United States will rely in the future on oil, nuclear power, solar power, or other forms of energy is still undetermined. In any case, however, so long as the development and production of energy remain dependent primarily on the private corporation, decisions on this issue will be made more on the basis of corporate (that is, profit) consequences than on long-range societal consequences such as environmental preservation or safety.

Although both government and university are also active in developing new technologies, their research is generally tied either directly or indirectly to the corporation. In fact, most of these efforts are jointly undertaken by government, university, and corporation. The research budgets of the federal government since the end of World War II have been dominated by the development of weapons systems, and such research has been done in close collaboration with those industries which ultimately produce these weapons.

Influence On the Mass Media

In chapter 2 we noted control over the flow of information as a power resource. In modern industrial societies, the mass media —newspapers, magazines, radio, and particularly television —are the carriers of information to the populace. As such they are in an extremely critical power position.

The corporation's influence over the media derives mainly from three sources. First, the mass media in the United States are private businesses and are dependent on advertising dollars for revenues. In this the United States is somewhat unique among advanced industrial societies. In all others, while newspapers generally remain private enterprises, television and radio are either state owned and operated or there is a mixed state/private system such as Canada's or Great Britain's. Thus although direct censorship over television programing or newspaper content in the United States is unusual, the media must pay heed to the wishes of top advertisers, mainly the large corporations.

Second, given the capitalist structure of the media, corporations monopolize their use. Access to the airwaves or the newsprint is dependent on ability to pay, and the cost of purchasing air time or newspaper space is prohibitive for most other groups. As a result there are only limited interpretations of events and issues —those selected by the media in conjunction with their clients, the large corporations. The consequences of this situation are spelled out by one media expert in the following way:

> With the exception of the news departments, the mass media provide no systematically operative outlets for the display of events and opinions about them. If you can't gain acceptance as a news item or feature, and if you can't pay for access, the chances that mass publics will learn of your predicament or views are extremely small (Rubin, 1977:4).

Third, the national media are large corporations themselves or are owned by corporate conglomerates. CBS, for example, comprises a huge media complex including book publishing firms, magazines, and several large local radio and television stations; NBC is part of the RCA Corporation, one of the world's largest. The concentration of power in the three major television networks is obvious enough, but what is not so obvious is the similar increasing concentration of power in the other media. Fewer and fewer cities have more than one daily newspaper, for example, and the ten largest newspaper chains account for over half of all newspaper revenues (Monaco, 1978:13). Moreover most newspapers rely on two or three news agencies, such as AP or UPI, to gather and prepare national stories.

In short, the tendencies of other industries —monopolization, concentration, and even internationalization (see Read, 1976; Schiller, 1969) —have been displayed by the media as well. The social and political impact of these tendencies is also similar. Thus, as the media are presently organized, enormous and increasing power to select and disseminate ideas and information for the society as a whole falls to a smaller and smaller media elite, those few who own, produce, and edit the society's newspapers, television and radio programs, magazines, motion pictures, and books. We shall have more to say about the role of the media in sustaining the society's prevailing ideology in chapter 12.

Corporate Power in Summary

To summarize the power of the corporation in the United States and other modern capitalist societies, it may be said that although its capacities are not unlimited, the giant corporation has greater influence on social and economic outcomes than any other societal institution, including in many ways the state. In the words of Berle and Means, "the modern corporation may be regarded not simply as one form of social organization but potentially (if not yet actually) as the dominant institution of the modern world" (1968:355).

CORPORATE OWNERSHIP AND CONTROL

Given the massive power of the corporation in modern capitalist societies, we must further ask who owns the resources of these organizations and who controls their allocation.

Ownership of Corporate Stock

Ownership shares in the corporation are in the form of stocks, and these tend to be highly concentrated among a small percentage of the society's individuals and key financial institutions. The wealthiest 20 percent of American families own almost 100 percent of all individually held corporate stock. The top 5 percent alone own 86 percent, and the top 1 percent own 62 percent (Turner and Starnes, 1976:118). Studies of stock ownership in the United States have revealed that the pattern of extremely great concentration of corporate wealth has not changed appreciably since 1929 (Kolko, 1962; Lundberg, 1968). These findings refute the notion of "people's capitalism," a belief that stock holding is no longer limited to only a few very wealthy families but is widespread throughout the populace (Anderson, 1974:113–115). Many corporations publicly boast of the great number of their shareholders, but none point out that the vast majority of their stock is held by a relative handful out of the tens and even hundreds of thousands of stockholders. Of all shareholders in General Motors, for example, 78 percent own 100 shares or less (Blumberg, 1975:87).

Perhaps the most significant aspect of the control of stock of the giant corporations is the influence of banks and other financial institutions. The extent of bank control of corporate stock in the entire range of the American economy is documented by a Senate report of 1974. Although the Senate committee which undertook the study was given only partial information by those corporations which responded to its request to identify their 30 top stockholders, enough information was gathered to reveal a clear pattern: a concentration of stock held among a handful of banks, primarily in trust accounts, in corporations representing almost every area of economic activity —utilities, manufacturing, transportation, communications, and retail trade. Of the 89 corporations which cooperated by submitting data, Chase Manhattan Bank (New York) held 2 percent or more of the stock in more than half (46) of the companies; Morgan Guaranty and First National City Bank, also of New York, held 2 percent or more of the stock in almost one-third (29 and 28) of the companies; and Bankers Trust of New York held 2 percent or more of the stock in almost one-fourth (21) of the companies (U.S. Senate, 1974:6). Control of as little as 1 or 2 percent of stock in a corporation is sufficient to exert great influence over company policy. Chase Manhattan alone was the largest stockholder in 20 giant corporations, including such familiar names as General Electric, RCA, Atlantic Richfield, Union Carbide, United Airlines, and Safeway Stores. Moreover, these figures represent a considerably understated picture of bank influence since only a fraction of the top corporations in America reported their ownership data to the Senate committee.

Banks have also strengthened their influence in nonfinancial corporations through interlocking directorates. Through membership on the boards of nonfinancial corporations, bankers can directly influence corporate policy, a power which is undergirded by their banks' large stock holdings. In 1970, First National City Bank of New York (Citibank), the second largest in the United States, was interlocked with 40 of the 300 largest industrial corporations (including 7 of the top 10), 6 of the 15 largest life insurance companies, 2 of the 4 largest retailers, and the 2 largest utilities (Leinsdorf and Etra, 1973:xxvii).

In sum, corporate wealth may no longer be solely the possession of the families comprising the super-rich,[6] but it is concentrated nonetheless. Today concentration is increasingly within institutions —that is,

6. Several studies have pointed out that the decline of family control and ownership of large corporate enterprises has not been as rapid or as substantial as has been commonly believed. It was reported in 1967, for example, that in approximately 150 American companies on the *Fortune* 500 list, controlling ownership rested in the hands of an individual or the members of a single family (Sheehan, 1970; see also Lundberg, 1968; Zeitlin, 1974).

banks, insurance companies, and pension funds. Economic power, then, is a function not of personal wealth but of institutionally controlled and managed wealth. If not owned, the society's wealth is *controlled* by a handful of men who occupy the top positions of the corporate world. These are the persons in decision-making positions who allocate the resources of the important economic organizations, and it is to those positions that we must look to understand how corporate power is applied.

The Corporate Elite

It is generally understood that ownership and management of the giant corporation are now largely separate functions, though the extent of that separation is still debated. This means that the real power to make corporate decisions is left to the managers, with stockholders maintaining little more than ceremonial powers. Civics book descriptions of the corporation portray the stockholders as effectively powerful since officers and directors are ultimately answerable to them. But this is a well-recognized fiction (Berle, 1959:69–76). Stockholders as a group rarely, if ever, challenge the power of corporate officers. The organizational impediments alone preclude such action. When stockholders are dissatisfied with corporate performance, they generally sell their stock and buy that of another corporation.[7] One observer of corporate government describes the power of management as "largely unencumbered by any workable mechanism of accountability to stockholders" (Nadel, 1976: 205). The almost absolute power of management is a generally recognized fact of the modern corporation.

Moreover, the power of corporate managers is aided by their ability to choose their successors. Top managers and directors are selected by corporate leaders themselves. The result is virtually unchallenged and absolute power to set the corporation's policies and to make its vital decisions. Whether the functional officers who run the daily affairs of the firm or the board of directors who set long-range policy are the real powers in the governing of the corporation is a disputed point. But the distinction may be of minor importance so far as delineating powerful positions is concerned. In either case there is a tiny number of individuals whose power, whatever its limits, is great; these people constitute the corporate elite.

In absolute numbers the corporate elite represents no more than a few thousand. Berle notes that within the 500 corporations that own

---

7. Hacker (1964:6) notes that one-third of all stock purchases are held for less than six months.

two-thirds of the society's industrial assets, the actual decision-making power is confined to a tiny group which he calls "the highest concentration of economic power in recorded history" (Berle, 1964:101–102).

Corporate Elite or Ruling Class?

Beginning with Berle and Means in 1932, it has been argued that the separation of corporate ownership from management has eliminated the power of the capitalist class in modern industrial societies. With increasing size, complexity, and bureaucratization, responsibility for running the corporate system falls upon a highly trained and specialized managerial class, which is concerned primarily with the technical problems of business and industry and not solely with the rapacious pursuit of profit, as was the traditional concern of the capitalist class. Managers rather than owners of corporations are now the effective holders of power since without their expertise corporations cannot function. It is claimed, therefore, that a ruling class in the sense of a cohesive and conscious unit whose power base is its economic wealth no longer exists; the important decisions of the society's dominant economic institutions—the corporations—are made by functionaries who do not own them. The power of ownership is thus minimized.

There are several reasons, however, why the distinction between owners and managers of the society's dominant economic institutions may be overstated. First, the two groups, owners and managers, share a common goal: maximizing corporate profits. So long as this remains the chief objective of the corporation, it is necessarily the same for its managers (Baran and Sweezy, 1966:39–40). In seeking personal success, corporate managers must conform to the imperatives of the corporate system. That is, personal success for the managers is attained by enhancing the place of their firms in the business world, and this means the constant need to generate profits. Thus, to argue that since the managers are not owners of the corporations they are not motivated by profit incentives is illogical.

Second, top-ranking corporate managers are not simply higher employees in the rank order of industrial workers, as some have contended (Galbraith, 1967). There are substantial qualitative differences between those at the top of the managerial hierarchy and lower-ranking managers (let alone nonmanagerial workers) in terms of the scope of decisions made, in the consciousness of their power, and in the nature of their rewards (Birnbaum, 1969).

Third, and perhaps most important, the picture of corporate managers as nonowners has been exaggerated. Kolko has shown that "the

managerial class is the largest single group in the stockholding population, and a greater proportion of this class owns stock than any other"
(1962:67). Of the 100 top paid corporate chief executive officers in 1971,
only 29 held less than $1 million of shares in their firms, and most were
well over this figure (*Forbes*, 1972:205–208). Barnet and Müller (1974:
292) calculated that the average market value of the stock holdings
of the chief executive in his own firm (based on a sample of 50 large
industrial companies) in 1972 was over $5 million; this had increased
from $1.6 million in 1960 (see also Blumberg, 1975). To speak of corpo-
rate managers as a group distinct from the ownership class is therefore
essentially erroneous.[8]

In addition to their ownership of stock, top corporate executives are
among the most highly paid individuals in the society. Of the 795 largest
corporations in the American economy in 1977, the average pay of the
chief executive officer was $300,000. The top four wage earners among
them each received over $1 million (Saunders, 1978:86–87).

Empirical evidence thus verifies that the very top managers of large
corporate enterprises are among the largest owners of corporate stock as
well as the largest income receivers. They are without question a significant element of the tiny economic upper class of America and other
contemporary capitalist societies.

But their ownership of great wealth merely complements the power
which derives from their authoritative positions. Even if they were not
among the important owners of corporate wealth, the fact remains that
they *control* the allocation of the society's industrial and financial resources, and that is the chief source of their power. As Mills has aptly
written, "If the powerful officials of U.S. corporations do not act as old-
fashioned owners within the plants and do not derive their power from
personal ownership, their power is nevertheless contingent upon their
control of property" (Mills, 1951:102).

In any case, ownership and control of corporate wealth are tightly
intertwined. The interests of the very wealthy are protected and pursued
by top corporate managers, who are themselves commonly among them.

Private Privileges and Public Powers

One of the paradoxes of the American political economy is the enormous public powers exercised by corporations at the same time that they

8. The top executives of most large corporations are not only paid a fixed salary but are
   awarded bonuses depending on the company's financial performance. Most of these
   bonuses are in the form of stock options, which are additional incentives for managers
   to maximize the profits of their firms (see Stern, 1974:78–79).

operate basically as private enterprises. Given the internal structure of the modern corporation, the accountability of corporate managers to stockholders is to all intents and purposes nil. Of greater concern to the society as a whole, however, is the inability to hold corporate leaders responsible for decisions and actions which have clearly public consequences. Decisions made by the corporate elite regarding the allocation of their companies' resources are far-reaching, with resultant effects on jobs, prices, the environment, and the general economic well-being of the society. But these are for the most part *private* decisions, not subject to public control. Despite governmental presence in many areas of economic decision making, the private corporation remains the chief molder of the society's economic condition, and its leaders are only minimally accountable to the public.

It is now commonplace to decry the capacity of government in modern industrial societies to enter into and shape almost every aspect of social life. The power of the state is seemingly limitless, including everything from granting a permit to build an additional bathroom in one's home to mobilizing the entire society for war. In its actions, the state taxes, the state may use violence and even kill, and the state alters the physical environment. *But all of these powers are presently within the capabilities of the giant corporations.* In effect they can exert the same kinds of power over citizens that governments can, including the ultimate power over life itself. Dahl (1973:11) has described the large corporation of today as a "political system," which, by its leaders' decisions and actions, exercises great power over people's lives much like any state political system: "It would take enormous semantic refinement and an excessive addiction to purely legalistic conceptions to establish that the city of New Haven, for example, is a political system while General Motors is not." In a sense, the 100 or so largest industrial and financial corporations in American society are "private states" whose power often exceeds that of government itself.

Despite the enormity of their public consequences and their pervasive impact on American society and the rest of the world, the actions of the corporate elite are mostly covert and not subject to public scrutiny, much less control. Decisions are made behind the closed doors of executive offices, and disclosures of the bases of those decisions are rarely made. It may be that what occurs in the executive offices of Exxon or General Motors is of greater consequence for the society than what occurs on the floor of the House or Senate. But what takes place in the latter are generally matters of public disclosure (or can become so with enough deliberate searching), while the former are almost entirely outside the realm of public information. That the corporate elite can operate outside the public view is itself a significant power resource.

One of the clearest illustrations of the difficulty in holding corporations publicly accountable is the lack of knowledge of who their dominant stockholders are and what the extent of their holdings are —in short, who actually owns the corporations. This information cannot be easily ascertained since corporations, as private entities, may simply choose not to reveal it. The previously cited Senate inquiry into corporate ownership, for example, requested 324 of the largest corporations to identify their 30 top stockholders and the amount of stock held; only 89 companies responded fully to the query. Thus, as to the relationships between banks and nonfinancial corporations, the ownership of such institutions, and the interlocking of personnel between them, the study concluded that "The Federal Government does not have sufficient information in these areas upon which to base reasoned public policy" (U.S. Senate, 1974:10). In an earlier Senate hearing, consumer advocate Ralph Nader testified that it is impossible to determine who actually owns the great wealth of America, not only because corporations may operate in virtual secrecy but also because of the inability of public agencies, ostensibly designed to control economic institutions, to extract such information (U.S. Senate, 1973:1056).

Big businessmen and even some social scientists argue that the new corporate elite, in contrast to the capitalist class of old, recognizes its public responsibilities. Excesses in corporate power are thus avoided by a self-imposed sense of social obligation on the part of corporate leaders. But to speak, as some have, of the "soulful" corporation or of a consciousness of social obligation is to assume that corporate violations of the public trust are unusual. However, revelations of corporate transgressions are so common that it is difficult to know whether these actions are exceptional or normative practices. Corporate officers in recent years have been implicated in price-fixing schemes, stock swindles, and knowingly producing and distributing faulty and unsafe products, as well as the more highly publicized political payoffs and illegal campaign contributions (see for example Ermann and Lundman, 1976; Heilbroner, 1972). Moreover, the view of the modern corporation as a self-policing institution with a social conscience rests on the assumption that corporate managers are only secondarily interested in maintaining high profits for their firms. This we have seen to be a highly dubious premise.

It is also paradoxical that, given the great power of economic decision makers, such individuals remain relatively anonymous personalities. In contrast to political decision makers, who at all levels of government are given much notoriety by the media and whose activities are under constant public view, the very identities of top corporate officials are unknown to most Americans. If one were to ask people at random to identify a few high-ranking politicians, almost all would be able to do so. But few would be able to name the chief executives of even the two or three largest corporations, despite the power of these men fundamentally to affect their lives. This anonymity further contributes to the unaccountability of the corporate elite.

Recognizing the vast and largely unrestrained power of the corporate elite should not lead to the conclusion that its power is unlimited. Corporate managers cannot simply set *any* price for their products, nor can they influence consumer demand beyond a certain point. And as we shall see, they cannot always rely on government to favor corporate interests. But the limitations on corporate power are very broad, allowing for a wide range of discretion within which to operate. Indeed, it is the enormous range of its power which distinguishes the corporate elite from others. As we will see in the following chapter, it can more easily extend its power into government, but it can also penetrate other institutions of the society more readily than other elite groups such as labor leaders, educators, or religious leaders. Porter (1965:216) notes that in Canada, like the United States and other Western societies, "Bishops or university presidents in the board rooms of large corporations are exceedingly rare; but corporation directors on the boards of universities or publishing chains, or as members of synods or councils of churches are quite frequent."

SUMMARY

Our analysis of power in the United States and other advanced capitalist societies is based on the assumptions that (1) political power is a synthesis of the actions of state and dominant economic institutions; (2) ruling elites make the important decisions in these two spheres, with little control by the masses; and (3) inequalities in political power reflect inequalities in wealth.

The corporation is the dominant economic institution in advanced capitalist societies. In the United States a handful of giant corporate enterprises, operating with basically monopolistic powers, determines the social and economic status of the society. Investment, jobs, education, material goods, technological change, and the mass media are all essentially shaped by corporate actions.

Ownership and control of corporate wealth are highly concentrated. A tiny percentage of the population owns most corporate stock, which is further concentrated in large banks and other financial institutions. The corporate elite comprises those top-ranking managers who control the allocation of (and often own great amounts of) corporate wealth and make key corporate decisions.

The corporation in America exercises enormous public powers while operating as a private institution. Decisions made by the corporate elite have sweeping societal impact, often even exceeding decisions of top government officials. But this group remains largely inaccessible and unaccountable to the general public.

REFERENCES

Adams, Walter. 1977. *The Structure of American Industry*. 5th ed. New York: Macmillan.

───────────, and **Horace Gray.** 1955. *Monopoly In America*. New York: Macmillan.

Allen, Michael Patrick. 1974. "The Structure of Interorganizational Elite Cooptation: Interlocking Corporate Directorates." *American Sociological Review* 39 (June):393–406.

Anderson, Charles. 1974. *The Political Economy of Social Class*. Englewood Cliffs: Prentice-Hall.

Aronson, Jonathan, and **Elliot Stein, Jr.** 1977. "Bankers Milk the Third World." *Progressive* 41 (October):48–51.

Baran, Paul, and **Paul Sweezy.** 1966. *Monopoly Capital*. New York: Monthly Review.

Barnet, Richard, and **Ronald E. Müller.** 1974. *Global Reach*. New York: Simon and Schuster.

Berle, Adolph A. 1959. *Power Without Property*. New York: Harcourt Brace and World.

───────────. 1964. "Economic Power and the Free Society." In Andrew Hacker (ed.), *The Corporation Take-Over*. New York: Harper and Row.

───────────, and **Gardiner C. Means.** 1968. *The Modern Corporation and Private Property*. Revised ed. New York: Harcourt Brace and World.

Birnbaum, Norman. 1969. *The Crisis of Industrial Society*. New York: Oxford U. Press.

Blumberg, Phillip I. 1975. *The Megacorporation in American Society*. Englewood Cliffs: Prentice-Hall.

Cincinnati Enquirer. 1978. "Want Your Child to Have 'Bumper-Sticker Mentality?'" (January 16):B-3.

Dahl, Robert. 1973. "Governing the Giant Corporation." In Ralph Nader and Mark J. Green (eds.), *Corporate Power in America*. New York: Grossman.

Dolbeare, Kenneth. 1974. *Political Change in the United States*. New York: McGraw-Hill.

Dooley, Peter. 1969. "The Interlocking Directorate." *American Economic Review* 59 (June):314–323.

Dye, Thomas R. 1976. *Who's Running America?* Englewood Cliffs: Prentice-Hall.

───────────, and **L. Harmon Zeigler.** 1978. *The Irony of Democracy*. 4th ed. North Scituate, Mass.: Duxbury.

Elzinga, Kenneth. 1977. "The Beer Industry." In Walter Adams (ed.), *The Struc-*

ture of American Industry. 5th ed. New York: Macmillan.

Ermann, M. David, and **Richard J. Lundman** (eds.). 1976. *Corporate and Governmental Deviance*. New York: Oxford U. Press.

Ewen, Stuart. 1976. *Captains of Consciousness*. New York: McGraw-Hill.

Forbes. 1972. "Who Gets the Most Pay?" 109 (May 15):205–236.

——————. 1977. "The Forbes 500s." 119 (May 15):156-290.

Form, William H., and **Delbert C. Miller.** 1960. *Industry, Labor, and Community*. New York: Harper and Row.

Galbraith, John Kenneth. 1967. *The New Industrial State*. Boston: Houghton-Mifflin.

——————. 1973. *Economics and the Public Purpose*. Boston: Houghton-Mifflin.

Green, Mark J. 1972. *The Closed Enterprise System*. New York: Grossman.

Hacker, Andrew H. 1964. "Power to Do What?" In Irving Louis Horowitz (ed.), *The New Sociology*. New York: Oxford U. Press.

Hartnett, Rodney T. 1969. *College and University Trustees: Their Backgrounds, Roles, and Educational Attitudes*. Princeton: Educational Testing Service.

Heilbroner, Robert. 1966. *The Limits of American Capitalism*. New York: Harper and Row.

——————— (ed.). 1972. *In the Name of Profit*. New York: Doubleday.

Hunter, Floyd. 1953. *Community Power Structure*. Chapel Hill: U. of North Carolina Press.

Kohlmeier, Louis M. 1976. "Snap, Crackle and Divestiture." *New York Times* 125 (April 25):III–1.

Kolko, Gabriel. 1962. *Wealth and Power in America*. New York: Praeger.

Leinsdorf, David, and **Donald Etra.** 1973. *Citibank*. New York: Grossman.

Lenski, Gerhard. 1966. *Power and Privilege*. New York: Macmillan.

Lundberg, Ferdinand. 1968. *The Rich and the Super-Rich*. New York: Lyle Stuart.

Means, Gardiner C. 1964. "Economic Concentration." In U.S. Congress, Senate, Committee on the Judiciary, *Hearings Before the Sub-Committee on Anti-trust and Monopoly*, 88th Cong., 2d sess. (July).

Mills, C. Wright. 1951. *White Collar*. New York: Oxford U. Press.

——————. 1956. *The Power Elite*. New York: Oxford U. Press.

Mintz, Morton, and **Jerry S. Cohen.** 1971. *America, Inc.* New York: Dell.

Monaco, James. 1978. *Media Culture*. New York: Delta.

Nadel, Mark V. 1976. *Corporations and Political Accountability*. Lexington, Mass.: Heath.

O'Connor, James. 1972. "The University and the Political Economy." In Milton Mankoff (ed.), *The Poverty of Progress*. New York: Holt, Rinehart and Winston.

Parker, Richard. 1972. *The Myth of the Middle Class*. New York: Harper and Row.

Porter, John. 1965. *The Vertical Mosaic*. Toronto: University of Toronto Press.

Read, William H. 1976. *America's Mass Media Merchants*. Baltimore: Johns Hopkins U. Press.

Rubin, Bernard. 1977. *Big Business and the Mass Media*. Lexington, Mass.: Heath.

Salamon, Lester. 1975. *The Money Committees*. New York: Grossman.

Sampson, Anthony. 1973. *The Sovereign State of ITT*. New York: Stein and Day.

Saunders, Dero A. 1978. "The Boss' Paycheck: Who Gets The Biggest?" *Forbes* 121 (May 29):86-87.

Schiller, Herbert I. 1969. *Mass Communications and American Empire*. New York: Augustus M. Kelley.

Schmookler, Jacob. 1959. "Technological Progress and the Modern American Corporation." In Edward T. Mason (ed.), *The Corporation in Modern Society*. Cambridge: Harvard U. Press.

Sheehan, Robert. 1970. "Proprietors in the World of Big Business." In Maurice Zeitlin (ed.), *American Society, Inc*. Chicago: Markham.

Smith, David N. 1974. *Who Rules the Universities?*. New York: Monthly Review.

Stern, Philip M. 1974. *The Rape of the Taxpayer*. New York: Vintage.

Turner, Jonathan H., and **Charles E. Starnes.** 1976. *Inequality: Privilege and Poverty in America*. Pacific Palisades: Goodyear.

U.S. Bureau of the Census. 1977. *Statistical Abstract of the United States: 1977*. Washington, D.C.: Government Printing Office.

U.S. Senate. 1967. *Hearings Before the Subcommittee on Monopoly of the Select Committee on Small Business*. 90th Cong., 1st sess.

——————————. 1973. *Hearing before the Subcommittee on Monopoly of the Select Committee on Small Business, Role of Giant Corporations, Corporate Secrecy: Overviews*. Part 2. 92d Cong., 1st sess. (November 1971).

——————————. 1974. *Disclosure of Corporate Ownership*. Subcommittee on Intergovernmental Relations, Budgeting, Management, and Expenditures of the Committee on Government Operations. 93d Cong., 2d sess.

Warner, W. Lloyd, et al. 1967. *The Emergent American Society*. Vol. 1. *Large-Scale Organization*. New Haven: Yale U. Press.

Weisskopf, Thomas E. 1978. "The Irrationality of Capitalist Economic Growth." In Richard C. Edwards, Michael Reich, and Thomas E. Weisskopf (eds.), *The Capitalist System*. 2nd ed. Englewood Cliffs: Prentice-Hall.

Zeitlin, Maurice. 1974. "Corporate Ownership and Control: The Large Corporation and the Capitalist Class." *American Journal of Sociology* 79 (March):1073-1119.

Zim, Marvin H. 1978. "The Inflation Isn't Over in TV Advertising Rates." *Fortune* 98 (November 6):52-55.

chapter 7

the corporate state

*Nowhere else does the captain of big business
rule the affairs of the nation, civil and political,
and control the conditions of life so unreservedly
as in democratic America.*

Thornstein Veblen

In this chapter we want to look at the place of the state in the power structure of American society — what are its functions and whose interests does it primarily serve? Underlying our analysis is the assumption that in advanced capitalist societies such as the United States, the first priority of government is to keep the economic system running smoothly and efficiently. All else takes second place to this basic need. Whatever else government may do is colored by its obligation to keep the economy on course. As political scientist Kenneth Dolbeare explains:

> Government is the revenue-raising agent, the rationalizer, and the stabilizer of society. But its priorities, its personnel, and its policies are either those of the economic system, or ones consistent with the imperatives of that system (1974:26).

It is for this reason that the bulk of public policy decisions concern economic issues.

This does not mean that the basis of state action is at all times founded on economic considerations. Obviously this is not so. But the basic rules, the framework or structure within which the political system operates, is essentially determined by the needs of the society's economic system. One need not adopt a Marxian view to recognize the prevailing influence of economic matters in what may seem to be strictly "political" affairs. Economic institutions may not necessarily shape all other social relations, but their primary place in shaping public policies and in bolstering established values is hard to question. Thus, economic leaders do not simply represent one more interest group; like top government officials, they play key decision-making roles, and their decisions are societal in consequence. In the structure of power these two groups interlock naturally.

Although the state is never a perfect representative of the interests of the society's dominant economic groups, it operates, as we shall see, in such a manner as to favor those interests when they are in conflict with those of other societal groups. In American society, then, economic power is generally transformed into political power.

THE AMERICAN POLITICAL ECONOMY

When describing power in the United States or any other society, we must keep in mind that power structures are not static; change is perhaps slow and often imperceptible, but certain nonetheless. Thus, what the American power structure looks like today is not necessarily what it looked like 50 or 100 years ago and is not necessarily what it will appear to be in the future. Despite these changes, certain institutional structures and relationships are relatively constant, repeating themselves for many generations. It is these repetitive characteristics that give the power structure coherence and definition.

Business and Politics

One of the most enduring features of the system of power in America is the focal place of business in the political process. No other institution has so thoroughly woven itself into the fabric of government as has business. As one observer of this relationship has written, "business goals have been indigenous to our national development, as have the efforts of those with economic interests to implement such goals through political means" (Epstein, 1969:21). Whatever historical changes have taken place in the power structure have been adaptive to a fundamentally capitalist system, in which the preeminence of business interests and values has never been seriously challenged. The relationship of government and business has fluctuated from era to era; at certain times business power has been predominant, while at others government has successfully countered that power. But at no time have other social institutions played such a coordinate power role.

The Corporation and Government

During the past five decades, the expanded role of government in American society has paralleled the growth of the corporation as the major form of business enterprise. Indeed, the growth of one institution has aided the growth of the other, to the extent that the two now maintain a symbiotic relationship. In a sense, government and corporation are mutually supportive and would find it impossible, in their current form, to operate independently.

As one of the two key institutions in the society, the corporation's power derives from its control of the society's wealth, the provision of jobs, and the production and distribution of material goods. But in exercising these powers, very close ties to the state are necessary. The corporation becomes dependent on government to help maintain social stability, to protect property, to provide tax benefits, subsidies and other financial aids, to finance much of its investment, and to consume much of what it produces. In short, those who own and control the society's private wealth need government to support and coordinate the corporate system and to protect traditional privileges and benefits which accrue from that control.

Conversely, government needs the corporation to assure social and political stability since it is within corporate institutions that basic decisions are made regarding economic growth, employment, and industrial output. That is, private leaders rather than public officials determine the society's basic economic patterns. Most simply, the overriding goal of both corporation and government is the economic well-being of the society, and it is through that mutual goal that the two have been bound together. In addition, since the end of World War II, the maintenance of a huge military establishment has served increasingly to merge the activities of business and government. As Barnet and Müller have written, "To a significant degree, Big Business and Big Government represent identical interests" (1974:252).

The Development of the American Political Economy

Although business interests have been actively involved in the political process since the founding of the society, the business-government relationship has been an adversary one throughout much of American history. Businessmen traditionally viewed government with suspicion and resisted any attempts to infringe on their milieu. Government's role was seen as a policeman whose purpose was to protect property rights and assure that the private power of business did not overly violate the public interest. But it was not to intervene directly in the economic process.

The period of industrial growth. Although this laissez-faire conception of business-government relations was never more than a figment of capitalist ideology, it was most strongly realized during the period of industrial growth following the Civil War. The industrial expansion that marked the Age of Enterprise was characterized by the unrelenting efforts —generally successful—of big business to assure the enactment of favorable government policies and to maximize its exploitation of government-controlled resources such as land, mining, and timber. At the same time, big business strongly resisted attempts at government control or regulation, again successfully in most cases. Business involvement in government in the 1880s often featured the active role of corporate leaders themselves in politics. The U.S. Senate in 1889 was known as the "Millionaires' Club" since it included numerous industrial magnates of the day (Epstein, 1969:26).

The Progressive Period. The emergence of the reform movement during the early part of the twentieth century, known as the Progressive Period, was based in large part on the belief that the corporation's octopuslike power had to be checked. Many now feared that as the dominant economic institution, it would eventually dominate the state as well. Government regulatory agencies were formed and antitrust legislation was enacted with the avowed purpose of arresting the corporation's power and political influence. Neither proved effective. In fact, corporate interests were consistently served in the years to follow.

The Great Depression. The period of the 1930s, however, marked a major change in the relationship of government and business. The most serious economic depression in American history gave rise to the active role of government as a maker as well as an influencer of economic policy. Government controls were now more direct in nature, and the fiction of laissez-faire was finally put to rest. Influenced most strongly by the economic theories of John Maynard Keynes, the federal government under the Roosevelt administration instituted a sweeping series of measures, the basic purpose of which was to stabilize the business cycle.

Earlier economists had argued that each economic recession or depression would reverse itself naturally, and this had generally been the case until the 1930s. The depression of that era, however, simply did not turn about, and the economy continued to stagnate. Keynes argued that during periods when private industry was unable to generate consumer demand, there was no necessary upswing and the level of production and employment might continue to remain low indefinitely, as had occurred in the 1930s. Keynes' solution was for the government to step in and stimulate demand through its own spending programs and through tax cuts. In the same manner, if consumer demand was excessive and inflation was threatening economic stability, government could reverse its policies by cutting its expenditures and raising taxes, thereby stabilizing the system. With these policies, government now assumed substantial responsibility for monitoring the economic system. Government investment was now deliberate, and public projects such as roads, hospitals, housing, dams, and airports were undertaken.

During the early years of the century, it had been feared that the corporation might come to dominate the state. Now, however, that fear was reversed, so that state power over business became the prevalent concern, particularly within the business sector. This, of course, did not take place, and business found its relationship with the state following the Depression to be even more vital and advantageous than previously. The militarized economy, developed during World War II and continued after the war, was an important addition to the mutual dependence of state and corporation.

The post-World War II era. The most forceful convergence of state and corporation took place in the post-World War II era. The rise of big government and its intervention in the economic process was now viewed by big business not as a countervailing threat (though some businessmen even today continue to voice the rhetoric of the "evils" of government interference)[1] but as a guarantor of a stable economy as well as a vital customer for its products and services. Likewise, government now came to accept the inevitability, and indeed the necessity, of the large corporate enterprise as the dominant form of business in the society. To sustain a healthy political atmosphere required a healthy economic atmosphere, and this in turn required the sustained well-being of the corporation. As Richard Barber (1970:189) states, "Today most executives of major corporations and most government officials have come to view themselves as allies who can accomplish much more by working together in common cause than by prolonging their age-old cold war."

THE CONVERSION OF ECONOMIC POWER INTO POLITICAL POWER

The dominant economic interests in the United States and other capitalist societies can, as Miliband points out, "normally count on the active good-will and support of those in whose hands state power lies" (1969:145). Historical evidence has indicated that the various elements of government, including the bureaucracy, the military, the judiciary, and the executive, can be expected to follow policies and decisions which are generally in line with the interests of dominant economic groups. But this does not eliminate the need for these economic groups to exert pressure on government, for as Miliband further notes, their power is never absolute. Government will not always pursue policies which are to their liking or which correspond with their needs. It becomes necessary, therefore, for the society's dominant economic groups, like other interest groups, to pressure government. To this extent the basic pluralist picture of American politics as an arena of competitive forces, each trying to maximize its benefits, is accurate enough. However, the competition is far less than perfect. The political resources that dominant economic

---

1. Political scientist David Vogel (1978) suggests that businessmen not only believe their propaganda vis-à-vis government, but their beliefs are even stronger than public statements indicate. This, he claims, has been a consistent pattern of thought among American businessmen for over a century.

groups, corporations in particular, can apply to the state far outweigh those of any other interest groups.

What are the resources and methods used by the corporation and other key economic groups to influence government? And what is the evidence that they are usually more successful than other interests? In considering the means of political influence, we will look at four which seem particularly important: (1) the business sector's control of the society's economic resources; (2) lobbying and advising government officials; (3) campaign financing; and (4) the interchange of personnel between top policy-making political groups and top economic groups.

As to the question of whether the corporation and other dominant economic groups are usually more successful in their pursuit of government favor, empirical evidence is not easily obtained. Despite the fact that government is a public institution, its daily operations are in many ways no less secretive and hidden from public view than the corporation's. Sociologist Joseph Kahl reminds us that "those who sit among the mighty do not invite sociologists to watch them make their decisions about how to control the behavior of others" (1967:10). This is hardly less true of public decision makers than of private ones. Furthermore, the fact that power is *potential* as well as actual *participation* in decision making makes its determination even more difficult.

As a means of trying to determine the extent to which economic interests can transform their economic power into political power, we can utilize two indirect methods. First, we can try to ascertain in whose interests political power is applied. Essentially our question here is, "On behalf of whom does government work?" This involves investigating the distribution of government benefits and looking at those groups which seem to be consistently favored by government policies. Second, we can look at the makeup of government—that is, who occupies positions of political power (authority) and who can more easily make his or her views known to political decision makers. If big businessmen and key professional groups (such as doctors) have easier access to government, we may presume that their interests will get a better hearing on public issues than others. Likewise, if political officials are predominantly of the same social class as business leaders or their occupational origins are rooted in dominant economic groups, there is a strong likelihood that their actions will reflect the interests of those groups.

Let us begin by looking at the primary means of corporate influence in government.

Control of Economic Resources

To understand the necessity for government to pay obeisance to the

needs of big business, we need only consider the range of power of the latter and its effects on the political fate of government officials. It is of greatest political priority to create and maintain an environment favorable to the health of the corporate sector since that is where control of investment, employment, and so on basically lies. Plainly, if the giant corporation does not prosper, the politician does not get reelected or reappointed. Thus, most of all it is the ability to decide the economic fate of the society and any of its constituent parts that makes the threat of corporate retaliation an effective weapon in resisting government efforts to limit its power. What congressman, for example, can ignore the needs of corporations when they control jobs for workers in his district, own plants which employ those workers, and manufacture the products that his constituents want and need? Political scientist Charles Lindblom (1978:A19) aptly describes the dependence of the politician upon business interests:

> If business is not induced to perform, the result is economic distress. When the economy fails, the Government falls. When the economy declines it is not a David Rockefeller but a Senator Daniel Patrick Moynihan who loses his job. Hence, no category of persons is more attentive to the needs of business than the Government official. Businessmen consequently do not need to strain or conspire to win privileges already thrust on them by anxious legislators and administrators.

Basically, then, the corporation's political power derives from the impact it exerts on the economic condition of the society. Since jobs, goods, and wealth are controlled by these institutions, government policy, at least in the long run, must reflect their needs. In short, corporations cannot fail, for government will not permit them to do so. The political shock waves of lost jobs, lost investment, and so on would be disastrous. The political power of the corporation and other dominant economic groups is most simply their ability to control the allocation of resources and the rate of economic development of the society (Baratz, 1956). Former Secretary of Defense Charles E. Wilson's famous declaration that "what is good for General Motors is good for the country" is basically correct, given the society's economic structure.

Thus, politicians come naturally to view the interests of dominant economic groups as fundamental to a prosperous socioeconomic system and are prepared to accede to their needs more readily than to those of other interest groups. Barnet and Müller explain this relationship as clearly understood and accepted by political decision makers:

> No government dedicated to steady, spectacular economic growth

as the prime tool for maintaining social peace can afford to take a tough line with big corporations. For those who have come to power in America in the last thirty years, the notion that there were any fundamental conflicts between corporate interests and the public interest simply did not arise. The power of the United States rested so clearly on the power of the great corporations (1974:248).

An obvious example of the reluctance of government to permit large corporations to fail, even when they are internally mismanaged, is the rescue of the Lockheed Corporation by the federal government in 1971. As a top defense contractor and an employer of thousands, Lockheed was threatened with bankruptcy since it could not secure needed loans from private financial sources. By a narrow margin, the Congress voted to underwrite $250 million in loans to Lockheed, which meant that it provided assurance to private investors that their loans would be guaranteed by the government should Lockheed have been unable to pay. Since then, Lockheed has recovered and is once again a viable corporation, doing most of its business with the government (Kraar, 1977). Similar government action was taken to rescue the Chrysler Corporation in 1979, when it was faced with financial insolvency. These cases also demonstrate the dual nature of the American economy and the relationship of the two business sectors to government. Small businesses, representing relatively little collective power, are dispensable and cannot expect government assistance when threatened with financial ruin. Large corporations, on the other hand, controlling the bulk of the society's productive resources, are indispensable, and their needs must be met by a cooperative government.

Lobbying and Advising

In addition to the influence corporations are able to wield simply on the basis of their control of the society's productive resources, there are other more direct mechanisms which are used in translating economic power into political power. Lobbying and advising government officials are two important means by which corporate leaders are able to gain access to political decision makers. These activities become vital communications links between government and big business sectors.

Lobbying. Trying to persuade legislators and other government officials through direct efforts—lobbying—is a practice which is well institutionalized in American politics. Indeed, the interest group system (described in chapter 3) revolves around such activities. But today lobbying efforts have become tools for groups whose economic resources permit them to retain permanent staffs of lobbyists in Washington and in state capitals, constantly working to further their political interests.

As might be expected, corporations, given their immense financial capacities, are predominant lobbying forces, not only through their support of industrial and trade associations which lobby for particular industries or business groups collectively (such as the American Petroleum Institute, the American Insurance Association, or the American Trucking Association) but also, and perhaps more importantly, through their own company lobbying staffs. There are currently an estimated 5,000 or more full-time lobbyists in Washington, 10 for each member of Congress. Among these it is estimated that 8 of every 10 of the nation's 1,000 largest corporations have their representatives in Washington, and at least a dozen new companies establish lobbies each year (Green, 1975: 29; see also *Congressional Quarterly*, 1974b).

In addition to the monetary and material benefits which lobbyists bestow on legislators and other government officials in hopes of favorable treatment on particular issues, lobbyists influence government in another, perhaps more important, way. They constitute a key source of information for legislators and other policymakers on general as well as specific issues. In this manner business groups, as the chief lobbyists, are better able than others to apply input into the shaping of government policies which affect their interests. When legislation arises concerning, for example, the oil industry or the trucking industry, necessary information is supplied by the companies themselves, usually through their lobbyists. Thus, during the energy crises of the 1970s, government officials relied primarily on figures supplied by the oil industry in considering measures to ease the alleged shortages.

This power of lobbyists is partially a consequence of the structure of federal and state legislatures. Lawmakers are burdened with an unending stream of various bills to consider and a limited staff with little financial wherewithal to research each measure adequately. This is also true of federal and state agencies which make policy. This being the case, legislators or administrators generally find themselves dependent on lobbyists to supply information. Such information will, of course, be slanted, reflecting the interests of the lobbying group. Government officials, however, come to see such efforts as helpful and even vital to their decision-making functions.

At the same time lobbyists provide information, they acquire information from their interaction with government officials and relay it back to their clients. Lobbyists, in effect, constitute what one observer calls an "informal intelligence network" which not only supplies information but also receives it and uses it for further advantage (Green, 1975:30). It is extremely valuable, for example, for a corporation to know in advance what legislators and other government officials are thinking on issues vital to its concerns as well as whether and when new policies may be considered.

Other interest groups, of course, maintain lobbies in addition to big business. Among the more important are those of organized labor and professional groups such as doctors, lawyers, and educators. Public interest lobbies such as Common Cause have also developed in the past decade, representing all-inclusive social groups such as consumers. On the major issues of the political economy, however, the collective power of business lobbies is most pervasive.

Corporations and other key economic groups have a disproportionate capacity not only to lobby lawmakers and other government officials but to influence public opinion. Through massive public relations efforts, they can sell their political views to the society in a manner which is financially and organizationally prohibitive to most groups and individuals. The case of Proposition 18 in California in 1970 illustrates the power of giant economic interests with money, organization, and influence to overwhelm a poorly funded, loosely organized citizen group. Proposition 18 was a modest proposal to divert highway funds to other forms of transportation in an effort to fight air pollution and improve mass transit. Opponents of the proposal included various segments of the highway lobby, made up primarily of oil companies but also including trucking associations, automobile clubs, and real estate associations. It was estimated that opponents of the measure outspent the proponents by about 15 to 1 (in media advertising by 43 to 1), with the most substantial contributions coming from oil companies such as Standard Oil of California, Shell, and Mobil. Supporters of the proposal, on the other hand, had to rely on small donations (Whitt, 1973). As might be expected, the proposal was soundly defeated.

Government advisory groups. Major business groups maintain close ties with agencies of the executive branch of the federal government through a network of business advisory councils. These groups, numbering from 1,000 to perhaps 6,000, are made up of businessmen who work in collaboration with government administrators, helping to shape economic and social policies having wide-ranging impact.[2] These are in addition to the very close relations corporations have established with the various

2. Various observers claim that it is difficult to determine accurately the actual number of these groups. Green (1975:17) claims 1,500; Epstein (1969:79) estimates from 5,000 to 6,000.

regulatory agencies, which we will look at later in this chapter. Such advisory councils, like lobbies, supply information to government officials on economic matters and in many cases become the chief or sole source of such critical data (see for example Roose, 1975). The National Petroleum Council, for example, serves as a key advisor for the Interior Department in its oil policies.

One of the most significant of these advisory groups is the Business Council. Though little public attention has been drawn to it, the Business Council's recommendations have been offered to a great many government departments in addition to the Department of Commerce, which it originally was designed to advise. The membership of this group has been primarily the highest-ranking officers of top corporations. Epstein notes that in one year "its approximately 160-man membership included the chairman or president of the top two automobile makers, of two of the three leading steel firms, of two of the Big Three in chemicals, and of two of the top four rubber producers" (1969:79). In its meetings with equally high public officials, it is difficult to gauge how much it has functioned as an advisory group and how much as a policymaking group. Moreover, the public versus private distinction of the Business Council is, according to political scientist Grant McConnell, "hopelessly lost" (1966:278; see also Domhoff, 1974:98–103; Domhoff, 1979:70–75).

Other particularly influential advisory groups on domestic issues are the Committee for Economic Development, described by Dye as "a central organization for developing elite consensus, researching national problems, and directing national policy," and the Brookings Institution, "the dominant policy-planning group for American domestic policy" (Dye, 1976:112–115; see also Domhoff, 1979:67–69). The makeup of these groups is a range of top business, financial, governmental, and academic personnel.

In the area of foreign affairs, the Council on Foreign Relations has been noted by many as one of the most significant policy-planning councils (Domhoff, 1970; Dye, 1976; Shoup, 1975). Its membership and financing are heavily supplied by major corporations as well as foundations such as the Rockefeller, Carnegie, and Ford. Domhoff calls it a "key connection between the federal government and the owners and managers of the country's largest financial institutions and corporations" (1970:121). Almost all important State Department officials have served on the CFR in recent administrations, both Democratic and Republican.

Another noteworthy policy-planning group of recent years is the Trilateral Commission. Established in 1972 principally under the direction of David Rockefeller, chairman of the board of Chase Manhattan

Bank, the Commission is made up of top officials of multinational corporations and banks as well as government leaders and scholars of the United States, Western Europe, and Japan. Its purposes have been to coordinate and set out long-range economic policy among these countries. Jimmy Carter, himself a former representative to the Commission, chose several key Cabinet officials from the Trilateral, including Secretary of State Cyrus Vance, Secretary of Defense Harold Brown, Treasury Secretary Michael Blumenthal, and National Security Advisor Zbigniew Brzezinski.

Campaign Financing

Being elected to political office today generally requires a great deal of money. This is particularly true of positions at the federal level, where campaigns are of a much broader scope than local ones, requiring costly television and other media advertising. Unless candidates are personally wealthy, they must turn to others for financial assistance. While labor unions and other interest groups provide substantial funds to many candidates, the bulk of campaign financing at the federal level is borne by big businessmen. This fact was thrust home by one of the U.S. Senate's most venerable members, Russell B. Long, a wealthy oil man himself:

> Most campaign money comes from businessmen. Labor contributions have been greatly exaggerated. It would be my guess that about 95 percent of campaign funds at the congressional level are derived from businessmen. At least 80 percent of this comes from men who could sign a net worth statement exceeding a quarter of a million dollars (quoted in Mintz and Cohen, 1971:158).

The growing extent of money in politics in the past three decades is illustrated by the fact that in 1952, when media techniques were not yet fully developed, the total cost of campaigns for all elective offices in the United States was $140 million; by 1972 it was $425 million, and television and radio accounted for almost $60 million of this total (*Congressional Quarterly*, 1977:58). In the 1972 presidential election, the Nixon campaign alone spent $60 million.

Since the Watergate disclosures of illicit financing in the Nixon campaign of 1972, more stringent federal laws have limited presidential campaign contributions. Nonetheless in the presidential election of 1976, $67 million was spent by the various candidates in the primaries, while $46 million was spent by the final two (*Congressional Quarterly*, 1977:58). Furthermore, congressional campaign financing has not been affected. Thus, in 1976, Senate candidates received $39.1 million in contributions while House candidates received $61 million. In the 1978 congressional election, $150 million was spent by House and Senate candidates.

Although corporations themselves are barred from contributing money directly to candidates, this prohibition is easily evaded by diverting corporate funds to individual officers who make personal contributions and by forming political action committees (PACs) which engage in political fund raising among company executives. The indirect methods by which corporations may contribute to candidates are numerous (Epstein, 1968).

The revelations of Watergate showed the lengths to which corporate contributors might go to make their donations count. Executives from 21 of the largest American corporations were convicted of making illegal campaign contributions in 1972, mostly to the Nixon candidacy. It was further disclosed that for years, many corporations retained political "slush funds" from which campaign donations were made to a variety of presidential and congressional candidates. The largest of those uncovered was that of the Gulf Oil Corporation, which acknowledged a fund of over $10 million that had been used for political contributions and "related activities" from 1960 to 1974 (Lukas, 1976:172; see also *Congressional Quarterly*, 1974a).

The excesses of corporate contributors in the 1972 Nixon campaign need not be considered typical, however, to understand the inherent upper hand which giant corporations retain in this regard. Even when campaign financing is conducted on a legitimate basis, corporations have a decided advantage over other individuals and groups in the society. Their contributions are a factor in explaining why, as former Senator Fred Harris puts it, "David Rockefeller gets a better hearing in the Congress than does the average American workingman or woman" (1977: 26).

The fact that business money is "the lifeblood of American campaign finance" (Thayer, 1973:210) should not obscure the role of other interest groups in this activity, particularly labor unions. Much the same techniques used by corporations to raise and distribute funds are used by labor groups. If Republican candidates are generally favored by business, the bulk of labor money flows to Democrats, though exceptions are common on both sides.

Some claim that the effectiveness of campaign contributions as a means of securing political influence is greatly exaggerated. However, if this is the case, it is difficult to explain the persistence of such contributions by various interest groups. Herbert Alexander (1976:14) perhaps best summarizes the function of money in campaigns by noting that although it is only one element in the equation of power, it is "the common denominator in the shaping of many of the factors comprising political power, because it buys what is not or cannot be volunteered." Though not necessarily decisive in all cases, money, notes Alexander, is at least "capable of reducing severe handicaps for most candidates," and contributors are cognizant of that fact.

At the same time, to view campaign contributions as a means of "buying" elections is an extreme and faulty argument. If politicians were so easily purchased, there would seem no need for dominant economic groups to make any other efforts to pressure government. Although the degree of effectiveness of campaign contributions as a direct means of political influence is a disputed point, what remains significant about them is that *they provide donors easier access to public officials*. In this sense, campaign contributions dovetail with lobbying efforts.

The Interchange of Personnel

Campaign financing and even lobbying are at best uncertain mechanisms in assuring favorable treatment by political decision makers. Moreover, they are aimed primarily at legislatures where members of the economic elite play only an indirect role in policy planning and making. At the higher levels of the executive branch of the federal government, however, there is a much clearer interaction of a direct nature between economic and political elites.

We have seen that through lobbies and advisory bodies, the society's economic leaders are able to maintain a fluid network of access to government officials. Within the executive this interface occurs not only through advisory groups but through the exchange of formal positions between corporation and government. It is common for high corporate officials to leave the private sector and assume top positions in government while the movement occurs in the opposite direction as well. Thus, there is a kind of musical chairs played by economic and political elites in filling power positions. Given a mutual understanding of what constitutes a healthy and progressive society and agreement that a stable corporate system is necessary to maintain that condition, corporate and political elites can interact with ease and can move back and forth between their two worlds with little difficulty.

Perhaps the clearest evidence of the interchangeability of government and corporate personnel is found in the federal regulatory agencies, whose ostensible purpose is to act as public watchdogs over the activities of business institutions. As they function, however, regulatory agencies generally become protectors of the very industries they are designed to control. One of the key factors in explaining this turnabout is the composition of these agencies in terms of personnel. Regardless of the party in power, most appointees to regulatory commissions are individuals who have had executive experience within the industries they are authorized to regulate. Thus, administrators of the Food and Drug Administration are commonly former executives of drug companies, officials of the Federal Energy Commission come from the oil and gas industries, those of the Interstate Commerce Commission from the railroad and trucking industries, and so on. Following their government service, they generally return to those same industries. One study of the ICC found that of the 11 former ICC commissioners who had served in that post from 1958 to 1967, 8 were involved either directly or indirectly in business activities coming under the domain of the ICC (Fellmeth, 1970:20–21). This is a very common practice. That the decisions of regulatory commissions generally reflect business interests should therefore not be surprising. Even if their intentions are to act objectively, it is not realistic to expect officials to divest themselves of a political perspective developed within the corporate world. We shall further discuss the interrelationship of government and corporate personnel in the regulatory agencies later in this chapter.

This revolving-door flow of personnel from the private to the public sector and back is evident not only in the regulatory commissions but generally in the highest echelons of all areas of the executive branch. As a typical example, in 1977 a large Chicago bank recruited the Comptroller of the Currency and the Under Secretary for Monetary Affairs, two of the Treasury Department's highest officials; each had played a major role in regulating banking policy. Moving into the private sector, the two became executive vice presidents of the bank. It is also instructive to consider their positions prior to their government posts: One had been a lobbyist for the American Bankers Association and the other a vice president of a large national bank (Goldwasser, 1977).

The crossover of personnel between the Department of Defense and industries producing arms is particularly strong. As of 1969, there were over 2,000 retired military officers of high rank on the payrolls of the 100 largest defense contractors. Moving in the opposite direction, civilian officials of the Pentagon are most commonly from the world of big business. Of the 8 men who have served as Secretary of Defense since 1953, 4 came directly from high positions in the corporate world and two others had corporate ties as board members of large firms.

Although the same pattern may not necessarily appear at lower levels of government or even in the different branches of the federal government, evidence confirms the common overlapping of economic and political elites within the highest ranks of the executive. We might consider the three most important cabinet posts: Secretary of State, Defense, and Treasury. Starting with the Eisenhower administration in 1953, 21 individuals have held these posts, 13 under Republicans and 8 under Democratic presidents. With only three exceptions, all were either the holders of top corporate offices, chairmen or board members of one or more large corporations, or members of corporate law firms.[3]

This back-and-forth movement is not a recent phenomenon, however, but has been quite regular since the emergence of the corporate economy at the turn of the century. In a study of the interlocks between big business and the presidential cabinet over a 75-year period, one researcher found that "all Cabinet posts are to a high degree interlocked with the elite business sector and that there appears further justification for concluding that personnel interchanges between the Cabinet and big business seriously question the notion of a plurality of elites in government" (Freitag, 1975:148; see also Mintz, 1975). The penetration of big businessmen into the top echelons of the federal executive grows in significance when we consider that it is in the latter that the most extensive growth in government power has occurred in recent decades.[4]

The interchange of government and corporate personnel is advantageous for each institutional sphere. Those who have served in government are particularly valuable to the corporation since they have firsthand knowledge of the inner workings of political agencies and have established networks of influence which can be used to further corporate interests. Because of their familiarity with government procedures and personnel, many former government officials become corporate lobbyists. This is also true of former congressmen. As Mark J. Green notes, the road from the floor of Congress to the lobby is well worn, with nearly every big lobby having at least one former member of Congress on its staff (1975:46). At the same time, given the government's dependence on the corporation to sustain a healthy economy and the corporation's role in dealing with various social as well as economic problems, government agencies quite naturally seek out recruits from the corporate world.

---

3.   Data compiled from various editions of *Current Biography* and *Who's Who in America.*
4.   The pattern of interchange is apparent even at the state level of government. Serber (1975:86) found that of 67 persons working at the staff level of the Pennsylvania Department of Insurance, 58 had a background in the insurance industry. Of the 12 top ranking officers in the department, 10 came from the insurance industry.

HOW THE STATE SERVES THE CORPORATE SYSTEM

Government's chief role in the symbiotic relationship between it and big business is to maintain the socioeconomic (corporate capitalist) system, to keep it running smoothly, and to assure a social climate amenable to growth and prosperity. In promoting these conditions, government uses certain direct tools. These are concentrated primarily in the federal government, though state and local units play supportive roles. Four key mechanisms are utilized to influence and support the corporate system: (1) regulation of business by various governmental agencies; (2) taxation and subsidies to the private sector; (3) consumption of goods and services; and (4) management of foreign policy.

With these capacities to influence the economy, it would seem that big government would act as a potential counterforce to the society's dominant economic interests, holding their power in check. Most pluralist interpretations of the American sociopolitical system do see the state playing such a countervailing power role. To determine whether these governmental powers in fact hold dominant economic interests in check or whether they actually promote concentration of economic power and thus intensify the maldistribution of the society's wealth requires that we look at their effect on various societal groups. In short, who benefits most consistently and in greatest measure from these structures and processes of government?

Regulation of Business

Virtually every business activity in the United States is linked to some government agency. Particularly important government-business ties are found in the independent regulatory commissions. Beginning with the Interstate Commerce Commission in 1887, a succession of regulatory agencies has been created by Congress whose general purpose is to regulate various parts of the society's commercial life. For example, the Interstate Commerce Commission (ICC) approves freight rates and routes covered by railroads and truck lines; the Civil Aeronautics Board (CAB) does the same with the airlines; new foods and drugs which are marketed must meet standards established by the Food and Drug Administration (FDA); television and radio industries are regulated by the Federal Communications Commission (FCC) which grants new licenses and maintains broadcast standards, and so on. Even those industries which do not come under the purview of a specific regulatory agency are covered by general purpose agencies such as the Federal Trade Commission (FTC). The regulatory bodies, then, serve as a key bridge between government and business. In theory these agencies have the potential to play a powerful controlling role over big business. It is not surprising, therefore, that they have become prime targets of corporate influence in government.

So effective has corporate influence been that today it is commonly recognized that the regulatory agencies have become representatives of the very industries they are charged with overseeing. As was earlier pointed out, instead of operating as public agents they more often operate as corporate agents, formulating and enforcing policies which promote and protect the supposedly regulated industry.

However, it is not only in recent times that big business has had such broad influence in government regulatory agencies. In a revealing study, economic historian Gabriel Kolko (1967) has shown that the formation of regulatory bodies and other measures designed to establish public control over the increasing power of big business during the Progressive Movement of the late nineteenth and early twentieth centuries was not a victory for the antibusiness forces but instead became a triumph of the large enterprises themselves. "The dominant fact of American political life at the beginning of this century," writes Kolko, "was that big business led the struggle for the federal regulation of the economy" (1967:57–58; see also Thelen, 1976). From the outset of government regulation of business, businessmen themselves have played a leading role in the regulatory agencies.

As Kolko explains, big business was not threatened by regulatory measures but saw them as mechanisms to control or eliminate competition, to create a favorable environment for their continued expansion, and, by cooperating in their initial formation, to influence all future government regulatory policies. Through state intervention the corporation could receive protection from foreign competition through the imposition of tariffs; it could receive federal grants to land and other natural resources; it could be afforded armed support against recalcitrant workers; and it could receive exemptions from tax payments. The attitude of big businessmen of this era is well illustrated by the remarks of Richard Olney, a prominent corporation lawyer who had been appointed Attorney General during the second administration of Grover Cleveland. Speaking to the president of a large railroad who sought his aid in persuading the administration to abolish the Interstate Commerce Commission, Olney replied that

> The Commission, as its functions have now been limited by the courts, is, or can be made, of great use to the railroads. It satisfies the popular clamor for a government supervision of railroads, at the same time that that supervision is almost entirely nominal.

Further, the older such a Commission gets to be, the more inclined it will be found to take the business and railroad view of things. It thus becomes a sort of barrier between the railroad corporations and the people and a sort of protection against hasty and crude legislation hostile to railroad interests. . . . The part of wisdom is not to destroy the Commission, but to utilize it (Bernstein, 1955: 265).

Olney's prophecy has been fulfilled not only in the case of the ICC, but, as McConnell states, "has gained the stature of a general rule of independent regulatory commission development in most fields" (1966:287).

Instead of taming the corporation, government regulation has fostered its growth, concentration, and noncompetitive nature. Today the means by which this is accomplished are similar to those used by big businessmen at the outset of government regulation: first, the infiltration of regulatory agencies by personnel who come from the regulated industries or are sympathetic to their interests; and second, the inherent structural weakness of the agencies in challenging business power.

We have already noted the tendency for personnel of the various agencies to come from corporate backgrounds. That is, government administrators have a familiarity with the industries they are charged with regulating since they frequently have held managerial positions in those industries prior to their government service and will return to them when they reenter nongovernmental careers. It would be naive to assume that such persons can impartially represent the public one day and big business the next. The promise of a well-paying position in the private sector following government service may be inducement enough to cater to industry interests.

Even if the factor of personnel crossover is discounted, however, regulatory agencies simply lack the financial and personnel resources to challenge corporate practices. The Food and Drug Administration (FDA) serves to illustrate. This agency is basically responsible for assuring the quality of all food, drugs, and cosmetics sold in the United States. In order to carry out this duty, it employs about 8,500 people and has an annual budget of roughly $300 million. But to attempt to monitor the activities of industries as vast and financially powerful as food and drug companies with such means becomes an almost futile undertaking. The food industry alone markets an average of one new product a day. As a result, the FDA comes to rely primarily on food and drug companies themselves to supply it with information on new products and to conduct tests on these products before they are released to the market. In effect, the food and drug companies regulate themselves. This pattern of self-enforcement is repeated in each of the regulated industries.

Competition within industries is also reduced by regulatory practices. The CAB, for example, approves airline routes and also sets rates that airlines may charge, in each case protecting interests of established carriers and virtually eliminating real competition among them. In essence the CAB merely rubber stamps rates determined by the airlines themselves, thus naturally creating inflated fares. The disparity between air fares of CAB-regulated carriers and those of intrastate carriers not under CAB jurisdiction attests to the monopolizing effects of airline regulation (Pillai, 1973:161). Similarly, the FCC controls the number of television channels serving a given area and the awarding of broadcast licenses, in effect protecting the television market for the major networks and the established stations (Moore, 1973). Such protective, noncompetitive policies are typical in each regulatory area.

Antitrust laws are another theoretical means of controlling excessive corporate power, but their ineffectiveness and lack of enforcement are as well understood as the nonregulation of regulatory agencies. The continued concentration of market power in almost every industry in the American economy affirms this. Between 1950 and 1967, there were over 14,000 mergers of industrial corporations in the United States, only 199 of which were challenged by the government. Half of those challenged involved smaller firms with less than $100 million in sales, and in only 58 cases were companies required to divest themselves of anything (Barnet and Müller, 1974:230–231; see also Green et al., 1972).

In sum, government regulation in theory holds powerful economic institutions under control and forces them to act in the public interest. In effect, however, the very opposite is the case. Government regulation of big business acts to solidify the power of large economic enterprises by stifling competition and providing the corporate elite steady access to government policymakers.

Taxation and Other Forms of Wealth Redistribution

A second area that we might consider in determining who benefits from the government's economic activities is welfare. "Welfare" is used here in a broad sense to denote all efforts of government to redistribute wealth through taxation and other fiscal measures as well as through the provision of services. How does the welfare system operate and who are its primary beneficiaries?

Government measures designed to redistribute wealth take several forms, the most important of which is taxation. Although the chief purpose of taxation is to raise revenues for government programs, a secondary objective is the redistribution of wealth. The progressive income tax is the major means by which such transfers of wealth are accomplished. The principle of progressivity means that people are to be taxed in accordance with their ability to pay. Thus, those with greater income will pay a higher percentage of that income in taxes. The intent is not to make the distribution of wealth perfectly equal among the populace but rather to reduce the more glaring inequities between those at the top and those at the bottom of the economic hierarchy.

However, the tax structure consists not only of the federal income tax, which at least in theory is progressive, but also of state and local taxes such as sales or property taxes, most of which are regressive in nature. In these cases, persons' ability to pay is not considered; everyone pays an equal percentage, thus shifting a higher relative burden to those who are lower on the economic scale. As a result, when taken in total, the system of taxation is mildly regressive and ineffectual in closing the gaps between income groups.

The most striking contradiction of the principle of progressivity in taxation, however, is evident in the federal income tax itself. Through a variety of devices popularly referred to as tax "dodges" or "loopholes," those individuals at the top of the economic hierarchy as well as the large corporations have substantially reduced their percentage of tax payments (see Stern, 1974; Tuckman, 1973; Turner and Starnes, 1976). Through such features as lower tax rates on capital gains (income derived from the sale of stocks or industrial equipment, for example), or the lack of any taxes at all on state and municipal bonds (100 percent of which are owned by about 1 percent of American families), the affluent few wind up paying a far smaller proportion than their incomes would seemingly require.

Large corporations have been particularly adroit at avoiding taxes on income due to a complex system of corporate tax laws which have been enacted over the past 50 or so years. In recent years American corporations have actually reduced their percentage of income taxes. In 1969, corporation payments accounted for about 20 percent of federal income taxes collected, whereas in 1978 they accounted for about 15 percent of the total (U.S. Congress, 1979:H5028). Some of the more striking inequities are reflected in the extremely low or, for some, non-existent tax rates incurred by the largest and most profitable firms. In 1977, for example, Mobil Oil, on income of over $4 billion, paid only 7.4 percent in federal income taxes; ITT, with income of over $650 million, paid 12.2 percent; some, such as American Airlines and U.S. Steel, on income of over $80 million each, paid no federal income taxes at all. In fact, 17 giant corporations with total income of over $2 billion paid no federal income taxes in 1977 (U.S. Congress, 1979:H5023-H5029).

In addition to tax advantages and government spending (which we will discuss later in this chapter), both of which are indirect welfare payments, corporations also benefit from direct government subsidies. These are payments made for the support of the economic health of certain industries or firms. Among the more highly subsidized industries are airlines, defense contractors, and commercial agriculture. As to the last, the bulk of agricultural subsidies such as price support payments are paid not to small farmers but to large corporate farm operations. In 1977, the largest 1.5 percent of all farms received 28 percent of all price-support payments (Suits, 1977:38).

Indirect forms of subsidization are of even greater significance. Mail order merchandising industries, for example, are subsidized by the postal service; the trucking industry is subsidized by highway construction, as are airlines and shipping companies by the building of airports and harbors; many industries, such as textiles and electronics, enjoy tariff protection against foreign competition; and the costs of cleaning up environmental damage created by industry, such as oil spills and water pollution, are borne by consumers and ordinary taxpayers, not only through higher prices of goods but through government environmental programs as well.

All of these government programs reflect the increasing socialization of investment and costs of production. While government subsidizes capital investment of large corporate enterprises, profits earned on that investment, however, remain private.

Some have maintained that through transfer payments—programs such as Social Security, unemployment insurance, Medicare, food stamps, and public housing—government has reduced income inequality. Although such programs have benefited those at the very bottom of the economic hierarchy, their overall impact has not sharply reduced the maldistribution of wealth in the society. The largest transfer payment, Social Security, is a tax that is regressive in nature and is actually a form of postponed income. Other transfer payments are designed to aid those who are extremely poor, leaving out the more sizable near-poor and working-class families. In any case, such direct payments in services cannot compare in significance with the direct and indirect payments to the affluent and the corporations. As sociologist Charles Anderson bluntly puts it, "Welfare in the narrow sense, so-called giveaway programs for the financially impoverished, is very small potatoes in the U.S. economy" (1974:260). Moreover, such government-provided services as health care and public housing ultimately redound to the corporations and the affluent few who are paid by the government to deliver them. The Medicare system, for example, has proven a gigantic financial boon to the medical professions and other elements of the health services industry, such as drug and hospital supply companies (Ehrenreich and Ehrenreich, 1971: Winter, 1977).

In sum, what is seen in various government welfare policies is a repetition of other government activities which disproportionately benefit the most privileged economic stratum and the large corporations. Instead of reducing the maldistribution of income and wealth in the society, they have the effect of accentuating it.

Government as Consumer

One of the most important ways in which government supports dominant economic interests is through its consumption activities. In short, government at all levels, but particularly the federal, is an enormous purchaser of material goods and services. Government purchases amounted to about 11 percent of the nation's output of goods and services in 1929; today they exceed 20 percent. And it is the giant corporations that are the chief suppliers, and thus the chief recipients of government spending. Whether pencils, computers, medical services, highways, airplanes, or missiles, it is private industry which generally supplies them. Government thus becomes dependent on the society's dominant economic groups—primarily the corporations—to serve its practical needs; and these groups, in turn, rely on government as a constant and essential customer.

The significance of government spending in different industries varies, but in no other area is the government's consumer role more obvious than defense. We shall concentrate our analysis on military spending because it represents such a substantial portion of the federal budget and because the mutual dependence of government and big business is so apparent here.

The actual percentage of total federal expenditures devoted to the military has declined in recent years to about 25 percent, but the dollar amount of spending has continued to climb. Most simply, the Department of Defense is the largest single consumer in American society. In 1980 the arms budget was $138 billion. Since the end of World War II the United States has spent approximately $2 trillion on arms.[5] In addi-

5. Estimates of military spending since World War II vary with the inclusion or exclusion of certain categories of spending. If such military-related expenditures as the space program, atomic energy, veterans' benefits, and foreign aid are included, higher figures are more realistic. So vast and complex is the system of defense spending, however, that, as one observer notes, not even the highest officials know precisely how much is involved (Sherrill, 1970). Comprehensive studies of the financial costs of the defense industry are Yarmolinsky's (1971) and Clayton's (1972).

tion to supplying the American military, arms production has become a vital segment of American exports. Sales of American-made weapons rose from about $2 billion in 1967 to $11 billion in 1975.

Few groups or institutions in the society do not benefit in some way from the production of weapons. But a few giant defense industries profit most of all. The chief producers and sellers of defense items are among the same large corporations which dominate the consumer market, though many of the largest defense contractors produce weapons almost exclusively. Indeed, the concentration of the defense industry is even more pronounced than that of the civilian sector (Ellsworth, 1973; Fox, 1974). Although there are over 20,000 firms engaged in the production of arms and other military items, more than 70 percent of all prime contracts go to the 100 largest contractors. The largest 25 alone receive more than one-half of the total awards.

Among the largest industrial corporations, the dependence on defense contracts varies. Some firms, such as Lockheed, rely on them for almost all of their business, while for others, such as General Motors, they constitute only a small percentage of total sales (Fox, 1974:50). In any case defense contracts are highly lucrative since government usually furnishes much of the capital for projects. For example, in 1971 two giant defense firms, Lockheed and General Dynamics, were each using over $200 million worth of government plants and equipment, which represented one-quarter of each firm's total manufacturing assets (Katznelson and Kesselman, 1975:188). Also, firms will often take the patents and technology for a weapons system, developed at government expense, and apply them to production for the consumer market. Boeing, for example, developed its 707 jetliner, sold to commercial airlines, as a direct outgrowth of its government-financed development of the KC-135 tanker, a military aircraft (Barnet, 1972:168). Such cases again illustrate the government-business relationship, in which investment risk is socialized while profits earned remain private.

Another reason for the lucrative nature of military contracts is the contracting firms' failure to guarantee against cost overruns. Thus, the final price of a weapons system may be many times the original estimate. Obviously corruption and waste are fueled by such an open-ended system. The cost overrun on production of the C-5A transport plane, for example, was $2 billion.[6]

6. The Pentagon official who first exposed the tactics used in this particular case by the Defense Department and the contractor (Lockheed) to pad costs, as well as the more general methods of profiteering practiced by the defense industry, was shortly thereafter fired from his job; only after successfully winning his case in court was he rehired by the Pentagon (see Fitzgerald, 1972).

The familiar term "military-industrial complex" implies the mutual interest of the American military establishment and American industry. But there is a third component in the order of defense production: the politician, who, in the end, underwrites the entire system by approving huge military budgets. Politicians become committed to large defense expenditures not simply for ideological reasons or because of beliefs in the need for a strong national defense. More importantly, defense spending represents a vital source of jobs and investment which politicians cannot ignore. Defense contractors and subcontractors are located in every state and in over 80 percent of U.S. congressional districts (Fox, 1974:41). In states such as California or Washington, where military spending constitutes over 10 percent of all economic activity, it would be politically suicidal for any congressman or senator, regardless of ideological persuasion, to vote against continued high defense budgets.

It is important to keep in mind that the power configurations created by military expenditures do not represent a conspiracy among industrialists, generals, and politicians. Instead they embody a natural coalition of interest groups with an economic and political stake in defense spending. This coalition includes not only the military, corporations, and politicians but also labor unions, which are vitally interested in creating and maintaining jobs in these industries. In short, there are many powerful institutions and organizations which find support of the defense industry beneficial.

Marxists have long maintained that huge military expenditures by government are necessary to assure a prosperous capitalist economy. The consumer market alone, it is argued, cannot absorb the goods which a capitalist system must continue to produce. Government spending must be relied on to sustain expansion, and military goods have been found particularly vital in stimulating the economy (Green, 1970; Greenberg, 1974; Reich, 1978).

But others, not simply Marxists, have also held that the military aspect of government spending is essential to the American political economy. The understanding of politicians and businessmen that military spending is an economic tool is no better illustrated than by the admission of the Secretary of Defense in Senate hearings in 1974 that the proposed record defense budget of that year had been dictated not strictly by military requirements but by domestic economic considerations as well (Finney, 1974).

If government expenditures are vital to the maintenance of a healthy capitalist system, one might question why a greater percentage of this spending is not channeled into more pressing social needs such as housing, education, and medical programs. In the 1960s, economist Seymour

Melman illustrated the social cost of defense spending by comparing military projects with their cost equivalents in socially oriented projects. One TFX airplane, for example, was estimated to be the equivalent of 13 elementary schools, 570 dwelling units in low-rent public housing projects, or 278 hospital beds; the cost of a Polaris submarine with 16 missiles would have purchased 331 elementary schools, 6,811 hospital beds, or 13,723 low-rent dwelling units (Melman, 1965:37).

Economist Michael Reich (1978) suggests that many kinds of non-defense social spending are resisted because they put government in direct competition with private industry. For example, government production of low-cost housing in large amounts would substantially reduce profits of private builders and landowners. Similarly, building truly effective mass public transportation systems would prove detrimental to the automobile producers and their satellite industries. Defense projects, however, do not threaten established markets.

Reich also notes that the provision of good social services fulfills real rather than created needs. Housing, transportation, medical services, and schools are among these basic human requirements. But providing them interferes with the very basis of capitalist production, which is production—and consumption—that relies on contrived rather than genuine needs. Public goods and services, then, upset the business system founded on constantly generating needs through advertising and other commercial mechanisms. But defense spending does not obstruct this system.

In sum, military spending as a form of government enterprise is acceptable to dominant economic interests. As Reich explains, "It does not interfere with existing areas for profit-making, it does not undermine the labor market, it does not challenge the class structure, and it does not produce income redistribution. Social spending does all these things and thus faces obstacles for its own expansion" (1978:417; see also Baran and Sweezy, 1966:ch. 6).

The Corporate State in Foreign Affairs

Throughout the twentieth century in capitalist societies there has been a close and supportive relationship between state and business in the area of foreign affairs. The same premises underlying the domestic confluence of these two institutions have been the rationale for their coming together abroad. Just as the government's chief purpose at home is the maintenance of social and economic stability, the foundation of foreign policy is the preservation of a stable *world* environment in which the society's economic interests can be maximized. During the nineteenth and early twentieth centuries, the promotion of Western capitalist interests in the nonindustrial world was served by policies of imperialism, in which direct political and economic control of foreign countries was maintained. Today such blatant techniques are no longer used, though the objectives remain essentially unchanged.

The overriding aim of any nation's foreign policy is national security, and in the case of the United States, this goal blends easily with the objective of security for American-based corporations. The activities of of the State Department and other elements of the foreign policy establishment cannot be explained as a preplanned design of business and government officials to shape policy in a way which automatically protects and enhances the profits and protection of American foreign investment. But just as it becomes only logical for politicians to support policies which benefit the affluent and the corporations in order to assure domestic political and economic stability, it becomes equally logical to do the same in foreign affairs.

Foreign affairs officials and policymakers thus come to see the goal of a successful foreign policy in much the same way as politicians see a successful domestic policy: a healthy and stable socioeconomic climate. Since it is the multinational corporation more than any other institution which controls such conditions, political interests abroad are equated with corporate interests. Above all, the aims of foreign policymakers become: (1) protecting American business interests abroad and assuring an investment climate favorable to those interests; (2) stimulating the establishment of markets for American business; and (3) assuring the continued flow of raw materials from the underdeveloped nations to American industry. National security, then, becomes synonymous with corporate security.

The common understanding of government and corporate elites of what comprises a successful foreign policy is fostered by the same interaction between these two groups as was seen in the domestic political economy. The exchange of personnel between the corporate world and the foreign policy establishment is very evident, particularly at the highest levels of decision making. Looking at the men who have held the very top positions of the foreign policy establishment (Secretaries and Under Secretaries of State and Defense, Secretaries of the Army, Navy, and Air Force, Chairman of the Atomic Energy Commission, and Director of the CIA), Barnet (1972:179) found that out of 91 men who held these offices between 1940 and 1967, 70 came from big business or high finance. A Brookings Institution study (1967:134) revealed that between 1933 and 1965, 64 percent of the top officers in the Department of Defense and 26 percent of the top administrative positions in the State Department were held by persons who were either businessmen or lawyers prior to their government posts. Kolko (1969:19) investigated the occupational origins of the top foreign policy decision makers from 1944 through 1960 and concluded that they were "intimately connected with dominant business circles and their law firms."

Also, we have already noted the heavily business-oriented policy-planning groups such as the Council on Foreign Relations which, though not officially part of the foreign policymaking apparatus of the government, work closely with it and exert substantial influence. Through this continual overlapping and interaction between official policymakers and the corporate elite, dominant economic interests have an undue influence in the foreign policy area, even though they do not actually make and administer that policy.

Corporate interests and the Third World. American foreign policy in the post-World War II years has increasingly focused on the underdeveloped or Third World nations since it is in these societies that political and economic stability have been most fragile, thereby endangering the firmness of the world market. Also, in recent years these nations have been an increasingly important target of American foreign investment. Although foreign investment of U.S.-based corporations remains much greater in the industrial world (primarily Canada and Western Europe), the rate of profit garnered from investments in the underdeveloped world is very high. Even though they account for only about 30 percent of American foreign investments, those in Asia, Africa, and Latin America provide about half of all overseas earnings (Szymanski, 1978: 207; see also Mankoff and Majka, 1975:70). Furthermore these nations supply vital raw materials and labor, unlike the economically developed nations, which act mainly as trading partners in finished goods. Given their increased economic importance, coupled with their instability, U.S. foreign policy has concentrated on maximizing and protecting American business interests in these nations.

Understanding that when the stability of Third World societies is threatened, the economic fate of American-based multinational corporations is also threatened, has led to the use of direct and indirect tactics to firm up or restore to power governments which are more receptive to the American economic presence. The emergence of socialist movements in these societies has been recognized by foreign policymakers as automatically unfavorable to U.S. interests. Not only are such movements seen as fostering political and social instability, but they are committed to the nationalization of industry, thus jeopardizing the very foundation of the American corporate influence. The strongly negative reaction to the Castro takeover in Cuba in 1959 and the direct attempts first to prevent the election of socialist Salvador Allende in Chile and then to undermine his government in 1973 are two of the more obvious cases of the impulsive antisocialist response of American foreign policymakers. In the post-World War II era, American inspired or assisted overthrows have also occurred in Iran in 1953, Guatemala in 1954, and the Dominican Republic and Brazil in 1965. In each of these instances, left-wing governments had come to power, threatening American economic interests.

The need to contain threats to American economic and political power in foreign countries has led to a strong response in *any* threatened area, regardless of the scope of the U.S. presence. In a sense, the jeopardizing of American interests in one country is seen as a symbolic threat to American interests in others as well. The rationale of the Vietnam War may be at least partially explained in this way. The level of American investment in Vietnam, as well as the dependence on raw materials from that country, was minimal. Nonetheless, foreign policymakers saw Vietnam as a symbolic testing ground between the United States as leader of the capitalist world and the perceived threat of socialist forces.

War is an extreme tool of foreign policy, however, and maintaining a favorable investment climate, assuring the uninterrupted flow of raw materials, and bringing about long-range stability in the Third World are generally accomplished through less coercive and more effective means. Nations of the underdeveloped world are induced to cooperate with the United States through the provision of military aid, economic assistance in various forms (primarily long-term loans), technical assistance in the areas of agriculture and industry, and less overt methods such as counterinsurgency activities.

Foreign aid. American economic interests benefit not only in a general way from the broad shape and practices of foreign policy but also more directly and immediately from the mechanisms which promote that policy. Foreign aid provides an example.

Immediately following World War II, a foreign aid program, the Marshall Plan, was developed by the Truman administration, basically designed to stabilize and strengthen the war-torn societies of Western Europe. It was feared that these nations' governments might collapse and fall to communist regimes, as had already occurred in Poland, Czechoslovakia, and Hungary. But the political objectives of the Marshall Plan were tied to the need to reestablish European markets for American exports. The purposes of aid were thus economic as well as political.

American corporations not only benefited from the revitalization of their European markets but received substantial direct benefits from the aid program itself. All of the commodities sent to these nations were purchased from American businesses and, as it turned out, this became a propitious opportunity for dumping surplus goods and thus protecting the prices of these commodities in the United States. Green (1970:126) has noted, for example, that "Between 60 and 80 percent of all the United States exports of corn, peanuts, copper products, oilseeds, wheat and flour, cotton and tobacco during the first nine months of 1949 went to Marshall Aid." He goes on to explain that American corporations exerted great pressure on the government at this time to have their products purchased for shipment abroad.

The primary focus of foreign aid shifted in the 1950s to the underdeveloped societies of Asia, Latin America, and Africa, but its objectives remained the same: resisting the threat of communist takeovers and establishing American markets. American corporations thus again became major recipients of the benefits of these programs. Rather than a "giveaway," as it has been popularly described by conservative politicians, economic aid to the underdeveloped nations has usually been granted as long-term loans which must be paid back by the receiving country. Furthermore, such loans have usually been in the form of export credits, whereby the recipient must purchase American-made products with these funds. As a result, foreign aid has served as a substantial portion of the exports of American corporations.

Other stipulations are generally placed on economic assistance in order to assure favorable trade terms with the United States and to guarantee the future dependence of these countries on American exports (Magdoff, 1969). Also, once American technology is introduced either in the form of machinery or information, receiving nations automatically incur long-range obligations to purchase future equipment, replacement parts, services, and training from the American supplier.

The bulk of foreign aid to the Third World since the end of World War II, however, has been in the form of military rather than economic aid. It is here that the production and sale of arms abroad becomes an important prop for many corporations in the American economy as well as helping to assure a favorable balance of trade for the United States. The ostensible purpose of military aid has been defense against communist incursions into these nations. However, no serious observer of world politics any longer recognizes this as more than political rhetoric. The chief purposes of military assistance have been the same as the more general purposes of foreign aid: to stabilize noncommunist governments (that is, those within the political and economic orbit of the United States) and to provide a source of benefits to American economic interests.

Military aid has been selectively doled out to those regimes which are clearly amenable to the presence of American political and economic interests. Stabilizing antisocialist regimes friendly to the United States, regardless of their internal character, has resulted in bolstering many authoritarian governments since the 1950s, including regimes in Taiwan, Spain, Greece, Vietnam, South Korea, Iran, the Philippines, and numerous Latin American nations. The selective nature of distribution has, of course, been evident as well in providing purely economic assistance. For example, when the left-leaning Goulart government came to power in Brazil in 1962, American aid dropped from $82 million to $15 million. Following Goulart's overthrow by a military coup in 1965, aid again jumped to over $120 million (Sherman, 1972:168).

In sum, foreign aid can be seen as an example of how government and business interests mesh in the area of foreign policy. Assistance programs to the underdeveloped nations or even to the war-ravaged Western European societies have never been designed on the basis of magnanimity alone. The altruism of America in the post-World War II world has in reality been shaped mainly by political and economic considerations.

THE STATE-CORPORATE NEXUS IN SUMMARY

We have presented a picture of the structure of power in American society as a duality: Two institutions, the state and the corporation, dominate the resources of power and the authoritative capacity to apply those resources. Power in both corporation and state is highly concentrated, on the one hand within a few hundred giant corporations and on the other within the top policymaking and administrative bodies of the federal government, particularly the executive. It is the leaders of these organizations—economic and political elites—who exercise maximum societal power; it is they who decide the issues which most basically shape the pattern of social life.

In their societal functions these two institutions are mutually supportive. The symbiotic relationship between them is one wherein the corporation controls the economic conditions which provide a favorable social and political climate, while the state, in turn, offers the corporation the assurance of growth and continued profits through a favorable tax structure, the provision of a market for surplus production, increasing socialization of investment, the regulation of fiscal policy, and a business-oriented foreign policy.

Within the context of a capitalist system, economic resources are usually convertible into political power. Thus, the policies of government generally tend to reflect the interests of the economically powerful—in American society, primarily the giant corporations. This is evidenced particularly in the areas of taxation, spending, and foreign policy. With virtually unimpaired access to government leaders through such mechanisms as lobbying, campaign financing, and the interchange of personnel, the corporation is enabled to exert constant influence on the shaping of public policy. But above all, government policy must reflect the general needs of the corporate system simply on the basis of the latter's control of the society's productive resources.

That big business interests are the chief beneficiaries of government policies and maintain ready access to political officials should not imply, of course, that other societal interests do not benefit from state functions; obviously they do. And it is equally clear that noncorporate sectors of the society often successfully pressure political decision makers through much the same mechanisms as the affluent and the corporations. Labor unions, for example, have been an extraordinarily effective interest group during the past four decades, and the demands of other groups, such as blacks and women, have also been gradually responded to by government at all levels. In these cases the pluralist perspective of American politics, stressing the actions of interest groups and the inability of any one of them to dominate public policy decisions continually, seems sound.

But despite such cases, the basic structure of the political economy remains intact. As such, the corporation is the nucleus of that system, with overwhelming power to control the economic status of the society and to apply effective political pressure. The application of government resources to various societal interests is therefore heavily weighted in favor of the corporation.

Moreover, no other segment of the society is so routinely active in the policymaking process as big business. The power of organized labor, for example, is not a function of its ability to influence the shape of public policies. Only rarely are labor leaders consulted about (or participate in) the formation of government policy, and then only on issues that are labor-related. This is considerably different from the constant interplay of business and government elites.

Of course, to assume that big businessmen can always influence government policy to their liking or that top corporate and government decision makers never disagree on various societal issues is nonsensical. Neither pluralists, elitists, nor class theorists would make such claims. Despite the facts that the functional positions of economic and political elites frequently overlap and that they maintain constant communication with each other, dominant business interests are not the decisive factors on all issues faced by government. What is most important, however, is that *business's views are actively solicited and play a key part in policy development*. The personnel of no other institution in the society are so carefully consulted on all key issues or have such ease of access to top public policymakers.

In the end, government cannot stray too far from the maintenance of a stable economic system. There is, in other words, a limiting framework which constrains government activity, and in American society that framework is drawn most clearly by the dominant economic institution, the corporation. Thus, government leaders, regardless of party, must ultimately submit to the basic needs of that institution. In the arena of interest group activity, the corporation retains a highly advantageous position. Whether the corporation executes power in any particular instance may be less important than the fact that it generally has the capacity to act if it so desires.

One need not see conspiracy among political and economic elites to recognize the mutuality of their interests. The state can do nothing without the support of the society's productive system, and the converse is also true. Thus, state and corporation are both integral parts of the capitalist socioeconomic order. Whether or not politicians and corporate executives collude is, in the final analysis, only incidental to the state-corporate relationship. Collusion may facilitate the relationship, but it does not shape it. In a class stratified society in which economic power is so highly concentrated, those at the top of the stratification system who own or control the society's wealth hold a tremendous advantage over other groups in gaining access to the state and making it work in their interests.

REFERENCES

Alexander, Herbert E. 1976. *Financing Politics*. Washington, D.C.: Congressional Quarterly Press.

Anderson, Charles. 1974. *The Political Economy of Social Class*. Englewood Cliffs: Prentice-Hall.

Baran, Paul, and **Paul Sweezy.** 1966. *Monopoly Capital*. New York: Monthly Review Press.

Baratz, Morton. 1956. "Corporate Giants and the Power Structure," *Western Political Quarterly* 9 (June):406-415.

Barber, Richard J. 1970. *The American Corporation*. New York: Dutton.

Barnet, Richard J. 1972. *Roots of War*. Baltimore: Penguin.

_____, and **Ronald E. Müller.** 1974. *Global Reach*. New York: Simon and Schuster.

Bernstein, Marver H. 1955. *Regulating Business by Independent Commission*. Princeton: Princeton U. Press.

Clayton, James L. 1972. "The Fiscal Cost of the Cold War to the United States: The First 25 Years, 1947-1971." *Western Political Quarterly* 25 (September):375-395.

Congressional Quarterly. a:1974. *Dollar Politics*. Vol. 2. Washington, D.C.

_____. b:1974. *The Washington Lobby*. 2nd ed. Washington, D.C.

_____. 1977. *Congressional Ethics*. Washington, D.C.

Dolbeare, Kenneth M. 1974. *Political Change in the United States*. New York: McGraw-Hill.

Domhoff, G. William. 1970. *The Higher Circles*. New York: Vintage.

_____. 1974. *The Bohemian Grove*. New York: Harper and Row.

_____. 1979. *The Powers That Be*. New York: Vintage.

Dye, Thomas R. 1976. *Who's Running America?* Englewood Cliffs: Prentice-Hall.

Ehrenreich, Barbara, and **John Ehrenreich.** 1971. *The American Health Empire*. New York: Vintage.

Ellsworth, Larry Paul. 1973. "Defense Procurement: 'Everyone Feeds at the Trough'." In Mark J. Green (ed.), *The Monopoly Makers*. New York: Grossman.

Epstein, Edwin M. 1968. *Corporations, Contributions, and Political Campaigns*. Berkeley: Institute of Governmental Studies, University of California.

_____. 1969. *The Corporation in American Politics*. Englewood Cliffs: Prentice-Hall.

Fellmeth, Robert. 1970. *The Interstate Commerce Commission*. New York: Grossman.

Finney, John W. 1974. "Military Budget Spurs Economy." *New York Times* 123 (February 27):9.

Fitzgerald, A. Ernest. 1972. *The High Priests of Waste*. New York: Norton.

Fox, J. Ronald. 1974. *Arming America*. Cambridge: Harvard U. Press.

Freitag, Peter J. 1975. "The Cabinet and Big Business: A Study of Interlocks." *Social Problems* 23 (December):137-152.

Goldwasser, Thomas. 1977. "The Official Flow to Private Industry." *New York Times* 126 (April 3):III-14.

Green, Felix. 1970. *The Enemy*. New York: Random House.

Green, Mark J. 1975. *Who Runs Congress?* New York: Bantam.

_____. 1972. *The Closed Enterprise System*. New York: Grossman.

Greenberg, Edward S. 1974. *Serving the Few*. New York: Wiley.

Harris, Fred R. 1977. "The Politics of Corporate Power." In Ralph Nader and Mark J. Green (eds.), *Corporate Power in America*. Baltimore: Penguin.

Kahl, Joseph A. 1967. *The American Class Structure*. New York: Holt, Rinehart and Winston.

Katznelson, Ira, and **Mark Kesselman.** 1975. *The Politics of Power*. New York: Harcourt Brace Jovanovich.

Kolko, Gabriel. 1967. *The Triumph of Conservatism.* Chicago: Quadrangle.
———————. 1969. *The Roots of American Foreign Policy.* Boston: Beacon.
Kraar, Louis. 1977. "How Lockheed Got Back Its Wings." *Fortune* 96 (October):199-210.
Lindblom, Charles. 1978. "The Business of America Is Still Business." *New York Times* 127 (January 4):A19.
Lukas, J. Anthony. 1976. *Nightmare: The Underside of the Nixon Years.* New York: Bantam.
Magdoff, Harry. 1969. *The Age of Imperialism.* New York: Monthly Review Press.
Mankoff, Milton, and **Linda Majka.** 1975. "Economic Sources of American Militarism." *Society* 12 (May-June):69–72.
McConnell, Grant. 1966. *Private Power and American Democracy.* New York: Knopf.
Melman, Seymour. 1965. *Our Depleted Society.* New York: Dell.
Miliband, Ralph. 1969. *The State in Capitalist Society.* New York: Basic.
Mintz, Beth. 1975. "The President's Cabinet, 1897-1972: A Contribution to the Power Structure Debate." *Insurgent Sociologist* 5 (Spring):131-148.
Mintz, Morton, and **Jerry S. Cohen.** 1971. *America, Inc.* New York: Delta.
Moore, Beverly C., Jr. 1973. "The FCC: Competition and Communications." In Mark J. Green (ed.), *The Monopoly Makers.* New York: Grossman.
Pillai, K. G. J. 1973. "The CAB as Travel Regulator." In Mark J. Green (ed.), *The Monopoly Makers.* New York: Grossman.
Reich, Michael. 1978. "Military Spending and Production for Profit." In Richard C. Edwards, Michael Reich, and Thomas E. Weisskopf (eds.), *The Capitalist System.* 2nd ed. Englewood Cliffs: Prentice-Hall.
Roose, Diana. 1975. "Top Dogs and Top Brass: An Inside Look at a Government Advisory Committee." *Insurgent Sociologist* 5 (Spring):53-63.
Serber, David L. 1975. "Regulating Reform: The Social Organization of Insurance Regulation." *Insurgent Sociologist* 5 (Spring):83-105.
Sherman, Howard. 1972. *Radical Political Economy.* New York: Basic.
Sherrill, Robert. 1970. "The War Machine." *Playboy* 17 (May):134ff.
Shoup, Laurence H. 1975. "Shaping the Postwar World: The Council on Foreign Relations and United States War Aims During World War II." *Insurgent Sociologist* 5 (Spring):9-52.
Stanley, David T., Dean E. Mann, and **Jameson W. Doig.** 1967. *Men Who Govern.* Washington, D.C.: Brookings Institution.
Stern, Philip M. 1974. *The Rape of the Taxpayer.* New York: Vintage.
Suits, Daniel B. 1977. "Agriculture." In Walter Adams (ed.), *The Structure of American Industry.* 5th ed. New York: Macmillan.
Szymanski, Albert. 1978. *The Capitalist State and the Politics of Class.* Cambridge: Winthrop.
Thayer, George. 1973. *Who Shakes the Money Tree?* New York: Simon and Schuster.
Thelen, David P. 1976. "Our Government: A Wholly Owned Subsidiary." *Progressive* 40 (December):15-19.

Tuckman, Howard P. 1973. *The Economics of the Rich*. New York: Random House.

Turner, Jonathan H., and Charles E. Starnes. 1976. *Inequality: Privilege and Poverty in America*. Pacific Palisades: Goodyear.

U.S. Congress. 1979. *Congressional Record — House* 125 (June 22):H5023-H5029.

Vogel, David. 1978. "Why Businessmen Distrust Their State: The Political Consciousness of American Corporate Executives." *British Journal of Political Science* 8 (January):45–78.

Whitt, J. Allen. 1973. "Californians, Cars and Technological Death." *Society* 10 (July-August):30-38.

Winter, Bernard. 1977. "Health Care: The Problem Is Profits." *Progressive* 41 (October):16-19.

Yarmolinsky, Adam. 1971. *The Military Establishment*. New York: Harper and Row.

chapter 8

institutional leaders

*The influential are those who get the most of
what there is to get . . . Those who get the most
are* elite; *the rest are* mass.

Harold Lasswell

Since the state and the corporation are the most important institutions of power in America and other modern capitalist societies, our attention now turns to those who manage and control these institutions. Governments and corporations do not run themselves. They are directed by living beings who each day make decisions involving the application of human and material resources. To think of political and economic institutions as self-generating is to reify —that is, to attribute an objective reality to social relationships or abstract concepts. One cannot "see" an economy or a state any more than one can "see" honesty, justice, or love. Thus, to speak of the economy as having its ups and downs or the government acting in this way or that is to imply that somehow humans themselves are not responsible for these actions, that organizations and institutions have an independent existence of their own. This is simply not the case.

Not only do people run economic and political institutions, but only a *few* people run them. As was explained in chapter 4, the organizational tendency toward oligarchy seems to be one of the few fairly stringent "laws" of sociology. At best, those who occupy the command positions of the American political economy number no more than a few thousand, a fraction of a percentage of the populace. The same, of course, is true of all industrial societies, and on this point there is little apparent difference between modern capitalist and socialist systems.

Our concern in this chapter is with the sociological composition of those who head the dominant institutions: the corporate and political elites. Basically we want to know who these people are in terms of social origins and how they have reached the top. Specifically we will concentrate on two areas of inquiry:

1. What are the *patterns* of elite recruitment in the United States? That is, from which class, ethnic, religious, and other social categories do institutional leaders come, and how have these patterns changed over time?

2. What is the *process* of elite recruitment? That is, how do people acquire power positions? Have the routes leading to power remained stable, allowing the same groups to reach the top for many generations, or has the process accommodated previously excluded groups, such as working classes and ethnic and racial minorities?

Determining the social backgrounds of top decision makers can tell us much about the power structure of a society. The decisions of institutional leaders are never made in a social vacuum but are greatly influenced by their social experiences. We are all captives not only of our society's culture but of its subcultures as well, especially those revolving around class and ethnicity. Like others in their society, leaders come to see social issues in different ways depending on the perspectives and attitudes acquired within different social environments. And those perspectives and attitudes subsequently influence their actions within the realms of power; elites do not reach decisions with totally objective minds.

Knowing the social backgrounds of elites also provides an understanding of the changing—or unchanging—nature of the power structure, what Pareto and Mosca referred to as "elite circulation." While determining the social characteristics of elites does not necessarily prove that one particular group or another controls the society's key institutions, it certainly shows to what extent there is equal access to power for all societal groups.

Furthermore, if knowing elites' social backgrounds cannot serve as a totally reliable means of determining which groups control key institutions, it can give us good leads. Political sociologists recognize the overriding influence of social background (class and ethnicity in particular) in mass political activities such as voting and ideological preference. In the same way it is reasonable to assume that leaders too will generally reflect their class and ethnic backgrounds in power actions. Thus, if elites are disproportionately drawn from certain class, ethnic, sex, and other social groups, we may infer that the interests of those groups will more readily be served by elites' collective actions and decisions.

Elites and Democratic Ideology

Equality of opportunity is one of the strongest elements of the ideology of America and other Western democratic societies. Differences in wealth, status, and power may exist (though even these are understated), but as long as the opportunity structure provides everyone an equal chance to maximize his or her share of society's rewards, the system is regarded as just. If there are no impregnable barriers to upward movement, social attainment is in the long run the result of individual ability and effort, whereby the most able and hard-working occupy the important and well-rewarding positions.

It is particularly within the power hierarchies of these societies that democratic ideology seems to insist most strongly on such an open placement system. Indeed in the minds of many it is the availability of power to all social elements that distinguishes democratic from authoritarian systems. Traditional views of Western social democracy have been altered somewhat with the general acceptance of the view that a *few always* rule, but the idea of an open process of elite recruitment remains fundamental. One notable study of elites, for example, proclaims that "Democracy differs from oligarchy not in the presence or absence of an elite who wield most influence, but in the closed or open, representative or unrepresentative, responsible or unresponsible character of the elite" (Lasswell et al., 1952:preface). Elite rule is recognized as necessary and unavoidable, but it is understood that democratic social structures are preserved so long as entrance into positions of power and privilege is not limited to a single group and that these positions are allocated on the basis of achievement rather than birth.

What is assumed in this ideal picture is an opportunity structure that does in fact permit individuals of various social backgrounds to begin the quest for wealth, prestige, and power at the same point, with the same social resources. A good analogy is a foot race. If the participants do not begin the race at the same point, the competition is obviously unfair; those starting closer to the finish line have a built-in advantage, and the winner does not necessarily represent the runner who is actually fastest. In the same way, only if all persons begin at the same point in the society's opportunity structure can we be sure that individual ability and effort are really the determining factors in the attainment of high social position rather than the result of built-in social advantages.

In reality, of course, the opportunity structure is *not* set up so that everyone is placed at a common starting point. Instead it is arranged so as to automatically favor some over others. Despite the fact that in modern industrial societies birth is no longer the key factor in determining one's place on the social hierarchy, those with higher class and status origins have considerable advantages over those of lower social origins. If the society's opportunity structure were in fact equal for everyone, we would find a random distribution of persons of various class, ethnic, religious, and other social backgrounds in the highest positions of wealth, prestige, and power. What we find, though, is a highly disproportionate representation of select social groups, particularly in the very highest positions of societal power.

ELITE PATTERNS

What are the dominant social characteristics of the holders of power positions in the United States and other advanced capitalist societies? And how stable have these patterns been over long periods of time?

Class Origin

Even in societies such as the United States, where mobility is valued, expected, and not uncommon, class origins remain, for most, the major factor in accounting for their ultimate social position. Where individuals finally end up on the social hierarchy is attributable to their family's class position more than anything else. It might be facetiously claimed that those who want to be successful must carefully choose their families! Class origin becomes a key determinant of social placement, for it sets into motion so many of the society's mechanisms for channeling persons: education, occupation, primary group interaction, and even marriage.

Determining the class origins of any group, even those at the top of a society's power structure presents some difficulties. First, the term "class" has been inconsistently used by social scientists. Some see class in terms of wealth, others see it as life-style, and still others as a combination of the two. Furthermore, in their studies, social scientists may use different indicators of class, such as occupation, education, or income. To confuse matters more, there is simply no general agreement on either the number or boundaries of different classes. But however class is defined and regardless of the indicators used, studies have verified the consistency of upper- or upper-middle-class origins of American political and economic elites.

Let us look specifically at the class origins of top leaders of each sphere.

The political elite. Political scientist Donald Matthews asserts that government offices are class-ranked: "The more important the office, the higher the social status of its normal incumbent" (1973:45). This hypothesis is clearly borne out in looking at the class makeup of the American political elite, as well as the top political leaders of other modern capitalist societies.

Almost all studies of the American political elite conclude that the majority of its members come from upper- or upper-middle-class families and have displayed such backgrounds since the founding of the nation. Charles Beard, in a well-known historical study (1913), found that the members of the Constitutional Convention of 1787 were mostly the economic and social notables of their time. They were professional men, merchants, and landowners who, according to Beard, benefited economically from the adoption of the Constitution as it was written. In terms of class origins, those who have occupied the highest posts of political power since that time have not basically changed. Mills (1956:400–404) shows, for example, that the 513 men who occupied the top political offices of president, vice president, Speaker of the House, Cabinet member, and Supreme Court justice between 1789 and 1953 were mainly from well-to-do professional or business families.

Studies of American government leaders in all three branches—

executive, legislative, and judicial—indicate the predominance of those with privileged backgrounds. Warner and his associates (1963:13) studied 11,000 top federal executives and found that well over half had fathers who were professionals, business owners, or executives; only 15 percent were the sons of laborers. A study of the Supreme Court shows that of the 92 men who served in that body up to 1959, only 9 were not from families of economic importance, social prestige, and political influence (Schmidhauser, 1960:32). Even in the Congress, where popular election is the means of attaining office, there remains a clear predominance of individuals with upper- and upper-middle-class backgrounds. Matthews (1973:44) studied the 180 members of the U.S. Senate who served between 1947 and 1957 and concluded that, with few exceptions, they were selected from "near the top of the society's class system." More recent studies of the U.S. Senate and House find no basic differences since then (see for example Zweigenhaft, 1975). In an examination of current elites, Dye (1976:152) finds that of the 250 or so top political decision makers, 86 percent are products of the upper or upper middle class.

In sum, throughout American history top political leaders have been drawn from a narrow social base, not typical of the general populace. They have been and remain, as Matthews puts it, "far from common men in either their origins or their achievements" (1954:23–24).

In this, however, the United States is not unique. A similar pattern holds for political elites of all other Western industrial societies. In Canada, for example, almost all top government officials have traditionally come from at least middle-class families and about one-quarter from the upper class (Porter, 1965:394–395). The domination of the highest political positions by those of privileged social background is also the general rule in Great Britain. The House of Commons, for example, like the American Congress, "is today anything but a microcosm of the nation" (Guttsman, 1963:373). Indeed, the prevalence of middle- or upper-class members of all elements of the political elite of most Western societies is a well-recognized fact (Keller, 1963; Miliband, 1969; Putnam, 1976).

Lenski (1966:327) suggests that the correlation between one's status in the political system and other statuses pertaining to occupation, education, and wealth is becoming stronger in the United States and other industrial societies. One reason for this, according to Lenski, lies in the decline in the number of low-level patronage positions which previously gave men of lower-class backgrounds an opportunity to enter the political arena. With the spread of civil service, based as it is on objective recruitment procedures, the traditional channels for upward mobility within the political system have been reduced. As a result, those who can best afford to finance their political careers are increasingly found at the head of political parties, and those with the better educations generally occupy the most important administrative posts. Persons of sub-middle-class origins are thus shut out of the political system to an even greater extent than they were in an earlier period.

The economic elite. If top-ranking political leaders generally display class origins higher than most in the society, leaders of big business are even more clearly from privileged backgrounds.

Knowing the backgrounds of economic leaders is often a question of judgment, for we must rely mostly on what business executives themselves tell us. Thus, there are more than the usual difficulties in determining class origins. Businessmen's perceptions of the extent of their upward mobility may be greater than what they have actually experienced. The public image of the poor boy who has made it to the top is far more favorable than that of an executive who has inherited his position or whose place at the top was never in doubt. Hence, business leaders may sometimes exaggerate the humbleness of their origins. Although this is also true of political leaders, their pasts are subject to much greater public exposure than is true of top officials of the business world; it is therefore more difficult to sustain a "born in a log cabin" image if this is not actually the case. Despite these methodological difficulties, however, it is a basic conclusion of most studies of the corporate elite of the United States and other advanced capitalist societies that their members' origins are usually from the top or near the top of the social hierarchy.

One important study (Warner and Abegglen, 1963:14–16) concludes that two of every three top American business executives come from families whose economic and social positions were well above the average for the nation. Most are sons of business owners or executives, or of professional men such as lawyers, doctors, and engineers; only 15 percent are sons of laborers. It is significant that this study investigated 8,000 business leaders from a variety of industries and geographic areas, a somewhat inflated economic elite. The study included, in other words, executives of not only the most important industries in the economy but a great many which are of only minor significance. Even with the inclusion of such a relatively large number, the researchers conclude that "Whatever our national hopes, the business leaders of America are a select group, drawn for the most part from the upper ranks" (p. 14).

Other studies have confirmed the upper- or upper-middle-class origins of the business elite since the emergence of the United States as an industrial society. Newcomer (1955:62), for example, looked at business leaders of 1900, 1925, and 1950 and found no significant differences at these times in the proportion of the poor among them, though there was some decline in the proportion of the wealthy and a corresponding increase in the middle-income groups. Keller's (1953) study of three generations of business leaders found that 57 percent in 1950 were from the homes of business owners or managers, while only one-fourth originated in lower-class homes. Going back even further, Lipset and Bendix (1959: 122–123) conclude that "since 1801 a majority of prominent businessmen have come from families already well-established economically," while "the proportion of business leaders coming from families of workers and small farmers has also remained relatively stable."

More recent studies indicate little significant change in these patterns. A 1970 study reported that only 16 percent of American corporate chief executives were sons of blue-collar workers or farmers. "All the rest got a firsthand view of the executive world from fathers with an entrepreneurial frame of mind or who closely served those who did. Forty-five percent of their fathers stood at the very top of the business hierarchy either as founder, chairman of the board, or president of a company, or as a self-employed businessman" (Diamond, 1970:323). A group profile of the American corporate elite compiled in 1976 showed an increasing number of top executives referring to their backgrounds as "lower middle class," indicating the apparent movement of more men of modest class origins into top business leadership. However, these executives' self-proclaimed class origins are belied by the fact that about three-quarters of their fathers held upper- or upper-middle-class occupations: business executive, professional, or head of the same corporation (Burck, 1976:174).

The predominance of upper- and upper-middle-class men in the business elites of other Western societies is even more pronounced than in the United States. For example, Porter found that almost one-third of Canadian business leaders in 1960 had inherited their positions from their own families or their in-laws. Using additional indicators, he concluded that 82 percent of the economic elite came from middle-class origins or above; few rose to the top from low positions (Porter, 1965: 291–292). An updated study finds even greater upper-class exclusivity among the Canadian business elite. Clement (1975:209) concludes that "Few members of the elite could be said to have been selected meritocratically in the sense that they have worked their way up through the corporate bureaucracy without the advantage of high class origins." A study of corporate presidents in six Western European nations (Hall et al., 1969) indicates an overwhelming presence of upper-class men in such positions, ranging from 69 percent in Great Britain to over 85 percent in France. Those from working-class families are an even smaller percentage than among the American corporate elite.[1]

Class origin in sum. As for class origins, then, it is quite apparent that the top leaders of government and business in the United States, as well as other modern capitalist societies, are not typical of the general populace. Prewitt and Stone (1973:137) estimate that the wealthiest one-fifth of American families contribute about nine of every ten leaders of the political economy, and the next wealthiest fifth contribute most of the remainder (Figure 8-1). When elites of education, the military, and the media are combined with those of government and business, the same general pattern is evident. Dye (1976:165) concludes that while the upper-class segment of American society is estimated at only 1 percent,

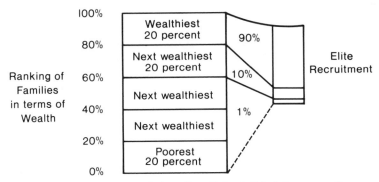

Figure 8-1 Class Origins of the Elite of the Political Economy. Source: From THE RULING ELITES by Kenneth Prewitt and Alan Stone. Copyright © 1973 by Kenneth Prewitt and Alan Stone. Reprinted by permission of Harper & Row, Publishers, Inc.

30 percent of these institutional elites are upper class in origin and 90 percent are either upper or upper middle class. Only 3 percent of those at the top are lower middle or lower class in origin. In sum, the Horatio Alger myth (the belief in great leaps in upward mobility during one's lifetime or from one generation to another) is, so far as top leadership positions are concerned, just that—myth more than reality.

1.   In Japan, the business elite's uncommon social origins are perhaps even more noticeable than in North America or Western Europe. Top executives come principally from the urban upper class, with only a tiny percentage from the working class or even the lower middle class, a pattern which has intensified in recent decades (see Mannari, 1974:215).

But elites of the political economy are not only atypical in their class origins. They display a similar uniqueness in other key social characteristics as well.

Education

Education is generally recognized as the key to upward mobility in all modern societies. There is a powerful relationship between one's position on the class and status hierarchies and the extent and quality of one's education. Most simply, those with the best educations obtain the highest rewarding and most prestigious positions. It is not surprising, then, that the top leaders of the political economy are almost without exception highly educated and disproportionately graduates of the top-rated schools. In short, elite educational levels are considerably higher than those of the society as a whole.

Nearly all top institutional leaders in the United States today are college-trained, and more than half hold advanced degrees. At the pre-college level, 18 percent of corporate leaders and 10 percent of governmental leaders attended private schools, a strikingly large percentage when one considers that when they were attending these schools, only 6 or 7 percent of the general population was enrolled in private schools (Dye, 1976:155–156). Similar educational patterns are evident among the elites of Canada and other advanced capitalist societies (Miliband, 1969; Porter, 1965).

In developing societies, it is to be expected that power elites will display much higher educational backgrounds than the general populace. But in modern industrial societies, it is usually assumed that the availability of higher education is less class biased. Indeed, in contrast to traditional, preindustrial societies, education in modern societies is often seen as a means of breaking the hold of the upper classes on the acquisition of elite positions. The formula is simple. Presumably, in bureaucratically organized corporate and governmental systems, objective qualifications and merit rather than class and status are the critical factors in the selection of personnel. Even for positions of leadership, a set of functional skills are called for which are attained through education, not family background. Thus, as those of lower class and status origins gain greater access to higher education, they can increasingly enter the ranks of economic and political power.

What this formula assumes, however, is that access to higher education is in fact equalized for all. This is not the case, though, even in the United States, where equality of educational opportunity has traditionally been more strongly supported than in most societies. As is seen in

TABLE 8-1 Social Class Origins of U.S. College Entrants (% of each class entering college)

Social Class	1920	1940	1950	1960	1970 Males	Females
Upper and upper middle	40	70	75	80	90	86
Lower middle	8	20	38	50	70	57
Upper working	2	5	12	25	48	32
Lower working	0	0	2	4	20	10
% of total age group entering college	6	16	22	33	53	41

Source: From Robert J. Havighurst and Bernice L. Neugarten, SOCIETY AND EDUCATION, Fourth
Edition. Copyright © 1975 by Allyn and Bacon, Inc., Boston. Reprinted with permission.

Table 8-1, educational access is heavily class biased. Those of the upper and upper middle classes attend college to a far greater extent than those of working- and lower-class groups.

It is also apparent, however, that an increasing number of working-class individuals are entering college, a trend evident not only in the United States but in all industrial societies. Does this mean that educational opportunities—and thus the base for elite recruitment—are broadening? Unquestionably access to higher education has become more equalized in terms of *amount* (though there remain great disparities among classes). But with the widening of higher education to larger numbers and diverse classes, the *quality* and *prestige* of one's education have become more important placement criteria. In previous times, those with college degrees automatically qualified for the pool out of which the political and economic elites were drawn. Obviously this is no longer so. As a result, the elite pool is now limited by the type of school attended and the prestige of the school rather than simply the possession of a college degree. There is a great variety among the 2,500 colleges and universities in the United States, and there is an evident relationship between social class and type of school attended. Those of privileged social origins attend prestigious Ivy League and other private institutions, while those from lower income groups go primarily to state colleges and universities or junior colleges (Karabel, 1972).

Merely being a college graduate, then, does not necessarily measurably increase one's chances at attaining an elite position. Those of higher class origins who are able to secure education at top-ranked schools hold a decided advantage since it is from those schools that elites are heavily recruited. This fact is borne out by Dye's finding that over half the corporate elite and almost as many of the governmental elite are graduates of 12 extremely prestigious private universities such as Harvard, Yale, and Stanford (1976:156). This seems to hold true for other Western industrial societies as well. Clement (1975:242) notes that in Canada, "Obviously, not only attending university, but which university, makes a considerable difference for movement into the elite."

Furthermore, many top positions in government and the corporation now require advanced degrees. Studies of both governmental and corporate elites show a consistent increase in the number of persons with postgraduate training (Warner and Abegglen, 1963; Warner et al., 1963). About 65 percent of the top corporate executives, for example, attended graduate school (Burck, 1976:175). The need for graduate training further filters out those of lower social classes, since those attending academically high-ranked and prestigious undergraduate schools enjoy a substantial advantage in gaining admission to graduate and professional schools.

Increasingly, then, elite positions in the political economy assume not simply higher education but particular *kinds* of higher education: certain schools, certain types of schools, certain degrees. Consequently, despite the expanded higher educational opportunities for working-class and lower-middle-class individuals, those at the top of the class structure retain a sizable head start in entering the pool from which elites are selected.[2]

Race, Religion, and National Origin

Among advanced capitalist societies, the United States and Canada are noticeably heterogeneous, both made up of a variety of ethnic, religious, and racial groups. In societies with such varied social complexions, there tends to develop a system of majority-minority relations wherein those of the dominant or majority ethnic group appropriate the most desirable occupational and social positions and relegate persons of lower ethnic status to the lesser ones. Ethnicity (that is, race, religion, national origin, or a combination of these) thus becomes a factor in the distribution of the society's rewards. In all heterogeneous societies there is a clustering of ethnic groups at various points of the economic and power hierarchies. Those at the top are disproportionately members of the dominant ethnic group, while those at the bottom are disproportionately of lower status —that is, *minority*—ethnic groups.

The dominant ethnic group in American society from the very beginning of its history has been white, Anglo-Saxon, and Protestant (WASP). Those who have been part of this group or whose origins have

2.   For a discussion of class differentials in education, see Rossides (1976:ch. 6).

been culturally close to it (such as other northwest European Protestants) have enjoyed easier access to positions at the top of the society's economic and political systems. As sociologists Nathan Glazer and Daniel Moynihan have written:

> The original Americans became "old" Americans or "old stock," or "white Anglo-Saxon Protestants," or some other identification which indicated they were not immigrants or descendants of recent immigrants. These original Americans already had a frame in their minds, which became a frame in reality, that placed and ordered those who came after them. Those who were like them could easily join them. It was important to be white, of British origin, and Protestant. If one was all three, then even if one was an immigrant, one was really not an immigrant, or not for long (Glazer and Moynihan, 1970:15).

Just as it has been commonly assumed that one's class of birth is no impediment to upward mobility, it has also been traditionally believed that ethnicity is not an obstacle for any particular individual in his or her quest for a higher social position. As collectivities, all ethnic groups are seen as following a similar developmental course, entering the society at the bottom but rising over a generation or so, dependent on the desire and initiative of its individual members. Again, the assumption of an equal opportunity structure for all is implied.[3]

But just as class serves as a gatekeeper to the society's top power positions, so too ethnicity is a strong factor in the process of elite recruitment. The myth of equal opportunity does not conform to the reality of ethnic discrimination. With slight changes from time to time and from sector to sector, WASP dominance has been the general rule at the highest levels of the political economy.

Indeed, other than class origin, ethnicity has been the predominant criterion of social placement throughout American history. For some groups, such as blacks, Hispanic Americans, and native Americans, it has even superseded class. Let us look specifically at the effects of ethnicity on the makeup of economic and political elites.

The business elite. The American business elite has traditionally been made up overwhelmingly of northwest European Protestants —specifically Episcopalians and Presbyterians —with Catholics and Jews, particularly of southern and eastern European origin, underrepresented.

---

3. This view has been commonly adopted not only by the general public but even among sociologists (Metzger, 1971:628).

Keller (1953) found that 89 percent of top business leaders in 1900, and 85 percent in 1950, were Protestant, most of British descent; Catholics in each of these years comprised 7 percent and Jews 3 and 5 percent, respectively. Other studies have corroborated these findings (Marger, 1974; Mills, 1956; Newcomer, 1955). By 1976 little had changed, with Catholics only 14 percent and Jews 6 percent of the corporate elite (Burck, 1976:175).

The absence of non-Protestants at the top of the business world differs for particular industries. For example, Jews have been markedly successful in reaching top positions in the motion picture and television industries and in retailing, while they have been almost wholly excluded from banking and utilities (Institute of Social Research, 1964; Kiester, 1968; Ward, 1965). Furthermore, where they have been successful in the corporate world, Jews have more commonly entered the elite through the growth of their own firms rather than by climbing the bureaucratic ladder of well-established corporations (Marger, 1974; Porter, 1965).

Although they have penetrated the top of other major institutions in small numbers in recent years, blacks remain almost totally unrepresented in the executive suites and board rooms of American corporations. Dye's assertion that "it is justifiable to conclude that very few blacks are in any positions of authority in America" is borne out in the extreme within the corporate world.

In Canada, the major historical ethnic division has been between Anglo- and French-Canadians, though in the last several decades a significant infusion of other ethnic groups has occurred. Though both British and French ethnic groups in Canada are "charter" groups, having been present at the society's founding, the British have generally been the dominant group, even in Quebec, where they constitute a numerical minority. The differences between Anglo- and French-Canadians in access to elite positions is particularly noticeable within the economic realm. Porter (1965:286) notes that even though those of British origin made up only one-half the Canadian population in 1951, the economic elite was almost exclusively British. French-Canadians were 33 percent of the population but only 6.7 percent of the economic elite. Other ethnic groups of neither British nor French origin were hardly represented at all. More recent findings show a continuing underrepresentation of French-Canadians in the economic elite, though a slight gain is evident. Other Canadian ethnic groups also remain heavily underrepresented (Clement, 1975:237).

The political elite. In the U.S. political realm, the predominance of WASPs at the top of all areas of government remains a clear pattern.

TABLE 8-2 Religious Makeup of the U.S. Congress

	1961		Overall Pop. (1966)	1979		Overall Pop. (1977)
	Senate	House		Senate	House	
Protestant	87%	77%	68%	76%	66%	60%
Catholic	12	21	25	15	27	28
Jewish	1	3	3	7	5	2

Sources: David T. Stanley et al., *Men Who Govern* (Washington: Brookings Institution, 1967), pp. 22–25; *Congressional Quarterly*, 37 (January 13, 1979): 43–52; *Religion in America* (Princeton: Gallup Opinion Index, 1977–1978), p. 37.

Although a Catholic was elected president for the first time in 1960, religious and ethnic minorities are severely underrepresented in the highest positions of the executive, legislature, and judiciary of the federal government. The Brookings Institution study (Stanley et al., 1967:15) of federal political executives, for example, found 77 percent Protestant, 19 percent Catholic, and 4 percent Jewish. One might expect a more proportionate representation of religious groups in the popularly elected Congress, but here too Protestants have been and remain a larger percentage than the overall Protestant population (Table 8-2).

Despite the considerable entrance of blacks into political offices at the local level of government in the past decade, this group remains practically absent at the highest ranks of the federal government. Only two blacks have served in positions of significant authority in the Carter administration: Andrew Young as U.S. Ambassador to the United Nations and Patricia Harris as Secretary of Health, Education, and Welfare. One other black in high office is Thurgood Marshall, associate justice of the Supreme Court, who was appointed in 1966 by President Lyndon Johnson. Marshall was the first black to sit on the Supreme Court. At present, no blacks are in the Senate, and only 17 serve in the House.

The Canadian political elite has been somewhat more equitable in ethnic representation than its American counterpart, though still clearly dominated by the British group. Porter states that "at the level of national politics, although underrepresented, the French have retained something of a co-charter group status with the British." In general, however, the Canadian political elite "has scarcely been representative of Canada's ethnic composition" (Porter, 1965:389).

Male Domination

The highest positions of leadership in the political economy of the United States and similar societies are almost exclusively occupied by males. In the corporate world, women are scarcely present in top-ranking posts. In 1972, of some 6,500 top-ranking officers and directors of the 1,300 largest industrial and nonindustrial American corporations, only 11 were women (Robertson, 1973).

The political elite has been hardly more accessible. At the national level only 1 woman occupies a Cabinet level post, 1 serves in the Senate, and 16 are in the House. No woman has ever been appointed to the Supreme Court. The absence of women from political leadership positions, however, is not limited to the United States. Plainly, the world of high politics is "almost universally a man's world" (Putnam, 1976:32–33).

What impact the women's liberation movement will have on future patterns remains to be seen. In any case, however, it will be many years before anything approaching parity of elite positions for men and women is reached. Since the push for black civil rights began in the late 1950s, only slight penetration of top national elites by blacks has been evident, and there is little reason to expect that the entrance of women into power elites will proceed at a significantly faster pace. We must be careful, of course, to distinguish between local and national patterns. Both groups seem to have been more successful at the local level of government, and in the corporate world too, both blacks and women have begun to enter lower managerial positions in greater numbers. It is at the uppermost echelons, however, that societal power remains a virtual monopoly of white males.

The Composite Leader

At the very highest levels of power in the United States and other advanced capitalist societies, the social backgrounds of leaders are noticeably similar. If we combine the dominant social characteristics of American power elites, the typical leader emerges as a highly educated white male, of northwest European ancestry, Protestant, and the son of an upper- or upper-middle-class family. Warner et al. (1963:31) observe that "the similarities between the executives of big business and those who occupy the top ranks of the federal government are more evident than the differences." The findings of most studies of institutional leadership lend credence to that general conclusion. In short, members of economic and political elites display strongly similar social backgrounds which undergird their close functional relations. Moreover this pattern has not changed appreciably throughout American history.

THE PROCESS OF ELITE RECRUITMENT

We have now seen that despite the rhetoric of equal opportunity, elites of the political economy have been and remain composed overwhelmingly of members of the society's dominant class and status groups. One's chances of entering the confines of political and economic power are determined mainly by the fortunes of one's birth. Does the critical importance of ascribed characteristics such as class origin, ethnicity, and sex mean, then, that individual ability and effort are not factors in elite recruitment? The answer is a qualified "no." Individual talent and effort do become important determinants in the selection of institutional leaders, but only after the competitive field has been thinned out.

The Achievement Factor

The recruitment process can be pictured as a system in which persons are chosen from a potential elite pool. In this reservoir of possible leaders are the individuals with the skills, education, and other qualifications needed to fill elite positions. It is here that competition *does* exist, that the highest achievers *do* display their abilities, and that the best qualified *do* generally succeed. Hence, what is most important is *entering this reservoir of qualified people* (Figure 8-2).

Many in the masses may have leadership abilities, but unless they can gain entrance into the elite pool, their abilities will go unnoticed. Those of higher class and status rank enter more easily into this competition since they have been afforded greater opportunities to acquire the needed qualifications.

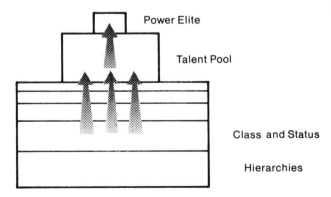

Figure 8-2 The Process of Elite Recruitment.

Self-selection

In addition to formal qualifications, there are less obvious social-psychological factors which tend to narrow the potential elite pool further. "Self-assertion" and "self-elimination" are processes by which those of higher social status assert themselves and those of lower social status eliminate themselves from competition for elite positions (Prewitt and Stone, 1973:140). A young man whose family has been active in politics, who has attended Harvard, and who has established a network of connections to the economic and political power establishments would not be unrealistic in aspiring to a high position in the business or political world. On the other hand, a young man with a less prestigious family background, no connections, and only a high school diploma or even a college degree from a state university would not likely visualize a future place for himself at the top. As Prewitt and Stone (1973:140) explain, such an individual "has few models to emulate, no contacts to put him into the right channels, and little reason to think of himself as potentially wealthy or powerful." Thus, self-selection aids in filtering out those of lower income and status groups from the pool of potential elites. Most eliminate themselves from the competition early in the game.

Social Connections

Following the acquisition of skills necessary to compete for elite places, one must then display them. There is, in a sense, a stage upon which potential elites must exhibit their qualities. Having access to that stage means not only achieving the formal requirements for entering the elite pool (education and others) but also interacting within social circles that count—that is, where incumbent elites are apt to take notice of a talented individual. These are the social connections which come more naturally to those of higher class and status groups and which further filter out otherwise qualified persons from power elites. The familiar adage that "it's not what you know but who you know" is quite applicable in the process of elite recruitment.

Ascriptive Factors

In the end, entrance into the potential elite pool is still only a necessary first step on the route to institutional leadership. The reservoir of qualified people is larger than the number of positions to be filled. It is at this point in the recruitment process that ascriptive factors become critical. Nonrational criteria such as class, ethnicity, and sex, in addition to formal qualifications, may be imposed by incumbent elites in selecting new members. Over these factors the individual has no control.

The case of Jewish absence at the top of the banking industry illustrates the effect of ascriptive factors. A study in the late 1960s reported that although Jews constituted from 12 to 15 percent of the graduates of the Harvard Business School —a favorite recruiting ground of top business and finance firms —only 1 percent of the Harvard Business graduates who ended up in banking were Jews (Kiester, 1968:11).

Elite Penetration by the Less Privileged

Despite impediments such as lower-quality education, minority ethnic status, or lack of social connections, some from the bottom rungs of the social hierarchy *do* penetrate the society's power elites. There is always room at the top for those few who overcome social handicaps, manage to enter the talent pool, and once there, excel. Incumbent elites, in other words, are not totally able to frustrate the entrance of lower-status individuals into positions of power. As Lipset and Bendix (1959:3) state:

> No elite or ruling class controls the natural distribution of talent, intelligence, or other abilities, though it may monopolize the opportunities for education and training. As long as many of those with high abilities belong to the lower strata (and many contemporary studies suggest that this is so), there will be leaders who come from those strata. The chance for potential leaders to develop the skills which will take them up from the ranks may be small, but sooner or later some will break through.

But the penetration of a few from lower social ranks should not be mistaken as common. On the contrary, such cases are clearly exceptional.[4] However, it is the entrance of the few from more humble backgrounds which strengthens the traditional belief that the process of elite recruitment accommodates all, regardless of class and status.

The Systemic Nature of Elite Recruitment

In sum, elite recruitment is most accurately pictured as a process in which the cards are heavily stacked in favor of the society's affluent and highest status groups. The structural forces of class, ethnicity, and sex,

---

4. It should also be obvious, of course, that those who are not qualified to run corporations or governments will not be selected even if they are of privileged class and status origins.

as well as the more subtle social-psychological forces of self-selection, tend to perpetuate the place of dominant groups in key power positions.

This need not be seen, however, as a conscious conspiracy on the part of a ruling class to preserve its power. Rather, the system of elite recruitment is well in place and is largely self-directing. The fact that the social composition of elites tends to be consistent from one generation to another reflects the structural nature of societal power and the selection of power holders. Those who are upper or upper middle class, white, Protestant, of northwest European origin, and male need not conspire to protect their favored social positions; they are automatically afforded easier access to the wealth, education, and connections needed for entrance into power positions. And by the same token, a cumulation of disadvantages automatically works to the detriment of those of lower-class, working-class, and ethnic and sexual minority groups. Lipset and Bendix (1959:198–199) explain this self-sustaining process:

> Occupational and social status are to an important extent self-perpetuating. They are associated with many factors which make it difficult for individuals to modify their status. Position in the social structure is usually associated with a certain level of income, education, family structure, community reputation and so forth. These become part of a vicious circle in which each factor acts on the other in such a way as to preserve the social structure in its present form, as well as the individual family's position in that structure.

Thus, top power holders in almost all institutional spheres quite naturally continue to come predominantly from the same social groups.

Moreover these repetitive patterns of elite recruitment come to be commonly expected among the masses, thereby further strengthening the hold of dominant social groups on top positions. Most people simply do not expect blacks and women, for example, to head giant corporations, to be nominated for the presidency, or to be five-star generals. Social expectations of who should occupy power positions are reinforced by widely held negative stereotypes regarding the capabilities of lower-class and minority groups, helping to make their underrepresentation in power elites a self-fulfilling prophecy.

SUMMARY

Our picture of elite recruitment is mixed, but only slightly so. We have seen that the system is not tightly closed, and thus some persons of lower social origins do find their way to the top. But these are not typical cases.

The outstanding fact of elite recruitment in the United States and other Western industrial societies is that leaders are chosen overwhelmingly from socially dominant groups, and have been for many generations. Patterns of recruitment into power positions indicate an unmistakable correspondence between wealth and power; those of upper- or upper-middle-class origins have considerable advantages in reaching the pinnacle of the political and business worlds. Skills, education, and connections with powerful persons are critical needs for movement into power positions, but differential access to these needs remains rooted in the society's class structure. When class is combined with other ascriptive factors such as ethnicity and sex, upward mobility in the realm of power, so fundamental to democratic ideology, becomes in fact difficult for most and virtually impossible for many. We might say, then, that the system is open, but only slightly so for those of lower social status.

REFERENCES

Beard, Charles. 1913. *An Economic Interpretation of the Constitution*. New York: Macmillan.

Burck, Charles G. 1976. "A Group Profile of the Fortune 500 Chief Executive." *Fortune* 93 (May):173–177/308–312.

Clement, Wallace. 1975. *The Canadian Corporate Elite*. Toronto: McClelland and Stewart.

Diamond, Robert S. 1970. "A Self-Portrait of the Chief Executive." *Fortune* 81 (May):181/320–323.

Dye, Thomas R. 1976. *Who's Running America?* Englewood Cliffs: Prentice-Hall.

Glazer, Nathan, and Daniel P. Moynihan. 1970. *Beyond the Melting Pot*. 2nd ed. Cambridge: MIT Press.

Guttsman, W. L. 1963. *The British Political Elite*. New York: Basic.

Hall, D. J., H. C. deBettignies, and G. Amado-Fischgrund. 1969. "The European Business Elite." *European Business* 23 (October):8–11.

Institute of Social Research. 1964. *Discrimination Without Prejudice: A Study of Promotion Practices in Industry*. Ann Arbor: University of Michigan.

Karabel, Jerome. 1972. "Community Colleges and Social Stratification: Submerged Class Conflict in American Higher Education." *Harvard Educational Review* 42 (November):521–562.

Keller, Suzanne. 1953. "The Social Origins and Career Lines of Three Generations of American Business Leaders." Ph.D. dissertation, Columbia U.

————. 1963. *Beyond the Ruling Class*. New York: Random House.

Kiester, Edwin, Jr. 1968. *The Case of the Missing Executive*. New York: American Jewish Committee, Institute of Human Relations.

Lasswell, Harold D., Daniel Lerner, and C. Easton Rothwell. 1952. *The Comparative Study of Elites*. Stanford: Stanford U. Press.

Lenski, Gerhard. 1966. *Power and Privilege*. New York: McGraw-Hill.

Lipset, Seymour Martin, and Reinhard Bendix. 1959. *Social Mobility in Industrial Society*. Berkeley: U. of California Press.

Mannari, Hiroshi. 1974. *The Japanese Business Leaders*. Tokyo: U. of Tokyo Press.

Marger, Martin. 1974. *The Force of Ethnicity*. Detroit: Wayne State U. Press.

Matthews, Donald. 1954. *The Social Background of Political Decision-Makers*. New York: Random House.

——————————. 1973. *U.S. Senators and Their World*. New York: Norton.

Metzger, L. Paul. 1971. "American Sociology and Black Assimilation: Conflicting Perspectives." *American Journal of Sociology* 76 (January):627–647.

Miliband, Ralph. 1969. *The State in Capitalist Society*. New York: Basic.

Mills, C. Wright. 1956. *The Power Elite*. New York: Oxford U. Press.

Newcomer, Mabel. 1955. *The Big Business Executive*. New York: Columbia U. Press.

Porter, John. 1965. *The Vertical Mosaic*. Toronto: U. of Toronto Press.

Prewitt, Kenneth, and Alan Stone. 1973. *The Ruling Elites*. New York: Harper and Row.

Putnam, Robert D. 1976. *The Comparative Study of Political Elites*. Englewood Cliffs: Prentice-Hall.

Robertson, Wyndham. 1973. "The Highest Ranking Women in Big Business." *Fortune* 90 (April):81–89.

Rossides, Daniel. 1976. *The American Class System*. Boston: Houghton Mifflin.

Schmidhauser, John R. 1960. *The Supreme Court: Its Politics, Personalities, and Procedures*. New York: Holt, Rinehart and Winston.

Stanley, David T., Dean E. Mann, and Jameson W. Doig. 1967. *Men Who Govern*. Washington, D.C.: Brookings Institution.

Ward, Lewis B. 1965. "The Ethnics of Executive Selection." *Harvard Business Review* 43 (March-April):6–39.

Warner, W. Lloyd, and James Abegglen. 1963. *Big Business Leaders in America*. New York: Atheneum.

——————————, Paul P. Van Ryser, Norman H. Martin, and Arvis F. Collins. 1963. *The American Federal Executive*. New Haven: Yale U. Press.

Zweigenhaft, Richard. 1975. "Who Represents America?" *Insurgent Sociologist* 5 (Spring):119–130.

chapter 9

the structure and behavior of elites

Competition among elites means very little to those at the bottom of the heap when the elites have very similar objectives and interests, as is the case in the United States today.

Barrington Moore, Jr.

We have now considered the social origins of power elites in the United States and other advanced capitalist societies and the social routes to power they have seemed to follow. In this chapter we want to look at the structure and behavior of elites—that is, how the powerful relate to each other and the manner in which they exercise their power.

We have noted that there is today little question among observers of politics in society that elites rather than masses actually exercise power, no matter what the society's political structure or ideology. The important question of power analysis, then, is not whether elites or masses rule, but rather *what is the character of elite rule?*

THE AMERICAN ELITE STRUCTURE

Much of the debate concerning power in America and other industrial societies has revolved around the questions of whether (or to what extent) the powerful in various spheres of societal life are centralized in structure, unified in their actions, and alike in social backgrounds. These questions have particular significance in Western societies since it has been assumed that greater concentration of power and cohesiveness among leaders breed a decline of their control by masses, the very antithesis of a democratic sociopolitical order.

The structural and behavioral relations of leaders at the top of the political economy in the United States have been interpreted in correspondence with one or a combination of the major theoretical perspectives of societal power described in Part Two. It will be recalled that both Marxists and elitists see power holders in society as a relatively cohesive group in structure, interests, behavior, and social origins. Pluralists, in contrast, see the powerful as disjointed, scattered among a variety of groups and interests, and unable to rule without basic disagreements on key issues.

Another question has centered on the functions of power elites in society. They may be seen either as exploiters who are unnecessary for the well-being of the society or as indispensable leaders who are entitled to an unequal share of the society's rewards (Prewitt and Stone, 1973:12–19). The first view is generally shared by Marxists and radical elitists, who see leadership groups ruling in their own interests. The second view is usually taken by pluralists and conservative elitists, who see ruling groups as essential, thus meriting their privileges.[1]

---

1. On the issues of societal power, it is often difficult to separate contemporary Marxists or class theorists from radical elitists since their perspectives are closely intertwined on various points. The more evident split, however, is between these two and the pluralists.

Most power structure studies of the past several decades have emanated from the United States and have naturally focused on the American system. Thus we have relatively fewer opportunities to make meaningful cross-national comparisons than would be desirable. However, the political and economic bases of other advanced capitalist societies are not basically unlike those of the United States. Thus much of the following discussion is also broadly applicable to those societies, though it primarily concerns American power elites.

We will briefly look at the most representative works of each of the main schools of thought on the structure, functions, and behavior of power elites and will then attempt to synthesize these views by extracting and combining the most valid points of each. Since they head the most powerful institutions, it is necessary that we look primarily at elites of the state and the economy. Leaders of other institutions such as education, religion, and communications exert power in their particular realms, but it is only in the economic and governmental areas that elite decisions are of broad enough scope to affect comprehensively all members of the society.

Mills: The Radical Elitist View I

More than any single social scientist, the late C. Wright Mills sparked the ongoing debate of the last two decades concerning power in the United States. Writing his most significant works in the 1950s, Mills was a maverick among sociologists of that time, disputing the generally accepted pluralist depiction of the American power structure. Some consider Mills' analysis Marxist (Anderson, 1974:216–222), but he seems to represent the radical elitist view best.

Mill's purpose and method. Mills' purpose in *The Power Elite* (1956), the most important of his writings on American political society, is quite simply the basic starting point of any political sociology: to explain who has power and how it is exercised. He begins by identifying the key institutions in the United States wherein the most consequential and far-reaching decisions are made. Issues involving war and peace, for example, or basic economic policy are those which have societal impact; they are not limited to local areas or specialized interests but affect everyone. The power to decide such issues is the kind of power to which Mills addresses his analysis. He concludes that in post-World War II America, institutions with such power are the giant corporation, the top echelons of the federal government, and the military. It is here that the society's critical policies are determined.

Next, Mills identifies the persons holding the top positions in these institutions, those who actually have the capacity to make basic decisions: in the corporation, officers at the head of the managerial hierarchy; in government, the president and other key political officials mainly of the executive branch; in the military, the Joint Chiefs of Staff. These, then, are the people who comprise the power elite. In Mills' words:

> By the power elite, we refer to those political, economic, and military circles which as an intricate set of overlapping cliques share decisions having at least national consequences. In so far as national events are decided, the power elite are those who decide them (1956:18).

The cohesiveness of the elite. Mills investigates the power elite's sociological characteristics and finds that members are quite similar in general outlook, interests, and social background. These persons have attended the same schools, exhibit similar career patterns, and have, for the most part, been exposed to common socialization experiences. They are, as a result, a socially cohesive group.

But in addition to their common social characteristics, and perhaps of greater importance as a builder of cohesion among them, is their close working relationship. Because their institutions overlap functionally, elites of business, government, and the military find themselves continually interacting with each other. Business leaders do not simply operate in an isolated business world, nor do government leaders or military chiefs function apart from other elites. Rather, the three top groups act as a loose coalition, coming together often on issues which are of mutual concern.

The three primary institutions overlap in the sense that the interests of one complement the interests of the others. Mills argues, for example, that post-World War II government in the United States has expanded its power most noticeably in the area of foreign affairs and has, as a result, established tremendous arms budgets. This, in turn, corresponds with the needs and world view of the military and with those of the giant corporations, which are the chief producers of arms and thus the chief economic beneficiaries of military spending.

Given the interconnections between institutional spheres, elite roles are interchangeable. Businessmen move easily into top government posts, generals retire to positions in the corporate world, and so on. There is a constant back-and-forth movement of personnel between the three realms of power. Thus there are not three power elites, but one.

In sum, given their similar social background the members of the power elite share the same outlook regarding the society's needs. In addition, the overlapping interests and functions of their institutions cause them to come together in a working relationship, further strengthening their common social and psychological orientations. They think the same and act the same because their social and career environments are the same. Like the elites described by Pareto, Mosca, and Michels, Mills' power elite constitutes a cohesive, relatively well-knit group:

> All the structural coincidence of their interests as well as the intricate psychological facts of their origins and their education, their careers and their associations make possible the psychological affinities that prevail among them, affinities that make it possible for them to say of one another: He is, of course, one of us (Mills, 1956:283).

Mills' approach, then, is one that relies not on personal traits to explain the power elite (à la Pareto) or even on organizational needs (à la Michels). Power is not an attribute of "naturally superior" persons, nor does it simply develop out of complex social structures (though Mills would not deny Michels' basic thesis). Rather, Mills explains that great power in American society, indeed in any modern society like the United States, is simply attached to critical institutional positions. Power inheres in vital institutions such as government and corporation, and those who occupy the command positions of these most important societal institutions thus constitute the power elite.

The vertical dimension of the power structure. Mills conceptualizes the hierarchy of power in the United States as a tri-level arrangement: the power elite at the top, the masses at the bottom, and a middle level of power wherein less consequential political decisions are made. This middle level consists essentially of Congress, organized labor, important state and local political officials, and various pressure groups. It is here that the "game of politics" is seemingly played, about which the media regularly report. In fact, however, this power level is of minimal significance when the most important issues of the society are decided: "Undue attention to the middle levels of power obscures the structure of power as a whole, especially the top and bottom. American politics, as discussed and voted and campaigned for, have largely to do with these middle levels, and often only with them" (Mills, 1956:245).

It is at this middle level that a balance of power exists. No one of these groups or institutions is able to dominate or to impose its will on the others at all times. But this plurality of interests is of little consequence so far as the society's larger issues are concerned. None of these groups have the effect of shaping *basic* policies to which they, like the

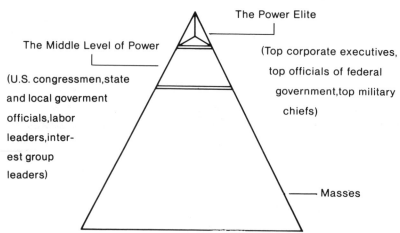

The Power Elite

The Middle Level of Power

(Top corporate executives,
top officials of federal
government,top military
chiefs)

(U.S. congressmen,state
and local goverment
officials,labor
leaders,inter-
est group
leaders)

Masses

Figure 9-1 Mills' Model of the American Power Structure.

masses, must respond. Mills calls this level a "semi-organized stalemate" (1956:297).

At the bottom, the bulk of the populace is relatively disorganized, inert, and in the process of becoming a "mass" —that is, a society which responds with no countervoice to decisions made by a centralized power elite. The transformation of the American public into a mass society is due largely to the nature of mass communications, in which most people only receive but cannot respond to opinions voiced by organized authorities. Political ends are accomplished through successful manipulation of the populace using such primary means as television. According to Mills, "the public is merely the collectivity of individuals each rather passively exposed to the mass media and rather helplessly opened up to the suggestions and manipulations that flow from these media" (1956:305).

Mills in summation. Mills neatly summarizes his view of the structure of power in America:

> The top of modern American society is increasingly unified, and often seems willfully co-ordinated; at the top there has emerged an elite of power. The middle levels are a drifting set of stalemated, balancing forces: the middle does not link the bottom with the top. The bottom of this society is politically fragmented, and even as a passive fact, increasingly powerless: at the bottom there is emerging a mass society (1956:324).

The outline of power in America as presented by Mills resembles the classical elitists' model: a powerful ruling group and a powerless, manipulated mass. But unlike Pareto and Mosca, Mills does not see elites in American society as rightfully occupying the important decision-making positions, much less acting in the interests of the masses. On the contrary, he speaks of a "higher immorality" in which leaders are intellectually mediocre and are neither responsive nor responsible to the public.

Mills in retrospect. The reaction among social scientists and other social observers to Mills' description of power in America was at first mainly negative. *The Power Elite* was published in 1956, and power in the United States during the 1950s was seen by most as a balanced plurality of various interest groups, none of which was dominant (see chapter 3). The idea that a small and relatively cohesive group could determine the basic shape of political and economic life in the society did not sit well with these pluralist assumptions. Not until the late 1960s, after the society had experienced the reality of bitter and often violent domestic conflict as well as the arrogance of presidential power in Vietnam, was Mills' thesis reconsidered. The changed social mood now seemed to make his view of the structure and process of power in the United States more valid.

One must keep in mind that Mills confined his observations to the United States and did not purport to draw any general conclusions regarding power in other societies or even the United States in other historical periods. In fact, he carefully detailed the changing character of the American power structure over the course of its political and social development. Mills' description of the power elite was as he saw it in the 1950s.

Perhaps the most important aspect of Mills' work is that it compelled political sociologists to rethink basic ideas about power in contemporary America. *The Power Elite* has become a classic work largely because of the controversy it initially aroused and still continues to provoke. Indeed, much of the research on power in the United States in the past two decades has been by and large a response to Mills' thesis. Though its details have been subject to much criticism, it remains in a broader sense fresh and stimulating.[2]

Hunter: The Radical Elitist View II

Floyd Hunter's study of top American leadership corroborates Mills' findings of a relatively cohesive power elite. Completed in 1959, three years after Mills' work was published, the stated purpose of Hunter's

2.   For critiques of Mills' power elite thesis, see Domhoff and Ballard (1968).

study was "to learn whether there was a definable national power structure decisive in shaping the general policy course of the country" (p.
160). The findings of a closely knit power elite were earlier offered by
Hunter in a study of the power structure of a single large city (1953),
and the methods employed there were applied to his study of power at
the national level.[3]

Hunter's method consisted of consulting management personnel of
key national interest groups such as the American Medical Association,
the U.S. Chamber of Commerce, the National Association of Manufacturers, the American Federation of Labor, and the Farm Bureau and
asking them to name those persons whom they felt were top national
policymakers. Hunter also surveyed important association officials in all
large population (100,000 or more) cities and asked them to name whom
they felt were top policy influencers in their communities. In these ways
Hunter traced a national leadership network. He then interviewed a
sampling of those named, in order to determine the interrelations of
these leaders and their roles in national policy development.

Through his interviews, questionnaires, and polls, Hunter identified
about 100 men who were consistently named top leaders. These men
knew each other, communicated with each other, and formed a cohesive
group (1959:172–173). Included among this core power group were
representatives of the three institutions Mills had considered critical:
government, military, and big business, the last clearly dominant. In fact,
Hunter concluded that policy issues of societal scope are determined by
big businessmen more than any other leadership group, including political leaders. Politicians, he found, play more of an enacting or administering role rather than actually formulating policy (1959:176). The corporation thus emerges in Hunter's analysis as the seat of greatest power,
a view closely parallel to Mills'. Corporate leaders do not play a direct
participating role in the political arena, but their influence among government officials is what makes them politically powerful.

Although he denies a monolithic power structure, Hunter sees interlocking among elites, particularly those of government and business: "It
is also apparent that each major, particular power structure is related
directly and indirectly, through its personnel, to every other structure"
(1959:138). Key policy decisions are thus communicated between various
elites even though they remain formally separated. Leaders in various
institutions are, as in Mills' analysis, a convergent group whose paths
commonly cross in the performance of their power positions.

The interchange of government and corporate elites is more the
product of a mutuality of functional interests than a natural coming to-

---

3.   This study is discussed in some detail in chapter 10.

gether of men with a strong class consciousness. Most simply, corporate and government leaders interact in their formal activities, and this functional interaction carries over into the social realm, where the power network is further solidified:

> National leaders tell me they have a wide acquaintance among other leaders. Some men are recognized as top policy makers, others as second- and third-rate figures of importance through informal discussions with the higher-ups, still others as front men for specific interests. The acquaintanceship is not confined to persons who serve on the same corporate boards or belong to the same political party or happen to have similar amounts of money in the bank. Friendships, committee work, clubs and recreational associations, customer relations, and financial matters all tend to intertwine definable action patterns. Policy development thus is a prime social function that defies confinement entirely within formally organized political or associational groupings (1959:38).

Hunter, then, sees a basic unity among America's top leadership, though not a formal, conspiratorial relationship. Leaders come together in a natural working arrangement when called for, but the national power structure is "not a single pyramid of influence and authority." Rather, it is "a kind of informal, potential group, representing many of the major influence groups, that acts on specific matters of policy as the need arises" (1959:176). Though disagreements may arise on specific issues, fundamental dominant interests —usually corporate interests —create a "workable unity within the total power structure" (1959:176).

Domhoff: The Marxist View

G. William Domhoff's analysis of power in America is closely akin to Mills' and Hunter's works but is characterized as well by a strong Marxian flavor. Domhoff seeks to show that the upper class in America is essentially a ruling class. If we recall the Marxian idea of ruling class in capitalist society, it is "that class which owns and controls the means of production and which is able, by virtue of the economic power thus conferred upon it, to use the state as its instrument for the domination of society" (Miliband, 1969:23). Domhoff posits that there is in fact a readily apparent relationship between those who own or control a disproportionate amount of the society's wealth and the governmental elite. Significant societal wealth is found within the corporation, and those who dominate this key economic institution through ownership or management do maintain maximum influence in the public policy-forming process. Domhoff calls this group a "governing class":

A governing class is a social upper class which receives a disproportionate amount of a country's income, owns a disproportionate amount of a country's wealth, and contributes a disproportionate number of its members to the controlling institutions and key decision-making groups in that country (1967:142).

Domhoff maintains that members of the upper class themselves occupy many of the top government offices, but where they do not, their political lieutenants work in their behalf: "Leaders within the upper class do not labor alone in dominating the political process. They have the help of hired employees: high level managers and officials in corporations, law firms, foundations, and associations controlled by members of the upper class" (Domhoff, 1971:106).

Unlike Mills and Hunter, who stress the structural factors which bring the power elite together, Domhoff emphasizes the social nature of the governing class. The cohesiveness of this ruling group is largely a product of their common upper-class ties. He identifies the upper class as those who are listed or have close relatives listed in the *Social Register* or its equivalent for a particular city; those having attended or having close relatives who attended a small group of elite prep schools; and those who are members of a small list of very exclusive private clubs or have close relatives who are members.

Through these common points of social interaction, the upper class consolidates a consciousness of purpose and effectively controls the power process. According to Domhoff, it is chiefly through elite men's clubs and through upper-class-dominated policy-planning organizations such as the Committee for Economic Development and the Council on Foreign Relations that the upper class formulates its policy preferences and communicates them to political decision makers. These clubs and organizations thus become major locations of upper-class interaction, not only for social purposes but for functional or working purposes as well (Domhoff, 1974).

Domhoff's emphasis on the social nature of the governing class and its members' mutual ties to recognized upper-class institutions is a serious point of criticism. Political scientist Thomas Dye, who has also closely investigated the nature of elite interaction, refutes Domhoff on the significance of elite club membership, for example. Dye maintains that members of prestigious private clubs are mainly from the corporate elite, with few government leaders represented. Moreover, members are selected *after* they have established themselves in power positions; rarely do they acquire power *because* of club memberships. In any case, so far as the exercise of power is concerned, the clubs, according to Dye (1976:163), "merely help facilitate processes that occur anyway."

Perhaps more importantly, even if there may be a strong presence of political and economic elites in upper-class organizations, to what extent their interaction within these organizations helps to promote control of public policy remains questionable. As Prewitt and Stone point out, "The overrepresentation of a social upper class no doubt gives some common tone and style to the elite circles, but it does not begin to explain what is politically critical about those circles" (1973:159). Sociologist Scott McNall's comment on this point is even more precise:

> No matter how many times it is shown that a few men belong to a few exclusive clubs at which both corporate executives and government officials dine together, this does not provide the information we need to conclude that there is a governing class which controls the government (McNall, 1977:15; see also Dibble, 1968).

Despite this criticism, many of Domhoff's basic conclusions are well founded. Whatever its significance, the social interaction of members of the corporate elite and top-ranking political officials is easily verified empirically. Also Domhoff has shown that even though political leaders may not be found as frequently as corporate leaders on upper-class club rosters, their presence is felt in other ways (Domhoff, 1974). More importantly, he has demonstrated the very clear upper-class participation in important policy-planning groups as well as the overrepresentation of members of the upper class in the most significant federal executive positions.

Baltzell: The Conservative Elitist View

Further evidence of a strong overlap between the upper class and those who head the powerful institutions of American society is provided by sociologist E. Digby Baltzell (1958; 1964). Baltzell's conclusions regarding the interrelations between the upper class and the society's chief power wielders are strikingly similar to Domhoff's: Essentially he sees a ruling class. But in contrast to Domhoff (as well as other elitists and Marxists), Baltzell's view is conservative in that he sees a ruling class as socially beneficial, its special privileges justified.

Baltzell distinguishes three groups at the top of the social hierarchy. First, there is what he simply calls the "elite," made up of top functional leaders of various spheres of social activity. These are the important decision makers of the corporation, the government, education, the media, and so on. Second, there is an upper class, composed of families of established wealth whose members are descendants of elite members of one or more generations ago and who make up a social upper class with a distinct style of life and primary group solidarity. Baltzell has studied closely the American upper class and concludes that unlike other classes, it comprises a distinguishable and self-conscious group. It is, in Weber's terms, a "status community." When this class combines its wealth and status with functional power—that is, when its members are simultaneously elite members—there exists a ruling class, or what Baltzell calls an "establishment." This conceptualization of the power structure closely resembles Domhoff's.

Baltzell sees the need for a society to maintain a system of power which combines the traditional authority deriving from the past with the infusion of new groups into positions of functional power: "The most difficult and delicate problem faced by democratic societies is that of balancing the liberal need for the continuous circulation of individual elites with the conservative need for maintaining a continuity of family authority" (Baltzell, 1964:72). Ideally, then, the establishment is made up of individuals whose power and prestige are inherited, but it remains open to the newly powerful, those who are recruited into the elite on the basis of talent and ability. This requires that members of the elite be accepted into the upper class regardless of ethnic origin or religion. Baltzell emphasizes that without the infusion of new blood from the elite, the upper class will degenerate into a group which neglects its leadership duties and concerns itself only with its rights to privilege. In a sense, Baltzell views the establishment as a "noble aristocracy" which is socialized into accepting its leadership role and understands its societal obligations.

Baltzell finds a great degree of overlapping of the upper class and the elite throughout American history. That is, those who have occupied positions of power in government, the corporation, and other societal institutions have been overwhelmingly representative of those of wealth and prestige. In recent years, however, the upper class has become more narrow in its social composition, excluding those of diverse ethnic and religious origins who have penetrated the society's functional elites. As more Catholics, Jews, and other ethnic and religious minorities have come into positions of power in government, the economy, education, and other areas, they have not been absorbed into the upper class, as they had been in past generations. Baltzell thus sees an open class system operating in the society's functional institutions, with upward mobility from the lower social ranks but an increasingly castelike status system, closing off entrance into the upper class for the new men of power.

Baltzell, then, unlike Domhoff, does not see a close interrelationship of upper class and power elite at the present moment in American history. Although it has done so in past eras, the upper class, according to

Baltzell, does not presently constitute or even necessarily control the power elite. Those of non-upper-class origin are able to enter into top positions of power and may exercise their power independently of the upper class, which is increasingly concerned only with protecting its status and privilege, not with exercising power.

Baltzell, however, views this development apprehensively. A closed upper class creates the possibility that power will be wielded by those who lack socialization to upper-class values and who therefore have little understanding of their larger social responsibilities. Their legitimacy may thus become questionable and force them to resort to coercion and deception to govern effectively. Baltzell might well have predicted, for example, the emergence of national political figures such as Richard Nixon and Spiro Agnew, each lacking upper-class credentials, whose concerns seemed almost exclusively the enhancement of personal power and wealth.

Rose: The Pluralist View I

As we saw in chapter 3, pluralists do not deny the existence of elites as power wielders, but they part with Marxists and elitists in their view of the structure and behavior of those elites. Essentially pluralists see the power structure as made up of separate and autonomous elites within various areas of social and political life (government, business, education, and so on) who do not necessarily maintain close working or social relations. In short, a variety of elites functioning in particular institutional realms deters centralization of elite power and assures at least some degree of mass control.

One of the leading exponents of the pluralist view is the late sociologist Arnold Rose. In *The Power Structure* (1967), Rose delineated what he called the "multi-influence" elite structure. Since it was written with the expressed purpose of answering Mills, Hunter, and those who saw a relatively cohesive and centralized power elite in America, this work is among the most important pluralist writings. Also, Rose's is one of the few pluralist studies to have focused on power at the national rather than the community level.

Rose's position as a counter to Mills is clearly stated in his own summation of his thesis:

(1) There are many power elites, each of which is somewhat specialized in the area in which it exercises its influence. (2) Power elites interlock only temporarily and on limited types of issues, with some issues being determined in a "democratic" fashion by the

great voting public when it occasionally mobilizes itself with interest and action on those issues (1967:89).

Rose denies the power elite theme of Mills and Hunter, both from a substantive and a methodological standpoint. He maintains that through the technique of questioning supposedly knowledgeable persons about the identity of the powerful, Hunter presented an *image* of the national power structure, not the power structure itself. He further contends that Hunter's methodology "naturally" led him to discover the predominance of economic over political leaders. Similarly, Rose criticizes Mills for failure to verify the relatively integrated nature of the elite structure he claims exists.[4]

Rose holds that decision makers of the economy and polity do not necessarily see eye-to-eye on all societal issues, even the basic ones, and therefore, no unity of purpose may be said to exist among them. He notes that the relationship between these two leadership groups in American society has been a constantly changing one, at certain times making for conflict and at other times for cooperation, "with each group influencing the other in changing proportion to some extent, and each operating independently of the other to a large extent" (1967:493).

In contrast to Mills and Hunter, Rose downplays the power of the business (economic) elite. Political officials are seen as counterbalancing and even exceeding its power. Rose points out, for example, that the Congress has approved measures such as Medicare and other social welfare programs, as well as labor reform, despite the opposition of big business interests. The president too has independent powers which have been used to counter the power of big business. Rose claims that it is only on issues relating to economic production that top business leaders are mainly influential. Even on issues affecting consumption and distribution of wealth, they exercise only "occasional" influence, and on noneconomic issues such as foreign affairs they exercise little influence (Rose, 1967:89– 94).

Moreover, Rose claims that members of the economic elite, even among themselves, do not constitute a unified group either in their actions and attitudes regarding various sociopolitical issues or in their social relationships. As he states, "neither the economic elite nor the political authorities are monolithic units which act with internal consensus and coordinated action with regard to each other (or probably in any other way) (1967:493). Cleavages are created within the economic elite by policies which benefit one industry or business sector but possibly harm

4. This is a charge which has been leveled at Mills by various critics. See for example Dahl (1958).

another. Also, Rose points to the traditional schism between big businessmen and small businessmen (a point not disputed by Mills or Domhoff), as well as regional differences such as those between the new business wealth of the Southwest and the old business wealth of the East.

Keller: The Pluralist View II

Sociologist Suzanne Keller has offered a general theory of elites (1963) which is applicable not only to the United States but to all modern societies. Her theory, which she calls "strategic elites," parallels the notion of elite-pluralism described in chapter 3.

Keller contends that due to the increased complexity of modern societies, no one group of leaders is capable of making critical decisions in all areas of societal life. As a result, there occurs a proliferation of specialized functional or "strategic" elites. Those in the political sphere are professional politicians and are not competent to make judgments about business matters, which is the domain of professional managers; military leaders know little about educational affairs, which is the specialty of professional educators; and so on. Each elite must operate within its own particularized field. Public officials run governments, businessmen run corporations, teachers and administrators run schools, and generals run armies. As Keller (1963:83) puts it:

> The President of the United States, the president of a giant corporation, the top atomic scientist and the leading writer of an era have little in common beyond their general cultural backgrounds and their achievement of prominence. How they arrived at their pre-eminent positions, what they must do to remain there and how they affect the lives and fortunes of other men through the exercise of their functional responsibilities differ for each.

The contrast to Mills' power elite thesis could not be more striking.

Functioning in basically different roles, the various elites, according to Keller, will be relatively autonomous. They will not be composed of the same persons, nor will they necessarily recruit their members from similar social classes. All of these factors tend to diminish the likelihood that an all-powerful elite will emerge with the capacity to dominate the society's power structure. Thus an equilibrium among power groups is sustained. Keller explains: "Strategic elites, representing specialized and separate centers, find their power to be specialized and limited. The only way to prevent abuses of power is to control the powerful, and the dispersion of strategic elites constitutes such a control" (1963:273).

Keller's thesis, then, relies on the understanding of societal elites as necessary and indispensable. On this point she is, like Baltzell, in line with the conservative view of the role of elites in society. But unlike Baltzell, Keller sees little crossover between the upper class and the functional or strategic elites. Positions in the society's power elites are dependent more on merit than on inheritance, though she does not deny the effect of the latter. And most importantly, Keller does not see the strategic elites as centralized. The society's functional needs obviate such a development.

Riesman: The Pluralist View III

One of the most widely cited versions of the pluralist view, one frequently used in comparison with Mills' power elite, is Riesman's "veto groups." Conceived in 1950 as part of his classic description of the character of American society, *The Lonely Crowd*, Riesman's portrayal of where power lay and how it was exercised blended naturally with the dominant pluralist notions of the 1950s.

In contrast to those who see a power elite (and even in contrast to contemporary pluralists, who recognize the presence and actions of elites), Riesman sees so many structural constraints on the power of decision makers in the United States that effective leadership rarely crystallizes. Power is "indeterminate" and "amorphous," constantly shifting from one source to another. Riesman's picture of the power structure is thus unique in that he sees virtually *no* forceful and powerful leadership. Not only does he recognize a lack of unity among elites, in line with other pluralists, but he does not see the ability of *any* elites to rule effectively in American society at mid-century.

Riesman's is a fitting complement to other group theory variations of pluralism discussed in chapter 3. He sees various pressure groups as so counterbalanced that no one is able to initiate action successfully; each can only block the actions of other groups. Hence the term "veto groups." Riesman explains:

> ... power on the national scene must be viewed in terms of issues. It is possible that, where an issue involves only two or three veto groups, themselves tiny minorities, the official or unofficial broker among the groups can be quite powerful—but only on that issue. However, where the issue involves the country as a whole, no individual or group leadership is likely to be very effective, because the entrenched veto groups cannot be budged: unlike a party that may be defeated at the polls, or a class that may be replaced by another class, the veto groups are always "in" (1950:254).

Riesman describes the veto groups as neither leader-groups nor led-groups:

> The only leaders of national scope left in the United States today are those who can placate the veto groups. The only followers left in the United States today are those unorganized and sometimes disorganized unfortunates who have not yet invented their group (1950:244).

Riesman's and Mills' power models parallel each other up to a point. Both recognize several basic changes in the American power structure over the course of the society's development. But where Mills sees the emergence since World War II of a centralized power elite, Riesman maintains that power in America remains dispersed widely among countless groups and interests. So dispersed is group power, in fact, that seemingly no one is actually in control. Power struggles among the various groups are limited in Mills' analysis to the "middle level" of the power structure; but for Riesman there is no higher level. It is here, at the level of interest groups, that societal issues are decided. In this view the masses are courted by various interest groups, not dominated by elites. The fact that they remain for the most part nonparticipants in the power process is due to apathy—not, as the elitists maintain, manipulation.

Riesman's view of power in America, then, discounts the place and significance of societal elites. Who such people are and what they do in the decision-making process is not at all clear, and furthermore is seemingly unimportant. In the end, it is not evident who makes power decisions and how they are made. One is led to conceive of interest groups and government bureaucracies as ends in themselves, self-generating and running in particular directions without the guidance of policymakers. Clearly with Riesman's veto groups we have run the full gamut of power models from the extreme of a cohesive ruling class to a situation of nonrule.[5]

THE CONFRATERNITY OF POWER

The issue of centralized leadership (power elite or ruling class) versus elite plurality has been persistent in American political sociology for the past several decades. Unfortunately, as in other aspects of the analysis of power in societies, this issue is not easily resolved by empirical investiga-

---

5. A precise comparison between Riesman's and Mills' models of the American power structure is made by Kornhauser (1968).

TABLE 9-1 Perspectives of Leadership of the American Political Economy

Perspective	Chief Power Group(s)	Elite Purpose	Relationship of Political & Economic Elites	Elite Social Relations & Origins	Elite Views on Societal Issues
Mills (R.E. I)	Power elite	Exploitive; unresponsive to needs of masses	Much functional and social overlapping	Similar social interests and common origins which color their attitudes, values, and policy actions	Agreement on basic issues, though some dissensus on minor issues
Hunter (R.E. II)	Power elite	"	"	"	"
Domhoff (Marxist)	Ruling class ("governing class")	"	Economic leaders are themselves political leaders or have political leaders act in their behalf	"	"
Baltzell (C.E.)	Ruling class ("establishment")	Necessary for stable system of authority	Close relationship based on common upper-class membership	"	"
Rose (P.I)	Multiple elites	Act in societal interests; ultimately responsive to needs of masses	Autonomous; no unity of purpose and action among them; little social cohesion	Origins and interests may or may not be similar; in either case, this has minimal bearing on attitudes and policies	Disagreement on many issues, even basic ones
Keller (P. II)	Strategic elites	Necessary to perform essential societal functions	Autonomous due to functional specialization	"	"
Riesman (P. III)	Veto groups	(Elites indeterminate)	(Elites indeterminate)	(Elites indeterminate)	"

tion since the actions of elites are never totally or even in large measure visible to nonelites. Porter (1965:523) reminds us that:

> When elites, the top decision-makers of the society, are called upon to make up their minds on matters which are far reaching for the society, they move through a long series of complicated discussions and negotiations, only fragments of which become public. Secrecy has always been an important weapon in power and in the deals which elites make with each other.

Simply put, the exercise of elite power is not easily observed by sociologists or laymen.

Another hindrance to a resolution of this debate is the question of methodology. Using varying definitions of power as well as different strategies in discovering it, researchers have been led to disparate findings almost automatically. Moreover, the ideological overtones of each model are strong, and as a result, advocates tend to marshall their evidence in such a way as to "prove" their theory in any case.

It will do us little good, then, to search, at one extreme, for cabals or conspiracies among elites or, at the other extreme, to try to locate irrevocable elite divisions. On the basis of what we can empirically observe, however, there is much to confirm the basic point of the elitist view: the relative integration of political and economic decision makers at the top of the power structure. From our analysis of the corporate system and its relation to government, it seems evident that societal power in the United States and similar societies is limited to a small number of individuals whose functional and social ties are unavoidably close, whether this elite constitutes a ruling class in the Marxian sense or a power elite in the Millsian sense.[6] At the same time, there is also at least some evidence to support the pluralist position. Let us briefly look at the major evidence supporting each view.

6. The idea of a "ruling class" is often confusing in political sociology due to the loose usage of the term in reference to any ruling group. It is sometimes difficult to detect any meaningful difference between what one political sociologist may call a *ruling class* and what another may call a *power elite*. Our understanding of ruling class conforms to the Marxian idea —that is, a group whose ownership or control of the society's productive resources enables it to control the political apparatus.

The Centralization of Elites

The Marxian-elitist notion is supported by the evidence of a strong coalition of political and corporate elites. These two leadership groups, and to a lesser extent elites of other societal institutions, are integrated along several lines.

Common functional organizations. As we have detailed in chapter 7, corporate and political elites come together in various policy-planning groups, advisory councils, and lobbying situations. Through these points of interaction, elites exchange views, come to know each other, and lay out long-range policy plans. Given these common sites of decision making, a natural confraternity of power emerges.

Interchange of personnel. We have also seen that business and government leaders frequently exchange positions, especially at the upper levels of national power. They are, in other words, functionally integrated to a significant degree. Much of this integration is simply a product of overlapping institutional interests. One need not interpret it as necessarily designed or contrived. As was explained in chapter 7, dominant economic institutions need the state, and the converse is equally true. Thus with basically similar interests, leaders of these two spheres naturally find themselves in a union of power. Corporate leaders and political leaders move back and forth between the private and public sectors as top advisors, Cabinet officials, and lobbyists. This constant interplay of functional power contributes to the development of a common frame of reference and a consensus regarding basic societal issues.

Common social backgrounds. We saw in chapter 8 that those who dominate the key institutions of the society exhibit strikingly similar social backgrounds. Most importantly, their class origins are relatively narrow, with most coming from the upper or upper middle classes. Even those who do move into power positions from lesser social ranks will have been exposed to similar later socialization experiences, such as higher education and occupational roles and affiliations. Indeed, these may be more important in molding common political interests than similar childhood experiences (Putnam, 1976:93).

Elite Differences

At the same time that elite integration is strongly evident, looking at the policy decisions of elites reveals that on many specific issues there are substantial divisions among them. These policy differences are most evident among political elites, but even within the corporate world, decision makers are rarely unanimous in their views and actions. It is this lack of consensus on many issues to which pluralists point in order to show that elites are not socially cohesive, attitudinally unified, and dominated by business interests.

Ideological differences. Noticeable ideological differences among elites are recognized not only by pluralists but in part even by those who emphasize the cohesiveness of institutional leaders, including Mills and Domhoff. Domhoff, for example, points to three major groups of the power elite (that is, those who, in his analysis, run the dominant institutions on behalf of the upper class) who maintain at least minimal political differences:

> The first is the CFR-CED-Business Council wing of the power elite, which is rooted in the largest corporations and has great influence in the centrist wings of both political parties. The second is the NAM-Chamber of Commerce-American Enterprise Institute wing of the power elite, with its economic base in smaller corporations and its political influence among ultraconservative Republicans and Southern Democrats. The third is the loose-knit liberal-labor coalition rooted in the trade unions, middle-income liberal organizations, university communities and the independent wealth of a few rich mavericks; its connections are to the liberal wing of the Democratic Party. The major strength of the CFR-CED conservatives is in the Executive branch through its numerous ties to the White House. The major strength of the ultraconservatives is in Congress. The liberal-labor coalition does not have any major stronghold (Domhoff, 1978:117–118).

Despite these differences, Domhoff makes clear that in this tripartite arrangement the moderate conservatives generally prevail, particularly on the major issues of the society.

Political observers have also noted the conflict in recent years between the previously dominant political and economic powers of the Eastern establishment and the newer financial and industrial powers of the Sunbelt region. Kirkpatrick Sale (1975) has referred to a "power shift" in which power within the society's political and economic institutions has gradually migrated, along with population and wealth, from the industrialized East and Midwest to the now economically powerful Southern and Western states. The oil industry and the burgeoning cities of Texas perhaps typify the new seats of financial and industrial power. This shift has given rise to a schism within the power structure between "Yankees" and "Cowboys" (Dye, 1976:181–186).

Divisions within the economic elite. In the United States today there is a definite schism between leaders of the big business (that is, monopoly) sector of the economy and those representing the small business or competitive sector. Small businessmen have not benefited from the accentuated role of government in the economy, as have big businessmen, and therefore have continued to resist the policies of the corporate state (see for example Burch, 1973). Within the ranks of big business itself the division may be less noticeable, but even here corporate leaders will not speak with a single voice on all issues, even those which directly concern economic matters. Domhoff (1978:120) notes the difference in policy perspective among the biggest of the big and "the run-of-the-mill multimillion dollar companies."

Divisions within the political elite. The substantive differences between the two major American political parties have been the subject of much debate among political observers. We will comment on this question in chapter 11. It is sufficient to say here that however similar the parties may appear in policy proposals and action, there remain ideological and symbolic differences between them which are reflected in the diverse sources of money that finance their campaigns. Most big business money continues to flow to Republican candidates, while labor contributes primarily to Democrats. Exceptions have occurred only when the candidates have been perceived as outside the mainstream of either party, such as the Goldwater presidential candidacy in 1964 and the McGovern candidacy in 1972. In those cases traditional patterns were discarded; much of big business supported the Democrat, Lyndon Johnson, in 1964, and many elements of big labor either tacitly or openly were supportive of Richard Nixon in 1972.

POWER IN AMERICA: AN INTEGRATED MODEL

How are we to explain a basic consensus among elites while still recognizing differences among them? The picture of elite power in the United States or any other society as either totally unified or totally disperse does not, of course, represent its true character.[7] Realistically the American power structure falls somewhere between these two extremes. Most contemporary Marxists and elitists would not deny many of the elite divisions we have delineated, nor would pluralists reject at least some degree of elite unification.

---

7. For a discussion of these two polar types see Aron (1950).

Moreover the shape of the elite structure and the nature of interrelations among its elements are not static. At certain times there are pressures which bring elites of power together and at other times which separate them. Some of these pressures are found in the society's class system, while others are the result of the structural nature of political and economic institutions. Rose's statement (1967:483) that "Political power in the United States, like any other social phenomenon, is changing its locus of concentration, its distribution, and its manifestations constantly" is well taken.

With these thoughts in mind, it is nonetheless possible to pick out key features of the American elite structure which define its essential character. Despite the validity of certain aspects of pluralist depictions, *power at the highest levels of policymaking in the United States is at present a basically centralized system.* Specifically, institutional leadership in the United States is best described as a *power elite* rather than either a ruling class in the vulgar Marxian sense or a pluralistic elite system. This view of top leadership in America reflects the description of power and the powerful presented in the previous three chapters. Let us look at some propositions which support this view.

Consensus on Basic Issues

Differences of opinion and action within the leadership of key institutions are present, but *these differences do not represent basic cleavages on matters which concern the essential nature of the political economy.*

Pluralists imply that disputes among elites on specific issues are indicative of more general disagreements about how the political and economic institutions should be structured and run. They point to central differences between the two major parties, for example, and within the parties themselves regarding economic policies, social welfare programs, or the tax structure. And in the same way they note internal differences within the corporate world regarding tariffs, labor policies, and the role of government in the economy. Simple observation verifies the fact that these disagreements are real. But these are disagreements on relatively superficial issues. On the fundamental shape of the political economy there is essentially no disagreement. As Miliband (1969:72) has aptly stated:

> To a much larger extent than appearance and rhetoric have been made to suggest, the politics of advanced capitalism have been about different conceptions of how to run the *same* economic and social system, and not about radically different social systems. *This* debate has not so far come high on the political agenda.

Those who question or openly advocate *systemic* changes are not likely to enter the circle of political and economic power to begin with, but if they do, their views are either ignored or tempered through cooptation or they are eased out of their positions. Take the case of Fred Harris. During the presidential primaries of 1976, Harris, a former Oklahoma senator, proposed policies and programs that, by his own admission, required fundamental changes in the society's distributive system (Harris, 1971; 1973). Nationalization of certain essential industries and basic changes in the tax structure that would have resulted in dispossessing the affluent and the corporations of some of their power and wealth were too much for established elites to accept. Harris' candidacy was not taken seriously. He was generally ignored by the Democratic party establishment and by the corporate and labor financiers of political campaigns. His candidacy was also treated lightly by the news media, which did not consider him one of the "real" contenders. His campaign collapsed after only a few months, a development which was easily predictable from the start.

While pluralists seriously underestimate the capacity of ruling elites to unite on fundamental issues, those who see a ruling class foster the equally erroneous notion that common social backgrounds and experiences of elites are sufficient to create attitudinal consensus on *all* issues. Mills (1956:280) reminds us, however, that "We cannot infer the direction of policy merely from the social origins and careers of the policymakers." There is, then, a strong but not invariable consistency between political behavior and social background.

That upper-class origins do not automatically assure sympathy for upper-class political values and interests is exemplified by political figures such as Franklin D. Roosevelt and, more recently, the Kennedys. Though possessing unquestionable aristocratic credentials, they often displayed concern for the interests of the working class and racial minorities, and their appeal among these groups was quite strong.

Of course, such condescending attitudes and policies by upper-class members may also be interpreted as an awareness of the need to surrender selective class privileges in order to protect the bulk of them. Thus various social welfare measures as enacted by administrations since Roosevelt's may be unquestioned today by ruling groups, who recognize them as necessary palliatives. But to interpret such measures as entirely self-serving is to deny any degree of altruism as a motivating factor. Even Domhoff admits that the political activities of some "fat cats," notably "a great many Jews" and a "handful of well-fixed maverick patricians," are impelled by a desire "to see a more humane society, which usually means in practice some expansion of civil rights and more reliable welfare measures for the bottom layers of society" (1972:17).

In sum, conflict does take place among the powerful, and there are noticeable differences in their attitudes and actions; but these are not fundamental rifts in either ideology or social perspective. Stability within the prevailing system is paramount; thus gradual and incremental rather than systemic changes are promoted. "The mark of a unified elite," claims political scientist Robert Putnam, "is not the absence of disagreement, but rather sufficient mutual trust, so that its members will, if necessary, forego short run personal or partisan advantage in order to ensure stable rule" (1976:122). Those at the top of the political economy are often sharply divided on various issues, divisions which are not to be minimized in either substance or effect. But on the norms of elite interaction and on the basic values and structures of the dominant capitalist institutions, these differences are put aside and a unity of purpose emerges (see Prewitt and Stone, 1973:146–158).

This fundamental agreement on basic social and economic issues is reflected in a survey of top American leaders in government, business, labor, and the mass media conducted in 1972 by researchers at Columbia University. The study found among all of these elites support for Keynesian economic policies and welfare for the indigent and unemployed; all, however, also *opposed* a top limit on incomes, taking large corporations out of private hands, and the belief that those of the working class cannot rise in the social hierarchy. Thus what is seen is "a clear consensus for capitalism among American leaders," albeit a capitalism modified by an active governmental role in the economy (Barton, 1975:522). Most importantly there is steadfast opposition among leaders of all spheres to basic changes in the prevailing power and reward structures.

Predominance of Economic Resources

Resources of power are varied and numerous, but economic resources are paramount in modern capitalist societies. Thus *economic leaders will generally, though not at all times, dominate the elite structure*.

Pluralists have overemphasized the role of governmental authority as the fundamental base of political power, a view which seriously underestimates the ability of economic institutions and their leaders to shape and affect public policies. As we have seen, economic power is generally transferable into political power in modern capitalist societies.

The independent power that political leaders sometimes exhibit should not lead to the assumption of a "balance of power" among elite segments. With its control of the society's productive resources, the economic (that is, corporate) elite is able to set the broad boundaries within which political decision makers must operate. Political leaders are thus influenced by the long- and short-range interests of economically powerful institutions (that is, corporations) more than any other factor. As Dolbeare (1974:26–27) has described the American political economy of today:

> The policies of government and of business are so intertwined and mutually supportive that no citizen can tell where one ends and the other begins. . . . Thus the first priority that underlies the entire pattern of government activity, social welfare and regulatory measures included, is the furtherance of the growth and other needs of the economic system.

Politicians at all levels of government quickly come to realize that political actions can never be completely divorced from economic consequences. Policies can be enacted only to the extent that economic circumstances will permit. And those circumstances are very much determined by individuals who, through their organizations, control the society's productive resources. This is the corporate elite.

Within those boundaries, of course, a great deal of conflict occurs among a variety of societal groups. In other words, though dominant economic interests establish the agenda of politics, they may not prevail on all issues which become part of that agenda. As was pointed out in chapter 3, on noneconomic issues in particular, the pluralist idea is essentially valid. On issues that do not affect the basic structure of the political economy, various groups will win out at different times.

Also it must be kept in mind that our analysis has been concerned primarily with political power at the national level in the United States and other advanced capitalist societies. At lower levels such as state and local government, there is general agreement (among class and elite theorists as well as pluralists) that political decision making is of a more pluralistic nature. Yet as we shall see in the following chapter, here too constraints imposed by dominant economic institutions set definable limits within which all groups must operate.

Although business leaders are the dominant element of the power elite, we should not assume that *all* political power even in advanced capitalist societies can be explained as a product of economic resources, a view which vulgar Marxists have seemed to take. The major issues of the society *are* generally decided on the basis of their impact on the dominant socioeconomic (capitalist) system, but it is not the case that political decision makers are *always* beholden to business leaders. Mills (1956:277) explains: "The simple Marxian view makes the big economic man the real holder of power, the simple liberal view makes the big political man the chief of the power system; and there are some who would view the warlords as virtual dictators. Each of these is an oversimplified view."

In sum, the power elite in the United States is not a balanced plurality of leaders from various institutional spheres. Rather it is dominated by leaders of big business, who shape the boundaries within which political debate and action take place.

Common Needs and Interests

Conspiracies or deliberate planning among members of the power elite are unnecessary since *common needs and interests, as well as relatively common social backgrounds, will generally assure elite consensus on basic societal issues.*

Pluralists have argued the importance of functional specificity as a factor preventing elite centralization. Most simply, different elites do different things in their institutional positions and thus cannot converge. But this division of labor among elites seems overestimated in significance, particularly at the top of the power structure. Increasingly, the skills needed to manage corporations are the same as those needed to manage government bureaus. The differences in duties performed by political leaders and, for example, the clergy or educational leaders are very obvious. But the functional differences between political and corporate leaders seem minimal. If this were not the case, the frequency of interchange among these two groups would not be so great. Also the training of political and economic elites has become similar, with a preponderance of lawyers in both spheres.

Pluralists have also stressed the lack of social cohesiveness among elites, a view which is not borne out by empirical study (Baltzell, 1958; 1964; Domhoff, 1967; 1971). In perhaps correctly dismissing the significance of upper-class social clubs and schools as unifying forces, they have overlooked the cohesiveness of the power elite, which derives if for no other reason from the close working relationships of its members. Although Mills describes the power elite as a socially homogeneous unit due to common socialization and frequent social interaction, he stresses the fact that elite members are cohesive simply because their institutional interests coincide, they work closely with each other, and they freely exchange positions. Given these objective conditions, it is foolish to think they would *not* display cohesiveness (Mills, 1956:278–297). They know each other (or of each other), they have compatible views of the society and their place in it, and they understand the need to preserve, protect, and defend the prevailing political, economic, and social institutions.

At the same time, however, this is not the cohesiveness of a castelike, conspiratorial ruling group. Those who see a ruling class in America have strongly suggested the capacity of the business elite to contrive consciously and systematically to further their political interests, particularly through participation in upper-class institutions such as exclusive clubs and schools. However, the function of upper-class institutions in creating a unity of purpose no longer seems as valid as it did in earlier periods of American social history.[8] Many who are part of the power elite do not attend Ivy League schools and are not part of exclusive social circles. And the converse is equally true: Those who are part of the inner social circles are not necessarily active in circles of power. Although the studies of Mills, Domhoff, and Baltzell have shown that economic and political elites *are* socially cohesive, this closeness is not necessarily by design; the power elite is not a club where members meet regularly to map out strategy for retaining power.

In sum, the power elite is composed of leaders who are functionally and to a large extent socially cohesive. Common interests and actions develop naturally given their mutual functional duties and obligations and their similar socialization experiences.

Canada: A Comparative Note

We noted at the outset that many of the patterns of elite interaction in the United States are similar in other advanced capitalist societies. This seems particularly so in Canada. Studies of the Canadian power structure have shown the existence of a close coalition of top corporate and political leaders throughout the twentieth century (Clement, 1975; Newman, 1977; Porter, 1965).

The same forces which drive the top leaders of the American political economy together operate in Canada as well: overlapping corporate and government institutions, interchanging elite positions, similar socialization, and similar class backgrounds. Furthermore various policy-planning organizations, boards, commissions, and councils serve as mechanisms for elite coordination in Canada just as they do in the United States (Clement, 1975:255–259; Porter, 1965:528–530).

The picture that emerges is very much like Mills' and Hunter's portraits of the American power elite. As Newman (1977:446–447) describes it, the Canadian power elite is not a monolithic establishment but "rings of establishments," dominated most of all by the corporate elite, which runs "most of the institutions that count." As with its American counterpart, the Canadian power elite is not a conspiratorial group but a leadership group whose members quite naturally think the same way on the important issues of Canadian society, given their broad consensual interests and social perspectives.

8. Studies have shown the declining influence of the social elite of particular communities among local political and even economic elites. See Dahl (1961) and Marger (1974).

Policy Implications

Given a relatively centralized and interlocking power elite, what policy implications does this have? Specifically, is a power elite consistently able to operate on behalf of narrow, primarily corporate interests in the face of opposition from a variety of societal interest groups? Pluralists have answered clearly "no" to this question, while class and elite theorists have answered "yes." Neither view, however, is entirely tenable.

Most basically, the pluralist model posits a balance of power among societal interest groups brought about by an inability of any one to dominate on all issues. Pluralists do not deny, however, that each of these groups is pursuing its own parochial interests, much like classical capitalist market behavior. Given the substantial corporate influence in government as well as the inordinate representation of upper-class persons in key power positions, it is only reasonable to expect these dominant economic groups to pursue their interests to the utmost with these resource advantages and thus to dominate the system. As one recent study points out, it is incumbent on pluralists to explain why this would *not* be the case (Kerbo and Della Fave, 1979:18). This touches upon what is perhaps the chief shortcoming of the pluralist model: the assumption of a balance of power among societal groups. This is not at all evident.

Unfortunately most of the empirical studies of power structures in American society, particularly those with a pluralist bent, have used local communities as their research sites and have not described power at the national level. As was pointed out, power may indeed be more equitably distributed among interest groups at the community level; but it is seriously faulty to extend findings here to the national level.

As for elitists, there is still a lack of substantial empirical evidence that the corporate rich are able to control the power elite as effectively as most seem to think. Our analysis has suggested plentiful evidence of the functional and social overlapping of top corporate and political leaders. But it still needs to be more clearly established that these corporate inroads translate into control of public policy making. Again, we have presented considerable circumstantial evidence that it does, but as McNall (1977:20) has pointed out, there needs to be "a reasonable test" to demonstrate this. Similar criticisms have been aimed at the power elite argument since Mills' work first appeared (see for example Dahl, 1958).

The Imperatives of the System

Finally, some, particularly Marxists or class theorists, have asserted that both elitist and pluralist views of the American power structure concentrate too specifically on the individuals and groups who wield power and, as a result, neglect the more important systemic biases which impel certain political actions regardless of who makes decisions and whether or not the decision makers are unified or fragmented (Block, 1977; McNall, 1977; Whitt, 1979). In this view the political economy is a structure which transcends the actions of any specific group or individual. Given the constraints of an advanced capitalist socioeconomic system, the state must act in the interests of dominant economic groups no matter who occupies the positions of authority. As Michael Harrington (1976:313) explains, "So long as private corporations remain the dominant production institution of society, no matter who is in power, the long-run trend in society will be to promote the corporate interest." Or, in the words of another observer:

> If socialists took over the Treasury tomorrow, the constraints upon their actions (e.g., flows of capital that are largely removed from political control, the ultimate possibility of investment strikes) would be the same as they are on the Treasury today, unless there were some general crisis in American capitalism (Dibble, 1968:473).

Sociologist Fred Block (1977:15) has noted that "those who manage the state apparatus—regardless of their own political ideology—are dependent on the maintenance of some reasonable level of economic activity." As was pointed out in chapter 7, politicians cannot hope to retain power if the society is experiencing serious economic difficulties. Moreover public programs enacted by the state are dependent on tax revenues which, in turn, are dependent on a healthy economic condition. Thus so long as the society's economic system is based on private ownership of productive resources and so long as investment and production decisions are privately made, primarily on the basis of profit and only secondarily on the basis of human needs, political leaders *must* pursue courses of action which benefit the society's dominant economic interests. This will be true irregardless of the degree of elite integration or fragmentation, the degree of elite attitudinal similarity, or the extent to which the upper class occupies positions in the power elite.

These systemic constraints operate as well on the business elite. Indeed, corporate leaders are no less immune to the dictates of capitalist institutions than are government leaders. David Vogel perceptively points out that business executives cannot easily change the basic orientations of their firms even if they may want to. Making corporations more accountable to the public, for example, "is fundamentally limited by the inability of a privately owned firm to pursue objectives that are incompatible with long run profit maximization, however loosely that objective is defined; a politically accountable corporation in a capitalist system is a contradiction in terms" (Vogel, 1978:225).

In sum, given the nature of political and economic institutions, the power elite-pluralist debate may be a hollow argument. In the end it may matter little *who* the wielders of power are. Whoever they are and whatever the nature of their interrelations, they will be driven in a basically similar direction by the imperatives of the political economy.

SUMMARY

Since it is elites who actually rule in any society, one of the key questions of political sociology concerns the nature of leadership: Are leaders unified in thought and action, or are they sufficiently divided to assure at least some degree of mass control? Two general groups of theories have clustered around each viewpoint, particularly as regards power in America.

Those positing a unified elite structure have been spurred by Mills' notion of a "power elite," composed of top leaders of the corporation, the federal government, and the military. Members of the power elite comprise a relatively cohesive unit due to their common social backgrounds and the common purposes of their institutions. With some variation, a generally similar picture of power in America is drawn by Hunter and Domhoff. Baltzell also sees unity of top leadership but, unlike the others, believes this is as it should be.

Another group sees power at the top as diffuse, with domination of no single group, even big business leaders. Rose most clearly responds to the power elite notion by asserting a "multi-influence" power structure in America made up of elites of different societal areas who are not in consensus on all important issues. The corporate elite is only one of many powerful groups, all of which are subject to the influence of the citizenry. Various issues are influenced in different degree by different elites—government, business, labor, and so on. Keller sees the decentralization of power groups as a natural outgrowth of specialization: In modern societies leaders of different areas are expert only in their own particular fields, thus precluding any overlapping or unification among them. Riesman suggests that in America power is so dispersed and counterbalanced that no group can initiate action; it can only block the actions of other groups.

There is at least some evidence to support each of these general views of the American power structure. Elites are integrated through the interweaving of their organizations (corporation and federal government in particular), their interchange of positions, and their common social backgrounds. At the same time, there is no absolute unity of purpose and belief among them. Political and economic elites do not always see eye-to-eye on issues, and there are splits even within each of these two power groups.

However, top leadership in America today seems closest to a power elite since (1) elite differences do not represent basic disagreements on essential issues of the political economy; (2) the corporate elite may not decide all issues, but they are able to set the agenda and boundaries of political debate; (3) the necessary overlapping of government and corporation gives rise to a natural elite cohesiveness, though not a conspiring group.

Some have maintained that a concern with the question of "Who rules?" or "What are the interrelations among the rulers?" overlooks the limitations imposed on elites by the structure of the political economy. Regardless of who leaders are and how they interrelate, they will be led along similar policy lines by the needs of the society's political and economic institutions.

REFERENCES

Anderson, Charles. 1974. *The Political Economy of Social Class*. Englewood Cliffs: Prentice-Hall.

Aron, Raymond. 1950. "Social Structure and the Ruling Class." *British Journal of Sociology* 1 (March/June):1–16; 126–143.

Baltzell, E. Digby. 1958. *Philadelphia Gentlemen*. New York: Free Press.

——————. 1964. *The Protestant Establishment*. New York: Vintage.

Barton, Allen H. 1975. "Consensus and Conflict Among American Leaders." *Public Opinion Quarterly* 38 (Winter):507–530.

Block, Fred. 1977. "The Ruling Class Does Not Rule: Notes on the Marxist Theory of the State." *Socialist Review* 7 (May-June):6–28.

Burch, Philip. 1973. "The NAM as an Interest Group." *Politics and Society* 4 (Fall):97–130.

Clement, Wallace. 1975. *The Canadian Corporate Elite*. Toronto: McClelland and Stewart.

Dahl, Robert A. 1958. "A Critique of the Ruling Elite Model." *American Political Science Review* 52 (June):463–469.

——————. 1961. *Who Governs?* New Haven: Yale U. Press.

Dibble, Vernon K. 1968. "Our Elusive Upper Class." *Nation* 207 (November 4): 470–475.

Dolbeare, Kenneth. 1974. *Political Change in the United States*. New York: McGraw-Hill.

Domhoff, G. William. 1967. *Who Rules America?* Englewood Cliffs: Prentice-Hall.
_____. 1971. *The Higher Circles.* New York: Vintage.
_____. 1972. *Fat Cats and Democrats.* Englewood Cliffs: Prentice-Hall.
_____. 1974. *The Bohemian Grove.* New York: Harper and Row.
_____. 1978. *The Powers That Be.* New York: Vintage.
_____, and **Hoyt B. Ballard.** 1968. *C. Wright Mills and the Power Elite.* Boston: Beacon.
Dye, Thomas R. 1976. *Who's Running America?.* Englewood Cliffs: Prentice-Hall.
Harrington, Michael. 1976. *The Twilight of Capitalism.* New York: Simon and Schuster.
Harris, Fred R. 1971. *Now Is the Time.* New York: McGraw-Hill.
_____. 1973. *The New Populism.* New York: Saturday Review Press.
Hunter, Floyd. 1953. *Community Power Structure.* Chapel Hill: U. of North Carolina Press.
_____. 1959. *Top Leadership U.S.A.* Chapel Hill: U. of North Carolina Press.
Keller, Suzanne. 1963. *Beyond the Ruling Class.* New York: Random House.
Kerbo, Harold R., and **L. Richard Della Fave.** 1979. "The Empirical Side of the Power Elite Debate: An Assessment and Critique of Recent Research." *Sociological Quarterly* 20 (Winter):5–22.
Kornhauser, William. 1968. "'Power Elite' or 'Veto Groups'?" In G. William Domhoff and C. H. Ballard (eds.), *C. Wright Mills and the Power Elite.* Boston: Beacon.
Marger, Martin. 1974. *The Force of Ethnicity: A Study of Urban Elites.* Detroit: Wayne State U.
McNall, Scott G. 1977. "Does Anybody Rule America?: A Critique of Elite Theory and Method." Paper delivered at American Sociological Association Annual Meeting, Chicago. (September). Mimeographed.
Miliband, Ralph. 1969. *The State in Capitalist Society.* New York: Basic.
Mills, C. Wright. 1956. *The Power Elite.* New York: Oxford U. Press.
Newman, Peter C. 1977. *The Canadian Establishment.* Toronto: Seal.
Porter, John. 1965. *The Vertical Mosaic.* Toronto: U. of Toronto Press.
Prewitt, Kenneth, and **Alan Stone.** 1973. *The Ruling Elites.* New York: Harper and Row.
Putnam, Robert D. 1976. *The Comparative Study of Political Elites.* Englewood Cliffs: Prentice-Hall.
Riesman, David. 1950. *The Lonely Crowd.* New Haven: Yale U. Press.
Rose, Arnold M. 1967. *The Power Structure.* New York: Oxford U. Press.
Sale, Kirkpatrick. 1975. *Power Shift.* New York: Random House.
Vogel, David. 1978. *Lobbying the Corporation.* New York: Basic.
Whitt, J. Allen. 1979. "Toward a Class-Dialectical Model of Power: An Empirical Assessment of Three Competing Models of Political Power." *American Sociological Review* 44 (February):81–99.

chapter 10

community power

. . . *the community is a primary power center and . . . it is a place in which power relations can be most easily observed.*

Floyd Hunter

The power of elites is evident at various levels of society. Our concern to this point has been primarily with the topmost level—that is, *national* power. It is there that the most encompassing and consequential issues are decided, where such decisions affect everyone in the society. But we are also affected by what happens at lesser levels of power, particularly within the cities and towns where we live and work. Indeed the decisions of community political and economic elites are closer and more comprehensible to us than at any other level. Local economic leaders are better known than executives of multinational corporations, and local political leaders or their agents are dealt with more frequently and directly than those of the federal government. Thus although less significant for the society as a whole, the structures and processes of power at the community level bear some attention.

Studies of individual communities have a long tradition in American sociology, dating from Robert and Helen Lynd's investigations of Middletown (a pseudonym for Muncie, Indiana) in the twenties and thirties (1929; 1937) and W. Lloyd Warner's studies of Yankee City (Newburyport, Massachusetts) in the forties (1941; 1942). These were comprehensive sociological portraits of these communities but dealt considerably with the specific issue of local power. "Who runs the town?" and "Who really counts?" were key questions investigated.

Drawing on this tradition, sociologists in the early 1950s began to concentrate more exclusively on the structure of power in the community. Beginning with Floyd Hunter's study (1953) of Regional City (Atlanta), community power became a well-studied topic. Community power also became the focal point of a most heated debate among sociologists and political scientists, a debate which has continued for the past 25 years, though its importance, as we shall see, has diminished.

Surprisingly, community power has been far more intensively studied than power at the national level. Domhoff (1978:151) notes that by the mid-1970s, community power structures had been the topic of over 300 journal articles and books, most of them written between 1955 and 1968. One apparent reason for the considerable coverage of community power—in contrast to national power—is its greater amenability to empirical study. Quite simply, national power is too remote and perhaps too mysterious to analyze with clear-cut procedures and testable hypotheses. At the local level, however, observing decision makers and power resources among various groups and individuals would seem less difficult. One can follow closely a city commission or a local industry, but to follow and observe so closely the president's cabinet or the daily activities of multinational corporation executives is simply not feasible.

APPROACHES TO COMMUNITY POWER

Given the greater visibility of elites and power resources, we would expect that studies at the community level would yield more definite, precise, and unarguable pictures of power, in contrast to the diverse descriptions of national power. However, this is not the case, chiefly because of the lack of agreement among researchers as to how the study of community power should proceed and, even more basically, what should be studied. Starting with different methods and with different concepts of power, it is not surprising that so little consensus has been reached in answering the question "Who has power in the community?" Indeed most of the same issues which generate different pictures of national power (pluralists versus elitists) are evident at the local level as well. Do elected political officials run the affairs of the city, or does a covert economic elite, made up of local business leaders, really pull the strings of power? And what is the relationship between these leadership groups? Answers to these questions and the methods for finding them have created a seemingly intractable debate among researchers.

In addition, much of the debate of the past 25 years regarding community power has been cast along disciplinary lines. Sociologists have preferred one method of analysis and have generally found one pattern of power, while political scientists have preferred another method and have found a correspondingly different pattern. To help clarify these issues, let us briefly look at the three main approaches to community power.

The Positional Approach

Most of the early community power studies employed what is called the positional approach. In this view, the holders of significant positions in the community's political, economic, and other important institutional spheres are seen as key figures of power. It is assumed that the occupants of these positions are powerful on the basis of the resources they control—wealth, jobs, votes, political offices, and so on. Thus the method of determining who has power is relatively simple: identifying the community's most important institutions and observing the top officials of each.

In this view, bank presidents, executives of the largest industries, top government officials, and leaders of other organizations and groups with substantial community resources ordinarily emerge as the most powerful persons of the community. The Lynds' Middletown study (1929) applied this approach, identifying in that community the dominance of a small business elite, which, in turn, was dominated by a single powerful family. This approach to community power is especially relevant to those who stress the importance of *potential* power held by persons rather than their participation in key decisions (Form and Miller, 1960:522–525).[1]

Several problems are apparent in this approach to community power, most important of which is the possibility of "hidden" power wielders. Influentials or power brokers operating behind the scenes are not as easily identified as those in top-ranking institutional positions. Also interpretations of which roles or positions control important community resources or even which institutions are of maximum importance in the community may vary.

Despite these problems, however, any investigation of local power must begin with an identification of the important formal leaders of the community. Thus the positional approach is fundamental to other approaches which have attempted to delve deeper into the mysteries of community power.

The Reputational Approach

A new technique was introduced to community power studies in 1953 by Floyd Hunter in his study of Atlanta. In order to discover the hidden power holders who might not be revealed by the positional approach, Hunter devised a method which relied on the judgment of informed people within the community, those who would seemingly be able to identify the most influential leaders. He assumed that if one wanted to discover who are the people in a city who really "run things," one would begin by asking those "in the know." This method, then, basically involved asking informants to name and rank those whom they felt were the major leaders in the community.

From top officials of key community institutions (business, government, civic affairs, "society") Hunter obtained lists of persons presumed to have power. From these he compiled a roster of 175 names which, through discussions with informed people in the community, was subsequently narrowed to 40 names. In order to confirm the choices, Hunter then interviewed over half of those selected as well as many more persons knowledgeable about the city's affairs. These interviews also provided insight on how these men actually exercised their power. From his rosters and interviews Hunter uncovered a power network in

---

1. Mills' analysis of the national power structure also adopted a basically positional approach. He began with the assumption that the holders of top positions in the most important institutions controlled key societal resources and thereby maintained the potential to affect the most consequential issues.

Atlanta, one dominated by leaders of the business sector. No single all-powerful individual or coterie was found but rather a number of cohesive leadership cliques, each composed of some element of the business sector, who regularly consulted one another on important community affairs.

Some variant of Hunter's method came to be favored by many sociologists, and those using it seemed to find consistently a relatively cohesive power elite dominated by businessmen, as Hunter had found in Atlanta. The picture that emerges is of a power structure with economic dominants at the top and political and civic leaders exercising largely administrative power. On important policy matters, political and civic community leaders are found to accept decisions already made by the business elite. At minimum, business leaders place limitations on the range of options available to public officials.

What is perhaps the chief underlying assumption of Hunter's technique is that power in the community is not necessarily what it appears to be. Knowing who formal institutional leaders are will not always tell us who in fact controls events in the community. Hunter found that the top business leaders of Atlanta, though actually most influential in community issues, were not in the public eye and did not garner the headlines, as did the political leaders. But as Hunter explained, "Organizational leaders are prone to get the publicity; the upper echelon economic leaders the power" (1953:86–87).

Hunter's approach was subjected to much criticism, mainly by political scientists, who questioned both its methodology and its findings. Many of the criticisms of Mills' power elite, described in chapter 9, were applied to Hunter's view of community power (Dahl, 1958; Polsby, 1963; Wolfinger, 1960). First, it was claimed that this procedure did not measure power as much as opinions about or reputations for power. Second, critics asserted that asking people in the community, no matter how informed, about power is apt to elicit erroneous responses due to different conceptions of power or misunderstandings of questions. Third, those using this approach, it was claimed, preconceived of economic leaders as dominant figures in the community and were thus led naturally to find them in that position. Fourth, critics maintained that the reputationalists assumed the structure of community power to be stable, not varying in form with different specific issues. Finally, it was pointed out that the very existence of a community power structure *per se* was assumed in advance of actually proving it. That is, Hunter and other researchers using his technique began their investigations by asking the question "Who runs this community?" rather than "Does anyone at all run this community?" (Polsby, 1960:478).

The Decision-Making Approach

These criticisms developed into a third approach to community power employed primarily by political scientists who favored a pluralist model of power. Their primary assumption was that nothing about power in a community can be preconceived. Those using the positional approach, it was claimed, had disregarded the fact that the power attached to control of key community resources had to be proven, not simply assumed; one might have great potential power but choose not to use it in community affairs. And those using the reputational approach had assumed that persons who were *reputedly* powerful were *in fact* powerful, and further, that some group in the community *had* to be dominant. Again, these assumptions were questioned.

Dahl and other pluralists accused Hunter and the reputationalists of invoking the "fallacy of infinite regress." That is, important power decisions were assumed to be made out of view of the public; thus a hidden elite could never be *dis*proved since, given this assumption, it always lies one step beyond the observable political affairs of the community.

How, then, did one go about determining who was most powerful (or whether there were any stable power groups at all) in a community? The pluralists' answer was: "a careful examination of a series of concrete decisions" (Dahl, 1958:466).

Instead of relying on informants to identify community power holders, this procedure uses participation in decisions as the chief criterion of power. The presumption is that we cannot know who actually runs things in a town or city unless we can determine how important community decisions are made and who makes them. The powerful are those who participate most effectively in such community decisions.

The logic of this technique seems clear enough. If one wants to find out who the powerful are, what better way than to observe the decision-making process on the community's most important issues? Observable and measurable leadership decisions thus become the focus of investigation. The technique is to select a number of important community issues and then trace the decision-making process — specifically, who was involved and what they did. Those who are found able to initiate or block key decisions are regarded as power holders. The decision-making approach, then, aims for a confirmation of who makes key decisions on vital community issues, not who is *reputedly* or *potentially* powerful. This, its proponents claim, is the only truly empirical method of determining the shape of community power: "How can one tell, after all, whether or not an actor is powerful unless some sequence or event, competently observed, attests to his power?" (Polsby, 1963:60).

The decision-making process in the community, of course, is observable only on strictly *public* issues —that is, those within the governmental realm. Thus it is here that attention is focused. Decisions are investigated regarding such issues as public transportation, public housing, and education. Given the necessary governmental focus of this technique, it should not be surprising that those using it have found government leaders in the community more powerful than reputational or positional studies have shown. Furthermore, those using the decision-making approach have found power to be dispersed and not concentrated in the community's economic elite. Shifting factions and coalitions are seen to form around different community issues.

The decision-making approach is best exemplified by Dahl's study of power in New Haven, *Who Governs?* (1961). Dahl found political leaders preeminent in public decision making and, most importantly, independent of the city's economic and social elites. In contrast to Hunter's picture of community power, Dahl concluded that business leaders were relatively insignificant in the resolution of important public issues and participated only in those issue areas of direct concern to them. Rather than a business-dominated power elite, as Hunter had found in Atlanta, Dahl described New Haven's power structure as pluralistic, with no single group that could be labeled dominant. Other researchers using the decision-making approach seemed to find similar pluralistic power structures in the communities they investigated (Banfield, 1961; Freeman et al., 1960; Jennings, 1964).

The elitists' response. Just as the reputational approach was strongly questioned by pluralists, the decision-making approach elicited a volley of critical commentary by elite theorists and sociologists in general (see for example Gitlin, 1965; Ricci, 1971:144–204). First, it was noted that the selection of "key" issues to be studied, no matter how explicit the criteria, is apt to be less than objective. Are the issues studied really the most important in the community, or are they of great importance only in the eyes of the researcher? If there are other more critical issues for the community that are not acted on in public, the process of discovering who makes key policy decisions may not be so straightforward after all.

The most telling criticism on this point was made by Bachrach and Baratz with their notion of nondecision making. As described in chapter 2, nondecision making is "the practice of limiting the scope of actual decision making to 'safe' issues by manipulating the dominant community values, myths, and political institutions and procedures" (Bachrach and Baratz, 1963:632). Thus powerful groups in the community might prevent issues detrimental to their interests from ever reaching the point of debate and resolution by community decision makers. By limiting their analyses only to observable decisions, Dahl and other pluralists disregarded the agenda-setting capacity of key groups and individuals in the community. If businessmen are absent from the decision-making process except on certain issues of direct concern to them, as pluralist studies have generally found, this may only reflect the fact that the power positions of businessmen or their economic interests are not at stake; that is, there is no need for them to expend resources on those issues. Instead of asking "Who makes decisions?" the more primary question may be "Which issues do leaders make decisions about and how are those issues selected for debate?" While elite theorists such as Hunter stressed the unseen face of power, pluralists using the decision-making technique looked only at the observable, thereby jeopardizing the validity of their findings.

Moreover, in their emphasis on public power, pluralists neglected the private power of dominant economic and other institutional groups in the community. The very title of Dahl's seminal work, *Who Governs?*, reflects this emphasis. Dahl is interested not in power *per se* but in who governs and how—that is, action in the realm of public affairs and government in general. It is the pluralists' contention that "the political arena is the sector of community life in which large groups in the community make demands upon one another and collectively determine policy outcomes" (Polsby, 1963:4). But this denies the independent power of significant economic organizations to render decisions in their own right which have communitywide impact.

The Debate in Summary

Much of the debate concerning community power during the past two decades has resulted from varying definitions of power and its manifestations. As political scientist David Ricci (1971:128) has noted, the difference between those using the positional and reputational approaches on the one hand and those using the decision-making approach on the other is not so much the method they employ—all three consider the community's key institutions and their leaders, gather their data by interviewing these leaders, and consult pertinent written sources of information—but in *what* is selected for investigation. Thus their contrasting findings may be most of all a product simply of different conceptions of what community power is. Does it consist of decisions in the public realm alone or in the private realm as well? Is community power the weight of resources a group or an individual may bring to bear on issues, or is it the actions people actually take to influence those issues? Is community power what a group or an individual can do potentially or must that potential be activated? These, of course, are some of the key questions which underlie the investigation of power at any level, national. local, or even within particular organizations.[2] As we have seen in chapter 2, little general agreement on these matters has been reached among sociologists and political scientists.

TABLE 10-1 Three Approaches to Community Power

	Method of Identifying the Powerful	Focus of Investigation	Usual Findings
POSITIONAL	Determining who occupies positions of authority and influence in key community institutions	Power resources controlled by institutional leaders (wealth, authority, and so on)	A power elite dominated by business leaders
REPUTATIONAL	Asking knowledgeable community informants about who is most influential in getting things done in the community	Reputations of power among those "in the know"	A relatively cohesive elite led by important businessmen
DECISION MAKING	Tracing those who are most influential in significant community decisions	Important community issues	A pluralistic power structure with government officials playing key roles

Also the findings of various community power studies have reflected a noticeable disciplinary bias. Several investigations of the many studies conducted in the 1950s and 1960s have found that the shape of the power structure portrayed by these different studies is very much dependent on the discipline of the researcher (sociology or political science) as well as the method employed. Sociologists using the reputational method tend to find pyramidal, concentrated power structures, while political scientists using the decision-making approach find factional, pluralistic structures (Aiken, 1970; Walton, 1966a; Walton, 1966b; Walton, 1970).

Political sociologists have devoted much attention to the conflicting issues of community power but comparatively little to the issues about which there is noticeably less discord. For example, the chief disagreement in findings is between those who conclude that community power is held by a relatively cohesive elite, dominated by businessmen, as op-

2. For an excellent discussion of variant definitions of power as used in community power studies, see Anton (1963).

posed to those who find a pluralistic power structure in which various groups, business only one among them, coalesce on different issues. Yet neither side denies that power is exercised by community elites; community power in a fundamental sense, then, appears little more democratic in terms of citizen input than power at the national level. Also all sides in the controversy recognize the overwhelming power of two sets of institutional leaders: those of government and of business. Thus, as is the case at the national level, there is less disagreement on *who* the participants in the processes of power are than on what roles they play.

Comparative Community Studies

Most of the studies of community power which appeared in the 1950s and early 1960s were case studies investigating the power structures of particular cities and towns. Although the participants in the community power debate recognized the dangers of applying findings for one city to *all* communities, Dahl's study of New Haven and Hunter's of Atlanta came to be seen by each side as prototypical, representative of the structure of power in American communities generally. Yet, as sociologist Peter Rossi observes, "One firm generalization emerges from the literature: the power structure of local communities and the decision making processes to be found therein show a significant range of variation" (1968:130).

Recognizing the limitations and dangers of generalizing on the basis of single cases, a second phase of community power studies began to emerge in the 1960s. These studies were of a comparative type and attempted to show what factors might account for differences in the structure of power from community to community. Sociologist Terry Clark (1968:83) has pointed out that the majority of the early studies applied the concept of "community" as if all towns and cities, regardless of size, economic base, and social composition, were the same. This new genre of studies now focused on economic, political, and social factors as important modifiers of community power structure. For example, what differences in the structure and processes of local power might be evident in towns with large absentee-owned industries as opposed to those with mainly locally based industries? Or what effect might a strong party system, as opposed to a nonpartisan electoral system, have on the local power structure? Studies developed along these lines (Bonjean and Olson, 1964).

Researchers were now mainly concerned with showing how community characteristics such as size, social makeup, political system, and economic base accounted for variations in patterns of community power.

Rossi (1968), for example, posited that in communities where public officials were full-time professionals, where the electorate was heterogeneous, and where class and status lines were clearly drawn, community power structures tended to be more pluralistic. Aiken (1970) also found more fragmented or pluralistic power structures in industrialized communities and those with many absentee-owned or controlled industries.

Also, many comparative studies now began to focus on the consequences or "policy outcomes" of different power configurations. The question here was: What differences in the implementation of community policies such as urban renewal or public housing could be related to particular types of power structures? (Aiken and Alford, 1970; Clark, 1968).

One of the more interesting findings of comparative community power studies is that in cities with reformed political systems — that is, where political machines no longer control city politics or where parties do not play a major political role — there is likely to be a more centralized or monolithic power structure (Aiken, 1970:449–501). In creating "good government" by cleaning up political corruption, the urban reform movement of the early twentieth century paradoxically contributed to more concentrated power in cities and less popularly controlled governments. By reforming city politics much blatant corruption may have been eliminated, but in the process some of the key mechanisms which had enabled working-class and ethnic minority groups to exert some power in local affairs — the machine, strong local parties, and election of representatives by ward — were destroyed. Thus, following reform, the structure of city government made it far easier for dominant economic and status groups to penetrate the power structure and to wield greater political influence (see for example Marger, 1979).

In sum, comparative studies have forced researchers to take recognition of the diversity of communities in accounting for differences in power structures and the policies they produce. No single model of community power, pluralist or elitist, is applicable to all towns and cities. Rather, differing economic, political, and social characteristics of the community will determine the nature of its power structure.

COMMUNITY POWER AND NATIONAL POWER

The community power debate has subsided in recent years, though the major issues around which the controversy originally swelled have yet to be resolved. It may very well be, however, that the traditional issues of community power are not as meaningful today as they may have been two decades ago. This is so mainly because the local community, regardless of the shape of its power structure, no longer exerts the kind of influence over public life it once did. The community in America, whatever its size, whatever its economic and social character, has been exposed to the processes of political and economic centralization, which have diminished local power over local issues. Put simply, increasingly the local community no longer controls its own affairs.

More and more the control of community affairs has fallen to the national level as economic, political, religious, educational, health, and even recreational institutions have tended toward concentration. Residents of a city buy their groceries, clothes, oil, and almost every other commodity from giant corporate enterprises whose production and distribution facilities may be hundreds of miles distant; workers are employed in the local factories of corporations whose headquarters are in New York or Detroit or Pittsburgh; small business owners are dependent on those same national corporations for the products they sell and, in turn, prevail upon their own nationally based trade associations for market protection; members of union locals take direction from national union leaders, who decide key issues involving wages, contracts, and strikes; local units of government—city, township, county—are dependent on the state and federal governments for sponsorship and financing of local projects such as roads, schools, and hospitals; local newspapers and television stations are affiliated with national chains or networks which provide the same news, entertainment, and advertising messages; students attend schools and colleges whose academic standards and curricula are set by national organizations; even churches and fraternal groups are increasingly directed by national bodies. In sum, "community life" is today largely a fiction. National economic, political, and social institutions now control the content and quality of life in the community more than local ones do.

Even the territoriality of the local community is no longer clear. Two decades ago one could still speak of the city as a definable unit; today that is no longer so. Our reference to "city" now ordinarily encompasses not simply one wholly integrated political, economic, and social unit but instead a group of diverse and loosely interdependent cities, towns, suburbs, and even rural areas. The city today is the "metropolitan area," the "urban area," or even the "megalopolis."[3]

The earlier community power students were aware of the tendency of decreasing local autonomy and dutifully acknowledged its impact on

3. A megalopolis is literally an urban complex encompassing several major cities. One investigation of the power structure of such urban units is Miller (1975).

the power structure. Nonetheless they went about their investigations as if local institutions and leaders were operating in a vacuum, detached from these growing national ties. So strong are these ties today that the whole focus of community power—who governs or who runs the community—may no longer be an issue of great relevance. Except in a few cases, the city may no longer be, as Hunter described it in 1953, a "primary power center" (p. 2). Indeed, this point was strongly made by one of the early community studies entitled *Small Town in Mass Society* (1968). In their investigation of a small community in upstate New York which they called "Springdale," Vidich and Bensman were led to conclude that the autonomy of the community was imaginary. Though Springdale's residents believed they were isolated from the influence of the larger society's culture and institutions, in reality the town was heavily penetrated by and dependent upon them.

In short, whether power at the community level is pluralistic or concentrated may matter very little if the consequences of public and private political actions at this level are not meaningful. It is now clear that important power centers are no longer located in each particular city (if indeed they ever were). As Alford and Friedland (1975:463) have stated, "The central city is not a closed system, nor is it a subsystem sufficiently differentiated to permit a theory of urban politics devoid of reference to the relationship between the city and the national political economy." Local power groups are now unavoidably dependent on the two key institutions of power in the larger society: higher-level government (federal and state) and the national (or multinational) corporation. Let us look more closely at how the local community and its power structure are vitally linked to these institutions.

The Community and Higher Levels of Government

Increasingly, local governments have come to play an implementing role for policies determined by leaders and organizations at higher levels of government. It is particularly in the realm of public finances that local governments depend more and more on state and federal agencies. In return for subsidies and grants, state and federal agencies place requirements on local communities to meet certain standards and regulations, thereby undercutting the discretion of local leaders. Policies set by officials in Washington or in state capitals thus impinge on the policy actions of community elites.

In a fundamental way, of course, cities owe their very legal existence to state governments, and almost everything they do in the way of financing and administering local programs is subject to regulations and guidelines set by state laws. More importantly, the local government's powers to tax are regulated by the state government, thereby placing serious financial constraints on all of its activities. Since cities as a group today acquire less than 60 percent of their revenues by their own tax collections (Gardner, 1978:356), needed revenue can be raised only by borrowing or by tax revenues shared by higher level—that is, state and, in recent years, federal—governments.

It is the latter method which is the primary supplement to local taxes. Such revenue sharing is usually in the form of grants-in-aid, whereby either the state or federal governments give tax monies they have raised to local governments for particular projects or for general spending purposes. Grants-in-aid are usually proffered on the condition that the city follow state or federal guidelines in administering programs financed in this way. Aid to local education for school construction or teachers' salaries, for example, obligates the community receiving these funds to follow state educational regulations such as teacher certification, curricular content, and so on. Federal funds likewise are contingent on meeting federal requirements such as racial balancing in district schools. Although most grants come from state government, federal grants are provided for such diverse local functions as antipoverty programs, urban renewal, crime control, medical care, education, environmental control, mass transit, and highways.[4] The stipulations tied to these grants contribute to the erosion of the independence of local political leaders.

The financial dependence on higher levels of government has been particularly critical in the past decade for larger cities of the Northeast and Midwest, whose tax bases have continued to erode. As higher income groups and corporations have left the central cities for the suburbs, these cities are left with an inordinately high proportion of those social groups most in need of public assistance—the poor, the aged, racial minorities—but least able to support higher taxes to pay for them. Changing demographic conditions have thus seriously affected large cities' ability to finance their services. Moreover larger cities have traditionally provided a greater variety of services to residents than have smaller towns, further contributing to their financial difficulties. Also the very costs of delivering those services have increased considerably over the past decade due to rising municipal workers' salaries and the effects of inflation. Consequently large urban units must turn more and more to state and federal agencies for assistance. The fiscal plight of New York City in the mid-1970s is symptomatic of most large Northern cities

4. The federal government supplies local governments with many indirect grants through grants made to state governments, which in turn pass them down to local communities.

in the United States. Indicative of this trend is the fact that federal aid to larger cities made up over 10 percent of their aggregate general expenditures in 1973–1974 as compared to .7 percent in 1951–1952 (Caraley, 1977:35). Both the Kennedy and Johnson administrations in the 1960s vastly expanded the scope of federal aid to cities, particularly programs whose targets were the urban poor. Though largely phased out by the Nixon administration, a residue was left in the form of revenue sharing, whereby the federal government provides lump sums to states and cities rather than monies for specific programs.[5]

As they have become increasingly dependent on state and federal governments for funds to finance basic services, larger cities have become captives of the decisions of government agencies and legislatures which may have no political interests or constituencies in these communities. Federal Cabinet members and agency heads, with no electoral ties to the cities, are nonetheless significant figures in determining what ultimately happens at this level of public policy.[6] Likewise in the case of state and national legislatures, big cities are dependent on lawmakers who may be more accountable, and thus responsive, to the small town or suburban interests which have elected them.

Ironically, then, at a time when the difficulties of cities are vast — crime, poverty, and the myriad problems stemming from institutional racism are most acutely manifested in the central cities — they lack the financial means to attempt to deal with them and must appeal increasingly to outside, often unresponsive, sources. Although the increasing dependence on nonlocal governments has been most apparent among larger cities, the tendency is characteristic of communities of all sizes.

The Community and the National Corporation

Just as higher levels of government now play a critical role in defining the public policy options of community elites, national corporations do the same in the economic realm. The giant corporation is the dominant economic institution in the community, as it is in the larger society. Ob-

---

5. On Nixon's — and later Ford's — negative response to the pressing financial needs of New York and other Northern cities, see Newfield and Du Brul (1977:ch. 3).
6. One journalist concluded in 1978 that in light of New York City's ongoing financial crisis, the most powerful group of leaders in shaping the city's future included not only such obvious persons as the Mayor and the Governor of New York but also national political figures such as Senator William Proxmire of Wisconsin, chairman of the Senate Banking Committee (which controlled the city's lines of credit), and then Secretary of the Treasury W. Michael Blumenthal. See Pileggi (1978).

viously the extent of any particular community's dependence on national corporations will vary, but none are immune to their influence. Heavily industrial cities or those where corporate headquarters are located will be more closely tied to these firms than will smaller towns or bedroom suburbs. Few communities of at least moderate size, however, will not be the site of a plant or retail branch of some national corporation. General Motors, for example, operates 121 plants in 73 American cities and another 7 in Canada. K-Mart operates over 1,500 retail stores in the United States and Sears, Roebuck almost 900. Plainly the economic life of most communities in American society today revolves around the activities of national corporations.

Resource power. The translation of the corporation's economic power into political power at the national level (chapter 7) is, in many ways, similar at the local or community level. This is particularly evident in its control of increasingly large proportions of communities' productive resources: financial capital, jobs, plants, and land. This resource power, according to Mott, increases "as the ratio of company resources to community resources increases" (1970:172). At one extreme are communities overly dependent on a single industry or company. Airplanes in Seattle or steel in Gary are such cases. Other communities are more economically balanced, with a greater variety of firms and industries. So interdependent is the industrial system, however, that all local communities are limited in their options by the investment decisions of the national corporate elite.

We have seen that pluralists have been content to judge the influence of businessmen in local power structures on the basis of highly visible political actions—that is, participation in key community decisions. The power of economic elites, it is held, is no greater than the extent of their decision-making roles in important community issues. On the other hand, those seeing a more centralized or elitist power structure have relied on businessmen's reputations of influence as a means of placing them in the community's power hierarchy. Both of these views, however, neglect the inherent resource power of large corporate enterprises and their officials. As sociologist William Spinrad has aptly noted:

> Those who are powerful in specific crucial institutional areas of community life may neither possess the appropriate reputations nor participate in many significant community-relevant decisions. Their power comes from the functions of their institutions. The decisions they make within their apparently limited sphere may be so consequential for the rest of the community or society that they are in-

herently "powerful," as long as the position of their groups are [sic] maintained (1965:344).

Thus, to conclude that economic elites are not significant power wielders because they do not directly participate in the political affairs of the community, or even that they are not reputedly powerful according to key informants, overlooks the power which corporate elites wield merely on the basis of their control of community resources.

As at the national level, economic resource control is easily converted into political influence. But direct means of political influence are minor in comparison with the indirect influence corporations exert on the decisions of political leaders merely through their control of the community's economic livelihood. Under such conditions, local officials can hardly afford to ignore the needs of large corporations in their midst. Like national political leaders, community leaders well understand that corporate interests *must* be catered to if the economic lifeblood of the community is to remain healthy. Thus dominant firms are usually granted special tax privileges, for example, or may be exempted from certain land use regulations. Such privileges are designed to either keep companies in the community or lure them to it.

With regard to the resource power of the corporation in American communities, Bachrach and Baratz's notion of nondecision making seems particularly relevant. When communities are dependent on large corporations for jobs, investment, and tax revenue, the views of political leaders will naturally reflect corporate interests. Issues will not emerge that seriously threaten the community's dominant economic institutions.

Value compatibility. The inherent power of corporate leaders in the community also stems from the similarities in interests and general social perspectives they share with community political leaders. So long as capitalist values predominate among these groups, a general consensus on important issues will prevail. Thus big businessmen need not be directly involved in political decisions so long as political leaders are likely to defend and advocate business interests in any case. As Mott (1970:172) explains:

> Policy decisions may be *made* by political leaders without any direct interpersonal influencing from economic dominants, but these decisions may be *shaped* in the minds of the political leaders by the social values they share with businessmen. Value compatibility is a form of power far more subtle and effective than persuasion, coercion, and the other traditional techniques of interpersonal influence.

Absentee control. With the concentration of economic power in fewer and fewer giant corporations and the centralization of corporate management, decisions concerning jobs, investment, and other corporate resources are increasingly made outside the local community. Hunter in 1953 had found an economic elite controlling the vital political decisions of Atlanta; but the elite he found was based in the community —that is, made up of local businessmen. Today, economic elites exercise community power *in absentia*. While a local manufacturing firm might once have wielded influence in a community where it was the largest employer and source of revenue (such as the Lynds found in Middletown), today the manufacturing company is most likely part of a national corporation whose important management decisions are made by top officials in headquarters far distant from the community itself.

Absentee ownership and control further deflate the power of local elites. Decisions to invest or to withdraw investment in communities by national corporations are not locally decided issues, despite their monumental local consequences. Youngstown Sheet and Tube Company's decision in 1977 to shut down its mill in Youngstown, Ohio, left 5,000 men jobless and threatened the economic well-being of the entire city. That decision, however, was made by officials of Youngstown Sheet and Tube's parent company in New Orleans. No community plebiscites were held among Youngstown's residents, and local leaders could respond to the decision only after it was made (Stuart, 1978:16). Although the numbers involved are not always as great, cases like this are not unusual.

The choice of a firm to locate in one city rather than another can mean an economic groundswell to the chosen community, just as the decision to abandon a city, such as the Youngstown case, can have disastrous effects. But these choices are not made on the basis of community need. The purposes of corporations in capitalist society are to earn profits and maintain steady growth. As a result, the interests of any particular community will take a primary place in the priorities of corporate leaders only if they coincide with the expectation of profit and growth. In short, the community's economic destiny is increasingly in the hands of a remote corporate elite who are not necessarily concerned with the community's long-range interests.

The national focus of corporations. Corporations in America are national or international in scope and they pursue, accordingly, national or world goals. It is on the federal government that the corporation in the United States relies to support and coordinate the corporate capitalist system; in this, local governments play only a minor role. Large corporations, therefore, are apt to be only minimally involved in community political affairs, limiting their activities to issues which specifically affect them or to public relations efforts aimed at fostering good will between themselves and the community (see for example Schulze, 1958). This may account for the apparent move toward a more pluralistic power structure in those communities dominated by absentee-controlled companies.[7] Spinrad points out that there is little reason for businessmen to expend resources on every community decision when their corporations' interests are not threatened: "As long as you can run your business, let the others have their particular decision areas" (Spinrad, 1965:346).

Sociologist Harvey Molotch argues that the key function of government at the local level is to sustain economic growth by attracting industry and commerce to the community. The people who are therefore drawn into city politics are those who have the greatest stake in the payoffs of local economic growth: "businessmen and, among businessmen, the more parochial sort" (Molotch, 1976:317). These are not corporation executives of large absentee-owned and controlled plants but those who are most interested in the distribution of local resources, particularly land, such as realtors, local bankers, land developers, and builders. Such persons profit by establishing those conditions which make the community attractive to large manufacturing and retailing firms — roads, housing, and so on.

The Community and the National Political Economy

In sum, power in the community can be understood only if we consider the community in the context of the national political economy. The cities, towns, and villages of America do not function apart from the national corporate structure or the state and federal governments. Many, perhaps most, key community issues are inextricably tied to the decisions of societal power elites whose actions are aimed at maintaining and stabilizing the corporate capitalist system. As a result, the ability of local power groups to affect decisions which vitally concern local interests diminishes.

Molotch's account (1970) of the experience of one American community in dealing with national power elites whose purposes do not always coincide with the community's interests is noteworthy. In 1969 the coastline of Santa Barbara, California, a city of 70,000, was ravaged by an oil spill from an offshore drilling rig. Community elites went into action immediately with efforts to rid the area of oil drilling activities. Appeals were made to state and federal governments; legal action was

---

7. For a bibliography of studies which indicate this pattern, see Mott (1970:523).

begun against the oil companies; rallies were held; a petition with 110,000 signatures was sent to the president and thousands of letters were sent to key congressmen appealing for legislation to ban oil operations offshore from Santa Barbara. In short, everything the established political system requires a community to do to protect its interests was done.

But the ensuing scenario revealed little or no support from higher levels of political power. Federal regulatory agencies, Congress, and the Interior Department defended oil's case almost totally. What is perhaps ironic is that Santa Barbara, unlike most American communities, did not vitally need the jobs and revenues derived from the presence of giant corporations (in this case, oil companies). As a relatively affluent community, it was, in a sense, immune to the threat of such large firms to "take their operations elsewhere." Even more ironically, the community of Santa Barbara derived almost no revenue at all from oil companies in the area since the oil was produced in federal waters. Given the tax privileges of oil companies and the artificially created price of oil, "the citizens of Santa Barbara, as federal taxpayers and fleeced customers were subsidizing their own demise" (Molotch, 1970:138). The residents of Santa Barbara had chosen to keep the oil companies out of their community but were in the end powerless to accomplish this.

From the outset of oil drilling operations in the area, local officials had been virtually excluded from participation in decisions made by oil company and Interior Department officials. No public hearings were held before drilling began since, as one Interior Department engineer explained in a note to the Assistant Secretary of the Department, "We preferred not to stir up the natives any more than possible" (Molotch, 1970:139). By influencing the media's portrayal of the events following the oil spill through staged events and distortion of facts, the power of the oil companies and federal agencies was complete. Their position could not be breached even by so comparatively well-to-do a community as Santa Barbara. Indeed, perhaps the most apparent irony in this case is the disproportionately upper- and upper-middle-class character of the community's populace, those who are ordinarily the chief beneficiaries of the corporate capitalist system!

Community power, then, must be placed in its proper perspective, given the workings of the political economy of the larger society. Obviously many issues of critical importance to the community's residents are decided at the local level. But community elites making those decisions are constantly constrained in their policy options by the decisions of corporate and political elites at the national level. And on issues which are vital to the maintenance of corporate capitalism (for example, offshore oil drilling), elites at the community level may be bypassed completely. The important question of community power today, then, is no longer "How is power organized?" (the major concern of earlier research), but whether and how community power can be restored.

SUMMARY

The study of community power has had an important place in political sociology for the past two decades. Beginning with Hunter's pioneering work, a debate ensued between proponents of two divergent methods of determining the structure of power in the community: asking knowledgeable persons to identify the most influential leaders or tracing them through their participation in key community decisions. Each method, in turn, seemed to lead to correspondingly discrepant findings: Reputational methods generally found a cohesive power elite dominated by local businessmen, while decision-making methods found a pluralistic power structure with political leaders playing key roles. Later studies of community power focused on the variant sociological characteristics of communities and offered models which could be used in comparing community power structures.

Early community power studies minimized the national context within which the community necessarily functions. Power in the community today must be placed into the framework of the larger political economy of the nation. With the increased dependence of local elites on the national power structure, the issue of "who governs" in the community seems less relevant today. Although not always vividly evident, the influence of the national corporation in the local power structure of most American communities is incontestable nonetheless. The same is true of state and, increasingly, federal governmental agencies and their elites.

What should not be forgotten through all of our analysis is the persistence of elite rule at the local level, identical to what was previously seen at the national level. The vital issues of the city are not decided by popular democratic means any more than are vital national issues; rather they are elite decisions, no matter what the shape or sociological makeup of the power structure. It is true nonetheless that local power elites, to the extent that they are able to make independent decisions on community issues, are bound to be more responsive to the general populace if only because their actions are more easily monitored and they are closer at hand. The power of nonelites is thus more significant here than at the national level.

It is to the general issues of nonelite power that we now turn.

REFERENCES

Aiken, Michael. 1970. "The Distribution of Community Power: Structural Bases and Social Consequences." In Michael Aiken and Paul E. Mott (eds.), *The Structure of Community Power*. New York: Random House.

_____, and **Robert R. Alford.** 1970. "Community Structure and Innovation: The Case of Urban Renewal." *American Sociological Review* 35 (August):650–665.

Alford, Robert R., and **Roger Friedland.** 1975. "Political Participation and Public Policy." In Alex Inkeles (ed.), *Annual Review of Sociology*. Vol. I. Palo Alto: Annual Reviews.

Anton, Thomas J. 1963. "Power, Pluralism, and Local Politics." *Administrative Science Quarterly* 7 (March):425–457.

Bachrach, Peter, and **Morton S. Baratz.** 1963. "Decisions and Nondecisions: An Analytical Framework." *American Political Science Review* 57(September):632–642.

Banfield, Edward. 1961. *Political Influence*. New York: Free Press.

Bonjean, Charles M., and **David M. Olson.** 1964. "Community Leadership: Directions of Research." *Administrative Science Quarterly* 9 (December):278–300.

Caraley, Demetrios. 1977. *City Governments and Urban Problems*. Englewood Cliffs: Prentice-Hall.

Clark, Terry N. 1968. *Community Structure and Decision-Making: Comparative Analyses*. Scranton, Pa.: Chandler.

_____. 1968. "Community Structure, Decision Making, Budget Expenditures, and Urban Renewal in 51 American Communities." *American Sociological Review* 33 (August):576–593.

Dahl, Robert A. 1958. "A Critique of the Ruling Elite Model." *American Political Science Review* 52 (June):463–469.

_____. 1961. *Who Governs?* New Haven: Yale U. Press.

Domhoff, G. William. 1978. *Who Really Rules?: New Haven and Community Power Revisited*. Santa Monica: Goodyear.

Form, William H., and **Delbert C. Miller.** 1960. *Industry, Labor, and Community*. New York: Harper and Bros.

Freeman, Linton, et al. 1960. *Local Community Leadership*. Syracuse: Syracuse U. Press.

Gardner, Wayland D. 1978. *Government Finance*. Englewood Cliffs: Prentice-Hall.

Gitlin, Todd. 1965. "Local Pluralism as Theory and Ideology." *Studies on the Left* 5 (Summer):21–45.

Hunter, Floyd. 1953. *Community Power Structure*. Chapel Hill: U. of North Carolina Press.

Jennings, M. Kent. 1964. *Community Influentials*. Glencoe: Free Press.

Lynd, Robert, and **Helen Lynd.** 1929. *Middletown*. New York: Harcourt, Brace and Co.

_____. 1937. *Middletown in Transition*. New York: Harcourt, Brace and Co.

Marger, Martin. 1979. "Ethnic Succession in Detroit Politics, 1900–1950." *Polity* 11 (Spring):340–361.

Miller, Delbert C. 1975. *Leadership and Power in the Bos-Wash Megalopolis*. New York: Wiley.

Molotch, Harvey. 1970. "Oil in Santa Barbara and Power in America." *Sociological Inquiry* 40 (Winter):131 – 144.

——————. 1976. "The City as a Growth Machine: Toward a Political Economy of Place." *American Journal of Sociology* 82 (September):309 – 332.

Mott, Paul E. 1970. "The Role of the Absentee-Owned Corporation in the Changing Community." In Michael Aiken and Paul E. Mott (eds.), *The Structure of Community Power*. New York: Random House.

Newfield, Jack, and **Paul Du Brul.** 1977. *The Abuse of Power: The Permanent Government and the Fall of New York*. New York: Viking.

Pileggi, Nicholas. 1978. "The 36 Who Run New York." *New York* 11 (January 9):30 – 33.

Polsby, Nelson W. 1960. "How to Study Community Power: The Pluralist Alternative." *Journal of Politics* 22 (August):474 – 484.

——————. 1963. *Community Power and Political Theory*. New Haven: Yale U. Press.

Ricci, David. 1971. *Community Power and Democratic Theory*. New York: Random House.

Rossi, Peter H. 1968. "Power and Community Structure." In Terry N. Clark, *Community Structure and Decision-Making: Comparative Analyses*. Scranton, Pa.: Chandler.

Schulze, Robert O. 1958. "The Role of Economic Dominants in Community Power Structure." *American Sociological Review* 23 (February):3 – 9.

Spinrad, William. 1965. "Power in Local Communities." *Social Problems* 12 (Winter):335 – 356.

Stuart, Reginald. 1978. "Youngstown Seeks a Grasp on Its Fading Steel Industry." *New York Times* 127 (June 20):16.

Vidich, Arthur J., and **Joseph Bensman.** 1968. *Small Town in Mass Society*, Rev. ed. Princeton: Princeton U. Press.

Walton, John. a:1966. "Substance and Artifact: The Current Status of Research on Community Power Structure." *American Journal of Sociology* 71 (January): 430 – 438.

——————. b:1966. "Discipline, Method and Community Power: A Note on the Sociology of Knowledge." *American Sociological Review* 31 (October): 684 – 689.

——————. 1970. "A Systematic Survey of Community Power Research." In Michael Aiken and Paul E. Mott (eds.), *The Structure of Community Power*. New York: Random House.

Warner, W. Lloyd, and **Paul S. Lunt.** 1941. *The Social Life of a Modern Community*. New Haven: Yale U. Press.

——————. 1942. *The Status System of a Modern Community*. New Haven: Yale U. Press.

Wolfinger, Raymond E. 1960. "Reputation and Reality in the Study of 'Community Power'." *American Sociological Review* 25 (October):636 – 644.

chapter 11

elite-mass linkages

The common assumption that what democratic government does is somehow always a response to the moral codes, desires, and knowledge embedded inside people is as inverted as it is reassuring. This model, avidly taught and ritualistically repeated, cannot explain what happens; but it may persist in our folklore because it so effectively sanctifies prevailing policies and permits us to avoid worrying about them.

Murray J. Edelman

Most of our concern thus far has been with power as it is exercised by those at the top of the social hierarchy, the power elites. In this chapter we will look at the position of nonelites in the structure of power—where they fit, what their political actions and attitudes are, and what effect they have on the decisions of the powerful. Political sociologists and political scientists have generally labeled the various political activities of the common man "political behavior." Studies in this area have included a wide array of topics, from the most encompassing, such as mass movements, to the most minute, such as the psychology of voting. Indeed, political behavior, particularly voting and party activity, has been the most widely researched aspect of politics in society. One reason political sociologists and political scientists have been so preoccupied with the behavior of nonelites is the ready availability of data in this area. Compare, for example, the ease of acquiring voting statistics or perceiving trends in party composition with the difficulty of observing and recording the decision-making processes of elites. Social scientists, given as they are to a preference for rigorous evidence, have thus naturally turned to these topics and sources of information.

Another explanation for the extensive study of nonelite political behavior lies in the general assumptions of pluralist democracy. As the dominant model of the society's power structure, pluralism postulates the importance of citizen activities such as voting as a means of controlling political leaders and assuring nonelite input into political decisions. Marxist and elitist models of power, on the other hand, do not see such activities as effective in either controlling elites or choosing them. Instead these models see elections and other forms of participation by the masses as responses to elite or ruling class manipulation. These views have customarily not been as popular as pluralism among most political scientists and sociologists. Thus traditional political analysts continue to see the electoral process as central to power in the United States and other Western societies and have studied it exhaustively.

No perspective of politics in society, however, whether Marxist, elitist, or pluralist, omits nonelites from the structure and processes of power. Obviously without masses there are no elites. Moreover the forms of nonelite political behavior in modern societies are varied; electoral activities are only one. Hence even Marxists and elitists recognize the potentiality of mass power. Indeed this is fundamental especially to Marxist (or class) theories. The frequent displacement of elites and at times even the alteration of entire sociopolitical systems by mass actions testify to this potential. To fully understand power in societies, then, it is vital to study the nature of nonelite participation and the factors which motivate it.

We will focus primarily on nonelite political behavior in the United

States and other Western capitalist societies, those which proclaim themselves democratic—that is, where the citizenry presumably maintains ultimate control over political leaders. Although the characteristics of democratic systems have been subject to varied interpretation, there seems to be general agreement that a sociopolitical system is democratic to the extent that leaders are held accountable to masses. This is accomplished through political institutions which facilitate mass participation in various forms, primarily free and competitive elections. Necessarily, then, much of our discussion will concern the electoral process.

But the technique of elections should not be confused with its final product. Indeed, if holding elections were the only requirement of a democratic system, most totalitarian societies would easily qualify. What is more important are the *effects* of citizen participation. The compelling questions, then, are "To what extent are leaders really held accountable?" and "To what extent are citizens' needs and desires fulfilled through electoral and other participatory institutions?" It is on these points that the democratic character of a sociopolitical system hinges. Electoral participation may be quite high and the institutional means for citizen expression vast; yet these are of little meaning if they do not provide some degree of real power to those who participate. Thus throughout our discussion we will take a critical look at democratic institutions, continually probing their effectiveness in affording nonelites a share of societal power.

Also we must remember the wide scope of politics in society. Although sociologists and political scientists have studied elite-mass linkages almost exclusively within the governmental realm, we should not think that political behavior is limited to the actions people take in regard to government alone. A major theme running throughout our previous discussions of power in society is the collateral power of economic and governmental institutions. This point must again be underscored in looking at the actions of nonelites. Regardless of what impact masses may exert on the policy decisions of government leaders, this represents only one key decision-making area. Events occur and decisions are made within economic institutions which impact enormously on people's lives. Thus we must also examine the extent to which masses are able to hold elites accountable here.

In what follows we will try to clarify first *who* among nonelites participates and *in what ways* they do so. Second, we will look at the chief instrument of mass political participation in Western societies, the mass party. Finally, we will deal with the *meaning* of mass participation—that is, the effect it may have on the structure of power and the distribution of the society's wealth.

NONELITE PARTICIPATION

Political participation in societies takes a number of forms. These activities may be divided into two categories: those which are institutionalized and those which are noninstitutionalized. Institutionalized forms of participation are the established and acceptable methods of citizen action, those recognized as legitimate by the prevailing political system. Voting, writing letters to political officials, working for a political party, demonstrating peacefully, and so on are institutionalized actions. *Non*institutionalized forms of mass participation are not recognized as legitimate, extending beyond the official definitions of what is appropriate citizen behavior. These might include civil disobedience, violent confrontations with authorities, and, most extreme of all, actions designed to overthrow the prevailing system. Certain noninstitutionalized forms of political participation will be discussed in chapter 13. Here we are concerned only with the institutionalized forms.

Who Participates?

Citizen action is fundamental in a democratic system. Yet one of the most salient facts of research in political sociology is the relatively low level of participation among nonelites in any form of political activity. This has been true in American society for most of the twentieth century despite the expansion of voting rights and other political opportunities to previously disenfranchised groups such as women, blacks, and other minorities. The low level of nonelite participation is not unique to the United States, however, but is quite the same in most Western industrial societies.[1]

Political scientist Lester Milbrath (1965) has constructed a hierarchy of political involvement (Figure 11-1) denoting various activities in which citizens might engage. These activities tend to be cumulative so that participation in one near the top of the hierarchy makes it likely that other lesser activities will also be engaged in. Those who are minimally involved, the "spectators," make up, according to Milbrath, about 60 percent of the citizenry: "they watch, they cheer, they vote, but they do not do battle" (p. 21). "Gladiators" participate in more meaningful activities requiring greater expenditures of time, energy, and money. These are

---

1. Research on political participation has been vast. One of the best introductions to the general findings of researchers is Milbrath (1965). Other basic works are Campbell et al. (1960), Lane (1964), and Flanigan and Zingale (1975). On other Western societies see Rose (1974) and Almond and Verba (1963).

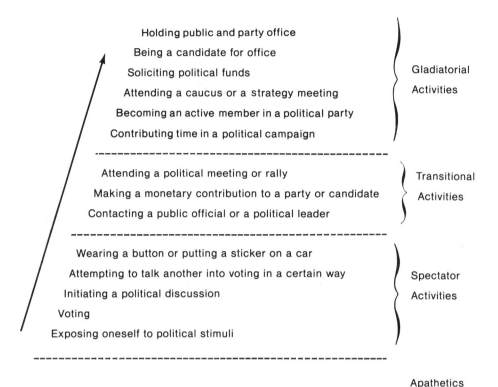

Holding public and party office

Being a candidate for office

Soliciting political funds

Attending a caucus or a strategy meeting

Becoming an active member in a political party

Contributing time in a political campaign

Gladiatorial
Activities

Attending a political meeting or rally

Making a monetary contribution to a party or candidate

Contacting a public official or a political leader

Transitional
Activities

Wearing a button or putting a sticker on a car

Attempting to talk another into voting in a certain way

Initiating a political discussion

Voting

Exposing oneself to political stimuli

Spectator
Activities

Apathetics

Figure 11-1 Hierarchy of Political Involvement. Source: Lester Milbrath, *Political Participation* (Chicago: Rand McNally, 1965), p. 18. Reprinted by permission.

the significant participants, but they constitute probably only 1 or 2 percent. This leaves about one-third of the American adult population who can be characterized as the "apathetics," completely outside the arena of participation. In most cases they are "unaware, literally, of the political part of the world around them" (Milbrath, 1965:21).

Political scientists Sidney Verba and Norman Nie have also investigated various nonelite political activities and some of their findings are shown in Table 11-1. As can be seen, only the act of voting is performed regularly by more than half the adult population, and this occurs only in presidential elections. In activities beyond voting, no more than one-third of the American citizenry takes part, and those requiring more than trivial amounts of time and energy are performed by no more than 10 to 20 percent. Nie and Verba note, however, that political participation is somewhat specialized; those engaging in one type of activity are not necessarily the same as those who engage in another. Thus the

TABLE 11-1 Percentage Engaging in Twelve Different Acts of Political Participation

TYPE OF POLITICAL PARTICIPATION	PERCENTAGE
1. Report regularly voting in presidential elections[a]	72
2. Report always voting in local elections	47
3. Active in at least one organization involved in community problems[b]	32
4. Have worked with others in trying to solve some community problems	30
5. Have attempted to persuade others to vote as they were	28
6. Have ever actively worked for a party or candidates during an election	26
7. Have ever contacted a local government official about some issue or problem	20
8. Have attended at least one political meeting or rally in last three years	19
9. Have ever contacted a state or national government official about some issue or problem	18
10. Have ever formed a group or organization to attempt to solve some local community problem	14
11. Have ever given money to a party or candidate during an election campaign	13
12. Presently a member of a political club or organization	8

Number of Cases: weighted   3,095
unweighted 2,549

[a] Composite variable created from reports of voting in 1960 and 1964 presidential elections. Percentage is equal to those who report they have voted in both elections.
[b] This variable is a composite index where the proportion presented above is equal to the proportion of those in the sample who are active in at least one voluntary association that, they report, takes an active role in attempting to solve community problems. The procedure utilized was as follows: each respondent was asked whether he was a member of fifteen types of voluntary associations. For each affirmative answer he was then asked whether he regularly attended meetings or otherwise took a leadership role in the organization. If yes, he was considered an active member. If he was an active member and if he reported that the organization regularly attempted to solve community problems, he was considered to have performed this type of political act. Membership in expressly *political* clubs or organizations was excluded from this index.
Source: From PARTICIPATION IN AMERICA by Sidney Verba and Norman Nie. Copyright © 1972 by Sidney Verba and Norman H. Nie. Reprinted by permission of Harper & Row, Publishers, Inc.

number who participate in *some* form of political activity is greater than these figures suggest. In any case, however, they reflect only a minimally active citizenry.

Although the percentage who vote regularly is higher, these patterns of participation are generally similar in Western European societies. In Great Britain, for example, those actually participating in anything other than voting in a general election are a small percentage and become smaller as the significance of activity increases (Butler and Stokes, 1974:20–23).

Moreover the general public remains ill informed about government and politics despite widespread dissemination of at least basic information through the mass media and the educational system. In a survey conducted by the Louis Harris Organization in 1973, most citizens admitted their relative ignorance of the workings and functions of government at any level. Slightly more than half, when asked, could correctly name at least one U.S. senator from their state, and only 46 percent could accurately name the congressman from their district (Harris, 1974). Surveys such as this have been conducted at various times for several decades, and the results have remained quite consistent (Glenn, 1972:274). Political scientists David Butler and Donald Stokes (1974:22) note a similar limitation of public awareness of politics in Great Britain. Indeed this seems to be a common pattern in democratic societies.

The first key point regarding political participation in the United States and other Western societies, then, is that *only a small number actually participate in any meaningful way.* Unless an issue is perceived as having direct personal significance, most people remain uninterested and uninvolved. As one sociologist has put it, "In nearly all political domains only the single most visible personality or headlined issue reaches the average person's awareness. Politicians almost invariably overestimate public attention to affairs that deeply concern them" (Stacey, 1977:114).

Social correlates of political participation. In chapter 8 we saw that the society's institutional leaders are not typical of the citizenry as a whole. We might expect, however, that political participation, slight though it may be, would extend rather broadly across the social spectrum. But in looking at participation in the United States and other Western societies, we find again that by and large the few people who do engage in political activities in any significant way are not representative of the general populace.

Who are the political participants? We may summarize the substantial research on voting and other forms of activism with a breakdown of the general patterns within key sociological categories[2]:

CLASS: Those of higher occupational positions, higher income, and higher levels of education participate more than those of lower oc-

2. In addition to those sources listed in footnote 1, see Lipset (1960:ch. 6).

cupational status, income, and education.
SEX: Men participate more than women.
RACE: Whites participate more than blacks.
RELIGION: Jews participate more than Catholics, who in turn partici-
pate more than Protestants.

Class and Political Behavior

The most significant of the correlates of political behavior is social class.
Whether and how one participates as well as one's general political attitudes are dependent more on this factor than any other. Merely knowing a person's class, of course, does not mean we can accurately predict
his or her political behavior at all times. We can, however, perceive fairly
clear differences in political behavior between different class *groups*.
Thus, by looking at these collective patterns, we can generalize for all
persons of a particular class, realizing that the pattern may not hold true
for any specific individual. This is the common sociological mode of
analysis.

Class and participation. The relationship between class and participation
is one of the firmest assumptions of political sociology, backed by a
wealth of empirical evidence. Indeed the importance of class as an
explanator of *all* forms of political behavior is recognized by all political
sociologists and political scientists regardless of theoretical persuasion.
Most simply, *the higher one's class, the greater the scope, intensity, and significance of political participation* (Lipset, 1960; Verba and Nie, 1972).[3]
Those at the upper end of the society's stratification system participate
most frequently and in the most effectual political activities. Whether
class is measured in terms of wealth and income, occupational status,
education, or a combination of these, this pattern remains exceedingly
strong in the United States and other capitalist societies. Thus the common notion that class and politics in America "do not mix" is not borne
out in reality.

   The relationship between social class and political participation
(specifically voting) may be seen in Tables 11-2, 11-3, and 11-4. It is
clear that regardless of the measure of class—income, education, or occupation—the pattern is much the same: Those at the upper levels of
the class hierarchy vote at much higher rates than do those at the lower
levels. Moreover these figures indicate only the minimal participatory act
and thus understate the difference in political participation between

3. For other studies that confirm this relationship, see Milbrath (1965:116).

TABLE 11-2 Percent Reported Voting, By Income, 1976

Under $5,000	45.6
5,000– 9,999	53.0
10,000– 14,999	60.4
15,000– 24,999	70.3
25,000 and over	77.2

Source: U.S. Bureau of the Census, *Current Population Reports*, Series P-20, No. 322, "Voting and Registration in the Election of November 1976" (Washington, D.C.: U.S. Government Printing Office, 1978), Table 13, p. 65.

those at the top and the remainder of the populace. Insofar as other more significant forms of political activism are concerned, those requiring money and serious effort, the upper income, occupation, and education groups virtually monopolize the political arena.

How might the varying rates of participation among different class groups be explained? Political sociologists have traditionally pointed to a combination of social and cultural factors. Those in higher class positions work in occupations which involve more politically relevant activities and which naturally extend their political skills and interests. Since such people have more education to begin with, it is argued that they will likely become more aware of and motivated to participate in political activities. Moreover those of higher social class have more free time to engage in politics; those at the other end of the class hierarchy simply lack energy for investment in political activity given their constant struggle for existence (Lane, 1964:233– 234; Lipset, 1960:198). In addition, middle-class people are, according to Lipset, more conforming to the society's norms, including those related to politics, and thus participate more dutifully than the lower classes. Such factors explain political activism as a product more of socialization than any rational calculation of

TABLE 11-3 Percent Reported Voting, By Years of School Completed, 1976

Elementary	0–4	29.1
	5–7	42.0
	8	51.4
High School	1–3	47.2
	4	59.4
College	1–3	68.1
	4	78.6
	5 or more	81.9

Source: U.S. Bureau of the Census, *Current Population Reports*, Series P-20, No. 322, "Voting and Registration in the Election of November 1976" (Washington, D.C.: U.S. Government Printing Office, 1978), Table 10, p. 57.

TABLE 11-4 Percent Reported Voting, By Occupation and Sex, 1976

Occupation	Male	Female
White-collar workers	73.8	70.4
Professional, technical, and kindred workers	78.2	78.6
Managers and administrators, except farm	73.0	70.2
Sales workers	71.2	64.3
Clerical and kindred workers	67.5	67.6
Blue-collar workers	50.6	45.9
Craftsmen and kindred workers	55.9	61.4
Operatives, except transport	46.7	42.1
Transport equipment operatives	47.7	59.7
Laborers, except farm	43.5	45.1
Service workers	56.5	50.6
Private household workers	—	47.2
Service workers, except private household	56.7	51.2
Farm workers	62.3	63.7
Farm workers and farm managers	77.0	69.6
Farm laborers and supervisors	34.7	61.3

Source: U.S. Bureau of the Census, *Current Population Reports*, Series P-20, No. 322, "Voting and Registration in the Election of November 1976," (Washington, D.C.: U.S. Government Printing Office, 1978), Table 12, p. 63

the advantages of participating. People of different classes are exposed to different cultural environments and thus learn different responses to the political process.

These presumptions have been subject to much scrutiny, however, and are by no means universally accepted among political sociologists. The lower rates of participation among working classes and the poor may also be attributed simply to lower expectations that political activism will yield measurable benefits, a notion, which, as we will see, appears to be by and large correct. And in the same way, the more extensive activism by those of higher social class may be seen as a product of quite rational decision, given their anticipated payoff from the expenditure of time, energy, and money. Thus differences in political behavior may be a result not so much of cultural factors as rational perceptions of the relative profits resulting from participation.

Moreover in recent decades low rates of political participation have been widespread throughout the populace. The absence of participation from electoral politics is too general today to dismiss merely as a characteristic of the poor, the uneducated, and racial minorities. Some have pointed to the mechanical obstacles to participation, such as cumbersome voter registration laws, numerous primary elections prior to general elections, and lengthy, complex, and confusing ballots (Kimball, 1972). But at best, these impediments can account for only some of the lack of voting and cannot explain the low levels of other more significant forms of political activism.

Others suggest that the low rate of participation in electoral politics may simply reflect satisfaction with the output of the political system. This argument seems weak, however, since studies have shown that the subordinate classes—those who participate least—do not see the system working in their behalf to the extent that relatively advantaged social groups do (Hamilton, 1972; Huber and Form, 1973; Verba and Nie, 1972).

Political alienation. A more compelling explanation for nonparticipation among a variety of class and status groups is disaffection with the prevailing political system. For the disaffected, electoral politics do not reflect their needs, and thus participation is without purpose. Various types and degrees of disaffection with the political system are generally termed political alienation. The concept of alienation was first applied in sociology by Karl Marx and has since been popularly used to describe a variety of psychological and social conditions, all denoting some sense of being cut off from or unable to control or cope with social institutions (see for example Fromm, 1955; Josephson and Josephson, 1962). *Political* alienation may be defined simply as a feeling on the part of an individual that he or she is not part of the political process (Levin, 1960:62). Persons see their votes as meaningless and believe that important political decisions are made by remote leaders who are not responsive to or interested in the needs of the average person. The politically alienated lack trust in decision makers and feel that societal institutions, particularly government, are run mainly for the benefit of special interests. Politics thus loses its meaning.

We might say that political alienation arises when the manner in which the political system is really believed to work does not coincide with people's expectations of how it *should* work. Political scientist Murray Levin (1960) explains that, ironically, the fundamental tenets of democratic theory, emphasizing the power of the masses in controlling elites, are key sources of political alienation since such a controlling role by nonelites is simply not realizable in modern societies. Classical democratic theory, according to Levin, "demands more of the individual citizen than he can realistically fulfill and promises more than can be delivered" (p. 73).

Although intense and long-lasting alienation has been usually evident mainly among lower class and status groups, recent trends in voting behavior and expressions of lack of confidence in leaders and institutions indicate that feelings of political alienation may extend far beyond the subordinate classes and racial minorities. Public opinion polls in the United States in the last decade have shown not merely a dissatisfaction with a particular party or administration but rather a growing disaffection with and distrust of the political system itself among a majority of the population. Increased feelings of powerlessness and meaninglessness have paralleled a noticeable decline in voting, even in presidential elections (Miller, 1974; Nie, Verba, and Petrocik, 1976).

The growing intensity and scope of political alienation are reflected in a 1979 survey developed by political scientist Alan Westin and conducted by the Louis Harris Organization. The researchers found that 38 percent of Americans felt voting made no difference in government actions. On feelings of trust in political leaders and institutions, three out of five felt that government could not be trusted to look after their interests. After collecting responses on several measures, the researchers created an index of alienation and found one-half of Americans to be either "highly" or "moderately" alienated. What is perhaps most significant is the lack of substantial difference the study found among various occupational, income, age, sex, or educational groups in this total index (Westin, 1979).

Undoubtedly the traumatic events of the Vietnam era followed by Watergate have been significant contributors to heightening disaffection with the political system. What consequences the apparent diffusion and intensification of political alienation will have on future nonelite political behavior remains a vitally important question.

Class and partisanship. Political partisanship, the party preferences and ideological leanings of people, is also strongly related to social class. Generally those of the working and lower classes tend to support parties and ideologies of the left, while those of the upper and middle classes support those of the right. This is true particularly on economic issues. Parties of the left, such as the Democratic party in the United States, the Labour party in Great Britain, and various socialist and communist parties in Western Europe and Japan, offer policies which proclaim the interests of the working class, while parties of the right, such as the Republican party in the United States, the Conservatives in Great Britain, and the Christian Democrats in West Germany and other Western European societies stand more strongly for the protection of business interests. Most importantly, nonelites interpret the differences in party offerings in this way.

When noneconomic issues are considered, however, less clear-cut class patterns are apparent. Lipset explains that while the poorer strata are more liberal or leftist on bread-and-butter issues such as wages, taxes, and trade unions, they display more conservatism on social issues such as civil liberties, social equality, internationalism, and so on. On these issues "The more well-to-do are more liberal, the poorer are more intolerant" (Lipset, 1960:92; see also Lipset and Raab, 1978). Whether these class patterns of partisanship are in fact valid, however, has been increasingly debated in political sociology and will be discussed later in this chapter.

Ethnicity and Political Behavior

In multiethnic societies such as the United States, various forms of ethnicity—race, religion, national origin—are additionally important correlates of political behavior. Blacks, for example, exhibit a lower rate of participation than whites, and Jews show consistently higher rates of activism than other ethnic groups.[4]

Ethnic factors are also important determinants of political partisanship, sometimes even superseding class factors. For instance, since the 1930s blacks and Jews in the United States have tended to vote overwhelmingly Democratic regardless of class position. Both of these groups solidly turned to the Democratic party during the New Deal of Franklin D. Roosevelt and have remained there ever since, given the party's clearer identification with working-class and minority interests. Jews have generally displayed a preference for liberalism on most political issues despite the fact that they collectively rank higher in income and education than most other ethnic groups (Fisher, 1979).

Other Social Factors

That class and, to some extent, ethnic factors are strongly related to political participation and partisanship in capitalist societies does not mean that political behavior can always be explained in these terms. In Canada, for example, politics is organized more around regional, and to some degree religious, groupings than classes (Alford, 1963:257; Schwartz, 1974). But even in the United States, obviously other social and political variables such as region, age, and even sex will have some

4. The lower rate of participation by blacks may be attributed largely to their generally subordinate class position but also to their historically disenfranchised status, particularly in the South. This view is supported by the fact that when blacks and whites of middle- and upper-middle-class status are compared, their rates of participation are similar (Verba and Nie, 1972:ch. 10).

bearing on political behavior, as will the particular issues and personalities which are presented to the citizenry. In fact, at times the class
factor seems entirely absent. Consider a recent example. Although the
affluent in the United States usually vote Republican and the working
classes and the poor vote Democratic, in the 1968 presidential election,
two of the wealthiest suburbs in the country—Beverly Hills, California,
and Scarsdale, New York—both gave a majority to the Democratic candidate while the Fifth congressional district of Kentucky, with a median
family income several hundred dollars lower than any other in the nation, gave almost 60 percent of its vote to the Republican.

Certain upper-class individuals sometimes display sympathy for liberal causes and policies which benefit the poor and the working classes.
In fact, Lipset (1960:319) suggests that progressive political behavior on
the part of the old-line wealthy families in America has been somewhat
traditional "as part of their struggle against the vulgar *nouveau riche*
businessmen." Similarly some individuals of lower socioeconomic status
may display more conservative political attitudes and preferences than
would normally be expected. But to concentrate on exceptions such as
these is to overlook the more general congruence between social class
and political behavior. The bulk of evidence points to a strong correlation between class position and both participation and partisanship.

In sum, the major patterns of nonelite political behavior are: (1) a
limited number participate in political activities of any kind; (2) participation in political activities of greatest significance is confined to the
society's dominant class and status groups; (3) political partisanship is
arranged for the most part along class lines.

POLITICAL PARTIES AND PARTICIPATION

To understand the dynamics of nonelite political behavior, we must look
at the structure within which that behavior occurs. In modern societies
political behavior takes place primarily in the context of mass political
parties. Nonelite participation involves mainly electoral activities, and in
the United States and other Western societies the electoral system is intertwined with the institution of political parties. Basically, then, it is
within and through the political party that the ordinary citizen can take
part in the political process.

In the Anglo-American societies, the dominance of two parties has
historically characterized the electoral system. As it has functioned in the
United States and Canada (and to a lesser extent Great Britain), the
two-party system has protected the stability of the dominant sociopolitical

and economic institutions and has discouraged changes in the prevailing class system. Two features of the party system in the United States stand out as reinforcers of the political status quo: (1) the lack of fundamentally divergent policy offerings by the two parties and (2) the nonideological nature of the parties, neither reflecting sharp class interests.

Elections and the Two-Party System

To begin with, given the two-party system in the United States, rarely are elections so clearly contests between two diametrically opposing groups. This is partially due to the mechanics of the electoral system. Most elections are within single-member districts wherein only one candidate can be elected no matter how many are on the ballot. In such an arrangement, the two major parties must aim for a centrist course in trying to appeal to as broad a range of the electorate as possible. The parties and their candidates thus do not sharply diverge. If minority party candidates are on the ballot, voters are discouraged from voting for them since to do so is in effect to waste their votes.

In multiparty systems, however, parties gain representation in government on the basis of their electoral percentage. Here many parties, each with a chance to gain offices, are encouraged to place candidates on the ballot. A variety of parties will thus be offered to the electorate, each reflecting relatively narrow, mainly class, interests. In such systems whereby parties need not appeal to the entire electorate, clear choices in policy are offered. And voters may ignore the major parties without fear of throwing away their votes. Today multiparty systems are found in France, Italy, and several other Western European societies.

In seeking appeal to the widest possible number of voters, American (and Canadian) parties tend to focus on trivial matters and issues of personality and to avoid serious issues concerning the structure and functioning of political and economic institutions. This is well illustrated by the 1976 presidential election. The chief controversies of the campaign centered on Gerald Ford's questionable competence (an image fueled by his statement during one of the televised debates that he could see no Soviet influence in Eastern Europe) and Jimmy Carter's interview in *Playboy* magazine in which he spoke frankly of his sexual lust. With the possible exceptions of 1964 and 1972, most recent presidential elections have focused on similar personality issues.

Whatever their differences, then, American political parties must present themselves to the electorate as moderate political forces rather than parties which seem to cater more strongly to one social group or another. The chief purposes of American parties are to nominate, campaign for, and elect candidates. Articulating issues and constructing policy programs play secondary roles. Indeed, spelling out specific programs and issues becomes an electoral liability. One political scientist has referred to American and many Western European parties of the post-World War II era as "catch all" parties in which their resources are used almost exclusively to attract as many voters as possible, thus deemphasizing specific issues which may frighten away potential votes (Kirchheimer, 1966:185–186). Neither party, as a result, can offer substantive policies of change.

Nonideological Parties

American parties have traditionally been "accommodationist," with no deep chasms of philosophical difference between them regarding the society's vital issues. "Ideological" parties, by comparison, engage in conflict over deep-seated differences in basic policy issues and philosophy. French political scientist Maurice Duverger has described the two American parties as "rival teams, one occupying office, the other seeking to dislodge it. It is a struggle between the *ins* and the *outs*, which never becomes fanatical, and creates no deep cleavage in the country" (1959:418).

In those instances when clear-cut differences seem to arise between the parties, the dispute is rarely one that can be traced to a fundamental disagreement in goals. The differences are generally related to the methods used to realize those goals and the degree of urgency each assigns to them (Lawson, 1968:44). Generally these boil down to the Democrats' preference for the greater use and speedier application of government means to achieve these mutually understood goals as opposed to the Republicans' preference for a slower pace, relying on private rather than government efforts. For example, both parties favor policies aimed at keeping the rate of unemployment as low as possible. But while Democrats will call for the creation of more jobs through direct government measures, Republicans will advocate leaving the task to the private business sector.

In addition to the electoral system, which contributes to their nonideological character, the centrism of American political parties may be due in large part to the society's nonideological tradition in which class divisions, though objectively acute, have historically been underplayed. The fact that the two parties have operated with little threat from class-based third parties during the course of American history may reflect the continual low level of class consciousness in the society. In contrast to contemporary France or Italy, where a wide variety of parties compete along very clear ideological lines, reflecting those societies' class divisions, American parties have continued to function by openly appealing to no single class. Ideologically specific parties have never been able to gain a foothold among the electorate even during economically troubled times. In the Depression election of 1932, for example, all the various Marxist parties together could win no more than 2.6 percent of the popular vote. More moderate socialist parties have fared little differently.

Mild ideological differences are evident within and between the two major parties, then, but almost never to the point of serious rifts. As sociologist Daniel Bell (1964:48) has described them, "Each party is like some huge bazaar, with hundreds of hucksters clamoring for attention. But while life within the bazaars flows freely and licenses are easy to obtain, all trading has to be conducted within the tents; the ones who hawk their wares outside are doomed to few sales."

A lack of ideological content has characterized party politics in Canada also. Like the Democratic and Republican parties in the United States, the Liberal and Progressive Conservative parties in Canada are "all encompassing," reflecting the interests of no particular social class. The electoral strategies of Canadian parties have thus closely paralleled their American counterparts (Ogmundson, 1975; Porter, 1965:368).

Though operating within a two-party system, the political parties in Great Britain, in contrast to the American and Canadian parties, have been more clearly linked to class groups and issues in their historical development. The Labour party, for example, is closely allied with British trade unions and tends to reflect their interests in its policy proposals and actions. As might be expected, class-based voting patterns are more evident in Great Britain than in the United States or Canada (Alford, 1963; 1972; Butler and Stokes, 1974).

Some do see American parties reflecting class interests, though less overtly. A classic study of American electoral patterns (Campbell et al., 1960:159) notes that although it lacks the overriding importance that it has in most Western European party systems, "class is clearly one of the underlying dimensions of party affiliation in the United States." Lipset (1960:230) also notes that "Even though many parties renounce the principle of class conflict or loyalty, an analysis of their appeals and their support suggests that they do represent the interests of different classes."

The relationship between party and class has in fact been fairly consistent in the United States. As might be expected, working- and lower-class persons have generally supported the Democratic party, while the Republican party has attracted upper- and upper-middle-class persons as well as certain segments of the lower middle class, notably small businessmen. And whether warranted or not, the parties have come to be associated in the minds of most voters with these class interests.

But the party-class connection in the United States should not be overdrawn. Few Americans of any class think in terms of class divisions and thus do not make political decisions on that basis. Party identifications, though divided along fairly clear class lines, are more the product of family socialization than of class consciousness. Indeed the fact that party loyalties are developed early in childhood helps to make the appeal of class- or ethnic-based minority parties ineffectual.

The American party system has clearly provided stability, consistency, and in political scientist Theodore Lowi's (1976:301) words, "a regular, even if modest, departure from absolute tyranny." The durability of this system has been fostered by the nature of the electoral system itself, by the nonideological character of the parties, and also by the built-in social and political impediments to the rise of effective third parties. In creating stability and consistency, however, the American party system has just as clearly frustrated any attempts at fundamental socioeconomic change through institutional means. Plainly the structure and workings of the two-party system have strongly aided the higher social classes in extending their domination of the political process.

The Declining Role of Parties

Many observers have expressed the view that the traditional role of parties in the American electoral system may be waning. Several factors are cited.

First, political conventions no longer seem to control the nomination of a presidential candidate, the single most important electoral prize for each party. Individual candidates have increasingly formed independent organizations to run their campaigns, thereby making conventions political "circuses" which merely ratify the choice already made through a series of primary elections. The Nixon campaign of 1972, for example, largely bypassed the regular Republican party apparatus. One political scientist suggests that the Democrats have had such relative difficulty in winning the White House in recent decades at the same time that they have dominated all other elective offices because "the presidency has come to have less and less to do with political party" (Ladd, 1977:215).

Second, the mass media, especially television, are now the chief sources of political communication. As a result, candidate image becomes more important than party identification, further releasing politicians from party commitments. This is particularly true of presidential candidates, who now engage in "gigantic acts of theater" (Ladd, 1977:215).

Third, there has been a distinct decline in the partisanship of the American electorate in recent years. In short, fewer and fewer people identify with either of the two major parties. By 1974, over one-third of the electorate referred to itself as "independent" (Abramson, 1976; Nie et al., 1976). This represented a steady decline in party identification since 1964. In addition to declining party identification, there has been a noticeable increase in independent voting behavior, with more ticket splitting in elections at all levels. What is particularly apparent is an increase in independent identification and voting among the higher educated, that group which has most consistently participated in the electoral process (Nie et al., 1976:276). One study investigating this tendency concludes quite simply that "The electorate is far more weakly tied to political parties now than at any time in the past century" (Ladd and Hadley, 1978:27).

However, the demise of party voting may be exaggerated in light of its relative stability in state, local, and even congressional elections. As Lowi (1976:280) puts it, "The situation in the electorate *below* the presidential level continues to be highly stable, composed of parties, strong party affiliations, tradition, habit, and an occasional issue or charismatic personality."

The imminent breakdown of the two-party system has been forecast at various times in American political history, and it is highly probable that it will survive the current round of dire prognostications, albeit in perhaps modified form. Whatever its future role and shape, however, its conservative effect on the body politic is not likely to change.

THE MEANING OF MASS PARTICIPATION

In looking at nonelite political participation, we have now seen that it is limited in scope, intensity, and breadth throughout the populace. Relatively few actually engage in political acts of any kind beyond voting, and those who do are ordinarily of the society's dominant class and status groups. These facts present several theoretical and practical questions with important implications.

First, what does the low level of participation mean for democratic politics? Since it is almost exclusively through the electoral system that nonelites can take part in the political process, the fact that so few actually do use this channel calls into doubt the very essence of a democratic polity.

Second, whatever the level of electoral participation, to what extent can this process serve as a check on elite power? Can it really assure that the will of nonelites is carried out by the powerful? In short, can mass needs and desires be translated into public policy through the electoral system?

Third, what means can nonelites employ to exert control over elites outside the governmental realm? In the end, electoral politics represents a mechanism which can be effective only within one institution—the state. But as we have seen, societal power—and thus elite power—is found in other institutional areas as well.

Let us look at each of these questions.

Participation and Democracy

Political sociologists are at odds over the implications of low levels of mass participation in electoral politics. Some see this development as detrimental to the maintenance of a healthy democratic polity. Verba and Nie's statement (1972:1) typifies this sentiment:

> If democracy is interpreted as rule by the people, then the question of who participates in political decisions becomes the question of the nature of democracy in a society. Where few take part in decisions there is little democracy; the more participation there is in decisions, the more democracy there is.

This is the traditional view of the purpose of participation in a democratic system and is a firm part of the political rhetoric of American society. Citizens are constantly urged to exercise their civic duty by, at minimum, voting, with the customary warning that failure to do so leads to the deterioration of democracy.

Perhaps a more pronounced view among political scientists and sociologists, however, is the belief that a very high level of participation is not necessarily in the best interests of democracy. Basically it is argued that there is no necessary correlation between the extent of citizen participation and the degree of responsible leadership in a society. If nonelite participation is too widespread, demagogues may exploit the masses, who are ill informed and thus incapable of making rational political decisions. That maximum participation does not ensure the election of responsible officials is a point verified by the heavy mass political activism in most totalitarian societies. The rise of the Nazi party in Germany in the 1930s, for example, followed the vitalization of many previously inactive groups. Hitler's success, we are so often reminded, was initially through the ballot.

The assumption among proponents of this view of democratic politics is that societal elites, along with the upper and upper middle classes—those who are the main participants in the system—are as a rule responsible people, basically concerned with protecting the interests of the society as a whole (see for example Banfield and Wilson, 1963). These classes are the chief defenders of democratic politics since they are the best informed and educated and the most conscious of the need to maintain the system's democratic character.

A corollary of this view is that the masses—specifically the working and lower classes—are prone to *un*democratic attitudes and actions. They are more easily given to the abandonment of civil liberties, minority rights, and other fundamental aspects of a democratic system. Lipset (1960:102) has referred to this tendency as "working class authoritarianism" and cites data from a number of societies, including the United States, indicating that the lower and working classes are much less committed to democratic principles. He attributes this largely to inferior education, lack of participation, and general isolation from the activities of democratic society. Secondarily these traits are the result of economic and psychological insecurity: "Acceptance of the norms of democracy requires a high level of sophistication and ego security" (Lipset, 1960:115).

In this view, then, maximal nonelite political participation represents a potential danger to the stability and continuity of a democratic system and is thus not to be encouraged. Rule in democratic societies quite rationally and necessarily falls to elites and their class peers.

How valid is the notion that the subordinate classes are less committed to democratic principles or, conversely, that the upper and middle classes are more committed to them?

Sociologist Richard Hamilton, with impressive evidence, dispels the image of working- and lower-class illiberalism. After reviewing a wealth of data, he concludes that the upper middle class, those who are occupationally and economically most secure and most educated, "do not appear to be especially responsible, either in matters concerning immediate economic welfare or in matters at some remove such as support for more adequate education" (Hamilton, 1972:519; see also Lipsetz, 1965). He also finds that they are no more supportive of civil rights than any other class group.

Form and Huber (1969) likewise find that the affluent are least likely to see government's role as properly one which involves equalizing social opportunity. Indeed instead of working-class authoritarianism, they suggest that "a case can be made that the syndrome amounts to an upper-class authoritarianism." Their findings lead to the conclusion that the ideas and attitudes of the dominant class regarding how power is and *ought* to be distributed in society "are no more systematic, idealistic, or coherent than those of lower income strata" (p. 30).

Those who fear greater participation by the masses in electoral politics assume that their judgments of candidates will be made on irrational bases rather than on careful study of issues. However, Hamilton's evidence indicates that mass ignorance of political matters is mainly the result of the avoidance of issues of major concern among political leaders and the use of "frivolous and distractive themes" (1972:520). Masses, in other words, remain unaware of important societal issues and respond instead to petty concerns because elites choose to concentrate on those concerns. The working and lower classes thus do not represent a threat to democratic politics as much as elites do.

The notion that the middle and upper classes are uniquely qualified to make electoral judgments is refuted by the fact that even the seemingly most informed voters do not exhibit a high level of information on candidates and issues. Moreover political decisions can be based on social factors (for example, party of one's parents, ethnic background) and irrational factors (for example, candidate's image) as much for these people as for any other social group.

Finally, as we have seen, even the common notion that the nonparticipants in electoral politics are mainly among the poor and working classes has been subject to increasing doubt. Nonparticipation is apparently widespread. Indeed one study of nonvoting concludes that "the differences between voters and refrainers are attitudinal rather than socioeconomic" (Hadley, 1978:30). By and large, those who do not vote are as a group not decidedly different in class, race, or education from those who do. If this is so, no particular class group can be singled out for exhibiting either sound or shallow electoral judgment.

Participation and Elite Accountability

The second key question in the analysis of mass participation concerns the effect of such activism on the behavior of political elites. We might ask quite simply, "What difference does it make?" Can the electoral process, regardless of who or how many engage in it, respond to the desires of nonelites? In short, what impact do electoral activities have on the policymaking process?

The classical view of democracy rests on the assumption that participation equates with citizen power. Political leaders are ultimately called to answer for their actions by the electorate and must therefore respond to its general needs and desires. This assumption, however, seems ill-founded for several reasons.

The class bias. First, the electoral process entails more than simply voting. And as we have seen, the serious participants in this process, those whose activism goes well beyond voting, are a distinct subset of the general populace—higher than average in income, occupation, and education. This would not pose serious problems if the needs and wishes of these upper- and upper-middle-class citizens coincided with those of subordinate classes. But "the participants differ substantially from the nonparticipants in the problems they consider salient and in the solutions they prefer" (Verba and Nie, 1972:15).

Those who participate most extensively bring their class perceptions and biases to the electoral process. As a result, to the extent that political leaders do respond to the electorate, they respond to the perceived needs of *these* classes rather than to the needs of the working and lower classes. Hamilton's previously cited study (1972) found that during the 1950s and 1960s, for example, the majority of Americans beneath the upper middle class consistently favored government efforts to establish various social welfare programs such as health care and guaranteed incomes. Yet throughout this period, legislators thwarted these desires and responded instead with generally conservative, status quo policies. A study of elite-mass linkages in Canada likewise concludes that "the sentiments of a considerable portion of our population have not been given a viable outlet by our two major political parties" (Ogmundson, 1976:8).

In any case, most legislators at the national level are from upper-middle-class backgrounds themselves and are thus not likely to hold views which reflect the needs of subordinate groups. Their perceptions of social problems will be quite consonant with those of the significant participants in the electoral process.

Legislative autonomy. Participation does not necessarily equate with citizen power for a second reason: In the policymaking process, lawmakers enjoy a great deal of autonomy vis-à-vis the general electorate. Many studies have indicated that there is little relationship between electoral preferences and the responsiveness of legislators to those preferences.[5] Indeed given the wide recognition by political scientists that voting behavior is less meaningful as a form of citizen influence than is regarded in democratic rhetoric, it is puzzling that they have continued to devote such substantial resources to its study.

The autonomy of legislators stems from several sources, some built into the electoral system itself. First, we have seen that within the two-party system, elections are hardly ever contests that draw sharp lines be-

5. For a discussion of these studies, see Alford and Friedland (1975:440–447).

tween candidates or parties. Almost always they aim for a middle position in hopes of attracting the widest possible portion of the electorate. Thus it becomes difficult, if not impossible, for nonelites to predetermine candidates' views on critical issues accurately. Candidates speak in generalities, not specifics.

In studying the campaign statements of recent presidential candidates, political scientist Benjamin Page concludes that campaign rhetoric about policy is extremely vague. Specific policy statements are rarely made, and those that are appear obscure, ambiguous, and evasive. "The infrequency and inconspicuousness of policy stands make it difficult for the ordinary voter to find them. But even the most diligent and successful seeker after information is frustrated by the fact that stands on policy, once found, turn out to be quite unspecific" (Page, 1978:162). Speeches designed for the general public are couched in ill-defined and empty phrases, while any specific policy stands are usually made before key interest groups, in relatively specialized magazines and journals, or in position papers, the contents of which are not reported by the press. And much of the inconspicuousness and ambiguity of candidates' policy stands, Page points out, cannot be attributed to poor media coverage; rather they are plainly deliberate. For example, Page reports that Richard Nixon's 1968 campaign statements on certain issues regarding the restriction of steel, meat, and textile imports (which would mean higher consumer prices), as well as the oil depletion allowance and the space program (which would mean higher taxes), were made before audiences friendly to those policies but not where they would be seen or heard by the general public.

Even if their positions are clearly spelled out, there is no guarantee that once elected, candidates will abide by their campaign commitments. A good illustration is Lyndon Johnson's campaign pledge in 1964 to deescalate American involvement in the Vietnam war. Following his victory over Barry Goldwater—who favored advancing the war—Johnson considerably expanded the American effort.

Moreover, political, economic, and social conditions may change quickly, making election promises difficult to keep even when there is a genuine intention to do so. Political officials therefore need not be seen as double-crossers who design strategies to fool the public. Although this may be the case in some instances, most elected officials are more likely to see their policy turnabouts as honorable and necessary in light of the vagaries of the political environment.

Also there is a wide communications gap between electors and elected. One study of the U.S. Congress which compared representatives' attitudes with their constituents' concluded that the two coincided only in some measure. In most cases the representatives appeared as having "very imperfect" information about their constituents' policy preferences and vice versa (Miller and Stokes, 1963; see also Prewitt, 1970).

If elections hardly clarify the issue preferences of candidates, neither do they necessarily clarify those of voters. Since electors can vote for only a single candidate, while there are many issues extant at any particular time, the successful candidate cannot know specifically which of his policy stands are actually favored by the voters (Lindblom, 1968: 47). Moreover electors often vote for a candidate not because they favor his or her policy stands but rather as a means of "punishing" the opponent. They vote, in other words, not *for* a particular candidate but *against* another. This further limits the perception of constituency preferences.

In the United States, the lack of party discipline is another contributing factor to the independence of elected officials. In contrast to the major parties in Great Britain and most European societies, as well as Canada, elected officials can ignore their party's leadership and policy lines without jeopardizing their standing or financial support in the party. Thus we find congressmen or senators from the same party often taking widely divergent stands on issues and displaying overall ideological differences. In the Senate, for example, Strom Thurmond, expressing ultraconservative views, and Mark Hatfield, usually proclaiming liberal views, are both nominally Republicans. Likewise, Southern Democrats for many decades have voted in Congress more consistently with Republicans and have generally followed a more conservative policy line than their Northern counterparts. Indeed there may be greater differences *within* either of the two parties than between them.[6] Party labels and party declarations of policy thus often mislead rather than inform the electorate.

Furthermore, having been released from party obligations, legislators can be more responsive to the interests of financially and organizationally powerful lobbying groups who can appeal to them personally instead of through party channels.

Power without participation. The fact that there seems to be a rather weak link between political elites and masses does not mean that elites can or do ignore mass opinions and desires at all times. Obviously this is not the case. Rather, the responsiveness of elites to masses is a matter of degree. As Verba and Nie (1972:7) point out, it is unrealistic in any case to expect leaders to be absolutely responsive to masses in a complex soci-

6.   For a comparison of American and Canadian parties on this point, see Epstein (1964).

ety in which elections are the only mechanism available to the latter. It is clear that any single citizen, through the ballot alone, can have little meaningful impact on the policy decisions of elites; and conversely, those decisions can perfectly match the desires of no more than a few citizens.

The more important questions, then, are (1) Which groups are able to have the greatest impact on the formation of the agenda of political elites? and (2) To what degree are the policy preferences of certain groups of the society more regularly met by political elites? In simple terms, who shapes the issues that government leaders debate, and who ultimately benefits most from their decisions? From our analysis of the corporate state (chapter 7), it seems apparent that the society's dominant economic groups score highest on both counts. Even if not by design, the imperatives of a capitalist political economy dictate this outcome. And it is an outcome which may have very little to do with participation in the electoral process *per se*.

Focusing attention on electoral behavior alone may cause us mistakenly to accept this aspect of the political process as the most significant wellspring of power. Electoral decisions, however, are only secondary to the establishment of the political agenda itself. Rather than deciding *who* will argue and act on particular issues, deciding *which* issues will become part of the political debate is a more primary act of power. Thus, under the most democratic of systems, with a maximum of citizen participation, the power of nonelites in decision making remains symbolic at best if they cannot influence the roster of issues to be debated and acted upon. Even when voters have the opportunity to choose between representatives of clearly opposing positions on particular issues (and it is obvious that they are rarely afforded this opportunity), their collective decision may mean little.

Alford and Friedland point out that the traditional pluralist perception of the political process assumes that the most important decisions are made at the point where legislation is proposed and debated. This, in the pluralist view, is where political power can be best observed and the responses of lawmakers to the electorate best measured. But this procedure overlooks the more important preemptive development of policy options by dominant—principally economic—interest groups. On these decisions, nonelites do not participate. In Alford and Friedland's words, "Mass publics can participate only at those points of political production where the power of dominant interests is *not* located" (1975: 455).

In any case, since the policymaking process is, to all intents and purposes, reliant on the cooperation of government and dominant economic groups, the latter are basically in a position to greatly influence the structure of state action even though they may play little formal role in participatory politics. Whatever government does is dependent on tax revenues, and the ability of government at all levels to raise revenues is, in turn, dependent on the production and investment decisions of dominant economic groups. In the United States these are the giant corporations. Thus, as Alford and Friedland (1975) stress, lack of participation is no indication of the extent of corporate power in the political process. This is "power without participation" (p. 447). And by the same token, mass participation in electoral activities, no matter how extensive, can be virtually meaningless. What social and economic programs are enacted by legislators are dependent more on the private decisions of economic elites than on the policy preferences of the electorate. Thus it seems only logical that legislators will respond more routinely to the interests of powerful corporations than to those of other societal groups.

Nonelectoral Forms of Participation

Although elections are the most essential form of nonelite participation in modern societies, there are other methods by which masses may impact on political decision makers. If the electoral process is dubiously effective in holding political elites accountable, what other means do nonelites have at their disposal and how effective are they?

Interest groups. Pluralists have traditionally considered interest group activity one of the most important instruments of citizen input into the policymaking process. If elections are not always effective in communicating the needs and desires of the people to political elites, interest groups, serving as intermediaries between people and government, may do so. This assumes, of course, that most of the populace will be active members of one or several interest groups. But as was noted in chapter 3, the popular image of Americans as a society of joiners is not accurate. The same holds true even more strongly in other Western societies (Almond and Verba, 1963:246–247).

As with participation in the electoral process, there is a definite link between the scope and intensity of activism in interest groups and one's class position. Most simply, the higher one's class, the greater the number of memberships and extent of participation in such organizations. Thus, like the electoral process, the interest group process is heavily class biased. Furthermore, the most effective interest groups are those which are firmly part of the lobbying system, which do not come and go with changing issues. These mainly represent dominant economic interests.

Nonelectoral forms of participation, such as interest group activity, are not stressed by the traditional democratic rhetoric. There is such an emphasis on voting as the chief form of citizen participation that people are encouraged "to rely on leaders' images and promises at election time, and to believe that they have nothing active or critical to do with the political system at other times" (Fellman, 1973:166). People are not as frequently exhorted to pressure their congressmen or lobby a government agency as they are to vote on election day. The very term "lobbying" connotes a somewhat disreputable activity. This further removes nonelites from interest group activity and enhances elite power. Political and economic elites are left to conduct the affairs of the interest group process free of public knowledge or understanding.

Noninstitutional political behavior. Perhaps the most consequential forms of mass political behavior in modern societies are those which fall outside the established political system. Demonstrations, acts of civil disobedience, riots, and various types of sociopolitical movements are tactics to which masses may turn when conventional forms of participation fail to elicit desired responses from elites. As we shall see in chapter 13, these forms of political activism have often served as effective nonelite power resources and have sometimes compelled changes in the society's distribution of rewards when traditional methods have failed.

The Functions of Electoral Politics

Most political sociologists and political scientists recognize the inadequacies of the electoral system as a form of citizen power. Though the purpose of elections as a means of holding leaders accountable is clearly spelled out by liberal democratic theory, most see them as effective mainly in letting the people choose leaders, though not in influencing specific issues (see for example Pomper, 1968:98). At best it is expected that political elites will reflect the general interests of nonelites. Of course, even in choosing leaders the electoral system may not work as we expect it to. As Max Weber pointed out, the formality of elections does not necessarily mean that appointment of candidates has not already been made by party chiefs (Gerth and Mills, 1946:200). Grass roots candidates may sometimes capture a party's nomination for an important office, but more typically places on the ballot are filled by those who have faithfully served the party and who have nurtured support within its higher echelons. Moreover the place of money and media exposure in the candidate selection process is so obvious as to need no elaboration.

Despite their limitations as an effective instrument of citizen participation in the shaping of public policy, electoral activities do serve less obvious functions. Sociologist Robert Merton (1968:117) has explained social phenomena as having "manifest" and "latent" functions. The manifest functions of a social trait or institution are its clearly spelled out, obvious purposes; they are *intended*. Latent functions are *un*intended and generally unrecognized consequences of the same trait or institution. Elections may be placed into this scheme. On the surface they are expected to serve as a method of citizen control of leaders. Beneath this obvious but largely unmet function, elections serve certain unplanned and usually unrecognized purposes. For one, ruling political elites must remain aware of the moods and general desires of the masses, and in this, elections often serve as a kind of warning mechanism.[7]

Most important, however, are the unintended *symbolic* functions of the electoral process. Democratic rhetoric fosters the notion that participation gives people at least some control over political decisions which affect their lives. Though this is clearly not the case for the majority of the populace, the illusion of democracy serves as a means of stabilizing the system and preventing serious mass movements. Political scientist Murray Edelman (1964:17) has keenly described this symbolic function:

> To quiet resentments and doubts about particular political acts, reaffirm belief in the fundamental rationality and democratic character of the system, and thus fix conforming habits of future behavior is demonstrably a key function of our persisting political institutions: elections, political discussions, legislatures, courts, and administration. Each of them involves motor activity (in which the mass public participates or which it observes from a distance) that reinforces the impression of a political system designed to translate individual wants into public policy.

While its effectiveness in translating mass wants and needs into public policy is questionable, a major function of the electoral system is to legitimize the dominant system of political rule. At the same time that they respond most regularly to the needs of the society's dominant socioeconomic groups, political elites are able to employ the symbolism of voting and other acts of participation to justify their actions and policies. Voting has a palliative effect on nonelites, helping to assure them that their voices can be at least collectively heard on the society's important issues. In sum, the electoral process serves primarily to deter serious noninstitutional challenges and thus maintain the status quo.

7. Sophisticated polling techniques may be supplanting elections in this regard. For a sobering analysis of the limitations—and dangers—of the use of public opinion polls, see Lowi (1976:231–241).

The Unaccountability of Nonelective Leaders

Let us assume for the moment that elections do serve their intended purpose. At best, they can only help to control the actions of elected political officials. During the past four decades, however, political power has passed increasingly from the legislative branch of government, where officials are elected, to the executive branch and to independent administrative agencies, where officials are appointed. The power (and public recognition) of a high-ranking senator or congressman, for example, is hardly comparable to that of a forceful Secretary of State such as Henry Kissinger despite the fact that the latter need never answer to an electorate.

More and more, political decisions regarding how, what, and to whom government resources are to be allocated and how laws are to be written and interpreted are made by autonomous bureaucratic agencies which are immunized from electoral controls. The passing of policymaking power away from elective legislative bodies is evident not only at the national level in the United States but at the state and local levels as well and generally in Western industrial societies. The net effect of this tendency is a further neutralization of mass political participation.

The drift of power to independent government agencies has also aided the penetration of state power by dominant economic groups (Alford and Friedland, 1975: 451). Such independent government agencies become reliant on those private institutions, mainly large corporations, which are the very focus of their policies. The capture of regulatory commissions by the regulated industries themselves, for example, was noted in chapter 7. Thus giant corporations and government agencies have become mutually dependent, leading to a natural alliance of economic and nonelective political elites in the public policymaking process.

The Unaccountability of Economic Elites

The past several decades have witnessed the inflation of public power of private institutional leaders, notably the corporate elite. Two factors have contributed to the extension of this group's societal power: (1) the growing union between government and corporation and (2) the increasing concentration of economic resources in fewer and fewer large organizations. In short, the capacity of the corporate elite to make, in effect, public policy through its interaction with government officials and through its own decision-making power is massive. Indeed, when considered in total, the decisions made by corporate leaders in regard to investment of resources, location of plants and equipment, employment levels, and so on are often of greater public consequence than those made by public officials themselves (see chapter 6).

Despite these far-reaching public consequences, nonelites have virtually no control over the decision-making process of the corporation. Representatives of interest groups or of the general public do not sit on corporate boards, nor do they participate in the selection of those boards. Corporate leaders do not seek input from the electorate. nor are they required to maintain even the nominal public responsibility of elected or appointed government officials. In sum, the multifarious powers of the corporate elite are simply not publicly controlled. Hence even if we accept the most favorable picture of the role of the electoral process in democratic politics, it can affect only a part of the mosaic of power in advanced capitalist societies, perhaps not the most critical part at that.

Collective consumer action. Outside the realm of government, citizens have few legitimate tools which they can use to influence institutional elites, particularly economic elites. In recent years, however, many consumer advocacy groups have sprung up whose purposes are to hold powerful economic organizations accountable to the general consuming public. Groups such as those led by Ralph Nader are designed to pressure corporations and to lobby government agencies, which may then intervene on behalf of consumers. Secondarily their purpose is to mobilize people for consumer actions such as boycotts and selective purchasing. To what extent can the efforts of such groups succeed, and how much pressure can they effectively apply?

Lobbying efforts of consumer groups must compete with the lobbying efforts of corporations themselves, and in terms of financial and political resources, the latter enjoy a heavy upper hand. Perhaps more importantly, consumer groups must try to penetrate the close and mutually dependent working arrangements maintained by government agencies and corporations. This places them at a decided disadvantage. Corporate executives, for example, routinely consult top government officials, presenting their side of consumer-related issues. Similar access to high public officials is not so easily available to consumers or consumer group leaders.

As to collective consumer actions such as boycotts, the structure of monopoly capitalism makes them generally ineffective. Where a great number and variety of producers and sellers are in real competition, consumers can effectively apply pressure to those businesses charging unfair prices or selling shoddy merchandise. But in an oligopolistic or in some cases monopolistic market, this is rarely possible. A neighborhood boycott of the corner grocer who is overcharging customers can be effective; a boycott of the local power company or of a national automobile company cannot.

A second factor which mitigates against the success of collective consumer actions is the simple fact of organization or, more correctly, *lack of* organization. Consumers are a huge and disparate group and cannot be mobilized as easily as collectivities whose interests are more specifically focused. The more specialized is a group's interests, the more effective it can be in pursuing and protecting them. Neighborhood or even community actions may sometimes be successful since groups at this level, though usually amorphous, are still small enough to organize effectively around a particular consumer issue. But to attempt such ad hoc movements at the societal level is extremely difficult. Trying to build a sense of group consciousness among so widespread and disconnected a collectivity as "consumers" requires financial and organizational resources which only dominant economic groups have—the very groups against which such movements are ordinarily aimed.

The public powers of corporate officials are, of course, not absolute, any more than are the powers of publicly elected or appointed government officials. David Vogel, in a study of the corporate accountability movement of the past decade (1978), claims that the corporate elite is under increasing pressure to justify its decisions in terms of the public welfare in addition to the welfare of company shareholders. But such pressures, he explains, have not been exerted so much by citizen movements themselves as by government.

In sum, citizen challenges to corporate power have had limited effect. As Vogel states, "Compared to either the government or trade unions, citizen challenges still provide relatively few constraints on corporate decision makers" (p. 13). He goes on to conclude that the corporate accountability movement "can hardly be regarded as a serious challenge to corporate authority in the United States" (p. 222). None of its demands have been of sufficient scope or significance to threaten corporate power seriously. In Ralph Nader's words, "Corporations could go on meeting the demands of activists challenging them directly at the current rate forever and still their wealth and autonomy would remain essentially unaffected" (quoted in Vogel, 1978:222).

MASS PARTICIPATION AND THE CLASS STRUCTURE

Can nonelite participation, particularly the electoral process, have any impact on the distribution of the society's rewards? Can it, in Lasswell's terms, affect "who gets what, when, and how"? In short, can it change the shape of the society's class and status hierarchies? Although participation might, as Verba and Nie (1972:342) point out, help one social group as easily as another under varying circumstances, given the social, political, and economic institutions in the United States, it presently benefits primarily those at the top of the stratification system. This tendency is similar in other advanced capitalist societies.

The class structure in the United States has remained amazingly stable during the past century. The distribution of wealth and power has not been fundamentally affected by the techniques of procedural democracy. Changes which have occurred in this time have been of a superficial nature. Even the Great Depression of the 1930s and the institutionalization of many welfare state measures did little to redistribute societal resources. Despite elections in which rhetorical pledges to change the society's reward system have been routinely voiced, such changes have not materialized in any but minor or symbolic form.

This is not an unexpected outcome, however, since the electoral process is dominated by two parties which are in essential agreement on sustaining class inequality. Take "tax reform" as an example. This has been a basic part of each party's campaign platform for many years. But basic reforms which might begin to redistribute societal wealth more equitably are never proposed by administrations or debated by legislatures. Even relatively mild tax reform measures are rarely acted upon. The issue of tax reform, then, is mainly symbolic, with little meaningful substance.

If the electoral process has the effect of stabilizing the opportunity and reward structures of the society, it is not surprising that those of higher social class and status should be its main participants. Indeed if participation through normal channels has little effect on government responses to the needs of subordinate groups and if the party system and other aspects of electoral politics frustrate these groups' effective mobilization, then low rates of participation by those at the lower end of the class and status hierarchies are, in Alford and Friedland's words, "neither analytically surprising nor politically irrational" (1975:472). Verba and Nie (1972:338) contend that the upper-class bias of participatory politics is not easily overcome even by lower-class groups who *do* choose to become politically active; their numbers among those whose activism involves more than only voting are too small to be an effective voice.

Political participation by nonelites, then, is simply not the same for all class groups since each has access to different resources which affect the ultimate payoff for participating. Participation is meaningful for those groups who bring to the political arena sufficient political and economic resources to make themselves heard. Those with the time, skills, organization, and money to participate convincingly—not simply voting or joining a consumer group—are apt to see the system working effectively, and indeed for them it *is* working effectively. It is to these groups that government leaders respond, thereby preserving the basic political economy and its attendant structure of inequality.

SUMMARY

Certain institutional means of mass participation in the political process have been explored, electoral activity in particular. The rate and extent of these activities are heavily class biased. Only a relative few participate in any significant way, and these few tend to be mainly from the society's top class and status groups.

Most political sociologists and political scientists agree that electoral politics has limited bearing on the policy decisions of political elites. Elections serve mainly a symbolic purpose to assuage citizen discontent and fears of powerlessness, and to discourage serious challenges to the dominant institutional structure.

In any case, elections can at best seek to hold accountable only those who are part of the political elite—specifically, elective office holders. Elections have little or no bearing on the selection or actions of decision makers of nongovernmental institutions, especially the corporation, nor on appointive political office holders. In recent decades the most significant policymaking powers have fallen to these latter groups. Thus the electoral process represents only a limited aspect of the panorama of societal power in the United States and other advanced capitalist societies.

In sum, the institutionalized means of participation available to nonelites—primarily the electoral system—function in a seriously limited manner in selecting and controlling societal elites.

However, the electoral process always represents an instrument of *potential* nonelite power. Ruling elites and the society's dominant class therefore cannot take for granted their ability to dominate this aspect of the sociopolitical system. Nor can they rely on it as the sole mechanism for assuring mass compliance. In addition to political, economic, and organizational resources, they must apply ideological resources in order to preserve the status quo. It is to these dominant ideologies that we now turn.

REFERENCES

Abramson, Paul R. 1976. "Generational Change and the Decline of Party Identification: 1952-1974." *American Political Science Review* 70 (June):469–478.

Alford, Robert. 1963. *Party and Society*. Chicago: Rand McNally.

——————. 1972. "Class Voting in the Anglo-American Political Systems." In Guiseppe DiPalma (ed.), *Mass Politics in Industrial Societies*. Chicago: Markham.

——————, and **Roger Friedland.** 1975. "Political Participation and Public Policy." In Alex Inkeles (ed.), *Annual Review of Sociology*. Vol. I. Palo Alto: Annual Reviews.

Almond, Gabriel, and **Sidney Verba.** 1963. *The Civic Culture*. Princeton: Princeton U. Press.

Banfield, Edward, and **James Q. Wilson.** 1963. *City Politics*. New York: Vintage.

Bell, Daniel. 1964. "Interpretations of American Politics." In Daniel Bell (ed.), *The Radical Right*. New York: Anchor.

Butler, David, and **Donald Stokes.** 1974. *Political Change in Britain*. 2nd ed. New York: St. Martin's.

Campbell, Angus, et al. 1960. *The American Voter*. New York: Wiley.

Durverger, Maurice. 1959. *Political Parties*. New York: Wiley.

Edelman, Murray J. 1964. *The Symbolic Uses of Politics*. Urbana: U. of Illinois Press.

Epstein, Leon D. 1964. "A Comparative Study of Canadian Parties." *American Political Science Review* 58 (March):46–59.

Fellman, Gordon. 1973. *The Deceived Majority*. New Brunswick, N.J.: Transaction.

Fisher, Alan M. 1979. "Where Is the New Jewish Conservatism?" *Society* 16 (May-June):5/15–18.

Flanigan, William H., and **Nancy H. Zingale.** 1975. *Political Behavior of the American Electorate*. 3rd ed. Boston: Allyn and Bacon.

Form, William H., and **Joan Huber.** 1969. Ideological Beliefs on the Distribution of Power in the United States." *American Sociological Review* 34 (February):19–31.

Fromm, Erich. 1955. *The Sane Society*. New York: Fawcett.

Gerth, Hans, and **C. Wright Mills.** 1946. *From Max Weber*. New York: Oxford U. Press.

Glenn, Norvall D. 1972. "The Distribution of Political Knowledge in the United States." In Dan D. Nimmo and Charles M. Bonjean (eds.), *Political Attitudes and Public Opinion*. New York: McKay.

Hadley, Arthur. 1978. *The Empty Polling Booth*. Englewood Cliffs: Prentice-Hall.

Hamilton, Richard. 1972. *Class and Politics in the United States*. New York: Wiley.

Harris, Louis. 1974. *Confidence and Concern: Survey Conducted for the House Subcommittee on Intergovernmental Affairs*. Washington, D.C.: U.S. Government Printing Office.

Huber, Joan, and **William H. Form.** 1973. *Income and Ideology*. New York: Free Press.

Josephson, Eric, and **Mary Josephson.** 1962. *Man Alone: Alienation in Modern Society.* New York: Dell.

Kimball, Penn. 1972. *The Disconnected.* New York: Columbia U. Press.

Kirchheimer, Otto. 1966. "The Transformation of the Western European Party Systems." In Joseph LaPalombara and Myron Weiner (eds.), *Political Parties and Political Development.* Princeton: Princeton U. Press.

Ladd, Everett C. 1977. "The Democrats Have Their Own Two-Party System." *Fortune* 96 (October):212–226.

——————, and **Charles D. Hadley.** 1978. *Transformations of the American Party System.* 2nd ed. New York: Norton.

Lane, Robert E. 1964. *Political Life.* New York: Free Press.

Lawson, Kay. 1968. *Political Parties and Democracy in the United States.* New York: Charles Scribner's Sons.

Levin, Murray B. 1960. *The Alienated Voter.* New York: Holt, Rinehart and Winston.

Lindblom, Charles E. 1968. *The Policy-Making Process.* Englewood Cliffs: Prentice-Hall.

Lipset, Seymour Martin. 1960. *Political Man.* New York: Anchor.

——————, and **Earl Raab.** 1978. *The Politics of Unreason.* 2nd ed. Chicago: U. of Chicago Press.

Lipsetz, Lewis. 1965. "Working Class Authoritarianism: A Reevaluation." *American Political Science Review* 30 (February):103–109.

Lowi, Theordore. 1976. *American Government: Incomplete Conquest.* Hinsdale, Ill.: Dryden.

Merton, Robert K. 1968. *Social Theory and Social Structure.* New York: Free Press.

Milbrath, Lester. 1965. *Political Participation.* Chicago: Rand McNally.

Miller, Arthur H. 1974. "Political Issues and Trust in Government:1964-1970." *American Political Science Review* 68 (September):951–972.

Miller, Warren E., and **Donald E. Stokes.** 1963. "Constituency Influence in Congress." *American Political Science Review* 57 (March):45–56.

Nie, Norman H., Sidney Verba, and **John R. Petrocik.** 1976. *The Changing American Voter.* Cambridge: Harvard U. Press.

Ogmundson, Rick. 1975. "On the Measurement of Party Class Positions: The Case of Canadian Federal Political Parties." *Canadian Review of Sociology and Anthropology* 12 (November):565–576.

——————. 1976. "Mass-Elite Linkages and Class Issues in Canada." *Canadian Review of Sociology and Anthropology* 13 (February):1–12.

Page, Benjamin I. 1978. *Choices and Echoes in Presidential Elections.* Chicago: U. of Chicago Press.

Pomper, Gerald M. 1968. *Elections in America.* New York: Dodd, Mead.

Porter, John. 1965. *The Vertical Mosaic.* Toronto: U. of Toronto Press.

Prewitt, Kenneth. 1970. "Political Ambition, Volunteerism and Electoral Accountability." *American Political Science Review* 64 (March):5–17.

Rose, Richard (ed.). 1974. *Electoral Behavior: A Comparative Handbook.* New York: Free Press.

Schwartz, Mildred A. 1974. "Canadian Voting Behavior." In Richard Rose (ed.), *Electoral Behavior: A Comparative Handbook*. New York: Free Press.

Stacey, Barrie. 1977. *Political Socialization in Western Society*. New York: St. Martin's.

Verba, Sidney, and **Norman H. Nie.** 1972. *Participation in America*. New York: Harper and Row.

Vogel, David. 1978. *Lobbying the Corporation: Citizen Challenges to Business Authority*. New York: Basic.

Westin, Alan F. "Survey Finds Public Still Feels Alienated From Political System." *Louisville Courier-Journal* 248 (May 6):1–1.

part four

stability
and
change
in
power structures

chapter 12

ideology and political socialization

A well-established ideology perpetuates itself with little planned propaganda by those whom it benefits most. . . . Systems of life which confer special benefits on the other fellow need no plots or conspiracies when the masses are moved by faith and the elites are inspired by self-confidence.
Harold Lasswell

In Part Three we saw that, contrary to commonly held beliefs, the democratic character of the American sociopolitical system is in many ways questionable. Access to the resources of power is hardly the same for all groups and individuals in the society, and power elites do not in the main resemble the general populace in their class origins and other sociological traits. Moreover the ability of nonelites to affect elite decisions through the electoral process is more symbolic than real. Given these facts, one might logically ask, "How is a system which seems to favor the interests of a relatively few powerful economic and political groups given legitimacy?" Why, in other words, do those lacking great wealth and political influence — a decided majority — accept a system which has been and remains so apparently inequitable?

What is perhaps even more puzzling is the fact that those with little societal power not only tolerate the prevailing sociopolitical system but, for the most part, consider it just and beneficial. In short, few ever question any of the basic assumptions of the society's major economic, political, and social institutions. People may recognize certain shortcomings from time to time, but the system as a whole is seen as fundamentally sound and the best that has yet been devised.

Might the explanation for this paradox be that support for the prevailing sociopolitical system is produced by force? Do the powerful few induce the masses to obey on the basis of fear? As was noted in chapter 2, coercion is always at the root of obedience to authority, and all states use force when the need arises. But coercive techniques are most common in societies in which the dominant system is not accepted by a significant part of the populace. In modern totalitarian societies such as South Africa and Chile, the powerful must often enforce their will through blatant forms of repression.

The use of raw force alone, however, cannot be effective in prompting compliance over long periods of time. The stability of sociopolitical systems which rely primarily on coercion is always precarious. For government and other supportive institutions to establish and sustain a system of rule which is popularly supported over many generations requires that power be legitimized in less repressive and direct ways. People must come to see the exercise of power by the few as natural and socially beneficial. Only then does power become authority — that is, legitimized rule. When this is accomplished, ruling groups need no longer resort to force as the principal means of assuring their will.

It is only when a society's economic, political, and social institutions are supported reflexively — almost unconsciously — by the masses that long-range stability is evident, as in the United States. Occasionally there are signs of discontent and even mild rebellion (the urban riots of the

1960s are a fairly recent example); but these are unusual instances and are generally squelched with a display of force or superficial concessions. The widespread and consistent support of the society's institutional system is not often seriously challenged. To assure this kind of legitimacy and thus to sustain the system's long-range stability requires the development of an effective ideology and its communication through the process of political socialization.

THE NATURE OF IDEOLOGY

An **ideology** is an explanation of how and why a sociopolitical system works as it does, as well as a justification for that system. Most simply, it is a set of beliefs and values which rationalizes a society's structure of power and privilege.[1] Ideologies can be propounded not only for the purposes of stabilizing and defending a prevailing system but also for changing it.[2] Ideology can therefore be an instrument for ruling groups or for those who oppose them. Our concern in this chapter is with ideology as a force for keeping the structure of power and privilege as it is. In the next chapter we will deal with ideology as a change-inducing phenomenon.

Dominant Ideologies

That ideology which explains and justifies the status quo —that is, the prevailing power and reward structures —is called the *dominant* ideology. Since power and wealth are never distributed equally in any society, some justification and explanation must be provided for those at the top who gain the most from the way the system works as well as for those at the bottom who gain the least. As Huber and Form have put it, "Dominant ideologies function to comfort those whom the system rewards and to justify the system to those who fail" (1973:79). A society's dominant ideology, then, explains and rationalizes existing institutions of power and privilege. To paraphrase Lasswell, it explains not only *who* gets what, when, and how but also *why*.

1. As with other key concepts of political sociology, "ideology" has been applied in a variety of ways. Some have used the term broadly to denote a society's entire belief system, while others have used it more narrowly to describe a specific program of action of a particular group or party. Our use of the term is less extreme than either of these two. On varying definitions of ideology see Shils (1968), Lane (1962), and Plamenatz (1970).
2. In a classic work, Karl Mannheim (1936) termed ideologies which seek to change a social system "utopias" and those that seek to keep them as they are "ideologies" *per se*.

It is not surprising that those at the top of the society's power and wealth hierarchies —elites —should believe in the justness of their positions. But why do the masses pay allegiance to the society's dominant ideology? Slightly different answers to this question have been given by elite theorists, class or Marxist theorists, and pluralists.

As elite theorists explain it, ideology which justifies elite rule is produced by the elite themselves as a means of manipulating the masses. Here we might recall Mosca's "political formula," that set of ideas used by the elite to legitimize their rule. Elites may claim their right to power through various rationales. The divine right of kings was an effective ideology during the Middle Ages in Europe, asserting that kings were rulers chosen by God. European colonialists of the nineteenth century claimed their right to power over native peoples on the basis of biological and moral superiority, a rationale also employed by whites in North America in their dealings with both blacks and native Americans. A common modern-day elitist justification for the maldistribution of power and wealth is the possession of skill or expertise. Here the right to elite positions is claimed on the basis not of biological superiority but of competence or expertise in a particular field of ruling affairs.

In the elitist view, then, ideology is an effective tool for justifying the continued power and privilege of the few at the expense of the many. As such, the state plays an important role in educating the masses to the dominant ideology.

For class theorists, ideology is similarly a tool for assuring the interests of the few over the many. But in this view, it is not so much the deliberate creation of a ruling elite as the natural product of the society's productive forces. As will be recalled, in the Marxian theory productive forces give rise to the society's class structure. Those who control the means of production are the ruling class. This class controls not only the means of economic production, however, but also the means of *mental* production. This assures that the ideas of the ruling class regarding all aspects of social life —government, religion, family, and so on —become those of the entire society. Institutions such as the school and the media, which impart political ideas, quite naturally disseminate those ideas which reflect the interests of the ruling class.

This predominance of ruling class ideas is often referred to in Marxist writings as "ideological hegemony." "Hegemony" is a term which refers to domination; ideological hegemony is thus the prevalence of one group's ideology over all others. Antonio Gramsci, an Italian Marxist writing in the 1920s, described this phenomenon as:

> The "spontaneous" consent given by the great masses of the population to the general direction imposed on social life by the domi-

nant fundamental group; this consent is "historically" caused by the prestige (and consequent confidence) which the dominant group enjoys because of its position and function in the world of production (1971:12).

Ideological hegemony is, in other words, a legitimation of the status quo wherein those values which favor the interests of the ruling group become the acceptable standards of subordinate groups as well.

In the Marxian explanation of ideology, the predominance of the ruling group's standards is dependent on the development and maintenance of false consciousness among the masses. False consciousness is a belief on the part of nonruling groups that the prevailing sociopolitical system works in their interests when in fact it works primarily in the interests of the powerful few. Although primarily a Marxian notion used to describe the deceptive effect of ruling class ideas on the proletariat in capitalist societies (see chapter 3), the idea of false consciousness is also used by elitists to denote the end product of the elite's manipulation of the masses through its propagation of ideology.

A third theory explaining how people come to accept the dominant ideology is employed by many pluralists and might be called the "systems theory." In this view individuals support the legitimacy of a sociopolitical system through neither elite manipulation nor false consciousness, but through what is called "diffuse support." This is a generalized support which individuals come to express through a series of stages during socialization. Beginning in early childhood, individuals develop a positive image of government and social control agencies such as police and courts, and they retain this image, in somewhat modified form, into adulthood (Easton and Dennis, 1969:62–69).

This theory does not emphasize the capacity of ruling groups to impose their version of social reality on the remainder of the society but instead emphasizes an evolutionary, nondeliberative transmittal of values from one generation to another. The focus is upon how children learn from adults. Most of the traditional literature on political socialization has adopted this approach, concentrating on the social-psychological factors involved in the socialization process (particularly in childhood) rather than the content of socialization itself.

As in our previous discussions of the structure of power in the United States and similar societies, we will stress a combination of the class and elite approaches in explaining the functions of ideology and the process of political socialization. We will begin by looking at some of the details of the dominant American ideology and the beliefs which sustain false consciousness among the masses.

THE DOMINANT AMERICAN IDEOLOGY

Describing the dominant American ideology can be, as Huber and Form write, at the same time simple and difficult:

> On the one hand, the stuff of the dominant ideology is embedded in political campaign literature, newspaper editorials, TV shows, civics textbooks, stories about Dick, Jane, and Sally, and Chamber of Commerce brochures. It is the sum and substance of what every child has learned about the way the American system works. It is what everybody *knows*. . . . On the other hand, what everybody knows sometimes turns out to be wrong (1973:3).

As we will see, the dominant ideology in America or any other society is accepted in full part only on an abstract level; when applied to their own individual circumstances, people interpret the ideology more selectively, picking and choosing parts, often in an inconsistent manner. Thus although the dominant ideology may be hegemonic in the sense that it pervades all societal institutions, it is not acknowledged as totally valid by all people at all times. Nonetheless there is a recognizable body of certain beliefs and values which strongly guides most people's political thought and action.

In looking at the dominant American ideology, we might divide it into two parts: one explaining and justifying the political system and the other explaining and justifying the economic system. The two overlap and complement each other; just as politics and economics are never separate processes and structures, so too political and economic ideologies are counterparts.

In the United States the fundamental premises of capitalism are the foundation of the prevailing economic ideology: private ownership of property, free enterprise, competition, and the profit motive. Government's role in economic affairs is reluctantly accepted so long as it remains as minimal as possible. In the political realm the sacred principles are basically those we have described in chapter 3 as pluralist democracy: an open system in which the people as a whole ultimately control their leaders through free elections and petitioning. Bargaining and compromise among a variety of groups prevent irreparable rifts in the system and make for stability and continuity. Both political and economic processes are seen as "free markets" in which the individual can choose from among competing groups — parties in the political realm, businesses in the economic.

Underlying these beliefs is the general value of individualism — specifically, the notion that each member of society is personally responsible for his or her social lot (see for example Slater, 1976). The society's opportunity structure is pictured as open, providing equal chances for all to achieve material success or political power regardless of their social origin. This being so, each individual controls his or her placement in the social hierarchy. Social success, then, is the result of one's willingness to work hard; failure is the result of lack of ambition or desire to improve oneself. Differences in wealth and power are not denied, but they are seen as the product of individual factors rather than the workings of a class system that automatically favors success for the well-born and failure for the poor.[3]

These basic principles will often seem to vary as they are expressed by different groups and individuals. Some, for example, advocate a greater role for government and a more equitably distributed social product. Certain liberal segments of the Democratic party and some industrial labor unions such as the United Automobile Workers will ordinarily adopt such ideological positions. On the other hand, ultraconservative elements of the Republican party, as well as business organizations such as the Chamber of Commerce or the National Association of Manufacturers, will call for less government and more of a truly laissez-faire economic and social system.

Yet all of these variations fall within the mainstream ideology. Although their differences are apparent, these are not *fundamental* differences. Established institutions and their leaders are in agreement on the basic explanations of how the economic and political systems do and should work. All accept the two-party political system, the capitalist economic order, and the unequal reward system as givens, not to be tampered with in any fundamental manner.

The Underlying Belief System

Much of the dominant explanation of how a sociopolitical system works is not entirely or even in large part accurate. Ideology is thus to a great extent myth: It comprises beliefs which through constant articulation become accepted as descriptions of the true state of affairs. In Part Three we outlined some of the major discrepancies between the ideological picture of the American political economy and the manner in which it actually functions.

One need not think of ideology, however, as conscious distortion of social facts. Although some elite theorists and Marxists stress the contriv-

---

3. For descriptions of the dominant American ideology see Williams (1970:ch. 11), Dolbeare and Dolbeare (1976), and Slater (1976:ch. 1).

ance of ideology by ruling groups, most agree that elites as well as masses accept the society's dominant ideology as valid. In this sense ideologies differ from propaganda, which, as Gouldner explains, "is not believed in —at least at first —by those spreading it." Ideologies, on the other hand, "are intended to be believed in by those affirming them publically and by all men, because they are 'true' and they thus have a universal character" (Gouldner, 1976:33).[4]

Despite their acceptance by both ruling groups and masses, the fundamental ideological values tend to accommodate mostly the interests of the society's ruling groups. In the United States, individualism, competition, and achievement favor those who are wealthy and can easily avail themselves of the opportunities for success. In a similar way the sanctity of private property mostly benefits those who are great property holders, not the masses. Yet in spite of these outcomes, rejection of the dominant system among the masses is exceptional. Let us look at some of the more specific ideas which together serve as a justification for the prevailing sociopolitical system and contribute to the development of false consciousness.

Unchanging human nature. The dominant system is not likely to be questioned when people view it as founded on unchangeable human traits. For example, a capitalist system wherein political and economic relations are based on avarice and competition can be explained and justified by declaring such behavior merely "human nature." Expressions such as "people are by nature greedy and will always seek to accumulate more than their neighbors" are commonly voiced. Indeed most people in capitalist societies believe the profit motive to be an innate human trait, despite historical and anthropological evidence to the contrary.

The neutrality of societal institutions. Another way in which false consciousness is bolstered is by the depiction of societal institutions as neutral, whose purposes are to serve not the interests of particular groups but the society as a whole. Governmental agencies or legislatures, for example, are not pictured as representatives of particular economic or regional interests but as objective public institutions. That certain societal groups and interests are far more resourceful than others in penetrating these public institutions is not stressed. Similarly law enforcement agencies such as the FBI are seen as disinterested crime-fighting organizations, not politicized groups who enforce laws more or less vigorously depending on who the criminal or what the crime may be. That particular

4.   On the difference between political propaganda and ideology, see Ellul (1965).

groups and individuals are more frequently singled out by police agencies as "deviant" or criminal (for example, left-wing rather than right-wing radical groups; street criminals rather than white-collar criminals) goes unnoticed by most. The public perception of crime thus emphasizes those acts which are clearly visible and blatantly offensive, such as street muggings and homicides, but not the more silent and invisible crimes such as corporate price fixing or the dumping of pollutants into the environment. Likewise political radicalism is understood as activities of socialist-flavored groups but not those of ultraconservative groups such as the American Legion or the Chamber of Commerce.

Giant corporations are similarly portrayed as neutral organizations which provide people with things they want and need. The basic thrust of corporate advertising and public relations is aimed at strengthening a belief in the naturalness and goodness of the prevailing economic system, of which the corporation is, of course, the chief element. That corporations are profit-seeking entities whose purposes are primarily to enrich those who own them is a fact which is rarely brought to public consciousness. Occasionally when it is (as for example when oil companies are seen as profiteering at public expense), there remains little question that there is simply no "realistic" alternative to the corporate economy.

The mass media—television, newspapers, and so on—also are generally understood to be objective in their presentations of news and entertainment. In the case of news, the media become reporters of events "as they occur," while in the case of entertainment, the public is given "only what it wants." That news events are selected by the media from among countless events of social significance and are presented in a predesigned manner is not often considered. Nor is the fact that in the United States the media are private business enterprises which rely for their revenues on commercial advertisers, who may have much to say about what will or will not be printed or televised.

Finally, schools, from the primary to the graduate levels, picture themselves and are generally seen by the public as nonideological institutions whose purposes are to train students in practical skills and to impart a variety of ideas. Schools are not seen as "political" in function despite the constant enunciation and glorification of dominant political and economic values. Also, the popular picture of the educational system in America is one in which no particular class or ethnic group is favored over others. This neutral image prevails despite the fact that schools serve as social placement agencies, assuring top places for those of higher class and status origins and making upward mobility for those at the opposite end of the social hierarchy difficult at best.

Fear of other systems. A compelling aspect of the society's dominant ideology is that, as it is propagated, other systems based on different ideologies are seen as neither viable nor credible. Thus even if there is doubt about prevailing values and the institutions built upon them, there are no workable alternatives. "The American system may have its shortcomings," leaders admit, "but the shortcomings of other systems are much greater." Such an admission, along with its implicit warning of the uncertainties and insufficiencies of other systems, serves to defuse efforts at mobilizing people around counterideologies.

As an example, controlling the power of private corporations by introducing more socialist elements into the economic system is viewed as detrimental to the society's best interests. Thus the failures of the Soviet system are stressed while the successes of the heavily socialist Swedish system are ignored. Or suggestions by counterideological groups to socialize particular industries are most often met with arguments pointing out the inefficiencies and inabilities of government-operated industries such as the postal system in meeting consumer needs. Rarely mentioned, however, are more efficient and profitable state-run enterprises such as the Tennessee Valley Authority, a federal industry supplying electric power to parts of the South since the 1930s.

Moreover when there is a recognition of institutional deficiencies in meeting social ideals, violence and serious social disturbances are averted by calling up the larger ideological principle that only within the prevailing political framework can changes eventually be realized. Groups calling for change are advised to "work within the system." The black civil rights movement of the fifties and sixties serves as an example. As white America became collectively conscious of the plight of blacks in all areas of social life, the movement was recognized as legitimate and justifiable. But only traditional methods of the political process—voting, lobbying, and so on—were deemed acceptable as part of the movement. Violence was not recognized as either legitimate or effective. Thus civil rights groups and leaders calling for direct and sometimes violent confrontations with the white power structure were denounced as "radicals" and their tactics labeled "counterproductive."

Individual responsibility. The dominant ideology helps to stabilize and perpetuate the prevailing sociopolitical system by emphasizing individual responsibility for social ills rather than the society's institutional structure. Poverty, crime, and other social problems are interpreted as the deficiencies of individuals who have failed to adjust to a basically healthy social system. If people are poor, it is because of their lack of motivation, not because of structural impediments to their mobility; if people commit crimes, it is because of their criminal nature, not because of the social system's failure to provide them with the conventional means of achieving "success." Placing the burden of responsibility for social problems on the individual has been referred to by some as "blaming the victim" (Ryan, 1975).

The belief in an open class system in which people may rise without limit on the basis of their own effort is strengthened by the few who actually do make spectacular leaps in class position during their lifetimes. Rising from poverty to great wealth is (and has always been) very exceptional in American society. Most mobility occurs within the middle ranges of the stratification system, and even there only in small incremental steps. Those at the two extreme ends—the poor and the affluent—tend to remain there from generation to generation. But the handful who, for whatever reason, break out of poverty and rise to the top are widely heralded, while the vast majority of those who remain poor are ignored. These few exceptional cases "confirm" the reality of the American dream, "proving" that success is mainly dependent on individual effort.

It is interesting to consider how persistent the belief in individual responsibility for one's social place seems to remain in American thought. In their classic study of a Midwestern community in the 1920s, sociologists Robert and Helen Lynd (1929) asked high school students whether they agreed with the statement "It is entirely the fault of a man himself if he does not succeed." Then 47 percent answered "yes." In a 1977 replication of this study, Caplow and Bahr (1979:13) asked the same question (among others) and got the same 47 percent "yes" response.

The forcefulness of the dominant ideology in this regard is reflected in the adoption of the individual responsibility model by a wide variety of class groups (Lane, 1962; Sennett and Cobb, 1972). In a national survey conducted in the 1960s, Free and Cantril (1968:29–30) found that while most affluent persons attributed poverty simply to "lack of effort," a majority of the poor also agreed that they were at least partially to blame for their own condition.[5] Emphasizing individual responsibility for people's fate has a significant political implication: It discourages *collective* efforts that may turn into sociopolitical movements seeking to alter the society's major institutions (Ossowski; 1963:154).

Even when individuals themselves are not totally faulted for their social disadvantages, their problems are not seen as deep-seated and

---

5. Most of the poor, however, combined "lack of effort" with "circumstances" in explaining poverty, unlike the affluent, who explained it more exclusively as a result of "lack of effort."

widespread but rather as marginal and amenable to relatively quick and easy solution. Poverty, after its rediscovery in the 1960s, was not seen as a creation of the normal workings of a capitalist socioeconomic order but as a minor imperfection of an otherwise healthy system; government leaders thus saw its alleviation as requiring only a "mopping up" effort, not basic institutional change.

Accommodation to change. The dominant system and the ideology underlying it are not, of course, totally inflexible. Indeed, selective changes contribute to their durability. Some institutional reforms may actually be adopted, while other concessions to challenging groups may simply be symbolic in nature. In either case the political and economic structures are not basically altered.

In the case of symbolic change, leaders will give the appearance of acting to deal with a problem or making more equitable the distribution of power and privilege. Changes in tax laws, for example, may be depicted by policymakers as effective reforms which diminish the special privileges of particular groups, while actually having little such effect. Another common symbolic action of the federal government in recent decades has been to appoint a presidential or congressional commission to investigate a pressing problem of the society. Once established, the commission's work and its subsequent report are generally forgotten or ignored.

Many of the institutions of government are basically symbolic rather than instrumental in their effect. We have noted the existence of regulatory agencies and antitrust laws, which theoretically control abuses of economic power but which in fact do little in this regard. These agencies and laws, however, serve an important symbolic function, assuaging public doubts and fears that citizens may be unprotected against such abuses (Edelman, 1964; 1971). Such actions and organizations need not be seen as purposeful deceptions on the part of leaders; many, if not most, may genuinely believe in their effectiveness.

Of course, not all sociopolitical changes are symbolic. Reform measures are frequently adopted which result in concessions to challenging groups and ideologies. Such measures serve as safety valves wherein dominant groups accept slight changes in order to avert more sweeping and radical ones. Since most groups seek change only on single issues, concessions by dominant groups may be made in those areas without jeopardizing the basic institutional structure. Welfare measures may be seen in this light. Providing welfare to the poor may be acceptable to the affluent and powerful since such measures check radical movements which seek a real redistribution of social wealth; the prevailing reward system is thus not basically affected. As Parkin (1971:127) notes,

> We should not lose sight of the fact that the attempt to remedy
> inequality by the welfare approach brings about relatively little
> disturbance of the stratification system. As a result it is much more
> palatable to the dominant class than certain other solutions would
> be.

Submitting to minor or symbolic changes serves as a means of
defusing opposition groups by offering evidence that the system is "open
to change." Furthermore such concessions serve as proof that the system
is amenable to input from the citizenry and that change can be effected
through conventional means such as voting and interest group activity.
They prove, in short, that "the system works."

Not only do dominant institutions change in order to assure the
stability of the sociopolitical system but the ideologies underlying them
also undergo changes as called for by new social conditions. Few in
ruling circles today question the welfare state, for example, a far cry
from prevailing attitudes prior to the 1930s. Similarly the racist and
sexist aspects of American ideology have been seriously altered in the
last two decades in response to black and women's movements.

ALTERNATIVE IDEOLOGIES

Despite the development of false consciousness, acceptance of the dominant ideology is never complete. Though it clearly shapes and guides
most of social life, the dominant ideology undergoes scrutiny and at
times even challenge by those who are not among the upper class or
ruling elites. Variations in interpretation and acceptance will be evident
among different ethnic, age, and particularly class groups.

Parkin (1971) claims that there is not one unified belief system in a
society by which all people explain and make judgments about the
society's economic and political systems and the inequality they generate.
Rather he denotes at least three such belief or value systems by which
different groups evaluate and accept in varying degrees the dominant
ideology. He calls these three the dominant, accommodative, and radical
meaning systems.[6] The dominant meaning system endorses the prevailing power and reward structures; it is the "official" explanation of social
inequality and is accepted, of course, by those at the top of the power

---

6. Although some theoretical distinction can be made between a *meaning system* and an
   ideology, for our purposes the two are synonymous. See Converse (1964).

and wealth hierarchies. We have already discussed the means by which false consciousness is engendered among the less affluent and powerful so that they too come to support this explanation widely. Let us look more closely at the other two meaning systems, which stand apart from the dominant one.

The Subordinate Meaning System

What Parkin calls the subordinate meaning system is primarily centered in the working classes of industrial societies. This is an *accommodative* interpretation of the society's structure of power and privilege rather than one which totally accepts it. Although it does not fully endorse the dominant system, neither does it fully oppose it; its stress is on adaptation to the institutional status quo. In other words, opposition to the dominant system takes the form of seeking a greater share of the society's rewards rather than changing the opportunity and reward structures themselves.

Although this meaning system is most evident among the working classes, it is not a form of class consciousness in the Marxian sense. There is no national subordinate ideology as there is a national dominant ideology, and there is no translation of the subordinate ideology into political activism whose purpose is to alter basically the prevailing sociopolitical system. This is particularly the case in the United States, where, unlike most other capitalist societies, there is no labor-based socialist political party.

One major element in this accommodative outlook is fatalism. Being inured to continual material insecurity, people will often adopt a "what will be will be" attitude, stoically accepting their place in the social scheme. Despite real (though unarticulated and largely inchoate) dissatisfaction, many may simply become resolutely apathetic and cynical, displaying various forms of political alienation. As Huber and Form (1973:7) note, "An ideology is effective when there is no need to defend it, when people believe that the system is working the way it should or *that they can do nothing about it if the system is operating unfairly*" (added emphasis). Thus, lacking viable alternatives, the masses need not necessarily enthusiastically support the dominant ideology to assure its effectiveness.

But accommodation may also give rise to a kind of "instrumental collectivism," as exemplified by the trade union movement. Here workers will seek to better their material condition through collective effort rather than individually accept their lots. Trade unionism, however, is quite compatible with adaptation and does not represent opposition to the dominant ideology. On the contrary, collective bargaining means an acceptance of the general system with a desire to gain a greater share of its rewards. It does not seek to destroy or replace the prevailing system of class and power relations. Most reform movements seek similar goals: not institutional change, but a greater portion of the social pie.

The accommodative meaning system is, as Parkin explains, a "negotiated form" of the dominant ideology rather than a restructuring of it. It is a means by which people take the dominant ideology and shape it to meet their personal situations. Thus people will accept the dominant explanation and justification of the society's sociopolitical order in their abstract forms but will modify them to fit individual circumstances.

Such a modified or negotiated interpretation of the dominant ideology was found by Huber and Form in their study of one American community (1973). General acceptance of the dominant ideological themes regarding economic, educational, and governmental systems was evident, but there was far less agreement on specific applications of those ideas. For example, when they were asked whether there was plenty of opportunity in America for those who worked hard, respondents of all classes strongly agreed that there was (though noticeably less strongly among blacks than whites). But when the question was posed as to whether a poor boy had the same chance to advance as a rich boy if they worked equally hard, far fewer among all class groups answered affirmatively, least of all among the poor. Likewise the researchers found that although the pluralist model of how government works in the United States was chosen by most respondents over the Marxian and power elite models, "Both rich and poor respond selectively to the ideology of pluralism and adhere to different elements supporting their situation or aspirations" (Huber and Form, 1973:133).

The accommodative meaning system, then, is not confined to the working classes or to nonelites in general. Selective acceptance of the dominant ideology is evident even among some who may be safely among the privileged and powerful.

The Radical Meaning System

The radical or opposition meaning system offers a view of social inequality as a natural product of the very structure of prevailing economic and political institutions. The explanation and justification of these institutions as presented by the dominant ideology are rejected and in their place a completely opposite meaning system is offered, generally of a socialist nature. It is truly a *counterideology*.

Parkin maintains that the strength of a radical meaning system lies in the ability of workers to link up with intellectuals, a relationship which is most feasible through the mass political party. Lacking access to socialist parties (or in the United States even the existence of such parties), the political influence of intellectuals is diminished, and they remain isolated from the working classes. The inability of radical intellectuals and workers to bridge the gap between them is very apparent in the United States, where the two groups remain culturally and socially apart. An opposition or counterideology is evident among certain intellectual and academic groups, but their activities are scattered and relatively unorganized.

The dominant, subordinate, and even radical meaning systems should not be thought of as mutually separate. More realistically, people of all social strata are exposed to each in varying degrees and will adopt different elements of them depending on particular situations. Again, we should not expect to find great consistency in people's ideological statements and actions.[7] Indeed most studies indicate the lack of a cohesive ideology on the part of the majority of Americans and only a slight understanding of democratic ideology itself (Converse, 1964; Mann, 1970; McCloskey, 1964; Prothro and Grigg, 1960).

Ideology and Political Conflict

While there are noticeable differences and inconsistencies in specific interpretations of the dominant ideology from group to group, it is nonetheless true that the United States has avoided the more apparent ideological cleavages and class politics of Western European societies. The past and present marks of a class system are not so pronounced, and thus it is a relatively simple step to conclude that in America class differences are minimal. A number of factors have contributed to the blurring of class lines in the United States, including the lack of a feudal past, a strong tradition of universal education, a mass consumption economy, and in recent decades the advent of mass communications media. It should not be surprising, then, that despite vast differences in income, wealth, prestige, and power, almost all Americans, when questioned on the subject of class, proclaim themselves middle or working class. In short, there is little class consciousness among most Americans.

As a result, political conflict in the United States ordinarily takes the

---

7. Also, the precepts of any ideology itself will not be consistent. The dominant American ideology, for example, espouses both equality of opportunity and capitalist economics, the latter assuring that the former cannot be realized.

form of dominant versus accommodative interests rather than confrontations between dominant groups and those supporting opposition or radical ideologies. Counterideologies which aim for a classless society fall on deaf ears since part of the dominant liberalist-capitalist ideology is that such a society has already been achieved. Even relatively moderate reforms which call for greater equality in the distribution of power and wealth do not arouse widespread support.

Political groups in the United States may be arranged on an ideological spectrum according to the degree of challenge they offer to dominant economic and political institutions (Figure 12-1). Republicans versus Democrats, labor groups versus industry, and so on typify the participants in political battle. Rarely do conflicts arise involving broad sociopolitical change. Most are simply conflicts *within* the given system, with each group seeking to maximize its political resources. Those at the opposition extremity of the spectrum, advocating basic systemic change, are usually tolerated but are not recognized by dominant groups as serious participants. The dominant-versus-accommodative nature of political conflict typifies most other Western societies as well, though the range of ideological tolerance may be extended somewhat and the intensity of conflict greater.

Occasionally, of course, we do see dominant-versus-opposition ideological conflict, in which case the society's dominant groups may employ strong repressive tactics. Certain elements of both the antiwar movement and the black movement of the 1960s represented a budding opposition ideology. It was against such groups (for example, SDS, Black Panthers) that suppressive tactics were employed by federal and local police agencies (Blackstock, 1976; Wise, 1978). We will further discuss sociopolitical movements of various types and degrees in the following chapter.

POLITICAL SOCIALIZATION

Now that we have looked at the role of ideology in stabilizing the sociopolitical system, we want to turn our attention to the manner in which the dominant ideology is transmitted and loyalty to the prevailing system is infused.

Political socialization is the process through which people learn political beliefs and develop patterns of political behavior. This involves not simply learning the political norms and values of the society but internalizing them, making them an integral part of one's way of seeing and making judgments about the political world. Most simply, political

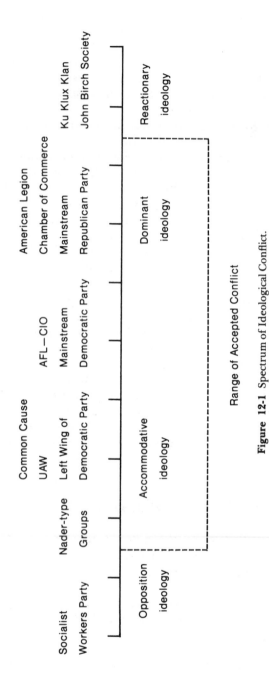

Figure 12-1 Spectrum of Ideological Conflict.

socialization consists of learning and accepting the rights and wrongs of political thought and action. If successfully imparted by socializing agents such as the school, the family, and the media, these beliefs very naturally become firmly accepted and their correctness is henceforth seldom questioned or even given much conscious thought.

In American society, for example, there is rarely any question regarding the desirability of applying democratic principles to power conflicts in all areas of social life. From choosing members of a neighborhood softball team to selecting members of Congress, the same basic notions of fairness and equality are assumed. From the time one begins to interact with peers, and particularly when the school enters the socialization process, the individual learns the "rightness" of democratic practices in social relations. The same is true of other basic political values.

It is important to stress that such beliefs and preferences are, like all other cultural values, imparted through various learning experiences. They are no more "natural" to the individual than is riding a bicycle or a preference for chocolate rather than vanilla ice cream. People of different societies are exposed to different ideologies and thus learn different political norms and values. What few people ever recognize, however, is that this learning process is aimed at acceptance of the dominant sociopolitical system. Political socialization is, as one political scientist describes it, "essentially a conservative process facilitating the maintenance of the *status quo* by making people love the system under which they are born" (Sigel, 1965:7). It is the subtle and essentially unconscious nature of this process which makes it so effective. The given system is accepted as seemingly natural; other systems become in our minds deviant or inadequate. As we have already noted, the effectiveness of socialization to the dominant ideology is revealed by the fact that even those who are permanently disadvantaged by the prevailing institutional arrangement come to accept, at least in the abstract, most elements of it.

What follows is a discussion of political socialization which focuses not on the social-psychological processes through which the individual learns his or her society's political culture[8] but on the process of political socialization at the societal level—that is, the transference of ideology from dominant to subordinate groups. We will concentrate therefore not on the various stages of cognitive and affective development of the person as political actor but on the carriers and transmitters of the

8. There is a sizable literature on the social-psychological processes of political socialization, particularly as it occurs during childhood. Some basic works are Easton and Dennis (1969), Hess and Torney (1967), Greenstein (1969), and Dennis (1973).

dominant ideology—specifically, the school and the mass media. This is not to minimize the importance of the individual in the process of political socialization. Obviously the content of socialization will be molded and mediated differently by different persons. Our stress, however, is on the socializers rather than the individual being socialized.

Political Socialization and the School

Socialization to dominant sociopolitical values takes place through the workings of many social institutions, beginning with the family. But it is in the school that this process is most deliberate and systematic. Social critic Ivan Illich (1971:37) sees the school in modern society serving a purpose similar to that of powerful churches in past eras: "It is simultaneously the repository of society's myth, the institutionalization of that myth's contradictions, and the locus of the ritual which reproduces and veils the disparities between myth and reality."

Some have pointed out that a distinction must be made between political or civic "education" provided by the school and outright political "indoctrination" (Coleman, 1965:226). However, the difference between these two concepts is highly subjective and often difficult to discern. For example, teaching students how a capitalist economy functions while ignoring other economic systems will be viewed as "educational" by dominant groups despite its indoctrinating character. In effect, education, no matter how seemingly neutral, is always political in nature. This is particularly evident in the areas of the social sciences and history. As the late political scientist V. O. Key (1964:316) has observed, "In the American setting the schools are not so obviously seen as arms of governance; yet in the large they play a significant role in the perpetuation of the values of the culture, including those habits, patterns of action, norms, and outlooks that are fundamental to the political order."

Deliberate political socialization. In a variety of ways the school imparts the dominant ideology. Some of these are quite straightforward. The content of civics and history courses, for example, is heavily biased in favor of the capitalist system. Although educators proclaim a spirit of objectivity in the content and methods of their teaching efforts, it is apparent that at all levels of instruction, from kindergarten to college, there is little real competition of ideas. When non-American sociopolitical systems and their ideologies are presented at all, it is ordinarily in a negative light.

Despite the pervasiveness of such direct techniques, research is inconclusive regarding their impact (Langton, 1969; Litt, 1963; Niemi and

Sobieszek, 1977:220–223). Several studies indicate that their effects may not be very great in actually molding political attitudes. High school civics courses, for example, appear to do little more than reinforce an already well-accepted ritual of the democratic creed (Dawson, Prewitt, and Dawson, 1977:143; Zeigler and Peak, 1970:126). In any case, however, these educational efforts complement those of other institutions in solidifying the legitimacy of the dominant system in the minds of students (Hess and Torney, 1967:106).

What students are *not* exposed to may be as important as what they *are* exposed to. Nowhere at the primary or secondary levels, for example, are students given a realistic picture of the acute economic and political stratification of the society. In this view, serious socioeconomic differences among class and ethnic groups simply do not exist, and the student is led to believe in the absence of societal conflict. "The categories of exploitation, dominance, structure, repression, class, and socialist perspectives," notes political scientist Murray Levin, "are not only not transmitted to the young, they are presented as antitruth, intellectually shallow, irrelevant, or utopian" (1971:267).

Efforts to assure that only dominant values will be taught in the schools have led at times to very explicit policing measures. During the hysteria of the Red Scare following World War I, for example, and during the McCarthy period of the early 1950s, teachers were often required to sign loyalty oaths; those suspected of espousing "un-American" ideas were admonished and in some cases even dismissed (Cante, 1978; Murray, 1955). Such blatant tactics to assure educational conformity, however, are usually unnecessary. In most cases teachers conform naturally to acceptable standards since they too are products of the same socialization process. School board members, and others in addition to teachers who determine the content and direction of schooling, tend to be recruited from business and professional occupations and are usually solid representatives of the dominant ideology (Charters, 1953).[9]

There is little question that freer expression of political ideas occurs at the college level and that the boundaries of tolerance imposed by authorities are much wider than in the public schools.[10] Yet, though less constrained, colleges and universities too necessarily operate in a cultural, political, and economic milieu which dictates their conformity to

9. In chapter 6 we noted the heavy influence of businessmen on most college and university boards of trustees.
10. Some maintain that the content of higher education in the United States has a natural tendency to undercut rather than reinforce traditional ideologies, unlike primary and secondary schools. See for example Milner (1972).

dominant ideas. Most institutions of higher education in the United States are heavily dependent on the state for operating funds and on corporations for developmental and research programs. Thus they cannot stray too far from acceptable political and economic values and objectives. The case of Bertell Ollman is illustrative. Ollman, a Marxist, was denied appointment as chairman of the University of Maryland's political science department by the university's president in 1978 even though he had been chosen as the most qualified candidate from among dozens and had been approved by the university's provost and chancellor. The political pressure imposed on the university president to block the appointment was a well-publicized matter.

Incidental political socialization. Direct forms of political instruction may be less important in the school's socialization role than indirect ones. Schools at all levels teach fundamentally individualist-capitalist values in a largely unintentional manner. Competition, for example, is an important incidentally imparted value of the classroom. From the first day of school to the conclusion of one's educational experience, competitive incentives are the chief tools used by the educational system—grades, promotion, awards, and so on. With few exceptions these are individualized competitive situations in which the person rather than the group is held responsible for his or her success or failure. Collective efforts, particularly in academic matters, are not encouraged. This solidly undergirds the principle of individual responsibility, so basic to the maintenance of the dominant ideology.

Another theme emphasized by the American educational system is the practical usefulness of education as opposed to its intellectual or abstract value (Williams, 1970:296). Education is seen as a means to practical ends—specifically, the improvement of one's place in the occupational world. With its emphasis on the acquisition of skills, education does not assume a questioning role for the student which a more theoretical or speculative approach might do. Students attend college mainly in the hope of acquiring a better job rather than to raise their political awareness or to ponder the dominant system. As a result, utilitarian curricula stressing science and technology are more highly valued than are philosophy, the humanities, or the social sciences. Preparing people for careers thus acts as an important mechanism in maintaining the status quo.

In sum, as one of the key agents of socialization in modern societies, the school must be viewed "as an instrument of power" (Spring, 1972: 23). While there is no general agreement as to which, if any, agent of socialization is most important in instilling political beliefs, there can be little doubt that the school plays at least a reinforcing role. We should not, however, overstate the effectiveness of the educational system in perfectly re-creating a political consciousness in each new generation. Obviously its success will vary from one historical period to another. Changes in educational method and approach are impelled by popular demand as well as by the educational system itself (Bowles and Gintis, 1976:129). And under any conditions the success rate of the school in turning out loyal and unquestioning citizens is never 100 percent. That social movements arise, some which question fundamental aspects of the dominant system, is a testament to this fact.

The Mass Media and Political Socialization

In modern societies the mass media—television, radio, newspapers, magazines, motion pictures—are extremely critical agents of socialization. They are the chief means by which people interpret the structures and events of their society, and they serve as the primary organs of political communication. Since their techniques are so pervasive, the capacity of the media as socializers supersedes in some ways even the family's and the school's.

The impact of the mass media in shaping political consciousness is two-fold: (1) the media are the major sources of information for the society's populace, and (2) the media are important means of building support for the society's dominant institutions and ideology. The mass media have, then, an *informative* function and a *persuasive* function.

The Media as Information Sources

That the mass media, television in particular, are the major information sources for modern societies is readily evident. A few statistics on the media in the United States illustrate: One copy of a daily newspaper is sold for every three persons in the society; paid circulation magazines number about 10,000; and almost 100 percent of American homes have radios and televisions, the latter viewed an average of six hours a day per home (Chaffee and Petrick, 1975:18–19). Most importantly the vast majority of the American public indicates a reliance on either television or newspapers as their primary source of information about important societal events (Roper, 1975).

Given these facts, the power of television news directors and newspaper editors in shaping reality for the society is substantial. Events become newsworthy only after they have been selected by the communications gatekeepers (Cohen and Young, 1973; Epstein, 1974; Gans, 1979;

Tuchman, 1978). Obviously what we see in one-half hour of television news each evening or even what we read in a daily newspaper is hardly representative of the total occurrences in any community, much less the society as a whole. The media, then, exert great influence in defining events. Media critic Ben Bagdikian (1971:xii–xiii) explains:

> As men gather in ever larger interdependent masses, communications technology becomes more important and increases the power of those who control it. In an isolated village of 50 persons who meet frequently, community events are learned in face-to-face contacts more effective than any formal medium. But in a country of 200 million self-conscious human beings, the power of news systems is infinitely greater: it is a source of reality itself. For most of the people of the world, for most of the events of the world, what the news systems do not transmit did not happen. To that extent, the world and its inhabitants are what the news media say they are.

Given the media's power of selection, news and political reportage, no matter how seemingly impartial, will be unavoidably biased in some way. But such bias is not so much the product of conscious decisions by media managers as it is the result of constraints brought about by the economic, organizational, and ideological frameworks within which the media operate. Let us look at some of these restrictive factors and how they work to reinforce the dominant sociopolitical system.

Economic constraints. The economic framework for the media in the United States is, of course, a capitalist system. Television networks and newspapers are private corporate enterprises whose major objective is no different from that of other business organizations: generating profits. What is often forgotten in analyzing the production and presentation of news is that it is a commodity to be bought and sold, much like other items. The intent of media corporations is to sell news to advertisers, who in turn use it to sell consumer products to the audience it attracts. V. O. Key cautions us to remember that communications industries, whether newspapers, television, or any other, are commercial entities, not public service institutions. "They sell advertising in one form or another, and they bait it principally with entertainment. Only incidentally do they collect and disseminate political intelligence" (Key, 1964: 378–379). News and public affairs programs have not been highly profitable by comparison with entertainment programs (Gans, 1979:215). As a result, whatever its makeup, news comprises only a slight percentage of television programing.

Organizational constraints. The organizational constraints of televised news are well described by Edwin Jay Epstein (1974), who relates that in most cases news items must be selected in advance by producers who operate with limited personnel and budgets. Camera crews, for example, cannot be in several locations at the same time, and so decisions must be made in advance about what will or will not be covered.

Similar constraints impinge upon newspapers. Newsman Lester Markel asks us to consider the most "objective" of reporters:

> He collects, say, fifty facts and out of these fifty selects twelve as the important ones, leaving out thirty-eight. First exercise of judgment. Then he decides which of the twelve facts shall constitute the lead of the story; this particular fact gets prime attention because many readers do not go beyond the first paragraph. Second exercise of judgment. Then the news editor decides whether the story is to go on page one or on page twenty-nine; if it appears on page one it has considerable impact; if it appears on page twenty-nine, it may go unread. Third exercise of judgment (Markel, 1972:161; see also Paletz et al., 1971).

Another organizational constraint on the media's ability to provide the society with political information objectively is their strong reliance on dominant political and economic institutions as *their* information sources. Often television and the press are forced to report only what government and corporate officials choose to make public. More and more, the state and the corporation themselves control the flow of information, which is then relayed to the public through the media. What they choose not to reveal may therefore go unreported, and what they choose to distort may be reported accordingly. The techniques of news control and manipulation by the Nixon administration are noteworthy. As an illustration, the massive bombing of Cambodia during the Vietnam war proceeded for two years before it was ever revealed to the general public or even to the Congress. And the crimes of Watergate might well have gone undetected had it not been for the persistent searching of two investigative journalists (see Bernstein and Woodward, 1974).

Techniques of presentation. A less obvious, but no less important, feature of the modern media which contributes to their distortion of social reality is their techniques of presenting information. One such technique, owing largely to commercial imperatives, is *fragmentation* of news events (Schiller, 1973). One seemingly unrelated item after another is thrown before the viewer or reader with little sense of totality. An evening news program of thirty minutes, for example, may contain twelve or fifteen stories, none of which is more than a few minutes in length. Furthermore, during this one-half hour, several interruptions will be made for commercial advertising messages. Indeed, as Herbert Schiller notes, "The total indifference with which advertising treats any political or social event, insisting on intruding no matter what else is being presented, reduces all social phenomena to bizarre and meaningless happenings" (1973:25). Viewers or readers are therefore not exposed to a holistic view of a social issue—that is, its root causes or systemic origins—but are offered bits and pieces in rapid succession which are digested as "information."[11]

The fragmented presentation of social and political events creates a kind of public desensitization. News becomes simply one more form of soporific entertainment rather than accurate and edifying reportage of events which galvanizes political action. Indeed, this manner of news presentation leads to apathy, resignation, and a superficial understanding of the workings of the dominant sociopolitical system. Communications expert Bernard Rubin (1977:11) has observed that:

> Unless news is directly perceived as signaling a potential or actual personal threat, most people accept such information in the same manner as they accept the sounds of the music they like. News is sensed rather than appreciated or analyzed. News has become so much *background stuff*.

In addition to their fragmented presentation, news events are communicated to viewers and readers as quickly as they occur. But the immediacy of presentation, rather than promoting understanding, leads to the opposite. The constant flow of "headlines" destroys any means of piecing events together and comprehending their larger meaning. Schiller (1973:28) explains:

> The mind becomes a sieve, through which dozens of announcements, a few important but most insignificant, are poured almost hourly. Information, rather than helping to focus awareness and create meaning, results instead in a subliminal recognition of inability to deal with the waves of events that keep breaking against one's consciousness, which in self-defense must continuously lower its threshold of sensitivity.

11. Much the same format is employed by the society's educational system, in which a variety of courses and materials is presented with little sense of holistic meaning.

Immediacy, then, along with fragmentation, contributes in an unperceived and perhaps even unintended manner to a neutralization of counterideological thinking and action.

The Media as Persuaders

We have now seen that the manner in which information is presented to the society by the media tends subtly and largely unintentionally to buttress the dominant system. Indeed the distinction between the media's "information" and "persuasion" functions is often hazy. Are there, however, more direct and deliberate persuasive functions of the mass media? Here we must look to the media's ideological drift. Few would deny that the American and most other Western media are more open and free than those of Eastern European and many Third World societies. But to dwell on the freedom of the media to collect and report information or to present a variety of entertainment is to lose sight of the implicit dominant ideological biases which characterize their content.

The media as big business. To begin with, given the economic and political context within which they function, the mass media cannot fail to be, as Miliband (1969:236) has described them, "predominantly agencies for the dissemination of ideas and values which affirm rather than challenge existing patterns of power and privilege." The pro-status quo position of media content is a product first of media ownership and control, which in the United States is totally private. Moreover the media are not simply private businesses but *big* businesses which are integral parts of the corporate political economy. Television revenues in 1976 were over $7.5 billion and newspapers over $11 billion (Monaco, 1978:286).[12] Moreover television stations and newspapers are commonly parts of large industrial conglomerates (Westinghouse Electric, for example, owns 7 radio and 5 television stations; General Tire and Rubber owns 17 radio and 4 television stations) or are owned by huge entertainment conglomerates composed of numerous radio and television stations as well as recording, publishing, and motion picture companies. Those who own and/or control the media are not, therefore, apt to use their communications power to undermine a system of which they are very much a part.

Media and politics. As noted, the free expression of ideas through the media is not, in general, a fiction in the United States and other Western

12. It is worth noting that almost 80 percent of newspapers' revenues were derived from advertising, while only 20 percent came from actual newspaper sales.

societies. Diverse interests do make themselves heard, even some which are noticeably contrary to the prevailing sociopolitical system. But as with other aspects of societal power, what is most important is the *degree* of influence upon and access to the chief instruments of public expression (that is, television and the press) which is available to various groups and individuals. The late newspaperman A. J. Liebling once wryly asserted that "freedom of the press belongs to those who own one." Since it is the society's dominant economic groups—primarily giant corporations—who pay the costs, it is they who have greatest access to and are thus the chief utilizers of the media in propagating their messages. As a consequence they exert at minimum an indirect influence on the political content of media presentations.

It is to be expected, then, that opposition or even accommodative ideological messages will receive little media attention. For example, the politics of the two major parties in the United States are covered fully by the media; minor parties, however, are not treated seriously and are given scant coverage. Their candidates and programs are portrayed as eccentric, whose ideas are not to be taken as "reasonable" or "responsible." They are, in short, treated as curiosities rather than legitimate alternatives. It is true that challenges to established authority are often given much attention by newspaper and particularly television journalism. But this is due primarily to the fact that "the logic of audience maintenance favors conflict between easily recognizable groups" (Epstein, 1974:269). Coverage is not provided in acknowledgment of the legitimacy of challenging groups or to present the substance of their protest.

The few instances in which the dominant system is subjected to media scrutiny and criticism (for example, the television weekly documentary *60 Minutes*) or the few moments of satirical comment on the dominant ideology (for example, the comedy show *Saturday Night Live*) do not reflect the bulk of television or general media content. Most simply, the society's power and wealth structures are not seriously questioned. Even when attention *is* drawn to societal shortcomings by public affairs or news programs or by investigative journalists, it is done in the spirit of the dominant ideology. That is, problems are presented as the products of deviant individuals or groups within the context of an otherwise healthy social system. The *systemic* origins of these problems are rarely recognized.

As with teachers within the society's educational system, the expression of dominant values by media managers, correspondents, and reporters is largely unconscious. They see themselves as objective news commentators, not bearers of opinion. That dominant values are implicit in their reportage is not often considered. As Gans (1979:39–40) notes,

"The values in the news are rarely explicit and must be found between the lines—in what actors and activities are reported or ignored, and in how they are described." As an example, the media's use of simplistic phrases such as "free world" as opposed to "communist world" projects an understanding of international affairs as a contest between the forces of good (that is, the United States and its capitalist allies) and evil (that is, the socialist societies).

We should not mistake their presentation of news as the mass media's only influence in creating support for the dominant sociopolitical system. As mentioned, news and public affairs represent only a small portion of media fare, particularly television. But the remaining entertainment, and especially the advertising which constantly augments it, is no less reflective and supportive of the society's dominant value system. (see for example Goldsen, 1977).

The Media in Summary

In concluding our discussion of the role of the mass media in political socialization, we should be careful not to overestimate their power, either as providers of information or as persuaders. As information providers, of course, there is little gainsaying their overwhelming influence. But even here the receptivity of the general public to all that the media offer is not open-ended. Although they are unarguably pervasive, their effectiveness in conveying the same messages to all readers or viewers is by no means certain. "The flow of the messages of the mass media," writes V. O. Key, "is rather like dropping a handful of confetti from the rim of the Grand Canyon with the object of striking a man astride a burro on the canyon floor. In some measure chance determines which messages reach what targets" (1964:357). In various ways people can and do screen themselves from mass media impact.

As to the power of the mass media in propagating the dominant ideology, it is surely not absolute. Although one must usually go beyond the popular media such as television and mass circulation newspapers and magazines to find dissenting views, they are presented in more specialized books, political journals and magazines, and the underground press. Moreover dissenting views are not always blocked even in the television and newspaper media, particularly after they have gained at least some credibility. For example, during the 1960s, antiwar and black civil rights movements eventually enlisted establishment media resources to counterattack successfully the policies of dominant groups. They did so, of course, only after they had reached such magnitude that they could no longer be ignored or overlooked.

The power of the media to shape and influence political ideas remains an issue of debate. Some claim that their impact here has been exaggerated (Seiden, 1974), while others recognize it as critical (Cirino, 1971; Rubin, 1977). Unfortunately most research on the political effects of the media have concentrated on political campaigns and elections rather than on the more general development of political attitudes and preferences. Moreover the study of media effects, particularly television, is still in its infancy. Most studies that have found minimal effects of television on political behavior, for example, were conducted in an era when the proliferation of television sets was not as widespread as today (Kraus and Davis, 1976:52).

In any case, the power of the media to control the flow of information in the society remains obvious. Since they control our vision of which are and are not vital social issues, they can go very far in shaping the agenda of political action (McCombs and Shaw, 1972). And it is here that their most far-reaching power may lie.

SUMMARY

Sociopolitical systems are stabilized and given continuing mass support through the development of ideology and its transmission through the process of political socialization. Dominant ideologies explain and justify the society's distributive systems of power and wealth. In the United States pluralist democratic and capitalist values shape the dominant ideology. Although slight variations are noticeable among political groups, there are few basic disagreements regarding the workings and legitimacy of the class system and its supportive institutions. Mass acceptance of the prevailing sociopolitical system is fostered through development of false consciousness, the belief that political and economic institutions are neutral, beneficial to all social groups, and superior to alternative systems.

The dominant ideology is pervasive mainly in the abstract rather than in real life application. Most people are nonideological in the sense that they do not articulate or even conceive a consistent, integrated set of ideas regarding political and economic life. Furthermore, acceptance of the dominant ideology, even in the abstract, is not total. Rather it is selectively interpreted by various social groups. An accommodative meaning system is evident, particularly among the working class, wherein people accept the dominant ideology as an adaptation to the status quo rather than as a full endorsement. A radical or opposition meaning system is propounded by some intellectual groups, but in the

United States it does not represent a serious challenge to the dominant ideology.

Political socialization is the process by which the society's dominant political beliefs are communicated and internalized. We have looked at two agents of political socialization—the school and the mass media—and their role in transmitting the dominant ideology. The role of the school as political indoctrinator appears less important than its role as communicator of dominant values. The impact of the media on political beliefs is less certain, but their importance lies in their role as the chief means of political communication and their ability to shape political and social reality. Both the school and the media have a reinforcing effect which, along with the family and other socializing agents, perpetuate dominant political beliefs.

Although we have emphasized the role of ideology and political socialization in assuring mass compliance in the United States, the processes described are similar in other modern societies. The content of ideology and the techniques by which it is transmitted may differ, but the effect of stabilizing the prevailing sociopolitical system is much the same.

REFERENCES

Bagdikian, Ben. 1971. *The Information Machines*. New York: Harper and Row.

Bernstein, Carl, and **Bob Woodward.** 1974. *All the President's Men*. New York: Simon and Schuster.

Blackstock, Nelson. 1976. *Cointelpro*. New York: Vintage.

Bowles, Samuel, and **Herbert Gintis.** 1976. *Schooling in Capitalist America*. New York: Basic.

Caplow Theodore, and **Howard M. Bahr.** 1979. "Half a Century of Change in Adolescent Attitudes: Replication of a Middletown Survey by the Lynds." *Public Opinion Quarterly* 43 (Spring):1–17.

Caute, David. 1978. *The Great Fear: The Anti-Communist Purge Under Truman and Eisenhower*. New York: Simon and Schuster.

Chaffee, Steven H., and **Michael J. Petrick.** 1975. *Using the Mass Media*. New York: McGraw-Hill.

Charters, W. W., Jr. 1953. "Social Class Analysis and the Control of Public Education." *Harvard Educational Review* 23 (Fall):268–283.

Cirino, Robert. 1971. *Don't Blame the People*. New York: Vintage.

Cohen, Stanley, and **Jock Young** (eds.). 1973. *The Manufacture of News*. London: Constable.

Coleman, James S. 1965. *Education and Political Development*. Princeton: Princeton U. Press.

Converse, Philip E. 1964. "The Nature of Belief Systems in Mass Publics." In David Apter (ed.), *Ideology and Discontent*. New York: Free Press.

Dawson, Richard E., Kenneth Prewitt, and **Karen S. Dawson.** 1977. *Political Socialization.* 2nd ed. Boston: Little, Brown.

Dennis, Jack (ed.). 1973. *Socialization to Politics.* New York: Wiley.

Dolbeare, Kenneth. 1974. *Political Change in the United States.* New York: McGraw-Hill.

————————, and **Patricia Dolbeare.** 1976. *American Ideologies.* 2nd ed. Chicago: Rand McNally.

Easton, David, and **Jack Dennis.** 1969. *Children in the Political System.* New York: McGraw-Hill.

Edelman, Murray J. 1964. *The Symbolic Uses of Politics.* Urbana: U. of Illinois Press.

————————. 1971. *Politics as Symbolic Action.* Chicago: Markham.

Ellul, Jacques. 1965. *Propaganda.* New York: Knopf.

Epstein, Edwin Jay. 1974. *News From Nowhere.* New York: Vintage.

Free, Lloyd A., and **Hadley Cantril.** 1968. *The Political Beliefs of Americans.* New York: Simon and Schuster.

Gans, Herbert J. 1979. *Deciding What's News.* New York: Pantheon.

Goldsen, Rose K. 1977. *The Show and Tell Machine: How Television Works and Works You Over.* New York: Dell.

Gouldner, Alvin. 1976. *The Dialectic of Ideology and Technology.* New York: Seabury.

Gramsci, Antonio. 1971. *Selections From the Prison Notebooks.* New York: International.

Greenstein, Fred. 1969. *Children and Politics.* Rev. ed. New Haven: Yale U. Press.

Hess, Robert D., and **Judith V. Torney.** 1967. *The Development of Political Attitudes in Children.* Chicago: Aldine.

Huber, Joan, and **William H. Form.** 1973. *Income and Ideology.* New York: Free Press.

Illich, Ivan. 1971. *Deschooling Society.* New York: Harper and Row.

Key, V. O., Jr. 1964. *Public Opinion and American Democracy.* New York: Knopf.

Kraus, Sidney, and **Dennis Davis.** 1976. *The Effects of Mass Communication on Political Behavior.* University Park: Pennsylvania State U. Press.

Lane, Robert E. 1962. *Political Ideology.* New York: Free Press.

Langton, Kenneth P. 1969. *Political Socialization.* New York: Oxford U. Press.

Levin, Murray. 1971. *Political Hysteria in America.* New York: Basic.

Litt, Edgar. 1963. "Civic Education, Community Norms, and Political Indoctrination." *American Sociological Review* 28 (February):69–75.

Lynd, Robert, and **Helen Lynd.** 1929. *Middletown.* New York: Harcourt, Brace.

Mann, Michael. 1970. "The Social Cohesion of Liberal Democracy." *American Sociological Review* 35 (June):423–439.

Mannheim, Karl. 1936. *Ideology and Utopia.* New York: Harcourt, Brace and World.

Markel, Lester. 1972. *What You Don't Know Can Hurt You.* Washington, D.C.: Public Affairs Press.

McCloskey, Herbert. 1964. "Consensus and Ideology in American Politics." *American Political Science Review* 58 (June):361–382.

McCombs, Maxwell E., and **D. L. Shaw.** 1972. "The Agenda-Setting Function of Mass Media." *Public Opinion Quarterly* 36 (Summer):176–187.

Miliband, Ralph. 1969. *The State in Capitalist Society.* New York: Basic.

Milner, Murray, Jr. 1972. *The Illusion of Equality.* San Francisco: Jossey-Bass.

Monaco, James. 1978. *Media Culture.* New York: Delta.

Murray, Robert K. 1955. *Red Scarce: A Study in National Hysteria, 1919-1920.* Minneapolis: U. of Minnesota Press.

Niemi, Richard G., and **Barbara I. Sobieszek.** 1977. "Political Socialization." In Alex Inkeles (ed.), *Annual Review of Sociology.* Palo Alto: Annual Reviews.

Ossowski, Stanislaw. 1963. *Class Structure in the Social Consciousness.* New York: Free Press.

Paletz, David L., Peggy Reichert, and **Barbara McIntyre.** 1971. "How the Media Support Local Governmental Authority." *Public Opinion Quarterly* 35 (Spring): 80–92.

Parkin, Frank. 1971. *Class Inequality and Political Order.* New York: Praeger.

Plamenatz, John. 1970. *Ideology.* New York: Praeger.

Prothro, James, and **Charles Grigg.** 1960. "Fundamental Principles of Democracy: Bases of Agreement and Disagreement." *Journal of Politics* 22 (May): 276–294.

Roper, Burns W. 1975. *Trends in Public Attitudes toward Television and Other Mass Media, 1959-1974.* New York: Television Information Office.

Rubin, Bernard. 1977. *Media, Politics, and Democracy.* New York: Oxford U. Press.

Ryan, William. 1975. *Blaming the Victim.* Rev. ed. New York: Vintage.

Schiller, Herbert I. 1973. *The Mind Managers.* Boston: Beacon.

Seiden, Martin H. 1974. *Who Controls the Mass Media?* New York: Basic.

Sennett, Richard, and **Jonathan Cobb.** 1972. *The Hidden Injuries of Class.* New York: Knopf.

Shils, Edward. 1968. "Ideology." In David Sills (ed.), *The International Encyclopedia of the Social Sciences.* Vol. 7. New York: Macmillan.

Sigel, Roberta. 1965. "Assumptions About the Learning of Political Values." *The Annals* 361 (September):1–9.

Slater, Philip. 1976. *The Pursuit of Loneliness.* Rev. ed. Boston: Beacon.

Spring, Joel H. 1972. *Education and the Rise of the Corporate State.* Boston: Beacon.

Tuchman, Gaye. 1978. *Making News.* New York: Free Press.

Williams, Robin, Jr. 1970. *American Society.* 3rd ed. New York: Knopf.

Wise, David. 1978. *The American Police State.* New York: Vintage.

Zeigler, Harmon, and **Wayne Peak.** 1970. "The Political Functions of the Educational System." *Sociology of Education* 43 (Spring):115–142.

chapter 13

sociopolitical movements

It cannot be denied that the masses revolt from time to time, but their revolts are always suppressed. It is only when the dominant classes, struck by sudden blindness, pursue a policy which strains social relationships to the breaking-point, that the party masses appear actively on the stage of history and overthrow the power of the oligarchies.

Robert Michels

As we have now seen, the continuity of ruling groups and the institutional structures which support them is considerable. Elites in modern societies are able to resist mass challenges to their power through control of the means of economic production, ideological dominance, and the coercive powers of the state. In chapter 11 we saw that the institutional means available to the masses in trying to influence the power structure are, in most cases, mainly symbolic in effect. And in chapter 12 we saw that the dominant ideology effectively creates false consciousness among subordinate groups, expressing itself most commonly as acceptance of things "as they are."

But neither the political behavior nor the political thought of the masses is always successfully dictated by elites and ruling ideologies. The means of political struggle are varied and are not limited to those endorsed by the dominant system. Political struggle also comprises *non*institutional actions and thoughts, those outside the established political framework. At certain moments large numbers of people defy some of the society's political norms and values which are ordinarily accepted routinely. And they do so collectively, not simply in random, individual actions. Many who usually accept the authority and legitimacy of leaders and their institutions now begin to question them; they no longer feel that existing structural arrangements are unchangeable or necessarily just. Most importantly, they begin to feel that dominant institutions can be successfully challenged. In any mass movement, then, there are changes in political behavior and consciousness (Piven and Cloward, 1978:4).

THE CHARACTERISTICS OF SOCIOPOLITICAL MOVEMENTS

Attempts by large numbers of people to change the society's dominant institutions in some measure are called social movements. Such movements can involve almost any social or cultural phenomenon, but we are interested primarily in those which culminate in political action and are intended to alter in some way the distribution of societal power. We shall refer to these organized political actions as **sociopolitical movements**. These movements may involve various class or minority groups who seek concessions from ruling elites. In all cases they represent challenges to the political and/or economic status quo. Sociopolitical movements, whatever their objectives, have several common features.

Organization

Sociopolitical movements are made up of clearly organized groups with specific programs of action. Thus we should not think of diffuse changes in the society's general political or economic environment as sociopolitical movements. The "industrial revolution," for example, denotes observable changes that have occurred in the way people produce their material needs, far different from an agrarian system. Or reference to a "sexual revolution" implies noticeable changes which have evolved in people's sexual behavior and attitudes. But neither of these "revolutions" represents a conscious effort on the part of specific groups to bring about those changes. Sociologists sometimes refer to such general changes or shifts in cultural emphasis as "cultural drifts." Out of these amorphous societal changes may emerge what sociologist Herbert Blumer (1939:258) has called "general social movements." These are sets of ideas expressed in various ways by people, but in a still uncoordinated way. The "women's movement" or the "labor movement" are such general social movements. From these unorganized movements ultimately grow specific movements with organization and strategy.

The general objectives of a sociopolitical movement may precede any formal organization, but it is organization that finely tunes a movement's goals, bringing them into clearer focus. As sociologist Lewis Killian (1964:433) has written, "For a social movement to develop there must be a vision, a belief in the possibility of a different state of affairs, and there must be an enduring organization devoted to the attainment of this vision." Although a sociopolitical movement will often revolve around a specific organization, there are usually a number of formal groups which comprise the movement. The black movement of the fifties and sixties, for example, consisted of at least a half dozen organizations, each with a somewhat different program but all basically concerned with the same goal—securing a more substantial place for blacks in the society's power structure and a greater share of the society's rewards. None of these organizations alone could be called "the movement."

The presence of organization distinguishes sociopolitical movements from spontaneous, momentary uprisings such as mobs, riots, and strikes. Out of such spontaneous actions, however, more formal movement organization may grow. During the 1930s, for example, many spontaneous work stoppages and sit-downs occurred in the automobile and other industries, marking the onset of clearly defined —and largely successful—movements to secure union recognition for workers in these industries (see Fine, 1969).

Noninstitutional Tactics

Since they are challenges to the status quo, it is usually necessary that sociopolitical movements employ tactics which go beyond the established political order. Indeed, were it not for their unconventional actions, they would not be distinct from electoral or interest groups pursuing their collective ends through legitimate means. Once their status is legitimized, sociopolitical movements become part of the established system and adopt fully conventional political methods. The industrial labor movement of the 1930s, for example, exhibited all the characteristics of a sociopolitical movement, including the use of illegitimate, often violent, tactics. But after labor unions were recognized by industry as legitimate bargaining agents of the workers, their tactics changed accordingly. Today union workers seek better salaries and working conditions through negotiations with company owners or managers, not through violent confrontation, as was often the case in the 1930s.

The use of illegitimate tactics will vary from movement to movement. Those seeking broader, more fundamental change will necessarily employ them almost exclusively, while others seeking limited institutional change will usually combine such tactics with legitimate means when they are strategically appropriate.

Ideology

Each sociopolitical movement proclaims an ideology—that is, a doctrine or set of beliefs which explains the need for change in the society's institutions. The ideology also spells out the target for the movement's actions, mobilizing people around a common awareness of who or what is responsible for their discontent.

Without a clearly defined ideology, discontent on the part of large numbers of persons will remain random and unorganized. Through ideology people develop a group consciousness and are mentally prepared to challenge the status quo. However, *dominant* ideologies, as we have seen, are not easily displaced in the minds of most people, and even movements which seek only minor changes in the society's institutional system must work arduously to attract a following.

Leadership

Leadership is critical to a sociopolitical movement. A group may be dissatisfied with its place on the society's hierarchies of power and wealth, but unless that dissatisfaction is articulated and structured into a specific program, it will not lead to a sociopolitical movement. A key function of leaders, then, is to explain and formulate the cause. "In the absence of leadership," writes Killian, "the most that can be expected to arise from such mass dissatisfaction is sporadic crowd behavior, often simply expressive, through which people give vent to their feelings but do not really attempt to change the social order" (1964:447). Black leaders in the 1960s such as Malcolm X and Martin Luther King were strongly charismatic figures who were able to employ their articulateness in spelling out the black movement's objectives and attracting great numbers of previously inactive or uncommitted persons.

In addition to charismatic figures, Killian specifies two additional types of leaders who are part of any movement: intellectual leaders and administrative or bureaucratic leaders. Each plays an integral role in the movement's developmental stages. The first type comprises the movement's ideologues, those who formulate and write its ideological principles. Thomas Paine, Leon Trotsky, and Che Guevara were notable revolutionary ideologues. Sometimes leaders of sociopolitical movements will combine charismatic and ideologue roles, as Lenin did during the Russian Revolution.

Administrative leaders emerge once the movement is stabilized and has a well-functioning organization. Here we might recall Weber's notion of the "routinization of charisma" (chapter 2). Charismatic figures lend themselves best to the tasks of galvanizing mass sentiment for action; indeed, they are the vanguards of social change. However their charisma can go just so far in keeping the movement afloat. Eventually resources must be acquired and larger, more complex organizations must be administered, tasks requiring the more practical skills of the bureaucrat.

TYPES OF SOCIOPOLITICAL MOVEMENTS

Collective attempts to alter the society's dominant power institutions differ, depending on the scope of change sought (sweeping or limited), the direction of change (progressive or regressive), and the methods used. On the basis of these features, three general types of sociopolitical movements may be distinguished: reform, revolutionary, and reactionary.

Reform Movements

Reform movements are the most common of the three types. This is to be expected since in terms of scope, direction of change, and methods, such movements are relatively limited. What is sought is change in the power position of some particular group (blacks, gays, women, poor people, and so on) or the resolution of a certain issue to the benefit of some group (nuclear energy, the Vietnam war, abortion, and so on).

Scope. A reform movement is not aimed at changing the institutional structure in any basic way or at replacing the society's ruling class or traditional power groups. Rather its goal is a greater share of power within the existing sociopolitical framework. The prevailing economic system and its unequal reward structure are not questioned, nor is the political system and its methods of choosing leaders and resolving issues. In short, reform movements seek only a larger piece of the power and wealth pies for certain groups.

Although its scope is quite specific, a reform movement can have wide-ranging effect on many areas of societal life. The contemporary black movement and the women's liberation movement illustrate how changes designed to secure greater power for one group will redound to the society as a whole. Indeed, it can be argued that in modern societies no reform, regardless of how limited its aims or how specific its intended beneficiaries, can avoid societal impact in some form.

Methods. Since there is no rejection of the dominant economic and political institutions, reform movements will often use conventional, institutionalized methods and strategies.[1] Rather than coercive tactics, various forms of persuasion will be used in trying to mobilize public opinion behind a group's cause and in pressuring elites to grant concessions. As sociologist Roberta Ash Garner (1977:6) puts it, the aim of a reform movement "generally is to manipulate or cajole the ruling class or state elites."

A reform movement is not a political party or an interest group, although it may use such channels in attempts to influence elites. Parties and interest groups operate exclusively within the established political framework. Reform movements, however, necessarily step out of that framework, at least from time to time, as conditions require. Consider, for example, the mixed tactics of the black civil rights movement. Sit-ins were illegal within the context of the laws of Southern states. While certain groups were implementing this strategy, others were promoting voter registration drives, a tactic clearly within the boundaries of established authority. As conventional means yield little success, a reform

---

1. Some contend that reform movements use *primarily* institutionalized means. Garner (1977:6), for example, explains the methods of reform movements as "fundamentally legitimate (albeit novel or slightly questionable) . . ." Our definition, however, assumes the need for action outside the established system.

movement may turn increasingly to illegitimate tactics. Thus with the frustrated success of nonviolent protest, certain elements of the black movement in the late 1960s turned to the use of confrontationist tactics, and even violence, when the situation seemed to call for it.

Direction. The intent of reform movements is not to change the entire sociopolitical system, or even a large part of it, but to make the system more effective or to establish social and political rights and economic benefits for certain disenfranchised or subordinate groups. Proposed changes are thus progressive or forward in direction. The industrial labor movement of the 1930s did not aim for a complete dismantling of the capitalist system, but only for a greater role for workers *within* that system. Similarly, the women's movement today seeks to modify the sociopolitical and economic institutions so that they better reflect the interests of women. Instead of appealing for a change in the system of power and the values which underlie it, a reform movement makes an appeal to the society to bring into the prevailing system the aggrieved group and in so doing reaffirm the society's moral values (Blumer, 1939:271). As sociologist Neil Smelser (1963:119) notes, adherents to reform movements (what he refers to as "norm oriented movements") "*justify* their program in terms of the higher values of a society." The ideology of the black or women's movement expresses the right of blacks or women to the economic and social rewards of the society within its *existing* legal and value systems, not those of an idealized society.

Although reform movements are generally of a progressive nature, we might also include certain conservative movements in this category, those which seek to prevent or slow down change. Such movements will generally arise as countermovements to reforms and, like reforms, will use noninstitutionalized as well as institutionalized methods, at least from time to time. The white citizens' councils which sprang up in the South during the 1950s, for example, were in direct response to the burgeoning black civil rights movement and sought to deter the changes inspired by that movement (McMillan, 1971).

Revolutionary Movements

Revolution is by far the most widely studied type of social movement and has occupied much of the attention of political scientists and historians, as well as sociologists.

Scope and direction. Reform movements concern specific issues or groups and do not seek alteration of the society's institutional system in any fundamental way; revolutions, however, are sweeping in scope and aim for a restructuring of societal institutions and ultimately the class system itself. This involves change in almost every aspect of societal life, including the society's value system. Franz Schurman (1971:20) has defined a revolution as "an overturning of fundamental hierarchical relationships in a society—what is below displaces what is above." Simply put, following revolution, what was socially defined as wrong may now be right, and those previously at the top of the social hierarchy may now be at the bottom.

Methods. Since its aim is basically to replace the existing social order, the methods of revolution are, of course, outside the established political framework. And they are bound to be coercive rather than persuasive; indeed, violence is usually assumed to be an integral element of revolution. Turning the social structure upside down obviously does not occur without the use of coercion by those seeking change and forceful retaliation by those resisting it. Ruling groups do not voluntarily relinquish their power. As Michels (1962:245) observed, "A class considered as a whole never spontaneously surrenders its position of advantage. It never recognizes any moral reason sufficiently powerful to compel it to abdicate in favor of its 'poorer brethren.' "

Given the scope and intensity of such change, it is not surprising that we have witnessed so few truly revolutionary movements in modern times. The first, and perhaps prototypical, social revolution occurred in France in 1789. Here the traditional ruling class made up of the landowning aristocracy was replaced by a new ruling class, the bourgeoisie, whose economic base was commerce and industry. An entirely new social order emerged based on the ideology of this now-dominant class. Other total revolutions which have basically altered class relations have occurred in Russia in 1917, China in 1949, and Cuba in 1959.

Political revolution. Rather than movements which bring about total social change, what is more common in the modern world is what might be called political revolution. Here either political institutions are radically changed or ruling political elites are forcibly displaced by a challenging group. But in either case the class system and other institutional relations remain basically intact. Where political institutions are altered, new rights and obligations of citizens and state may be drawn up (as in a new formal constitution). But so long as class relations are unaffected, the revolution is confined to such governmental changes. That class which controls the means of economic and ideological production is not displaced, and ruling elites continue to be recruited from the society's established ruling groups. Most revolutions of former colonial societies involve such basic changes in political institutions, while other aspects of societal life remain relatively unaffected. The American Revolution is a case in point. Although state power was transferred from England to an independent American government, the society's class structure was left essentially unchanged. Established ruling groups continued to maintain their places on the power and wealth hierarchies.

The other type of political revolution, in which one elite forcibly displaces another, is commonly referred to as a *coup d'etat*. Power personnel change, but the class structure and its underlying ideology do not. Thus, societal life outside the inner circle of governmental power may proceed quite normally, with little interruption or disjuncture. The frequency of *coups* in many Latin American societies during the twentieth century reflects the limited nature of such "palace revolutions." In Venezuela, for example, there have been 80 such illegitimate political successions in the last century and several hundred unsuccessful attempts (Rapoport, 1969:73). Argentina has experienced 6 forcible overthrows of the government by military juntas since 1955 (U.S. Dept. of State, 1977). But in all of these cases nongovernmental institutions were not affected in any basic manner. In fact, even the government bureaucracy ordinarily remains intact in the face of such intense, often bloody, takeovers, continuing to administer governmental affairs as usual.

Political revolutions, then, are limited to personnel or constitutional changes, with little or no effect on the society's class system. They should not be confused with *social* revolutions, which leave no area of societal life untouched (such as the French, Russian, Chinese, and Cuban revolutions). Social revolutions are, most simply, *total* revolutions. The shape of the class structure is radically altered and, most importantly, the society's ideological or value system is replaced with a new set of justifying principles. Not only is one group replaced by another at the top of the political order, but the ruling class itself, that group which controls societal wealth and ordinarily supplies institutional elites, is now displaced. A social revolution is, of course, also a political revolution. Indeed, political revolution is a necessary first step in such total social change. But movements that do not go beyond the replacing of political elites or changing governmental organizations —clearly the most common type —are not social revolutions. In the wake of social revolution, fundamental change is generated in every institutional area —economic, political, educational, religious, and even the family. In this sense only a handful of sociopolitical movements have occurred in the modern world that may be accurately classified as genuine social revolutions.[2]

2.   On the distinctions between various types of revolution see Johnson (1966:ch. 7).

Reactionary Movements

The basic distinction between revolutionary and reactionary movements is the direction of change sought. Whereas revolutions are progressive movements, seeking to establish new societal institutions and relations, reactionary movements are regressive, designed to re-create conditions which existed in an earlier time. We might think of this as inverse change.

In contrast to revolutionary movements, reactionary or right-wing movements seek to perpetuate or even intensify existing inequalities in the society. Their objectives therefore are to enhance the social privileges of certain groups at the expense of others. To explain and justify these goals, right-wing ideologies are predicated on claims of cultural and physical superiority of some social groups and the inferiority of others. As a result, those groups labeled inferior are targeted for oppression or perhaps even elimination—Jews for Nazis, blacks for the Ku Klux Klan, and so on (Moore, 1978:423).

Reactionary movements may differ as to the scope of change sought. A movement such as the Ku Klux Klan, for example, is aimed at reestablishing earlier forms of race relations but is not concerned with most other aspects of the social system. The Nazi party in Germany during the 1930s, however, proclaimed the re-creation of the total German society, based on what the movement's leaders saw as a once glorious past. Regardless of the scope of change sought, however, the methods of reactionary movements are, like revolutions, heavily illegitimate.

Table 13-1 illustrates the contrasting types of sociopolitical movements. According to Garner (1977:194), movements have certain choices:

between single issue demands and multiple demands;

between class-conscious demands and demands that do
not attack the legitimacy of present distributions
of wealth and power;

between influencing elites (or even incorporating
movement members into the elite) and attempting
to replace elites.

In terms of these alternatives, we may say that reform movements choose to focus on single-issue demands which do not question the legitimacy of the power and wealth structures. Revolutionary movements choose to focus on a broad range of demands and seek to replace elites and possibly the entire distributive system of power and wealth. Reac-

TABLE 13-1 Types of Sociopolitical Movements

Type	Purpose	Scope of Change Sought	Direction of Change Sought	Principal Methods Employed	Examples
Reactionary	Re-create a past social order	Broad; many institutions affected	Backward (regressive)	Coercive, non-institutional	Nazism, Ku Klux Klan
Conservative	Resist change in some aspect of the social order	Limited	Stationary	Mainly persuasive, but coercive and noninstitutional may be used	Wallace movement, anti-abortion
Reform	Promote change in some aspect of the social order	Limited	Forward (progressive)	Mainly persuasive, with some use of noninstitutional	Black civil rights, women's liberation, environmentalism
Revolutionary a. Political	Forcibly change political personnel or rules	Political institutions	Forward	Coercive, non-institutional; violence ordinary	American Revolution
b. Social	Forcibly change the entire social order	Sweeping; all institutions basically affected	Forward	Coercive, non-institutional; violence ordinary	Russian Revolution, Cuban

tionary movements choose similar options as revolutions but seek to re-establish a former societal condition rather than create an innovative one.

FACTORS IN THE EMERGENCE OF SOCIOPOLITICAL MOVEMENTS

The most compelling fact of the various types of movements aimed at altering power in a society is that most people do *not* participate. Thus, like the conventional modes of citizen action, the unconventional ones are utilized by very few. If, as we have seen, engaging in institutional politics is the exception rather than the rule, engaging in noninstitutional activity is even rarer. This should not surprise us, given the strength of the dominant ideology and its effect on the shaping of most people's consciousness. Most individuals, quite simply, are socialized into believing in the inherent justness and correctness of the prevailing system and are not apt to question it seriously unless driven to an extreme point where their personal crises are consciously linked to the way the society's institutions work. Sociologists have long observed the tendency for oppressed groups ordinarily to endure their subordinate place rather than challenge the status quo. Indeed, as Barrington Moore (1978:49) has noted, it is perhaps as important to ask why people do *not* revolt as to ask why they do.

Yet movements do arise which challenge parts of, or even the entire, dominant sociopolitical system. Sociologist Ralph Turner (1969:391) has written that "A movement becomes possible when a group of people cease to petition the good will of others for relief of their misery and demand as their right that others ensure the correction of their condition." What are the social and psychological conditions which seem to create such a mood, driving people to begin to challenge ruling groups and established ways?

Several general theories purport to explain why sociopolitical movements occur. Some concentrate on the psychological factors which motivate individuals to participate, while others emphasize the sociological factors—that is, the structural forces in society which seem to propel movements. Still others are what may be called social-psychological, combining both sociological and psychological factors. Let us look at some of the more prominent theories.

Psychological Theories

The key question asked by psychological theories of sociopolitical movements is, "Who takes part?" Such theories are mainly concerned with the personality traits of participants and suggest that there are certain types of persons who are especially attracted to movements.

The true believer. One of the more popular accounts of the membership of movements is Eric Hoffer's *The True Believer* (1951). Hoffer, a self-educated longshoreman, wrote this small classic as an attempt to describe those who join movements of all kinds, but extremist political and religious movements in particular. According to Hoffer, the potential convert to a movement is a fanatic and, for any number of reasons, a social misfit. Such persons are the society's disaffected, who may be found in all walks of life but especially in the categories Hoffer labels the poor, misfits, the inordinately selfish, the ambitious, minorities, the bored, and the sinners. Such people see themselves as discarded and rejected, their present lives ruined. Thus, according to Hoffer, they are more willing to join a mass movement which may promise a hope of salvation. Also they recognize an opportunity to dissolve their meaningless selves in a communal undertaking. In this view, participation in sociopolitical movements is an escape mechanism for frustrated individuals who cannot succeed in the mainstream society.

This is a conservative theory which does not question the societal conditions out of which people's behavior derives; rather it concentrates on individual motivations and actions. As such it is a theory that is attractive to those who would defend the established system. People who participate in sociopolitical movements are labeled "aberrant," "demented," or "riffraff" by authorities, and civil disorders or other actions which illegitimately challenge the dominant system are explained as the work of such maladjusted troublemakers. Police officials and mayors of American cities where riots by blacks occurred in the 1960s commonly credited the outbreaks to thugs, hoodlums, and other criminal types. Even some social scientists adopted a modified version of this explanation of the riots, maintaining that they were the actions of lower-class youth, primarily the uneducated and unemployed, who were merely rioting for "fun and profit" (Banfield, 1974). Most studies of the riots, however, failed to support this thesis. Rather than maladjusted, rioters were found to be relatively better educated and less alienated than nonrioters. They did not differ strongly in terms of income or unemployment, though they were more likely to be employed in dead-end, unskilled jobs and were less satisfied with their occupations than nonrioters (Blauner, 1972; Caplan and Paige, 1968; National Advisory Commission on Civil Disorders, 1968; Sears and McConahay, 1973).

Hoffer's thesis and others like it complement the society's dominant ideology. Focus is placed on the inabilities of individuals to adapt to the society rather than on the society's lack of adaptability to individual needs. Sociopolitical movements are thus seen as the product of deviant individuals, not individuals rationally responding to their objective conditions. In this view, dominant institutions are not at fault, and the suppression of such movements can therefore be justified. Obviously such theories lend themselves to a maintenance of the status quo.

The authoritarian personality. One of the most influential ideas in explaining participation in extremist movements is that of the "authoritarian personality." This account of movement participation rests heavily on the work of a group of German social scientists working in the United States after World War II who were motivated by a desire to determine the psychological foundations of such destructive and regressive movements as Nazism. Their focus was thus primarily on those who supported right-wing extremist movements.

In their main work, *The Authoritarian Personality* (1950), Theodore Adorno and his research associates theorized that there is a definite psychological type who is prone to engage in right-wing extremist movements. Such persons, they argued, are highly conformist, disciplinarian, cynical, intolerant, and preoccupied with power. They are particularly authority-oriented and are thus attracted to movements which require submission to powerful leaders. Such personality traits extend well beyond the individual's political beliefs and are reflected in all aspects of his or her social life. In the family, for instance, authoritarians will subject their children to strong disciplinary action and in their religious beliefs will emphasize submission and obedience. In sum, such persons are strongly supportive of conservative values and are highly resistant to social change.

Adorno and his associates constructed a test to measure these authoritarian traits called the "f-scale." Those scoring high on the various measures are presumably more authoritarian and thus attracted to Nazi and fascist-type movements. The f-scale, as well as the general premise of the authoritarian personality, have been the subject of much debate among social scientists. Some have questioned the methodology used in measuring authoritarianism, while others have criticized the theory's limited application only to movements of the right (see for example Pettigrew, 1958). Other studies, however, have seemed to confirm the basic notion of an authoritarian personality, and it has been used in explaining the behavior of blatantly prejudiced persons who tend toward right-wing extremist movements such as the Ku Klux Klan, the John Birch Society, and other antiblack, anti-Semitic, and superpatriot groups (Bell, 1964; McCloskey, 1958).

The psychological approach in explaining sociopolitical movements seems limited in a number of regards. First, it does not account for the actual development of movements. Indicating which types of personalities are more apt to participate is putting the cart before the horse; a movement must be in place before individuals can join. Second, a psychological emphasis neglects the situational conditions out of which movements arise, conditions which participants may be rationally seeking to change. As Rudolf Heberle (1968:441) notes,

> While many early leaders of radical movements have been maladjusted personalities and while frustrated individuals are often attracted by such movements, mass adherence is gained by rational reaction to economic or other social conditions which are felt to be intolerable.

For example, although the Nazi movement undoubtedly drew many adherents from among the social misfits and authoritarian personalities of Germany in the 1930s, studies have shown that the movement's appeal was across a wide social spectrum. Most who joined were responding to their objective economic condition, which had been eroded by a disastrous depression during these years. Sociologist Hans Gerth (1940) explains that people who suffered losses in status or income were to be found in every stratum of German society —workers, artisans, shopkeepers, professionals, industrialists, intellectuals. The belief in Hitler and the Nazi movement for these varied groups was the result of a common despair, economic insecurity, and frustrated status and occupational goals.

Turner and Killian (1972:365) write that it is probably more valid to conclude that different kinds of motivations draw people to different kinds of movements than to conclude that there is a movement-prone type. It is likely that personalities which Hoffer and Adorno describe do constitute some of the membership of extremist movements. But it is unlikely that they constitute most or even a majority. Moreover the inordinate focus on extremist movements overlooks the fact that most sociopolitical movements are not revolutionary or reactionary but are more moderate protest or reformist movements. Thus psychological theories do not account for those persons who become participants in such milder actions of challenge to the status quo.

In sum, the psychological explanations of sociopolitical movements do not explain the movements *per se* so much as they try to account for those who join them. But even in this they are too limited in explaining the myriad social types who may comprise any particular movement, of the left or the right. Clearly, other factors—namely, social, economic, and political forces—must be combined with these theories to explain more fully the origins of sociopolitical movements.

Structural Strain

Some sociologists see the emergence of sociopolitical movements as closely tied to changes in the social structure. In this view, societies are ordinarily balanced and cohesive social systems which may be thrown into disequilibrium by extensive structural change. For example, societies may face the large-scale upward mobility of formerly deprived groups, the influx of large numbers of immigrants, or basic alterations in political institutions. Such changes induce stress on the part of large numbers of people who feel threatened by these changes or by the groups involved. Widespread discontent is apt to lead to social unrest and the increasing likelihood of the development of sociopolitical movements.

Chalmers Johnson (1966) has theorized that the social problems created by structural changes demand adjustments by the society's ruling elites; if they are incapable of managing the changes which must be made to restabilize the system, the conditions for revolution are favorable. Neil Smelser (1963) has also emphasized the introduction of some source of strain into an otherwise cohesive social structure as the spawning force of social movements. He defines strain as "the impairment of the relations among parts of a system and the consequent malfunctioning of the system" (p. 384).

As an example of structural strain generating sociopolitical movements, we might consider the periodic waves of nativism which have been evident in the United States. Historian John Higham (1975:4) explains nativism as "intense opposition to an internal minority on the ground of its foreign (i.e., 'un-American') connections." During several periods of American history, nativist movements on a grand scale erupted in response to the influx of large numbers of immigrants. In the 1840s and early 1850s political parties such as the Know Nothings and the Native American party arose whose messages of fear and hatred were directed primarily at the waves of Irish immigrants who had flooded cities such as Boston and New York. Again in the 1920s a broadly based nativist movement reemerged. Such groups as the Ku Klux Klan, with its strongly anti-Catholic, anti-Semitic, and antiblack ideology, attracted national followings, and even establishment political figures called for the rapid and complete "Americanization" of Southern and Eastern European immigrants (mainly Catholics and Jews) who had arrived during the preceding 40 years. This wave of nativism resulted in the enactment of restrictive immigrant quotas, thereby putting an end to large-scale immigration. Both of these nativist movements coincided with changing economic and political conditions. In the 1840s and 1850s sectional cleavages (North versus South) had come to a head, threatening national unity, and in the 1920s the society faced the disruptions caused by World War I. Irish Catholics in one period and Catholics, Jews, blacks, communists, and other minorities in the other served as convenient scapegoats for the frustrations created by these social strains. As Higham (1975:107) writes, "In desperate efforts to rebuild national unity men rallied against the symbols of foreignness that were appropriate to their predicament."

This approach to sociopolitical movements is almost diametrically opposed to the psychological approach. It concentrates not on the motivations of individuals but on the social forces creating the conditions which seem to give rise to movements. However, it is difficult to identify those social forces which actually cause strain. Indeed, there may be a kind of circular reasoning involved here since sources of strain may be evident only after the fact—that is, following the emergence of a movement. Also, the very determination of strain becomes somewhat arbitrary. As Wilson (1973:35) notes, "Societies are always experiencing change and for this reason strain is endemic in all societies. At this stage the question clearly arises of how it is possible to separate those conditions which are exceptional enough to demand noninstitutionalized responses."

The structural explanation of sociopolitical movements also rests on an implicit understanding of a movement as a symptom of the society's malfunctioning. It is an "abnormality" rather than a reflection of what might be a common tendency of the society. If societies are seen as striving for balance, a movement is an indication of *im*balance; thus one is forced to look elsewhere for an explanation of the movement's causes rather than to the society's internal, perhaps usual, workings. But rather than generally stable or balanced, societies may just as easily be seen as constantly in flux, with a built-in conduciveness to sociopolitical movements (Wilson, 1973:55).

Even if sources of social strain can be identified, we are still left wondering *why* people join movements. Whereas the psychological approach generally ignores the social conditions out of which particular persons emerge to become movement activists, structural analysis seems to move in the opposite direction, neglecting the motivational factors of individuals. Not all persons will respond similarly to the same objective conditions of societal change. As Hans Toch (1965:9) notes, "The focus of a problem is not in the problem situation, but in its *impact* on individual people." To attribute protest movements or urban violence to "social conditions" or "structural strain" will not explain why certain groups and individuals respond to these conditions with noninstitutional behavior while others seek change within the dominant institutional system or simply continue to tolerate their discontent. It is how those conditions affect people and what response they make to them which determine why and when people will choose to challenge established norms and beliefs regarding the distribution of power and wealth.

Deprivation Theories

People's interpretations of and responses to changing conditions are the focus of "deprivation" theories. According to these theories, certain social conditions alone do not "cause" people to challenge established authority. Such conditions may be prevalent for long periods without the development of sociopolitical movements. It is only when people come to see those conditions as oppressive or unfair that they may be impelled to act and thus form the basis of a movement. In this view sociopolitical movements are the product of people's changing interpretations of what is happening in their society as well as their feelings about their present and future place in the society's power and wealth hierarchies.

Deprivation and political action. The essential meaning of deprivation is a condition in which people lack that which is thought to be necessary or desirable. Tying this notion to sociopolitical movements, the logic is simple: Those who are deprived in some way—materially, status-wise, politically—are those who are most likely to be dissatisfied with the existing political and economic systems and will thus become the participants in sociopolitical movements. This common sense explanation tells us that as people experience frustration and discontent, they organize themselves in an attempt to force institutional authorities to better their condition. Economic poverty or political oppression, it is assumed, leads people to take action when their situation becomes so bad that there is seemingly nothing to lose in revolt. In *The Communist Manifesto*, Marx and Engels, in a now familiar phrase, encouraged workers to unite since they had "nothing to lose but their chains."[3]

Looking at historical examples, however, this common sense explanation of sociopolitical movements appears to have little basis in fact. Oddly enough it is not extremes of poverty or oppression alone which seem to generate challenges to established authority. As so many observers have pointed out, the frustration created by economic deprivation or political persecution does not necessarily lead to activism to alleviate those conditions. Turner and Killian (1972:247) note that "Long continued frustration characteristically leads to hopelessness and preoccupation with immediate and momentary survival problems, which mitigate against participation in the promotion of any reform." Steady poverty or oppression may thus paradoxically be the best assurance of political *in*activity among the poor and oppressed. W. G. Runciman (1966:9) explains that "if people have no reason to expect or hope for more than they can achieve, they will be less discontented with what they have, or even grateful simply to be able to hold on to it." So long as they recognize no hope of improving their lot, the poor and the oppressed will resign themselves to the status quo and will fear and even resist change. Those who are totally consumed with staying alive from day to day do not have the physical or psychological will to create challenges to institutional authority. Hoffer (1951:17) well expresses this idea:

3. Like so many ideas of Marx and Engels, their view of the development of a revolutionary mood among the workers has received different interpretations. Some maintain that the simple notion of increasing misery, ultimately leading workers to revolt, is *over*simplified and is "vulgar Marxism." They emphasize Marx's explanation of *relative* impoverishment among workers in capitalist society. On this point of debate see Anderson (1974:22–24).

When our mode of life is so precarious as to make it patent that we cannot control the circumstances of our existence, we tend to stick to the proven and the familiar. . . . There is thus a conservatism of the destitute as profound as the conservatism of the privileged, and the former is as much a factor in the perpetuation of a social order as the latter.

History has shown humans to be remarkably resilient and compliant under the most vile and inhumane conditions of social and political life. That people do not revolt under extraordinarily oppressive conditions is well illustrated by the two most evident systems of human degradation of modern history: American slavery of the eighteenth and nineteenth centuries and the Nazi concentration camps of the 1930s and 1940s. In both cases rebellions of the oppressed were rare, short-lived, and mostly unsuccessful (Elkins, 1949).

This does not mean that poverty or oppression may not lead to anger, frustration, and other forms of discontent. But as Turner and Killian point out, the intensity of emotion felt by people is no indication of their conduciveness to create or join a movement. Intense anger is apt to lead to spurts of violent release such as riots, but not to the development of organized movements; these require staying power and are more than merely sporadic and momentary outbursts.

Ironically, then, it is only after conditions have *improved* that the social and psychological prerequisites for sociopolitical movements are in place. Only then does pressure for change begin to emerge among certain groups who now see themselves as unjustly deprived of power or wealth. Toch (1965) notes that before people are ready to join a movement, they must feel that they can affect their situation. At the very least they must feel "that the status quo is not inevitable, and *that change is conceivable*" (p. 11). Those at the very bottom of the social hierarchy are not likely to be political activists since they suffer *absolute* deprivation and do not expect change. Rather the supporters of movements will be those who suffer *relative* deprivation. These are the people whose expectations are rising but who feel held back in their upward movement by the prevailing political and economic institutions.

Relative deprivation. Political scientist Ted Robert Gurr (1970:13) defines relative deprivation as "a perceived discrepancy between men's value expectations and their value capabilities." Value expectations are those things to which people believe they are rightfully entitled, and value capabilities are the things they believe they are actually able to attain in their present condition. Simply put, people who suffer relative deprivation feel they are entitled to more than they are getting. The greater the gap between what they expect and what they can attain, the greater will be their frustration and sense of injustice.

In order for such feelings to crystallize, however, people must be able to compare their situations with others in the society. As Runciman (1966:9) explains, if people "have been led to see as a possible goal the relative prosperity of some more fortunate community with which they can directly compare themselves, then they will remain discontented with their lot until they have succeeded in catching up." In shaping their expectations, people use reference groups with which to compare themselves that are clearly visible and close at hand. Those who feel economically deprived in the United States, for example, do not compare their personal standard of living with people in India but with other groups in the United States. It is important to understand, of course, that people's feeling of deprivation may have no relationship to their real situation. What is critical is that they *think* they are being deprived of something they deserve. What their level of income is, for example, is less important than what they believe it should be.

Rising expectations. Sociologists have developed several more specific hypotheses regarding the general theory of relative deprivation, each pertaining to a somewhat different social condition or group (see Gurr, 1970: ch. 1). Perhaps the most common type of relative deprivation is what has been called "rising expectations." People may experience an improvement in their condition of life but, at the same time, experience a rise in the level of their desires. Thus their capabilities do not keep pace with their expectations. As the gap between expectations and capabilities grows, presumably greater frustration is experienced and people are impelled to engage in noninstitutionalized forms of political activism (Figure 13-1). Gurr refers to this as "aspirational deprivation."

Rising expectations are thought to be a key factor in the occurrence of revolution. Many have observed that revolutionary movements seem to take place when social conditions are actually improving rather than deteriorating. DeTocqueville (1955:175), in his analysis of the French Revolution, noticed that "those parts of France in which the improvement in the standard of living was most pronounced were the chief centers of the revolutionary movement." And historian Crane Brinton (1952:30–31), in his comparative study of four revolutions, concludes that England, the United States, France, and Russia, prior to their revolutions, were all on the upgrade economically. In these cases a period of improved conditions, particularly for certain classes, produced the expectation of and desire for further improvements. That such improve-

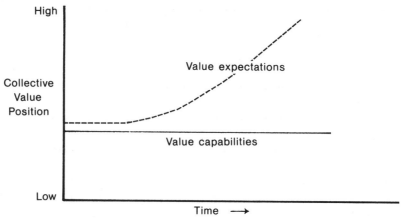

Figure 13-1 Aspirational Deprivation. Source: From Ted Robert Gurr, *Why Men Rebel* (copyright © 1970 by Princeton University Press; Princeton Paperback, 1971): Fig. 2, p. 51. Reprinted by permission of Princeton University Press.

ments did not develop as rapidly as anticipated contributed to the revolutionary climate.

When a society is experiencing general economic progress, not all groups reap the same proportional benefits. Thus, improvements in living standards for some groups may be real but, relative to more prosperous groups, may represent little or no improvement. In describing the plight of workers in capitalist society, Marx perceptively explained how their wages might increase but, by comparison with the capitalists, they might still experience a decline in their position:

> A noticeable increase in wages presupposes a rapid growth of productive capital. The rapid growth of productive capital brings about an equally rapid growth of wealth, luxury, social wants, social enjoyments. Thus, although the enjoyments of the worker have risen, the social satisfaction that they give has fallen in comparison with the increased enjoyments of the capitalist, which are inaccessible to the worker, in comparison with the state of development of society in general (Tucker, 1972:180).

Marx goes on to explain that our expectations—what we see as "needs" as well as "wants"—are socially determined and will change as the standards of the society change:

> Our desires and pleasures spring from society; we measure them, therefore, by society and not by the objects which serve for their

satisfaction. Because they are of a social nature, they are of a relative nature (Tucker, 1972:180).

Perhaps the best contemporary example of the relation of rising expectations to the development of a sociopolitical movement is the black revolt of the 1960s. Since blacks had experienced the effects of societal racism throughout American history, one might logically ask why a viable black protest movement arose in the 1960s rather than an earlier time. Many sociologists point to rising expectations. Rather than absolute deprivation, blacks had experienced an improvement in most social indicators during the immediately preceding two decades: occupational status, income, education, and so on. However, as blacks were improving their social positions, whites were improving at an even greater rate (Geschwender, 1964). Feeling that they were not progressing as rapidly and as substantially as they should have been, the social and psychological conditions were suitable for the emergence of a black protest movement.

Downward mobility. Another type of relative deprivation pertains to groups and individuals experiencing downward mobility—that is, a loss in economic or social status. When people experience downward mobility, they feel indignation over the loss of what they once had or believed they could have. Such persons experience relative deprivation by comparing their present position on the social hierarchy with where they were in the past (or where they feel they could have been). An economic depression in which fortunes or life savings are wiped out may generate such feelings. Under these circumstances people must adjust their expectations to a lower level, always a difficult and painful process. The Nazi movement in Germany and the Italian Fascist movement seemed to draw disproportionately from such "declassed" persons (Cantril, 1941; Fromm, 1941; Gerth, 1940). With the loss or threatened loss of their former positions, a significant gap was created between their expectations and their capabilities for satisfying them. Gurr refers to this type of relative deprivation as "decremental deprivation" (Figure 13-2).

Persons experiencing downward mobility are not the longstanding deprived but the newly deprived, and are thus likely to experience exceptionally great frustration. Their response is apt to be correspondingly extremist in nature. Gurr (1970:51) notes that "Men are likely to be more intensely angered when they lose what they have than when they lose hope of attaining what they do not yet have." Since they seek to restore a former social condition, movements which arise in response to downward mobility will usually be reactionary.

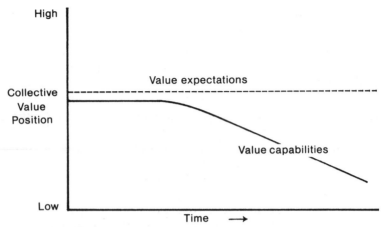

Figure 13-2 Decremental Deprivation. Source: From Ted Robert Gurr, *Why Men Rebel* (copyright © 1970 by Princeton University Press; Princeton Paperback, 1971): Fig. 1, p. 47. Reprinted by permission of Princeton University Press.

This type of relative deprivation may produce what some have called "status politics"—that is, political movements which appeal to persons who fear or resent the upward mobility of other groups or who are disoriented by abrupt changes in traditional social patterns and who, in response, collectively seek to maintain or improve their own status (Hofstadter, 1964; Lipset, 1964; Lipset and Raab, 1978). Whites who fear the upward movement of blacks, or doctors and small entrepreneurs who see increasing government intrusions into their businesses are examples of such groups. They do not necessarily suffer an economic loss, but rather a loss of status and a threat to their established way of life. Indeed, Lipset posits that it is precisely in times of economic prosperity that status politics are strongest. Frustrations arising from economic losses are apt to provoke rational responses—calls for a redistribution of income, for example. But those deriving from status losses, explains Lipset, are not so easily redressed by government action. In fact government may be the very source of the threat. Thus sociopolitical movements among those who perceive a loss of prestige or of life-style are commonly right-wing movements, which target particular groups who are seen as the status threats. Various nativist, antiblack, anti-Semitic, antilabor, and anticommunist movements throughout American history have been explained in this manner. In recent times the Wallace movement of the late 1960s, as well as other right-wing groups and political candidacies, have been interpreted as movements made up largely of those who have felt a status loss to newly emergent ethnic, occupational, and behavioral groups such as blacks, Jews, government bureaucrats, gays, and women.

Status inconsistency. Another deprivation-type explanation of participation in sociopolitical movements is found in the notion of status inconsistency. This describes a situation in which persons find themselves ranked variably on different measures of stratification. For instance, some may work in prestigious occupations that do not pay at a similar level (college professors, for example) or some may earn high incomes but rank low on the society's ethnic hierarchy (successful minority businessmen, for example). Such persons are thought by some sociologists to be prone to strong political activism in response to the social frustration they experience in these inconsistent statuses (Lenski, 1954; Goffman, 1957). Most simply, persons of inconsistent status (the taxi driver with a college degree, the uneducated millionaire, the black physician) will be treated on the basis of their lower rather than their higher social status, causing frustration and dissatisfaction with the dominant system; they will therefore be inspired to join sociopolitical movements which challenge established institutions.

The emergence of the black movement in the 1960s has been at least partially explained by the status inconsistency thesis. As blacks improved their status in terms of income, occupation, and education in the 1940s and 1950s, their ethnic status remained low. Also black advances in education were outpacing their advances in occupation and income, thus leading to a second source of status inconsistency (Geschwender, 1964:254).

Most studies of status inconsistent persons have maintained that they tend toward movements of the left. However, the type and direction of movements to which such people are attracted may differ depending on different status combinations. One study, for example, found a tendency toward right wing extremism among those who were high on income and low on education. Where high education was combined with low income, however, the political leanings were toward the left (Rush, 1967).

Relative deprivation in sum. Theories of relative deprivation seem especially well suited to sociopolitical movements, since their prime focus is on people's views of their power and wealth positions and their motivations to change them. But like psychological and structural theories, studies of relative deprivation have yielded much inconsistent evidence to substantiate the basic theory (Orum, 1974). Moreover, most of these studies, like those testing psychological and structural theories, have focused on extremist movements rather than more common reform movements. In any case, the dissatisfaction arising from people's interpretations of their power positions is not adequate alone to account for sociopolitical movements. Just as psychological and structural theories present only partial analyses of movements, relative deprivation too must be combined with these and other theories to produce satisfactory explanations of why people collectively challenge institutional authority.

THE RESOLUTION OF SOCIOPOLITICAL MOVEMENTS

Having looked at several types of sociopolitical movements and the factors which create them, we are left with one final query: What are the eventual outcomes of such mass actions? In what ways, when, and why do they succeed or fail in attaining their objectives? Sociologists have often described movements as having "life cycles" or "natural histories," and have explained in detail the various stages through which they pass (Blumer, 1939; Hopper, 1950; Mauss, 1975). But as Killian (1964:452) reminds us, "The significance of social movements, of course, lies not in their careers but in their consequences for the larger society and its culture."

In the United States during the past two decades we have witnessed a number of sociopolitical movements, most nonviolent and reformist in nature but some marked by violence and a few with even revolutionary overtones. Beginning with the black civil rights movement in the 1950s, movements focusing on a diversity of groups and issues have unfolded, including the anti-Vietnam war movement, student rights, women's liberation, gay rights, consumerism, the environmental movement, and antinuclear power. With the exception of the anti-Vietnam war and student movements, these are ongoing affairs whose main objectives have remained unchanged, though their ideologies, strategies, and organizations have undergone many revisions. Perhaps the most formidable of these, however, is the contemporary black movement, whose duration, maturity, and societal impact have surpassed the others. For this reason most of the examples cited in the following discussion are drawn from this sociopolitical movement.

The Responses of Ruling Elites

More than anything else, a sociopolitical movement's success or failure is dependent on the response it draws from ruling elites. Organization, tactics, and leadership will obviously affect a movement's ultimate outcome, but none of these factors is as critical as the capabilities of the society's power groups in meeting the challenge. If a regime is solidly in control, both physically and ideologically, movements seeking broad, fundamental changes will have little chance at reaching their goals. Groups and ideologies which present themselves as threats to established institutions and elites will be dealt with harshly and thoroughly in any society, regardless of its propensity to settle disputes peacefully and through procedural methods. The use of official violence to quell racial, labor, and political movements of various kinds throughout American history confirms this fundamental fact of political life. The violent stage of the contemporary black movement came to an end, according to Killian, not because the racial crisis had passed but because the white power structure effectively demonstrated the dangers of such tactics by imprisoning, assassinating, or forcing into exile the most "dramatically defiant" black leaders (Killian, 1975:155). More specific reform movements, of course, stand a better chance at reaching their goals in at least some form, since they are semilegitimate to begin with and do not pose a threat to dominant institutions. But even the successes of most reform movements are heavily diluted by ruling elites who are able to moderate demands, assuring that whatever concessions are eventually granted result in only minimal change in the sociopolitical order.

Let us look more closely at the power resources possessed by ruling elites and the strategies they employ in meeting the challenges of sociopolitical movements.

Violent Repression

As was pointed out in chapter 2, the authority of government in society is absolute since this institution, through police and military, controls the legitimate means of violence. But violence as a response to a sociopolitical movement is used in a most circumspect manner by established elites since its application can create unpredictable countereffects. Victims may become martyrs and public sympathy for the movement may grow. The brutal treatment —in some cases murder —of civil rights activists by police and vigilante groups in the South during the 1960s received national attention and aided in building public support for the movement.

Neither established authorities nor their challengers ordinarily resort to violence until other methods have proved futile. However, when violence is used, it is usually initiated by authorities attempting to squelch the movement rather than by the movement's participants. As Oberschall (1973:335) notes, although authorities do not espouse violence frivolously or indiscriminately, nevertheless "it is their actions or reactions that start violence, and, when the confrontation is under way, their actions that produce the bulk of the casualties." The urban black riots of the 1960s illustrate this. In the Newark riot, for example, 23 persons were killed, 21 of whom were blacks; in Detroit, 33 of 43 persons killed were blacks, and most of the white deaths appeared to have been accidental (National Advisory Commission on Civil Disorders, 1968:69,107). Similarly, the history of the American labor movement is replete with violence, most of its victims being either striking workers or those seeking union recognition (Taft and Ross, 1969).

Official violence may be severe even against movements which are basically reformist in nature, but it is particularly forceful when applied against movements which are perceived as revolutionary. Indeed, revolutionary movements are rare mainly because they are crushed so completely once they are seen by ruling elites as threatening. The Black Panther party, for example, that segment of the black movement with the most avowedly revolutionary aims, was subjected to official police repression in several cities even though the extent of its threat to established institutions was highly overdrawn.

The profits of turbulence. Despite the fact that it is officially deplored, violence has been an ever-present technique not only of established authorities but also of challenging movements throughout American history. "The fact that violence is a common consort of social protest in the United States," writes Gamson, "is not a matter of serious contention" (Gamson, 1975:72). It is commonly believed that violence is counterproductive to the group using it in a political confrontation. Yet, evidence shows that when ruling elites make concessions to challenging groups, or conversely, when movements are effectively stifled, violence or the threat of violence on the part of the successful group looms large in the picture.

For example, Piven and Cloward claim that protest movements such as black civil rights and the industrial labor movement did not gain establishment concessions because of their organizations or leadership, but because of the social turbulence they created. They argue that government relief programs such as welfare and unemployment payments are set up not so much because of moral incentives as by the need to quell mass disorder created by protestors. The relief measures of the 1930s Depression, for instance, were a result not of economic distress but of "the rising surge of political unrest that accompanied this economic catastrophe" (Piven and Cloward, 1971:45). Elites did not respond to widespread economic destitution until unrest became imminent. The expansion of relief benefits to the poor in the 1960s is explained in the same way. Common explanations of the substantial increase in welfare payments during this time point to the continued migration of poor blacks to Northern cities, the upgrading of benefit levels, and the presumed deterioration of the black family. With a good deal of evidence, Piven and Cloward refute these explanations. For example, they point out that more black families had moved North in the 1950s, yet increases in benefits by Northern states were three to seven times larger in the 1960s. Piven and Cloward conclude that it was the threat of increasing urban black turbulence which finally forced both local and federal governments to act. As with the unemployed of the Depression, "the expansion of the welfare rolls was a political response to political disorder" (Piven and Cloward, 1971:198).

Thus, rather than by working "through the system," as challenging groups are urged to do by ruling elites, it appears that any but the most moderate concessions are won by militant protest. Gamson's study (1975) of protesting groups in American society lends further weight to this view. He studied 53 voluntary associations that were active between 1800 and 1945, all of them challenging groups in the sense that they sought some degree of change in the power structure. As might be expected, he found that the less the group represented a challenge to the institutionalized system, the greater its success rate in achieving its aims. Most important, however, he found that of the 8 groups among the 53 which used violence as a tactic (either as aggressors or in self-defense), 6 gained advantages; among the nonviolent groups little more than half gained advantages (Gamson, 1975:79). While other factors are surely important, this and other studies (for example, Lamb, 1975) dispel the notion that violence is not profitable as a tactic in sociopolitical movements. Of course, when concessions are granted under these circumstances, they may be only superficial, momentary, or symbolic. In short, their long-range effect may not be great. Piven and Cloward (1971) explain, for example, that government relief to the poor and unemployed is usually withdrawn once social order has been restored.

Discreditation

Where violence is not called for, less severe methods are used by ruling elites to counter challenging movements. One such method is discreditation. Discrediting a movement involves the use of propaganda, voiced by institutional leaders, to malign and cast public doubts on the movement's program and objectives. The vilifications of Vice President Spiro Agnew against the anti-Vietnam war movement are notable. Most famous of his remarks were his references to protesting students as "an effete corps of impudent snobs who characterize themselves as intellectuals." J. Edgar Hoover, as director of the FBI, attempted to convince the American public that the black movement was "communist inspired" and made particularly crude efforts to defame its chief leader, Martin Luther King (Wise, 1978).

In such efforts at discreditation, ruling elites have huge power advantages over challenging movements due to their control of the society's key agents of socialization, particularly the mass media, as well as their greater credibility in the eyes of the general public. Indeed, dominant ideologies are ordinarily so deep-seated that little serious effort will be needed to discredit movements which seek to change longstanding norms and values. The effects of false consciousness are not easily overcome. It is not surprising, for example, that the women's movement of recent years has had only limited success in developing a consciousness of women's interests among women themselves. Similarly, the efforts of dominant economic institutions to neutralize the environmental movement have been partially successful due to the firm public belief in the growth ethic—that is, the need for unabated economic expansion. Giant industrial corporations—the chief source of environmental damage—have spent great sums of money informing the public of the "economically unrealistic" nature of environmentalists' objectives. Lost jobs, closed plants, and other economic hardships is the social price, they claim, for environmental programs. Thus, clean air and water standards are reduced or target dates for meeting them are repeatedly extended.

Cooptation

Cooptation, absorbing the movement or parts of it into the dominant system, is frequently an effective method of ruling elite control. Obviously such a technique can be effective only with reform movements and, more specifically, those whose objectives do not represent serious challenges to the dominant sociopolitical system. Cooptation can take two forms: bringing elements of the movement, usually leaders, into the elite structure or adopting all or part of the movement's program. On the cooptation of members of challenging groups, we might recall the notion of elite circulation advanced by Pareto and Mosca (chapter 4). Both viewed the entrance of new groups or individuals from lower strata into the elite as a critical control mechanism of ruling groups, helping to stave off serious challenges from below. As an example, Piven and Cloward (1978:30) point out that in the 1960s, organizers of the black movement took jobs in the federal government's Great Society programs, and when rioting erupted in the ghettos, street leaders were encouraged to "join in 'dialogues' with municipal officials." Some were even offered positions (largely insignificant in terms of power) in municipal agencies. Indeed, the militant ideologies and strategies of the black movement may have been quelled by the early 1970s partially because much of its leadership and the most activist middle-class segments of the black community had been coopted into the dominant system.

If ruling groups adopt in total the challenging movement's program, the movement, of course, will rapidly decline. Such a complete embracing of movement objectives, however, is rare. More commonly, ruling groups will adopt many of the symbols of the movement rather than its substance. Official statements will stress those values of the challenging movement which, it is claimed, are shared by established institutions. Oil companies, for example, regularly advise the public of their environmental concerns through television, newspaper, and magazine advertisements. Social historian Christopher Lasch (1973:109) asserts that "Through its control of mass communications, the ruling class coopts dissident styles of culture and politics and identifies them with its own version of the good life." In a sense, ruling groups have the resources to "buy out" dissent and even use it for their own purposes. During the 1960s, at the height of the black urban riots and police-student confrontations on many campuses, the Chrysler Corporation was urging Americans to "join the Dodge rebellion!"

Cooptation, however, is not always a victory for dominant groups. Yielding concessions—in any form—to challenging groups represents at least some degree of power shift. Furthermore, at times substantive, not merely symbolic, aspects of a sociopolitical movement are adopted by ruling elites, making parts of the movement's goals and organization irrelevant. Much of the vitality of the black movement, for example, was drained despite its incomplete goals by the incorporation of a great deal of its ideology and objectives by established institutions. Third parties have never been serious challengers in American politics for much the same reason: Their programs have usually been adopted in some form by the two major parties. Cooptation, then, is a two-way proposition (Gamson, 1968:137; Smelser, 1963:282–286).

Institutionalization

If a sociopolitical movement is successful, its objectives and ideology become part of the established order. Revolutionary movements, of course, totally displace the dominant social order and implant a new one. The revolution becomes the new status quo, giving rise inevitably to counter-revolutionary movements which challenge the new system. The success of revolutionary movements aimed at total social displacement is extraordinary, however. Reform movements are more likely to see their goals reached at least to some degree, so long as they remain specific enough not to threaten wide portions of the power structure and the society's class system. "The broader the goals of a social movement, the more central its focus, and the greater its threat to class structure," writes Garner, "the less likely it will be to succeed" (1977:12). The industrial labor movement is perhaps the best example of a successful reform movement in recent decades. Although in the eyes of the capitalist class it seemed to represent a serious challenge to the class system, once legitimized the labor movement's goals and ideology were considerably modified, and it was absorbed into the politicoeconomic establishment.

Sociopolitical movements may be institutionalized even if their goals are not reached. In such cases established authorities will recognize the problem around which the movement centers, and the movement's organizations may operate almost entirely within the dominant system, much like a party or an interest group. The consumer and environmental movements appear to have reached this stage. Likewise, although the ultimate social and economic goals of blacks have not been reached, certain black advocacy groups such as the NAACP or the Urban League are well established and recognized pressure groups, functioning totally within the prevailing system. Thus, although prejudice and discrimination persist, there is no longer any doubt on the part of societal elites that the basic objectives of the black movement as professed by these groups are fundamentally just and legitimate.

It is likely that more sociopolitical movements fail than succeed. Yet the successes or failures of movements are not always easily perceptible, except in retrospect and after a relatively long period has elapsed. The success of ruling elites in extinguishing a movement, or on the other hand, of movements achieving changes in laws or power personnel, are noticeable immediately; but changes in values, attitudes, and behavior patterns do not occur so swiftly or distinguishably. Thus movements which at first glance appear unsuccessful may actually effect a strong influence on the society. For example, it is obvious that blacks and women have a long distance to travel before they attain the level of power and status currently held by whites and men. But to view either the black or women's movement as a failure on the basis of these unfulfilled goals overlooks the less obvious success they have attained in changing social perceptions of blacks and women.

Just as seemingly unsuccessful movements may have lasting societal impact, so too the achievements of apparently successful ones may be more limited than they appear. This seems particularly true of revolution. Even if subordinate groups sweep ruling elites from power and establish new political and economic structures, this does not mean that the movement is successful in the sense of changing societal values. Ruling elites were replaced and major institutions fundamentally altered in Russia in 1917, but the flowering of a communist society in which people's actions are founded on nonacquisitive and nonindividualist values is still today hopelessly remote. Other revolutions of modern times must be seen in a similar light (see for example Ross, 1966).

Moreover, Michels' contention that organizations, even revolutionary ones, must inevitably degenerate into new oligarchies with attendant bureaucracies seems well confirmed by these and other successful movements. The remarks of Czech novelist Franz Kafka, when asked if he favored expansion of the then still young Russian Revolution, seem appropriate in this regard:

> As a flood spreads wider and wider, the water becomes shallower and dirtier. The Revolution evaporates, and leaves behind only the slime of a new bureaucracy. The chains of tormented mankind are made out of red tape (Janouch, 1971:120).

SUMMARY

Masses do not always limit their attempts to influence the society's power structure to institutionalized forms of conflict such as voting and interest group activity. At times sociopolitical movements arise which challenge ruling elites and dominant ideologies in varying degrees through noninstitutionalized methods.

Reform movements seek limited changes and do not challenge the basic institutional structure of the society. They seek only a greater share of power and rewards for certain groups. Revolutionary movements, by contrast, seek to change political, economic, and perhaps all other societal institutions fundamentally. These are movements which alter the society's class relations. The tactics of reform movements are principally legitimate, though noninstitutional means will sometimes be used. Revolutionary movements, seeking as they do total societal change, necessarily operate outside the established political system. Reactionary movements are essentially revolutions of the right, designed to move the society backward to a previous condition.

Several theories accounting for the emergence of sociopolitical movements have been offered by sociologists and psychologists. Psychological theories concentrate on the individuals who make up movements, particularly extremist movements of the left and right. Here participants are recognized as deviants or zealots. Such theories, however, fail to account for the bulk of movement participants who are neither eccentric nor fanatic. A more sociological explanation is "structural strain," wherein movements are seen as emerging from profound changes in the social structure, such as modifications in the class and status hierarchies or in the composition of the society's population. Deprivation theories are social-psychological and explain sociopolitical movements as the result of people's interpretations of their objective social conditions. If people see themselves as unjustly deprived of wealth, power, or status, they may become the nucleus of a movement which they believe will change that condition.

The success or failure of a sociopolitical movement is, more than anything, dependent on how ruling elites respond to it. Those movements seen as serious threats to the dominant power structure (that is, revolutionary movements) will be harshly repressed, often violently. Less intense methods, such as discreditation or cooptation, will be used to counter reform movements. Movements are said to be institutionalized when their objectives and ideologies are adopted, in part or in total, by the established order.

REFERENCES

Adorno, Theodore W., Else Frenkel-Brunswick, Daniel J. Levinson, and **R. Nevitt Sanford.** 1950. *The Authoritarian Personality.* New York: Harper and Row.

Anderson, Charles. 1974. *The Political Economy of Social Class.* Englewood Cliffs: Prentice-Hall.

Banfield, Edward. 1974. *The Unheavenly City Revisited.* Boston: Little, Brown.

Bell, Daniel (ed.). 1964. *The Radical Right.* New York: Anchor.

Blauner, Robert. 1972. *Racial Oppression in America.* New York: Harper and Row.

Blumer, Herbert. 1939. "Social Movements." In Robert E. Park (ed.), *An Outline of the Principles of Sociology.* New York: Barnes and Noble.

Brinton, Crane. 1952. *The Anatomy of Revolution.* Rev. ed. New York: Prentice-Hall.

Cantril, Hadley. 1941. *The Psychology of Social Movements.* New York: Wiley.

Caplan, Nathan S., and **Jeffrey M. Paige.** 1968. "A Study of Ghetto Rioters," *Scientific American* 219 (August):15−21.

deTocqueville, Alexis. 1955. *The Old Regime and the French Revolution.* Trans. Stuart Gilbert. New York: Anchor.

Elkins, Stanley M. 1949. *Slavery: A Problem in American Institutional and Intellectual Life.* New York: Grosset and Dunlap.

Fine, Sidney. 1969. *Sit Down: The General Motors Strike of 1936-37*. Ann Arbor: U. of Michigan Press.

Fromm, Erich. 1941. *Escape from Freedom*. New York: Holt, Rinehart and Winston.

Gamson, William A. 1968. *Power and Discontent*. Homewood, Ill.: Dorsey.

——————. 1975. *The Strategy of Social Protest*. Homewood, Ill.: Dorsey.

Garner, Roberta Ash. 1977. *Social Movements in America*. 2nd ed. Chicago: Rand McNally.

Gerth, Hans. 1940. "The Nazi Party: Leadership and Composition." *American Journal of Sociology* 45 (January):517–541.

Geschwender, James A. 1964. "Social Structure and the Negro Revolt: An Examination of Some Hypotheses." *Social Forces* 43 (December):248–256.

Goffman, Irwin W. 1957. "Status Consistency and Preference for Change in Power Distribution." *American Sociological Review* 22 (June):275–281.

Gurr, Ted Robert. 1970. *Why Men Rebel*. Princeton: Princeton U. Press.

Heberle, Rudolf. 1968. "Types and Functions of Social Movements." In David Sills (ed.), *The International Encyclopedia of the Social Sciences*. Vol. 14. New York: Macmillan.

Higham, John. 1975. *Send These to Me: Jews and Other Immigrants in Urban America*. New York: Atheneum.

Hoffer, Eric. 1951. *The True Believer*. New York: Harper and Row.

Hofstadter, Richard. 1964. *The Paranoid Style in American Politics*. New York: Knopf.

Hopper, Rex D. 1950. "The Revolutionary Process: A Frame of Reference for the Study of Revolutionary Movements." *Social Forces* 28 (March):270–279.

Janouch, Gustav. 1971. *Conversations with Kafka*. 2nd ed. New York: New Directions.

Johnson, Chalmers. 1966. *Revolutionary Change*. Boston: Little, Brown.

Killian, Lewis M. 1964. "Social Movements." In R. E. L. Faris (ed.), *Handbook of Modern Sociology*. Chicago: Rand McNally.

——————. 1975. *The Impossible Revolution, Phase II*. New York: Random House.

Lamb, Curt. 1975. *Political Power in Poor Neighborhoods*. Cambridge: Schenkman.

Lasch, Christopher. 1973. *The World of Nations*. New York: Knopf.

Lenski, Gerhard E. 1954. "Status Crystallization: A Non-Vertical Dimension of Social Status." *American Sociological Review* 19 (August):405–413.

Lipset, Seymour Martin. 1964. "The Sources of the 'Radical Right'." In Daniel Bell (ed.), *The Radical Right*. New York: Anchor.

——————, **and Earl Raab.** 1978. *The Politics of Unreason*. 2nd ed. Chicago: U. of Chicago Press.

Mauss, Armand L. 1975. *Social Problems as Social Movements*. Philadelphia: Lippincott.

McCloskey, Herbert. 1958. "Conservatism and Personality." *American Political Science Review* 42 (March):27–45.

McMillan, Neil R. 1971. *The Citizens' Councils: Organized Resistance to the Second Reconstruction, 1954-64*. Urbana: U. of Illinois Press.

Michels, Robert. 1962. *Political Parties.* New York: Free Press.

Moore, Barrington, Jr. 1978. *Injustice: The Social Bases of Obedience and Revolt.* White Plains, N.Y.: M. E. Sharpe.

National Advisory Commission on Civil Disorders. 1968. *Report.* New York: Bantam.

Oberschall, Anthony. 1973. *Social Conflict and Social Movements.* Englewood Cliffs: Prentice-Hall.

Orum, Anthony M. 1974. "On Participation in Political Protest Movements." *Journal of Applied Behavioral Science* 10 (April-May-June):181–207.

Pettigrew, Thomas. 1958. "Personality and Sociocultural Factors in Intergroup Attitudes: A Cross National Comparison." *Journal of Conflict Resolution* 2 (March):29–42.

Piven, Frances Fox, and **Richard A. Cloward.** 1971. *Regulating the Poor.* New York: Pantheon.

_____. 1978. *Poor People's Movements: Why They Succeed, How They Fail.* New York: Vintage.

Rapoport, David C. 1969. "Coup d'Etat: The View of the Men Firing Pistols." In Carl J. Friedrich (ed.), *Revolution.* New York: Atherton.

Ross, Stanley R. (ed.). 1966. *Is the Mexican Revolution Dead?* New York: Knopf.

Runciman, W. G. 1966. *Relative Deprivation and Social Justice.* Berkeley: U. of California Press.

Rush, Gary B. 1967. "Status Consistency and Right-Wing Extremism." *American Sociological Review* 32 (February):86–92.

Schurman, Franz. 1971. "System, Contradictions, and Revolution in America." In Roderick Aya and Norman Miller (eds.), *The New American Revolution.* New York: Free Press.

Sears, David O., and **John B. McConahay.** 1973. *The Politics of Violence: The New Urban Blacks and the Watts Riot.* Boston: Houghton Mifflin.

Smelser, Neil. 1963. *The Theory of Collective Behavior.* New York: Free Press.

Taft, Philip, and **Philip Ross.** 1969. "American Labor Violence: Its Causes, Character and Outcome." In Hugh Davis Graham and Ted Robert Gurr (eds.), *Violence in America.* New York: Signet.

Toch, Hans. 1965. *The Social Psychology of Social Movements.* Indianapolis, Bobbs-Merrill.

Tucker, Robert C. 1972. *The Marx-Engels Reader.* New York: Norton.

Turner, Ralph H. 1969. "The Theme of Contemporary Social Movements." *British Journal of Sociology* 20 (December):390–405.

_____, and **Lewis M. Killian.** 1972. *Collective Behavior.* 2nd ed. Englewood Cliffs: Prentice-Hall.

U.S. Department of State. 1977. *Background Notes —Argentina* (June). Washington, D.C.: U.S. Government Printing Office.

Wilson, John. 1973. *Introduction to Social Movements.* New York: Basic.

Wise, David. 1978. *The American Police State.* New York: Vintage.

epilogue: a note on political action and change

Very simple political maxims: Learn how to re-fuse the existing orthodoxies. Learn also how to refuse the would-be orthodoxies of tomorrow. Participate in the lives of others, but think your own thoughts. Accept "alienation" —it is the price of freedom. Learn how to stand apart.
                                        Peter L. Berger

Our major themes have revealed the fact that democracy in America is more myth than reality. Power and privilege are concentrated in a few hands, and political institutions work most fundamentally in the interests of those few. Moreover our prognosis for change in this state of affairs through participatory means, institutional or noninstitutional, has been bleak. Where does this leave us? Is societal politics merely the succession of one ruling group after another, with masses either spectators or pawns? Is this process inexorable? Can no basic political change presently be effected in the United States and other advanced capitalist societies?

While I have presented a rather negative, almost fatalistic view of power in America, my intention has not been to encourage readers to resign themselves to a system of rule they cannot influence in any meaningful way. Rather my purpose has been to raise questions in the minds of readers about how dominant institutions and elites in the society work, why they work as they do, and whose interests they ultimately serve. I have also tried to show how the prevailing sociopolitical system methodically molds our political thinking, and thus our political actions, to support of the status quo.

Throughout our analysis I have made no calls for change, though my doubts regarding the capacity of current American political institutions to achieve more than a semblance of authentic democracy within a society providing a fundamentally inequitable opportunity structure should be apparent. I would agree with sociologist Robert S. Lynd (1957:41), who has fittingly remarked that "The 'problem of democracy' as it exists in our society concerns principally the fact that purportedly democratic political institutions operate upon a factually undemocratic class base appropriate to capitalism."

Offering in conclusion a formula for political change or even a scenario of what the future may hold for America and other like societies in an era of diminishing environmental capacities and constricting economic conditions seems presumptuous and inappropriate. One need not look far for any number of such proposals and prognostications. I would suggest, however, that so long as the democratic goals of the society remain valid—maximizing the capacity of all persons to participate in their own governance and creating the fullest and most equitable conditions of life—political and economic institutions must be reshaped and the values upon which they are founded reexamined. This involves much more than changing personnel within the existing sociopolitical framework or stimulating more citizen participation. As long as the political ground rules and resource distribution remain unchanged, those groups who have traditionally reaped the benefits of the dominant political and economic arrangements will continue to do so regardless of who occupies positions of power or how many are politically active.

As we have seen, however, radical sociopolitical change is not an easy process, nor are its eventual outcomes ever certain. We should be extremely wary, therefore, not only of political and economic elites who impulsively extol the virtues of the prevailing system but also of those who promise instant utopia through revolution. Moreover we must not forget that no sociopolitical system in the modern world has yet averted the duality of elites and masses. Thus future political forms, however radically changed, are not likely to eliminate or even diminish power differentials in society.

If, then, prevailing as well as proposed orthodoxies are to be questioned, and if meaningful change is not possible within the dominant sociopolitical framework, does this not leave us in a state of political paralysis?

I would argue that developing political awareness —that is, understanding how and why political and economic institutions work as they do, and questioning official explanations of political and economic outcomes —is in itself a gigantic step in the direction of substantive change. Indeed, it is a necessary antecedent. In the United States, restructuring centralized, elite-dominated institutions in the shape of more authentic democracy can begin only with a critical examination of how those institutions currently operate to frustrate democratic goals. If action within the dominant sociopolitical system cannot lead to fundamental change, that fact must first be understood. Otherwise efforts at change will be wasted on futile endeavors.

In short, political awareness means constant skepticism and critical examination of dominant and challenging systems. Persistent questioning, of course, has its price. It makes for a good deal of mental discomfort. Most of us want to feel that societal leaders are telling us the truth and that they are in command of affairs. As a result, most of us accept unquestioningly the greater part of what elites tell us. Moreover the strength of the socialization process in instilling confidence in the dominant system is not easily overcome, as was explained in chapter 12. Hopefully, however, we have now taken the first step.

I would further suggest that seeking change through political action even within the dominant system is never totally unproductive. Power elites may be inevitable, but their power is never invincible. Apathy or resignation may seem logical responses considering the futility of most political effort. But they make the rule of dominant elites more relentless and less accountable and eliminate the possibilities of any change, slight though it may be. Furthermore reforms are not always symbolic or superficial in effect. To think otherwise is to deny the reality of significant changes in the social position of several sizable groups in the United States during the past four decades.

The emergence of elites —and in modern industrial societies, bureaucracies —may in fact be unavoidable, as Pareto, Mosca, Michels, and Weber have told us. If this is the case, the key questions are not how democracy and social equality in the ideal sense can be realized but how the control of societal institutions and elites by masses and the equalization of the society's resources can be maximized. Gaps between those at the top and those at the bottom may persist beyond the efforts of any sociopolitical system to eliminate them. But this does not mean that those gaps cannot be reduced in size. Likewise, large, impersonal institutions can be, if not eliminated, humanized.

Despite the unlikelihood of radical change in political and economic institutions in the near future, then, there is no reason to adopt a stance of hopelessness and resignation. Reforms cannot change social outcomes of injustice and inequality which are endemic in the structure and workings of dominant institutions; but they can make them more tolerable. As social historian Barrington Moore (1967:413) has put it, in the United States "we do have some room to think and act on behalf of—if not a decent society —at least something a great deal less indecent than what actually exists." If a more decent society is the best that can presently be hoped for, it is still far from a realization. Thus political action is not entirely futile, even within the context of prevailing institutions.

REFERENCES

Lynd, Robert S. 1957. "Power in American Society as Resource and Problem." In Arthur Kornhauser (ed.), *Problems of Power in American Democracy*. Detroit: Wayne State U. Press.

Moore, Barrington, Jr. 1967. "The Society Nobody Wants: A Look Beyond Marxism and Liberalism." In Kurt H. Wolff and Barrington Moore, Jr. (eds.), *The Critical Spirit: Essays in Honor of Herbert Marcuse*. Boston: Beacon.

index